W9-CNV-367

Robert Oppenheimer

LETTERS AND RECOLLECTIONS

Edited by
Alice Kimball Smith
Charles Weiner

HARVARD UNIVERSITY PRESS
Cambridge, Massachusetts
London, England 1980

LIBRARY OF CONGRESS CATALOGING IN PUBLICATION DATA

Oppenheimer, J. Robert, 1904–1967.
    Robert Oppenheimer, letters and recollections.

    "Scientific papers by Robert Oppenheimer": p.
    Bibliography: p.
    Includes index.
    1. Oppenheimer, J. Robert, 1904–1967—Correspondence. 2.
Physicists—Correspondence. 3. Oppenheimer, J. Robert,
1904–1967—Biography. I. Smith, Alice Kimball. II. Weiner, Charles.
III. Title. QC16.O62A4 1980   530'.092'4 [B]   80-10106
ISBN 0-674-77605-4

Preface

HOWEVER FUTURE GENERATIONS may view Robert Oppenheimer's place in history, in his own time he symbolized one supremely important event of the mid-twentieth century, the harnessing of nuclear fission in a devastating weapon. In the public mind he personified the newly dramatized link between science and national policy. And for students of the tragic theme in human history he exemplified the hero fallen from favor, the great man betrayed by faults ignored in lesser men.

To many of his contemporaries Oppenheimer was a brilliant scientist, a dedicated public servant, and a fine human being in whom virtue far transcended defect and fully compensated for it. Others saw a man of flawed judgment, sometimes devious or affected in personal relations or in public posture, whose actual contributions did not match his reputation as a physicist. Oppenheimer is often described as complex, but complexity is not (in itself) a trait of personality; it indicates rather that the observer is puzzled. What can confidently be said on the basis of Oppenheimer's early letters is that, even when he was a young man, the world around him, the choices it offered, and the human beings with whom he associated were not simple or easily defined. As Oppenheimer's personality became an object of wider interest, he still maintained an air of privacy, suggesting an inner self withheld from public view. People reacted to this quality with either fascination or displeasure. Throughout his life he sometimes showed an uncanny ability to cut through confusion with clarity and precision. At other times he groped his way toward answers and spoke and acted with an ambiguity that puzzled or antagonized those of a different cast of mind.

Yet this man—so difficult to classify, so selective in his preoccupations and his friendships, most at home in abstruse reaches of mathematical physics, who never courted approval outside a small social and intellectual circle, who was considered unpredictable and temperamental even by admirers—became the disciplined leader of the project that built the atomic bombs dropped on Japan in August 1945, thereby revolutionizing warfare and international relations. Oppenheimer's subsequent role as weapons adviser and as a leading architect of American nuclear policy was likewise an unexpected one.

The letters presented here were written by Oppenheimer between the autumn of 1922 when he entered Harvard College and the autumn of 1945 when he resigned as director of the Los Alamos nuclear weapons laboratory. They help to explain this man who played no small part in shaping the events and character of an era. One hundred eleven of these letters were written prior to 1942, when he became involved in the atomic bomb project. They represent a substantial portion of Oppenheimer's correspondence that survives from the prewar years, during which he saved neither letters he received nor copies of those he wrote. The prewar letters were collected by the editors specifically for this volume. Few were easily accessible; in fact, scholars were previously unaware of the existence of most of them. In March 1962 Oppenheimer wrote to Thomas S. Kuhn that "in those days I kept nothing. Since I learned different, if not better, during the war, I have kept things."

From 1942 on, the volume and character of available correspondence changes radically. The letters and memorandums in Chapter IV have been selected from a large archive of Oppenheimer's communications to his associates in order to illustrate how he carried out his awesome wartime responsibilities.

A few letters addressed to Oppenheimer over the years are also included because they show the character of a particular relationship, complete an episode, or offer a contrast in epistolary style.

The editors have not attempted to locate every item of institutional correspondence, such as Oppenheimer's replies to academic job offers and references he wrote for his students. We *have* followed every clue to possible sources of personal and scientific letters. Others will be found as scholars explore the papers of his contemporaries, but much has apparently been destroyed, including letters to his parents. More than half of the pre-1942 letters in this volume were preserved by individuals who were close to Oppenheimer during portions of the period: his brother Frank, his friend Francis Fergusson, his high school English teacher Herbert Winslow Smith, and the physicist George Uhlenbeck. The remainder come from other personal files and from institutional archives.

It was Herbert Smith's concern about the disposition of letters Oppenheimer had written to him from Harvard that led to consultation with us in 1974 and subsequently to the search for more letters and the decision to publish them. For even a preliminary reading confirmed Smith's view that the early letters—spontaneous, articulate, often troubled—revealed a relatively unknown Oppenheimer and explained much about the public figure who emerged after 1945. When we turned to Frank Oppenheimer and Francis Fergusson for advice, they generously turned over to us their own collections.

Part of Oppenheimer's attraction, at first for his friends and later for the public, was that he did not project the popularly held image of the scientist as cold, objective, rational and therefore above human frailty, an image that scientists themselves fostered by underplaying their personal histories and the disorder that precedes the neat scientific conclusion. Oppenheimer's foibles, his vulnerability, his capacity for enjoyment and affection are fully apparent in the early letters. We see a sensitive, sometimes awkward young man growing in self-assurance and finding satisfaction in a widening circle of friends, especially when personal compatibility strengthened a bond in physics. We note the development of Oppenheimer's legendary versatility—his skill as a linguist, his familiarity with literature, his knowledge of history and philosophy—and observe how solidly based it was in wide reading, hard study, and in his own creative torment as poet and storyteller. The Harvard letters, in fact, suggest a literary man in the making rather than a scientist.

Later letters shed light on Oppenheimer's role in physics in the 1930s when his own interpretation of what he liked to call style in science was influencing colleagues and students. They show that certain qualities of Oppenheimer the charismatic leader did not appear overnight—an engaging blend of hedonism and asceticism, a tough-minded skepticism tempered at times by a compassion born of his own struggle into adulthood, and a hard-won capacity for self-command. Yet the precocious Harvard freshman and the graduate and postdoctoral student in Cambridge, Göttingen, and Zurich, making a place for himself in the new world of quantum physics, was very much father to the distinguished theoretical physicist and the successful wartime leader. Many of the prewar letters that we have located deal with science. Some of these convey Oppenheimer's sense of excitement and a growing confidence in his ability to understand and extend the new physics unfolding all about him; others express his frustration in attempting to resolve the difficult problems inherent in the theory of quantum mechanics. Mathematics was the powerful tool that promised to illuminate the fundamental nature of physical reality, and it was the international language spoken and written by Oppenheimer and the other young theorists of his generation. A few of these letters and portions of others are so highly mathematical that they could be termed technical notes, and we have omitted them from this edition. We have retained most of the material relating to Oppenheimer's three principal scientific interests: quantum field theory, cosmic rays, and nuclear physics. Even to readers without knowledge of science or mathematics these letters will convey some understanding of the informal processes of scientific communication as Oppenheimer shares with his fellow students, mentors, and colleagues his thoughts on physics problems of mutual interest, describes his own research, throws out ideas for discussion, and passes on news of other physicists' work.

But correspondence is not biography. Apart from what these particular letters do not say about Oppenheimer's day-to-day activities, there are significant time gaps and dimensions of his life that we bridge with a minimum of biographical information. The most important one occurs after 1936, when Oppenheimer became involved in social and political causes. We have found little correspondence relating to this by no means minor hiatus or to a few others that knowledgeable readers will readily detect. Oppenheimer himself provided some information about his activities and associations of the late 1930s in the autobiographical sketch with which he replied in March 1954 to the withdrawal of his security clearance by the Atomic Energy Commission and in responses to questions directed to him throughout the subsequent hearings.

A unique autobiographical statement, quite different in character from replies to official charges or to inquiries from reporters and commentators, is contained in a taped interview with Oppenheimer conducted by Thomas S. Kuhn in November 1963 for the Archive for History of Quantum Physics. The primary purpose was to record Oppenheimer's recollections of the early days of the quantum revolution and its consequences. Kuhn's skillful questioning elicited valuable information about how Oppenheimer's own scientific interests developed and how they were channeled into this new field. Extensive excerpts from this interview, published here for the first time, complement the correspondence.

Taken together, the letters and the excerpts from the Kuhn interview constitute a previously unpublished collection of primary biographical sources. For decades anecdotes have circulated about Oppenheimer as student and Berkeley teacher. These stories enliven the pages of popular biographies and numerous brief sketches; some are included in our editorial comment. They are amusing and often illuminating, but they tend to emphasize the bizarre and erratic in Oppenheimer's behavior and show him through the eyes of others. In his own letters and recollections, Oppenheimer speaks for himself.

To provide background for the letters we have drawn upon published and archival sources, including correspondence and oral history interviews with physicists of Oppenheimer's generation which were conducted prior to the initiation of this project. However, the letters themselves introduce persons and episodes mentioned briefly or not at all in these interviews. In order to explain such references we have talked at length with people to whom and about whom Oppenheimer wrote. Even when they had no letters to offer, friends and former colleagues willingly shared their early impressions, recounted anecdotes, and searched their memories to explain Oppenheimer's comments on people, books, and midnight rambles by the sea. Interviews conducted specifically for this volume may be biased in Oppenheimer's favor. Not everyone who knew

Robert Oppenheimer longed to be his intimate friend, but those who did not like him tended to remain outside the ambience created by his personal correspondence. By drawing upon recollections, we hope to have made the letters more comprehensible, historically more meaningful, and generally more enjoyable for most readers.

In the course of these interviews a substantial archive of taped and transcribed material has accumulated that will be useful to historians and future biographers of Oppenheimer and his contemporaries. The transcripts are deposited in the Institute Archives and Special Collections, Massachusetts Institute of Technology Libraries. (See Sources and Style at the back of this volume.)

Intense intellectual and emotional experiences, as well as time, separated the eighteen-year-old Harvard freshman from the weary forty-one-year-old administrator who tried briefly after the war to resume a quiet life of teaching and research. Yet Oppenheimer's view of himself as a private person, even at Los Alamos, is reflected in the letters of the intervening years. No matter what choices he made after August 1945, this image could not have survived the glare of public attention focused upon him once it was known that the bombs that destroyed Hiroshima and Nagasaki had been developed under the direction of a man named J. Robert Oppenheimer. This change markedly affected the tone and content of Oppenheimer's correspondence and is a principal factor in the decision to conclude this edition of his letters with the year 1945.

Our decision was made only after extensive exploration of Oppenheimer's personal papers, which were deposited after his death in the Manuscript Division of the Library of Congress. (Oppenheimer's files as director of the Institute for Advanced Study remain in Princeton and are not open to the public.) Many papers in the Library of Congress relate to official and public activities after late 1945. A small segment consists of correspondence connected with his wartime work. In sharp contrast to the surviving letters that Oppenheimer wrote before the war, most of the later correspondence is voluminous, formal, and guarded. As Oppenheimer came to symbolize not only the atomic bomb but problems associated with it, his incoming mail assumed awesome proportions. A predictable increase in correspondence relating to government committees, to organizations, and to the resumption of basic research in physics was further augmented by hundreds of letters from worried citizens of the atomic age, including statesmen, school children, and ordinary folk seeking Oppenheimer's views on science, education, and international affairs. At first his replies addressed each individual concern; with time the answers became brief and formal.

Not only formal but cautious. By the end of the war Oppenheimer's defenses were up. His duties as director of Los Alamos, the probing into his prewar associations by security officers, and the discretion demanded of a government consultant combined to make him careful about what he put on paper. As a consequence, the copious materials in the Library of Congress are in many respects less revealing than the fortuitously preserved letters in the first three chapters of this volume.

The altered character of the postwar correspondence reinforced our belief in the unique quality of the early letters. Therefore, we have chosen to present the less familiar Oppenheimer—learning, playing, making friends, doing physics, winning recognition—as yet unburdened by the actuality of the bomb, by fame, and by public responsibilities. The wartime letters demonstrate the importance of the transition that took place at Los Alamos.

Acknowledgments

Many people have participated in the making of this book. Our primary indebtedness is to Herbert W. Smith, Frank Oppenheimer, and Francis Fergusson, whose letters form the nucleus of this collection and whose encouragement gave us the confidence to expand it. Frank Oppenheimer's role was crucial as donor of letters, as a source of factual information, and as a reader with both a deep affection for the subject of the volume and a concern for accuracy. We gratefully acknowledge his help and support, as we do that of Robert Oppenheimer's children, Peter Oppenheimer and the late Toni Oppenheimer Silber. Throughout the project we have benefited from the knowledgeable advice of Robert Serber, Oppenheimer's student, colleague, and friend.

George L. Weil initially brought the Harvard letters to Herbert Smith to our attention. Names of all individuals who supplied letters will be found in the chronological list of letters in the section on Sources and Style at the back of the volume. Our debt to them is obvious, and we appreciate their generosity. The list also notes the institutional archives in which we found the remaining letters. We are grateful to the archivists responsible for these collections for assistance and advice as we consulted the documents in their care and for their courtesy in providing copies. We thank particularly Ronald S. Wilkinson and his staff in the Manuscript Division of the Library of Congress, Judith Goodstein at the California Institute of Technology, and Arthur L. Norberg and J. R. K. Kantor at the Bancroft Library, University of California at Berkeley. We frequently consulted Spencer Weart of the American Institute of Physics Center for History of Physics, where Joan N. Warnow and Amy Weiner provided valuable help and reference services. Staff members of the Ethical Culture School searched its files for information. Harold Argo of the Oppenheimer Memorial Committee at Los Alamos was most helpful in locating photographs.

Thirty-three people were interviewed specifically for this project. To some we returned repeatedly for confirmation of details and with further questions. If the commentary in this volume contributes to a fuller understanding of the young Oppenheimer, those whose names appear in the list of interviews deserve much credit. We appreciate their cooperation and their patience. The list also includes several earlier interviews with scientists which contain useful information about Oppenheimer and his times. Quotations and observations from these sources are attributed to the persons interviewed and are used with their permission.

Oppenheimer's own recollections fall in a special category. We are grateful to Thomas S. Kuhn, who recorded the interviews with Oppenheimer in 1963 for the Archive for History of Quantum Physics. Kuhn's dialogue with Oppenheimer stimulated the illuminating reflections which provide the context for many of the early letters.

The extent to which we have drawn on the research of others is apparent in the citations. A brief list of relevant published works is included in the Bibliography.

We deeply appreciate the comments and criticism of those who read the manuscript or portions of it: Laurie M. Brown, Francis Fergusson, Hilde Stern Hein, Evelyn Fox Keller, Martin J. Klein, Thomas S. Kuhn, John H. Manley, Philip Morrison, Frank Oppenheimer, Robert Serber, and Spencer Weart.

In the long and arduous task of copying letters, transcribing taped interviews, and typing a complicated manuscript we have had the assistance of Johanna Kovitz, Roberta Towner, Myriam Barenbaum, Ruth Davidson, and Sharon Youland. An efficient system of cross-referencing letters and notes, set up by Adele Stanton Croft, greatly facilitated our work.

We wish to give special thanks to Nancy Seasholes. At a critical stage we benefited enormously from her skills in research and editing and from the intelligence and dedication with which she applied them.

Partial support for our research was provided by the Oral History Program and the Program in Science, Technology, and Society at the Massachusetts Institute of Technology. An American Council for Learned Societies Grant-in-Aid to Alice Kimball Smith for 1976 is gratefully acknowledged.

January 1980   *Alice Kimball Smith*
                                                        Charles Weiner

Contents

Biographical Chronology

1904, April 22	Robert Oppenheimer born in New York City.
1911, September	Entered the Ethical Culture School in the second grade.
1912, August 12	Birth of brother, Frank Friedman Oppenheimer.
1917, September	Entered the high school division of the Ethical Culture School.
1921, February	Graduated from the Ethical Culture School.
1921, summer	Contracted dysentery while traveling in Europe; spent the following year at home recuperating.
1922, summer	First trip to New Mexico and the West Coast.
1922, September	Entered Harvard College.
1925, June	Received A.B. summa cum laude in chemistry from Harvard College (as of the class of 1926).
1925, September	Admitted to Christ's College, University of Cambridge; until August 1926 did research at the Cavendish Laboratory under Professor J. J. Thomson.
1926, September	Continued graduate study in physics with Professor Max Born at the University of Göttingen.
1927, March	Received the Ph.D. in physics from the University of Göttingen; remained in Europe until July.
1927–1928	National Research Council Fellow (September–December at Harvard University; January–July at the California Institute of Technology).
1928–1929	National Research Council Fellow (September–December at the University of Leiden and the University of Utrecht; January–June at the Eidgenossiche Technische Hochschule, Zurich).

1929, August	Commenced concurrent appointments as assistant professor of physics at the University of California, Berkeley, and at the California Institute of Technology.
1931, October 17	Death of mother, Ella Friedman Oppenheimer.
1931, October	Promoted to associate professor at the University of California and the California Institute of Technology.
1936, August	Promoted to professor at the University of California and at the California Institute of Technology.
1937, September 20	Death of father, Julius Oppenheimer.
1940, November 1	Married Katherine Puening Harrison.
1941, April	Elected member of the National Academy of Sciences.
1941, May 12	Birth of son, Peter Oppenheimer.
1942, May	Appointed coordinator of fast neutron research in the United States Government's S-1 project to develop an atomic bomb.
1942, November	Appointed director of the proposed laboratory for design and fabrication of the atomic bomb.
1943, March	Moved with family to the new laboratory at Los Alamos, New Mexico.
1944, December 7	Birth of daughter, Katherine Oppenheimer, called Toni.
1945, May– October	Member of Scientific Panel of the U.S. War Department's Interim Committee on postwar atomic policy.
1945, October	Resigned as director of the Los Alamos Laboratory (effective October 16).
1945, November	Moved to Pasadena to resume professorship at the California Institute of Technology.
1946, January– April	Member of Board of Consultants to the U.S. State Department's Committee on International Control of Atomic Energy.
1946, March 4	Received the U.S. Medal for Merit (Presidential citation) for direction of the Los Alamos Laboratory and development of the atomic bomb.
1946, June– 1947	Adviser to U.S. representative to the United Nations Atomic Energy Commission.
1946, August	Moved to Berkeley to resume professorship at the University of California.

1947, January 3	Commenced six-year term as member of the General Advisory Committee to the U.S. Atomic Energy Commission (AEC); elected chairman.
1947, October	Assumed directorship of the Institute for Advanced Study, Princeton, New Jersey.
1948	President, American Physical Society.
1952, July	At conclusion of term on AEC's General Advisory Committee, appointed consultant to AEC.
1953, December 23	Clearance for access to classified data suspended by AEC.
1954, April 12–May 6	Participated in hearings before the AEC's Personnel Security Board on his eligibility for clearance.
1954, June 29	AEC confirmed the Personnel Security Board's recommendation that clearance not be renewed.
1958, spring	Awarded the Legion d'honneur by the French government.
1963, December 2	Received the AEC's Enrico Fermi Award from President Lyndon B. Johnson.
1966, Spring	Requested early retirement from directorship of the Institute for Advanced Study, effective June 30.
1967, February 18	Died in Princeton, New Jersey.

"I think that the world in which we shall live these next thirty years will be a pretty restless and tormented place; I do not think that there will be much of a compromise possible between being of it, and being not of it."

ROBERT OPPENHEIMER TO FRANK OPPENHEIMER
August 10, 1931

Introduction

J. ROBERT OPPENHEIMER was born in New York City on April 22, 1904, at his parents' home on West 94th Street. His father, Julius, born in Hanau, Germany, in 1871, had come to the United States at the age of seventeen to work in a textile importing business owned by relatives. He later headed his own company, which specialized in imported lining fabrics. On March 23, 1903, Julius married a young artist, Ella Friedman of Baltimore, whose forebears had come from Germany in earlier generations. Whether the "J" in Robert's name stood for Julius or, as Robert himself once said, "for nothing" may never be fully resolved. His brother Frank surmises that the "J" was symbolic, a gesture in the direction of naming the eldest son after the father but at the same time a signal that his parents did not want Robert to be a "junior."[1]

Robert was too young to remember a brother who died in infancy. He was eight when another brother, Frank Friedman Oppenheimer, was born on August 14, 1912. The household of Robert's childhood included his Grandmother Friedman and, as a rule, two servants. Shortly before Frank's birth the family moved to a large apartment on the eleventh floor of 155 Riverside Drive near 88th Street. From its comfortable high-ceilinged rooms one looked up and down the Hudson River and over the city to the south. There was nothing ostentatious about the Oppenheimers' style of living, but there was money for a summer house on Long Island, family trips to Europe when Julius went on business, private schooling for the boys, and a small collection of modern paintings of which Julius, and later

Robert and Frank, were justly proud. There was also money to indulge a penchant for generous gestures to friends which passed from father to son.

The boys' contemporaries remember Robert's father as affable and out-going, his mother as lovely, though reserved. One friend, Paul Horgan, re-called how they appeared to him in the summer of 1923: "She was a very delicate person . . . highly attenuated emotionally, and she always pre-sided with a great delicacy and grace at the table and other events, but a mournful person. Mr. Oppenheimer was . . . desperately amiable, anxious to be agreeable, and I think essentially a very kind man . . . The household was run with luxury but simplicity at the same time, every com-fort and great style and charm . . . and a sadness; there was a melancholy tone." According to Frank, the "melancholy tone" was not typical. If the atmosphere was seldom hilarious, it was dominated by "a sense of warmth and concern for friends and non-friends and by the discovery of recountable pleasure in everything that was going on." Another young visitor, Francis Fergusson, remembers Julius as a great arguer and talker who loved opening up big topics for discussion at the dinner table. His wife sat quietly and lis-tened with apparent approval, but did not join the conversation.[2]

Before her marriage Ella Friedman had studied art in Europe and given drawing and painting lessons. She taught for a time at Hunter College. Rob-ert and Frank thought of their mother as an artist. Occasionally she took out paints, brushes, and easel and worked on a canvas for a few days, but her talent was expressed chiefly in the careful decoration of the apartment and the quiet elegance of her own clothes. If she did not initially kindle her hus-band's interest in art, it was one of numerous bonds in a successful marriage. The mysterious glove that Mrs. Oppenheimer always wore impressed her sons' friends, mysterious because no one alluded to it. Frank explains it sim-ply: she was born without a right hand; the glove contained a primitive prosthetic device, a spring between the artificial thumb and forefinger.[3]

All agree that the Oppenheimers were genuine people, not concerned with making an impression. They seemed to be a united family, and what-ever the restraints imposed by a maternal sense of order and propriety, Op-penheimer hospitality was something that young guests remembered. Mr. Oppenheimer's favorite restaurant was Voisin's. Robert sometimes spoke of it scornfully, but dining there helped to set his standards of good eating and of entertaining friends.

The Oppenheimers were Jewish but maintained no active temple affili-ation. They belonged to the Ethical Culture Society, founded by Felix Adler in 1876, of which Mr. Oppenheimer was a board member from 1907 to 1915. Frank remembers family attendance at Sunday morning meetings of the society, but this became less regular in his later boyhood. Commitment to its nonsectarian ethical principles did not preclude mild teasing: a bio-graphical poem written by seventeen-year-old Robert for his father's fiftieth birthday included the line "and he swallowed Dr. Adler like morality compressed."[4]

Adjacent to the society's headquarters on Central Park West near 63rd Street was the Ethical Culture School. Robert entered the second grade in September 1911; he graduated from the high school division in February 1921.

A scientific bent developed early. "I have a fairly vivid recollection of how this set of interests started," Oppenheimer told Thomas Kuhn in 1963.[5] "I was given a perfectly conventional tiny collection of minerals by my grandfather who was living in Germany; I was there at the age of five and the age of seven, but I do not know which of these two times it was . . . He was an unsuccessful business man, born himself in a hovel, really, in an almost medieval German village, with a taste for scholarship. He gave me also, in addition to the mineral collection, an encyclopedia of architecture which I still have. It was clear that one of the great joys in life for him was reading, but he had probably hardly been to school. He knew that I was interested in architecture and so he gave me these books; what caused him to give me the mineral collection I don't know—perhaps just because it was the sort of thing one gave to a very young child. And it was nothing; it was a box with maybe two dozen samples labelled in German . . ."

"From then on I became, in a completely childish way, an ardent mineral collector and I had, by the time I was through, quite a fine collection . . . This was certainly at first a collector's interest, but it began to be also a bit of a scientist's interest, not in historical problems of how rocks and minerals came to be, but really a fascination with crystals, their structure, bi-refringence, what you saw in polarized light, and all the canonical business . . . When I was ten or twelve years old, minerals, writing poems and reading, and building with blocks still—architecture—were the three themes that I did, not because they were something I had companionship in or because they had any relation to school but just for the hell of it. I gave up the blocks probably at the age of ten, and the minerals became a charming preoccupation. I started trying to understand them. I had very great trouble because I didn't always know the vocabulary; I think it was a month before I realized that 'intercept' could be used as a noun as well as a verb and this was the bane of me."

While still a schoolboy Robert became by far the youngest member of the prestigious New York Mineralogical Club, to which he read a paper when he was about twelve. Club members were chiefly interested in showing new finds, Oppenheimer explained to Kuhn. This inspired him to go to diggings and add to his own collection, but his real knowledge about minerals came from books.

At school Robert's agile and original mind distinguished him even among Ethical Culture's bright and strongly motivated students from moderately prosperous upper West Side families. The teachers, who represented at this period all that was at once sound and innovative in the progressive education movement, recorded their opinion of Robert in consistently high grades. But he was more than a good student. "Bob was delightful to teach," recalled his Greek and Latin instructor, Alberta Newton, after he died. "He received every new idea as perfectly beautiful." Matilda Auerbach, who taught him math, coped with his restlessness in class by sending him to the library to do advanced work, which he was later allowed to explain to the other students.[6]

Two members of this highly competent staff had special influence upon Robert—Augustus Klock in science and Herbert Smith in English. Talking to Kuhn some forty-five years later, Oppenheimer emphasized his debt to Klock. "I think the most important change came in my junior year in high school . . . The teacher of physics and chemistry was Augustus Klock . . . He was marvellous; I got so excited that after the first year, which was physics, I arranged to spend the summer working with him setting up equipment for the following year and I would then take chemistry and would do both. We must have spent five days a week together; once in a while we would even go off on a mineral hunting junket as a reward for this. I got interested then in electrolytes and conduction; I didn't know anything about it but I did fiddle with a few experiments [although] I don't remember what they were. I loved chemistry so deeply that I automatically now respond when people want to know how to interest people in science by saying, 'Teach them elementary chemistry.' Compared to physics, it starts right in the heart of things and very soon you have that connection between what you see and a really very sweeping set of ideas which could exist in physics but is very much less likely to be accessible. I don't know what would have happened if Augustus Klock hadn't been the teacher in this school, but I know that I had a great sense of indebtedness to him. He loved it, and he loved it in three ways: he loved the subject, he loved the bumpy contingent nature of the way in which you actually find out about something, and he loved the excitement that he could stir in young people. In all three ways he was a remarkably good teacher."

As he moved from the collection of minerals to crystallography and properties like bi-refringence, Oppenheimer did some laboratory work at home. "I had a microscope and I had a polarizer; that limited what I could do at home except for the most primitive sort of field tests of minerals. I think I didn't complicate physics and chemistry at school very much with mineralogy . . . I loved [the laboratory aspect]. This whole bifurcation belongs to a later period. I think if you had asked me then, I would have been somewhat doubtful whether there was such a thing as a vocation of science apart from mining engineering, chemical engineering or teaching, but if I had thought about it, I'm sure I would have thought that it was inseparable from doing experiments because I still thought that three or four years later."

In the interview with Kuhn, Oppenheimer touched upon other aspects of the high school years: "I should admit that . . . I was always formally a very good student which I guess I enjoyed but which fogs everything because I don't have any recollection of real difficulty. I wrote an essay for an English class and I wrote it about oxygen. My teacher, who was also a remarkable man and later became a very prominent educator, said, 'I think your vocation is to be a science writer.' Well, I didn't think so, but I found it interesting in retrospect."

This other "remarkable man" was Herbert Winslow Smith, who joined the English faculty in 1917 as Robert was entering high school. Smith had completed his undergraduate work at Harvard in 1911 and obtained the master's degree in English there. He was teaching concurrently at Harvard and M.I.T. with his eye on a Ph.D. when he was offered the job at Ethical Culture. The philosophy of the school aimed to bring out what students were good at and relate it to their course work, and this approach appealed to Smith. He had so much fun that he never went back to Cambridge. His students had fun, too, especially the freshmen, including Robert, who were assigned to Smith's first homeroom, over which he presided until they graduated. Smith was an inspiring teacher. After class students clustered around his desk to talk. He invited them to his home in West Orange, New Jersey, and encouraged them to write. Later, from Poughkeepsie and Cambridge poems and short stories came back for his critical appraisal. Francis Fergusson, whose letters from Robert form an important part of this volume, remembers Smith as "very, very kind to his students . . . He took on Robert and me and various other people . . . saw them through their troubles and advised them what to do next."[7]

Oppenheimer also spoke of his parents' role in his intellectual growth. "I think my father was one of the most tolerant and human of men. His idea of what to do for people was to let them find out what they wanted. I think that both he and my mother were pleased that I was a good student, were pleased that I was highbrow, were perhaps somewhat mockingly proud of my vigor in collecting and learning about minerals, and were quite content with that aspect of my life. I think my mother especially was dissatisfied with the limited interest I had in play and in people of my own age, and I don't know over what years but I know she kept trying to get me to be more like other boys, but with indifferent success. My mother had a reasonable education; she was a painter and her real interests were not scientific; we never, as far as I know, talked about this. I may sometimes have tried to explain something miraculous, but I have no concrete recollection."

Robert's friend from New Mexico, Paul Horgan, who first visited the Oppenheimers after Robert went to Harvard, thought his parents had handled their precocious son very well. They knew they had a changeling in Robert, and a sometimes moody one at that, he later recalled.[8] They did not allow this fact to dominate the household but tried instead to create an environment in which independence and talent could flourish.

Direct impressions of the young Oppenheimer that can now be retrieved date largely from his high school years. Robert did not have a large circle of friends at school, but in Herbert Smith's homeroom group he was an easy, even gay, participant. Other contemporaries saw a physically awkward boy, bushy hair worn long, who blushed easily and seemed different and absorbed, traits that were on occasion translated with youthful imprecision into a common nickname of the day, "Booby" Oppenheimer.[9]

The shy awkward side of Robert's personality came to the fore the summer he was fourteen when he went to a summer camp run by Dr. Otto Koenig, principal of a school for boys in New York City. The boys came from well-to-do Jewish families like Robert's, but his preference for intellectual over physical activities, his tendency to show off his knowledge, his refusal to fight back, so effectively set him apart that he became the butt of name calling and physical tormenting well beyond the bounds of normal adolescent teasing. Steady harrassment culminated in his being locked naked in an icehouse overnight. Robert eventually told Herbert Smith about the night in the icehouse. Years later Smith described the episode as retribution for Robert's having written to his parents that he was glad he had come to camp because he was learning the facts of life. This news prompted a visit from the Oppenheimers and a subsequent crackdown on the circulation of dirty stories that was quickly attributed to Robert's tattling.[10]

In the more sheltered environment of the Ethical Culture School Robert could afford to be different. Memories of him as a schoolboy tend to be shaded by time and the commanding image of the later Oppenheimer. Not so those of his classmate Jane Didisheim, who became the wife of French journalist Jacques Kayser. Interviewed in Paris more than fifty years after their graduation from high school, Jane Kayser's memories of Robert "at something like fifteen" were far more vivid than those of the famous man she later saw in Paris and Princeton. Images of other girlhood friends had become pale and flat; the one of Robert was extraordinarily alive:

"He was still a little boy; he was very frail, very pink-cheeked, very shy, and very brilliant of course. Very quickly everybody admitted that he was different from all the others and very superior. As far as studies were concerned he was good in everything . . . Aside from that he was physically—you can't say clumsy exactly—he was rather undeveloped, not in the way he behaved but the way he went about, the way he walked, the way he sat. There was something strangely childish about him . . . There was a sort of *déséquilibre*. He was abrupt when he came out of his shyness but with all that a very polite sort of voice. He never seemed to want to come to the front of anything . . . If he did it was because he couldn't do otherwise . . . because he was so extraordinarily gifted and brilliant—that just pushed him."[11]

In his last year at Ethical Culture, Robert found a thoroughly compatible spirit in Francis Fergusson from Albuquerque, New Mexico. To prepare for Harvard Francis had attended a public high school in the Bronx, then transferred to Ethical Culture for his senior year. Oppenheimer later recalled that he shared an interest in poetry and literature with several people in his high school years—referring to Jane Didisheim and other members of Herbert Smith's homeroom and English classes—but he made a special point of his association with Francis Fergusson: "I had a very good friend who came . . . from New Mexico . . . and who at that time had some interest in biology. But his main interests were really a young man's philosophic interests; he was preoccupied with the old difficulty that if everything is natural how can something be good, in the form [in] which the 19th century writers had sharpened this. He is to this day one of my closest friends and our paths have crossed often . . . [He] became a producer, a writer of plays, a critic, and a historian of the arts—the theater primarily."

Robert and Francis saw little of each other in the 1930s and lost touch during the war, but they saw each other frequently after 1947, when Oppenheimer became director of the Institute for Advanced Study in Princeton and Fergusson became University Professor of Comparative Literature at nearby Rutgers. Trying to isolate early impressions, Fergusson remembers principally superior intelligence and competence. As a high school senior, Robert had lost some of that odd disequilibrium that his friend Jane remembered. He was, of course, manager of the Science Club, but Fergusson was also impressed by the "superhuman efficiency" with which he ran a major school affair—probably "The Bazaar" described in an undistinguished bit of doggerel that appeared over Robert's initials in the school paper.[12]

Robert graduated from Ethical Culture in February 1921, Francis, in June. They expected to enter Harvard together that autumn. As was the custom with February graduates, Robert spent the spring on a special project at the school; later, he went to Europe with his parents and Frank. "I went off on a long prospecting trip into Bohemia into the old mines, Joachimsthal, and I came down with a heavy, almost fatal case of trench dysentery. That and its aftermath kept me out of school for a year . . . I had planned to go [to Harvard] immediately, but it was called off because I was sick abed—in Europe, actually, at the time."

Robert spent the year 1921–22 recuperating, first at home in New York, then on trips, south in the spring, and west the following summer. Jane Didisheim was taking art courses in New York that winter and in a comradely, unromantic way she saw something of Robert during his convalescence. Visiting the Oppenheimer apartment occasionally at his parents' invitation or at the urging of Herbert Smith, she sensed that Robert had mellowed and gained assurance. "He had become less shy. I think he had become gayer also . . . In spite of the fact that he must have been ill at the time, I remember somebody much more *ouvert* . . . than he had been before." Jane saw him as not really happy, but not as deeply troubled either.[13]

This growth in self-confidence that Jane noted as Robert emerged from adolescence made possible the friendship with Francis Fergusson and other close and significant relationships for which Robert demonstrated so marked a talent in the coming years. Some of these developed during the summer of 1922 when, in the hope of completing the cure of the colitis that followed Robert's attack of dysentery, his parents asked Herbert Smith to serve as his companion on a trip to the Southwest. Smith had made a similar expedition the previous year with a nephew of Felix Adler's. For Robert, a seasoned European traveler, the trip opened a new world of natural and human experiences. It not only introduced him to the Pecos Valley in New Mexico, where a few years later their father leased a small ranch for Robert and Frank; it also gave pupil and teacher additional friends and interests in common and created the personal attachment so evident in the letters Robert wrote to Smith during his three years at Harvard.

In Albuquerque, Smith and Robert visited Francis Fergusson and his family. Robert enjoyed this household of lively young people, including Harvey, who had already begun his career as a novelist, and Erna, whose books on the Southwest would become classics. Through Francis, Robert also met Paul Horgan, their own age, like them intellectually precocious, and an avid reader. All three were propelled by as yet unfocussed talents and drives that would bring each distinction, Robert as scientist, Fergusson as literary scholar, Horgan as novelist and historian.

It is not clear how much time what Horgan variously describes as "this pygmy triumverate," "this great troika," all "polymaths," actually spent together. After two years at Harvard, Fergusson went on to Oxford as a Rhodes Scholar. Horgan experimented with music and painting before finding his vocation in writing. But until Robert went to England in September 1925, he and Horgan met whenever possible in New Mexico, Cambridge, or New York. At least twice, in 1923 and 1925, Horgan visited the Oppenheimers' summer home at Bay Shore. Horgan recalls: "There were high spirited goings on all the time. I think it is perfectly right to say that even then—and all my life I've felt this—he was the most intelligent man I've ever known, the most brilliantly endowed intellectually. And with this, in that period of his life, he combined incredibly good wit and gaiety and high spirits."

Horgan thought of Robert as special but not odd or unusual, "because he had this lovely social quality that permitted him to enter into the moment very strongly, wherever it was and whenever it was. So one didn't see him as eventually the incredibly great scientist or the celebrity at all. He had a great superiority but great charm with it, and great simplicity at that time." Horgan also noted Robert's consideration for others and his "exquisite manners . . . I've always been puzzled by later reports of his arrogance and his self-centeredness . . . I can't identify that in him at all."[14]

To Horgan, as to Jane Kayser, the young Oppenheimer was still a vivid presence in 1976. While enjoying the stimulation and gaiety of Robert's companionship, Horgan, however, was aware of a basic unhappiness. "Robert had bouts of melancholy, deep, deep depressions as a youngster," recalls Horgan. "He would seem to be incommunicado emotionally for a day or two at a time. That happened while I was staying with him once or twice, and I was very distressed, had no idea what was causing it." Horgan always had silent or oblique reassurance from Robert's parents.[15]

Herbert Smith too observed the trauma of Robert's growing up with interest and concern. He thought the persistent colitis was psychosomatic and while he deplored the prescribed treatment—bed and inactivity—as better suited to a tired businessman than to a seventeen-year-old genius, he was sure he understood what lay behind the illness, especially after their western trip. In the intimacy of travel and campfires Robert had revealed what Smith, who was well-versed in the psychological theories then current in avant-garde educational circles, interpreted as a pronounced oedipal attitude toward his father. In Smith's view, Julius Oppenheimer was often maladroit, as in his response to Robert's report of sex talk at summer camp. Smith thought that Mr. Oppenheimer's outgoing affability embarrassed his shy son. And Robert was self-conscious as well about the family's association with trade (though this cannot have been unusual among Ethical Culture families). Once on the western trip Smith was packing in a hurry and asked Robert if he would fold a jacket for him. "He looked at me sharply," Smith later recalled, "and said, 'Oh yes. The tailor's son would know how to do that, wouldn't he?'" Smith realized how deeply Robert felt the fact of being Jewish when he asked to travel west as Smith's brother, a suggestion that was firmly turned down. As the surrogate parent that even well-adjusted teenagers often seek, Smith was no doubt privy to anxieties and tensions that Robert's contemporaries did not notice. Some of them find this story hard to believe. Being Jewish, they say, was not a problem at Ethical Culture, where Jews and non-Jews among faculty and students mixed comfortably together. On the other hand, Fergusson believes that Robert may have felt "his Jewishness and his wealth, and his eastern connections, and [that] his going to New Mexico was partly to escape from that."[16]

Even in the 1920s escape was not the worst form of youthful rebellion. Robert's friends at school and at Harvard were not aware of special antipathy toward his father or of abnormal resentment of parental guidelines or family folkways. The early letters to Smith from Harvard do indeed indicate that the process of detachment—of establishing identity, we would now call it—was going on. Yet there was always a certain kindness in Robert's references to his parents and, as later letters show, in the years following Mrs. Oppenheimer's death in 1931, a remarkable willingness on Robert's part to share his life and his friends with his father.

The New Mexico trip not only initiated Robert's friendship with Paul Horgan and strengthened his ties to Francis Fergusson and to Smith, but introduced him to Cowles, a small community twenty miles up the Pecos Valley in the Sangre de Cristo Mountains northeast of Santa Fe. There he and Smith stayed at Los Pinos, a guest ranch run by Katherine Chaves Page and her husband, Winthrop, married the previous year. Friends of the Fergussons, the Chaveses were an old hidalgo family of which Katherine's father, Don Amado, was the current head. Katherine herself, then twenty-eight, is variously described as beautiful, charming, warm, imperious. Paul, Francis, and Robert, especially Robert, found her a fascinating and romantic figure. With her he developed a warm friendship which, although it decreased in intensity as he formed other attachments, lasted until her death in 1961. But according to Smith, acceptance of the insecure young New York Jew by the aristocratic Chaves circle, in which for "the first time in his life . . . [he] found himself loved, admired, sought after," was an important factor in the growing assurance that Robert's friends observed in him at this period.[17]

The Cowles visit also opened for Robert the magic world of the high country. He became an enthusiastic and expert horseman. With Katherine, Smith, and others he explored the slopes and valleys that led west and north to Lake Peak, the two Baldys—Santa Fe and Pecos—and the less accessible heights of Truchas. Smith was astonished at the endurance of his frail-looking and supposedly ailing young companion. There and elsewhere on their trip Robert displayed a fatalistic attitude toward physical danger that made him absolutely intrepid.

That Robert's first ride across the Rio Grande and up to the Los Alamos Ranch School on the Pajarito Plateau later determined the site of a great wartime laboratory has become a familiar part of the Oppenheimer legend. Robert's association with Los Alamos was in fact the dramatic epilogue to a quarter century of deep attachment to people and places in northern New Mexico. "I first knew the Pajarito Plateau in the summer of 1922," he later recalled, "when we took a pack trip up from Frijoles and into Valle Grande. We came back to it often from our ranch in the Pecos."[18]

The freedom and openness of this first western experience left a deep impression, and it was with broadened horizons, both geographic and social, that the young New Yorker returned to the east coast to commence his college education in Cambridge, Massachusetts.

Robert Oppenheimer, about age six, on a visit to Europe with his parents, Julius and Ella Oppenheimer. (Courtesy of Frank Oppenheimer.)

Robert Oppenheimer and his brother, Frank, about ages fourteen and six. (Courtesy of Frank Oppenheimer.)

Robert Oppenheimer, 1925, for the Harvard 1926 class album. (Courtesy of Harvard University Archives.)

I | "Work . . . frantic, bad and graded A"

HARVARD, 1922–1925

ROBERT OPPENHEIMER entered Harvard College as a freshman in September 1922. He received the A.B. degree in chemistry in June 1925. With one exception, the letters that survive from these three undergraduate years were written to people with whom he shared literary rather than scientific interests. Oppenheimer's contemporary comments on people and books, and on the poems and stories he was writing, represent a side of life that was very important to him at the time, but for significant information about how he learned science one must turn to the retrospective interview with Thomas Kuhn.[1] These reminiscences lack the immediacy of the letters, but Oppenheimer's searching and tentative replies to Kuhn show a young man pursuing a somewhat devious path toward a not yet clearly defined goal, a picture consistent with what the early letters have to tell. "I remember talking to some older colleagues [at Harvard] as to whether I should study chemistry or . . . mineralogy with the idea of becoming a mining engineer because I loved that kind of life . . . One of my friends said, 'Study chemistry; there are always summer vacations.'"

As to whether he took chemistry on the presumption that he would be a teacher, "I expect that wasn't a question that crossed my mind. It was a desire to learn which probably was much, much too uncalculated, but what I really wanted was to study physical chemistry because this was the thing whose glimmering I liked in elementary chemistry . . . It's only honest to add that at school and at Harvard I learned a lot of things that had no immediate connection with chemistry or with physics. I learned Greek at

11

school which was even then somewhat exotic . . . and I continued doing things like that at Harvard on a quite massive scale so that the notion that I was travelling down a clear track would be wrong. I determined to get a mastery of French and its literature which I knew very poorly; I had a very exciting time reading *The Principia* with Whitehead."

Oppenheimer presumed that apart from the "quirk about mineralogy and the abnormality of Greek," he probably had what was then a good high school background and not much more. "I knew what the calculus was, I knew what analytical geometry was, but I had had no formal training in it. I had probably looked at some texts. About physical chemistry I had read, but in a completely unenlightened way, a good deal more than one normally would but again with no discipline or coherence."

Because the Harvard years were intellectually stimulating, they were relatively satisfying, if not always happy, ones for Oppenheimer. They also saw the development of greater assurance in personal relationships, as foreshadowed by the experience with Francis Fergusson and Paul Horgan. During their one overlapping year at Harvard before Fergusson left for Oxford, this friendship was very important to Robert—caustic comments to Smith notwithstanding. Fergusson, who lived in a non-Harvard house at 96 Prescott Street while Robert was in a dormitory, recalls that they were in and out of each other's rooms all year.[2] Through Francis, Robert met a group of seniors and graduate students, including John T. Edsall and Jeffries Wyman. He joined the Student Liberal Club and a science discussion group. By the end of the year he had formed a second triumverate with two scientist classmates, Frederick Bernheim and William C. Boyd, which supplemented the literary one with Fergusson and Horgan.

AS HARVARD COLLEGE opened on September 25, Oppenheimer was settled in a single room, D 12 Standish Hall, a freshman dormitory facing the Charles River. (With the establishment of the house system in 1930, Standish became the west unit of Winthrop House.) A week later Robert wrote to Herbert Smith who had himself been a Harvard freshman fourteen years before.

D 12, Standish,
Cambridge, Mass.
October 2, 1922.

My dear Shylock,

Have mercy, great usurer! Here is the next installment of my debt. Then it will be for you to fulfill your contract of a letter for every two of mine. I hope you will not be tempted to do it as gracelessly as I. But even at that I await your answer with all the eagerness of those hectic days at [San] Diego.[a]

The tragic truth, however, is that I have no other legitimate reason for writing than that I hope thereby to elicit a brief but precious epistle from you. Harvard has so far been most delightful; it has crushed none of my romantic illusions of what it ought to have been; the only thing about which I might possibly display any righteous indignation is Dean Briggs' "College Life."[b] And the innate tact for which I am famous prevents even that bit of enthusiasm. There is no need my recounting to you the Freshman reactions: you know well enough the thunderous platitudes of the beginnings of philosophy and the painful phonetics of French. You may even remember the benign Lowell joining the Harvard locomotive,[c] and certainly you cannot have forgotten the disgust of the victim when he discovers to which English A instructor he has been assigned. In this, though, my shudders are all anticipatory: I have [Jess H.] Jackson, and Francis [Fergusson] says that meticulous spelling and plausible punctuation are all that will save me with him. By the way, I have written a theme, and this note is Freudian.

And you probably know too that I have not suffered from loneliness. There are plenty of amusing fellows with whom to read, talk, play tennis and make expeditions into the hills and toward the water (Freud again).

Two other things of which I should like to remind you: our scheme to involve Francis in the Yale game, and Mrs. Page's address.

As I am still in the hunt and peck stage of typewriting, my index finger is getting sore. So most of my brilliant witticisms will have to go unwritten (Gratia Dei).

Most sincere best wishes to you and Mrs. Smith,

Bob

You can excuse your delay in writing on the ground that you were waiting to tell me how much you disliked the books. The transcontinental alibi won't work. But I forgot; you never apologize.

A real P. S. —I had a letter from Scurlock at Diego.[d]

a. The first installment of the "debt" has not survived. In San Diego the Oppenheimers' friends, the William Templeton Johnsons, had shared with Smith responsibility for deciding whether Robert's colitis permitted a return home via the Canadian Rockies. He seemed much better, and the longer route was approved.

b. The edition of Dean Le Baron Russell Briggs' *College Life* current in 1922 contained four essays: "The Transition from School to College," "The Mistakes of College Life," "College Honor," and "Routine and Ideals."

c. A. Lawrence Lowell was president of Harvard University, 1909–1933.

d. J. C. Scurlock was a dealer in minerals in California. Robert considered his prices exorbitant. In 1948 Scurlock, manager of Western Engineering Associates, wrote to Oppenheimer that he need not have apologized for being late for their recent appointment "when I was twenty-six years getting you a tourmaline crystal with an 'unusual terminal' which you wanted"; Scurlock to Oppenheimer, June 22, 1948, Scurlock File, Box 65, J. Robert Oppenheimer Papers, Manuscript Division, Library of Congress, Washington, D.C.

Throughout the Harvard letters "Francis" is Francis Fergusson, who as a freshman had written frequently to Herbert Smith. Although he never admitted to Robert's outright satisfaction with Harvard, their attitudes were similar. Francis had hoped for a job on some one of the college papers but found that "writing" meant copying lists of students. "I decided that I preferred the life of the misanthrope," he told Smith, "so I now spend the time I should otherwise have spent in the competition reading Cabell's 'Beyond Life' as an antidote to Briggs' 'College Life.' "[3] As a sophomore, with Robert there to share his disdain for the typical collegian of their day, Francis took a more positive view of Harvard. Nevertheless, he diligently pursued the Rhodes Scholarship that would take him to Oxford for the remainder of his undergraduate work.

Robert failed to read the fine print in the catalogue which explained how to avoid freshman English, described as Rhetoric and English Composition. His other first year courses were: Elementary Organic Chemistry, followed second semester by Qualitative Analysis; French Prose and Poetry, Corneille through Zola; Analytic Geometry and Introduction to Calculus; and History of Philosophy.[4]

That some of these courses filled requirements did not spoil them for the young Oppenheimer. He truly did want to know French literature, and he remembered Philosophy A with Ralph Eaton, "a wonderful man," as "a really very good course . . . [I] had a nice time with it." Always, he told Kuhn, he audited two or three courses in addition to those listed on his transcript and learned so much in this way that in retrospect he could not distinguish them from those taken for credit.[5]

FREDERICK BERNHEIM was a class behind Robert at the Ethical Culture School, and they became friends as freshmen in Standish Hall. During their remaining two years at Harvard they occupied adjacent rooms in a house at 60 Mount Auburn Street.

By 1922 the Student Liberal Club, formed three years earlier to sponsor lectures and discussions, attracted those disillusioned with the postwar settlement in Europe and the Harding–Coolidge regime at home. Senior John Edsall, dining occasionally with Robert at the club's rooms at 66 Winthrop Street, spotted him as an exceptional freshman, more mature intellectually than socially. Forty years later Oppenheimer remembered only that he "felt very much a fish out of water," that he had provided a name for the club magazine, and had written something for it. The four surviving issues of *The Gadfly*, first published in December 1922, carry a quotation in Greek describing Socrates as the gadfly of the Athenian people. At Edsall's urging, Oppenheimer served as an assistant editor of the first two numbers, but his name is not among the later distinguished sons of Harvard who signed articles.[6]

2 | TO HERBERT W. SMITH

> Standish, D 12.
> Cambridge, Mass.
> November 14, 1922.

Dear Mr. Smith,

Fred Bernheim has performed the precarious experiment of entering two applications for the Yale game; he has as yet heard no anticipatory rumblings of vengeance, and there is at least a chance that he will get two or three tickets. He has promised me that, should this happen, he will give you one of them. It is, of course, too bad that we can not be together, but I believe that you will not have to search quite as diligently as you feared for your seat. If you can procure another ticket without too much difficulty and expense, that would surely be the safer course. I shall let you know as soon as I have more definite news.

Harvard has a serene and ridiculous appearance. The assinine pomposity of the Liberal club, the methodical expletives of our drunken patriots, the creative struggles of Francis's company and the quiet futility of most of the courses are as amusing as *Crome Yellow,* and are at least delightful in a somewhat Pecosian way.[a] Francis expects his Rhodes scholarship. Jackson is almost completely subjugated. And I am planning for next summer. I am hesitating, in my present deliberations, between Bolivia and a laboratory course in Cambridge. The proximity of East Brewster is a powerful argument in favor of the more conservative plan.[b]

15

I have been writing a good many variably execrable abominations.

Please tell me about your frivolities. Is the school still in existence after your ravages? Good luck to you all.

Bob

a. Refers to the Pecos Valley in New Mexico and the new circle of friends at Cowles.
b. East Brewster was the village on Cape Cod where Herbert Smith's Winslow ancestors had lived for generations and where Smith and his family usually spent their summers.

If Robert did not find himself at home in the Liberal Club, he fitted easily into the only other recorded extracurricular activity of his undergraduate years that could conceivably be called organized. He later recalled that for two years he had belonged to "a little science club which was partly faculty but mostly graduate students and which talked about scientific questions and philosophical questions related to science."[7] His letters to Smith do not mention the science group, but Francis Fergusson, writing to Smith in midautumn of 1922, commented on its origin and participants:

"I am one of four people who are starting a sort of organization whose purpose is to get professors to say interesting things . . . We meet Mondays in one of the members' rooms—a big room, with a fireplace and deep chairs. We invite a professor to come and address us on anything he wants. When he has finished we discuss. Such at least is the plan . . . I have seen something of Robert lately, who is one of our members. His conversation this year is a caricature of yours, ornamented with some of Paul's and my more elaborate affectations. I wonder what it will be like after a spell of this group, which contains an aberrant Cambridge Puritan, a boy from Atlanta, a New York German, learned in chemistry, a Minnesota exquisite, a Greek assistant in philosophy, a mathematics genius, and many other diverse and highly flavored fishes."[8]

ROBERT SEEMS regularly to have spent the Christmas holidays, a few days after the midyear examinations, and the spring vacation in New York. Usually he saw Herbert Smith. Fifty years later Smith displayed his de Maupassant volume as an example of the young Robert's extraordinary thoughtfulness.[9]

D 12 Standish,
Cambridge, Mass.
January 6, 1923.

Dear Mr. Smith,

Your Maupassant is being assembled. All the available editions were bound in ugly and inappropriate yellows and olive and pink mottling; and the one I am having made up will be ready in a publisher's week. As soon as I can wrest the Santayana from an aesthetic person from Minnesota—paradox—I shall return it and the even more precious socks; you should be delighted to learn that I have had the tact not to lend them.

The scoundrel Scurlock is trying to use me as one of a number of intermediaries in transferring a five thousand dollar mineral collection from an indeterminate Spanish engineer to the Agassiz museum. Fortunately I never had intended concentrating in geology.

For the remainder of this letter I should like to say 'thank you' again to you and Mrs. Smith. The two delightful days I spent with you were oases of civilization in the barren orgies of my vacation.

If you should have time to write, please do. I shall retaliate.

Very sincerely,

Bob

THE "AESTHETIC INTELLIGENCE TEST" mentioned in the following letter had originated two or three years earlier at a gathering of students, including Robert, at Smith's home. By way of entertainment, Smith had produced a set of questions fresh out of Teachers College which attempted to test poetic judgment by offering a choice of several selections, only one of which was genuine. Saying "we can do better than that," the students developed their own literary quiz game, which continued to circulate after they went to college. Smith thinks that his former students missed the easy exchange of their coeducational days at Ethical Culture and used this game as a way of keeping in touch.[10]

D 12, Standish,
Cambridge, Mass.
January 12, 1923.

Dear Mr. Smith,

God is most emphatically in his heaven; otherwise I should certainly have missed the delight of your letters; for they have reached me by the most extraordinary orbits. Yesterday there came a mysterious envelope with two copies of your aesthetic intelligence test—only that and nothing more. Today came a glittering letter of October third, which, even in its abridged form, did much to explain the bewildering discontinuities of our correspondence; and last of all came another consoling note and another challenging copy of *Innisfree*. This last was furnished with an appendix from Francis, setting a date for a walk. The interpretation of these remarkable phenomena takes a keener scientific brain than mine; all I can do is to say thank you again and again, and gloat in the reception of so many papers from your apt typewriter.

The only one of the poems that I very much like is the third. But "you are so clever, and I am so dull" that I tremble at calling that the original; it is really beautiful to my ears, but I do not consider you incapable of such gross deception. If, in the fourth, the sense and the verse were not engaged in such bitter battle, that would not be impossible. I think the first two are abominable. The deed is done.

In a few days Jane will be in New York. I have just received a letter from her; it is so strange that I am sending it to you. Even the queer idiom cannot explain it. But I should like it back, later; it is a fitting finale to a very poignant series. When you see the lovelorn lass, will you give her my most glib and convincing congratulations, please? Of course I shall write as soon as I know how to reach her. I suspect that Mama is mad.

I am again in the toils of a short story. It is not to be as pretentious or subtle as the last, and so there is some chance of its not being as vile. At least I think you will be interested in the setting. —A young mining engineer is starting his career at the Humboldt mine. I introduce the fellow as he dismounts from his horse and begins the climb. He has courage enough to enter the amphitheatre on the cable car; it is good fun to give his first impressions of the place when the cable gets high enough for him to see. He is a sophisticated and introspective person, and the filth, the phosphorescent manager, and the miserable, indifferent miners only make him laugh and look smugly at the sunset. But, by a simple mechanism, he discovers that the superintendent, who is a pretty unprepossessing person, is, like him, a graduate of an eastern college; and that he was, at one time, an intimate friend of the young fellow's aunt. He realizes that he, too, is rather likely to disintegrate just as the manager has; and his complacency vanishes. He is really miserable, and is perfectly willing to listen to a disgusting and doddering syphilitic, with whom, earlier in the day, he would have nothing to do. And he no longer sees anything at all risible in the mine. Observe the three unities. Anyway, it is rather fun, and I shall be too busy after this to do it.

It will take me eons to pay my literary debt to you. But another letter and some mangled verses will come soon. Good luck.

Very sincerely and gratefully,

Bob

Robert's friend Jane Didisheim had returned briefly from France prior to her marriage to Jacques Kayser. In 1974, thanking Herbert Smith for sending her copies of some of Robert's early letters, Jane Kayser wrote: "How many, both friends and adversaries who supported, judged, condemned him later on, during his brilliantly successful and desperately tragic career, could ever have guessed who Robert really was. To the adjectives you used to describe him . . . I should add: 'vulnerable.' Half a century after the letters were written, they give me food for much thought and awaken a consciousness of regret and sorrow—How innocently—or stupidly—callous I must have been, never to have sensed the thin-skinned delicacy of his attachment."[11]

5 | TO HERBERT W. SMITH

D 12, Standish,
Cambridge, Mass.
January 21, 1923.

Dear Mr. Smith,

Your last letter was so tactfully pregnant with catastrophe that I am quite unable to conceal my impolite curiosity. Are you again, O fortunate wretch, to spend a summer in New Mexico? Are you to assist in chaperoning Mrs. Page's maidens? Or are you about to import a third neurotic freak, even more unpresentable than the last two, into the wilds of Sprague's?[a] This importunate clamour is merely the typographic manifestation of much gloom; for I sit here seeking for plans by which to avoid the unavoidable sailboat and estate; and I glance with tear-blurred eyes from your poignant sentences to the three magnificent photographs on my wall. I fear that you are to blame for any signs of romanticism that I may show in future.

Yet if you had announced that you were on the point of departing for Siam, you could not have surprised me more than by your *Innisfree* pronouncement. For the second was the only one upon which Francis and I had vented our combined disapproval; and though I am lost in shame at the admission, I fear that we still do. I have mouthed the deceitful lines time and again, yet scarcely a trace of their poetic significance has reached my prosaic ear; the rhythm annoys me, and the figures seem to me unreal and colorless; I can not conceive of peace dropping to where the cricket sings, and I am, unfortunately, no doubt, acoustically incapable of hearing the dusk in my deep heart's core, or any where else, I fear. I have tried the wretched thing on two friends; one of them chose the third, and the other, mirabile dictu, the right one. He claims to have a true sense of poetry, and after a few professional contortions of his mouth, he pointed to the second and said "This." But in spite of him, Quiller-Couch, and you, I remain an unrepenting philistine.

Next week Francis and I shall concoct a retaliatory quiz. And I shall send you my story, which, at present, is complete but illegible. It is certainly adequate testimony of the mangling that I gave the other one, that it should seem untrue. For it is taken with scarcely any colitic revisions from an incident of my cousin with my uncle and my aunt.

Thanks for psychoanalysing Jane. My experience in matters marital is, and will always be, alas, so much less fortunate than yours, that I accept your dictum without a squirm.

Please give my best wishes to Mrs. Smith, and write when you have time. Very sincerely,

Bob

a. According to Herbert Smith, Mrs. Page hoped to recruit some girls as guests at Los Pinos to provide company for the boys brought by Smith. However, none came; Smith to Alice Kimball Smith, July 28, 1976. Sprague's was a guest lodge in Estes Park, Colorado.

"THE PINK THINGS FROM VASSAR" mentioned in the following letter related to the aesthetic intelligence game and came from Inez Pollak, a classmate of Robert's at Ethical Culture who was a sophomore at Vassar. In January 1923 she and her freshman sister Kitty each reported to Herbert Smith the reactions of Vassar friends to the various choices, enclosed their own versions of the game, and asked for Francis's and Robert's. Kitty concluded: "This new game is proving very popular, though the poetic appreciation isn't much better than at school."[12]

The Oppenheimers' summer home was at Bay Shore on the south side of Long Island, where they had first rented a house, then bought one a year or so after Frank's birth in 1912. Robert usually wrote Bay Shore as one word, for which Frank has no explanation other than that was the way they said it.[13]

6 | TO HERBERT W. SMITH

Standish D 12,
Cambridge, Mass.
January 28, 1923.

Dear Mr. Smith,

This is to be little more than a placard of procrastinations; the story is not yet legible; and so far the verses that Francis and I were to send have gone no further than a few revengeful mutterings. But after the midyear period,[a] so inappropriate for frivolity and impossible for thought, I may come down to the city for a day or so, bearing literary thunderbolts.

Nor can I say anything more definitely damning about the pink things from Vassar. Again I defend myself with a platitudinous and comprehensive scorn of the entire lot. But it seems to me less likely that Inez should have written about sky-pavilioned land than about Apollo's steeds, empty joys, or spanning skies. So, with the customary hesitation,—the third. Francis threatens to show me another set; as yet I have not seen it, but I suspect that my unprejudiced judgement would be more fortunate than the later ones that take into account such irrelevancies as the excellence of the verses.

The outlook is so dismal that I can't be at all successfully flip. Imbecile examinations, weeks of slush, tantalizing courses in chemistry that it will take me years to reach, and Bayshore threatening to absorb the summer vacation—is it not sad? But you can't be sentimental on a typewriter, so so long, and good luck.

Bob

a. Midyear examinations had begun on January 25.

ROBERT WENT "down to the city" before the second semester opened on February 12.

February 11, 1923.
Train North.

My dear Mr. Smith,

Our meeting yesterday was so short, & so much complicated by pleasant but Philistine company, that I am nearly as tragic as if I had not seen you at all. And Mrs. Smith couldn't come: no, it was a very unsatisfactory family reunion.

So may I be rude and intrusive by mail? For you reminded me more, yesterday, of El Paso than of Cowles; and I want to beg you to soothe your excitable conscience and work less heroically. If you had anything as annoying as this to say, you would, of course, do it tactfully and dynamically. I can't. And yet I would so much rather see all of Ethical go to college barbarously illiterate than know that you were losing weight on anything but me!

Adios; and perhaps it was only your dentist.

Bob

8 | TO HERBERT W. SMITH

Stillman Infirmary
Harvard University
February 18, 1923.

My dear Mr. Smith,

You were very wrong, really, to infer from my last impertinent note that you were not charming at our party; you were, and you scintillated more than any of that dismal gathering. Mrs. Page started bravely enough, but soon grew silent under the weight of paternal banalities and Ethical gossip;[a] and Jane's sighs of happiness came disastrously near, I thought, to groans of despair, when someone asked her if she had ever been out west. No—you were the only civilized person there; I apologize for any incompatible implication.

Francis told me, when he called here yesterday, that you had definitely decided to go west with your two new neurotics. F. F. is at present planning a trip for you four to the Hopi country, and chortling with much incoherent delight. Of course I am insanely jealous. I see you riding down from the mountains to the desert at that hour when thunderstorms and sunsets caparison the sky; I see you in the Pecos "in September, when I'll want my friends to comfort me, you know", spending the moonlight on Grass Mountain; I see you vending the marvels of the upper Loch, of the upper amphitheater at Ouray, of the waterfall at Telluride, the Punch Bowl at San Ysidro—even the prairies around Antonito—to philistine eyes. Do you remember that first evening in Denver, when we scrambled our luggage?

Does Mrs. Smith expect to meet you again next summer? And will you trust again to the five minute connection at Santa Fe? Wouldn't Mrs. Smith like to spend a few days at the shore, with us? There is lots of water, a sailboat, horses, & all that; & I'll be sure to be there at whatever time she says.

I have had a terrific fever, and have read another Conrad. So this may sound a bit strange.

But good luck.

Affectionately,

Bob

a. Katherine Page was instructor in Spanish at Finch Junior College in New York City during the academic year 1922–23; Consuelo Chaves Summers to Alice Kimball Smith, October 29, 1976.

9 | TO HERBERT W. SMITH

Cambridge, Mass.
March 31, 1923

Dear Mr. Smith,

This time I can again begin my note with the standard Ethical opening: I am sorry that I could not write before, but I was so dreadfully busy; for instance—

But in this time quite a stack of trivial news has managed to get itself collected; and so I shall sacrifice the proverbial unity and logical lucidity of my letter in its favor.

1. A letter has just come from Mrs. William Templeton Johnson, sending regards to you, inviting us both to return, urging California Tech and Joyism.[a] It seems that, among our literary calisthenics, my letter to the Johnsons went to the Dead Letter Office but has now been rescued.

2. A letter from home just before the great event well garnished with invitation, thanks, regrets, and trepidations.

3. A letter from Mrs. Page! She is coming down to the shore with Francis and the family on the fourteenth. Can't you possibly manage to tear yourself and Mrs. Smith away for a day or so? Again much invitation and laments.

4. The Pollaks have camped up here for the week. Francis and I have, ac-

cordingly, been spending most of our hours not claimed by lab and Widener [Library] in heterogeneous expeditions up to the Sachs estate.[b] It's all over.

5. You and Francis are going to have a great time. Mrs. Page and Francis have spared me none of the harrowing details, and I am dissolving in impotent jealousy.

6. Fred and I are about to become landed gentry. We propose to buy, rent, or otherwise appropriate a ramshackle cottage way out on Cape Ann. It lies way above the water, amid huge cliffs of yellow granite, and looks across a miraculously blue ocean to the shore line of Maine.

7. On the same expedition I received another inspiration to write a story. It is very short, exceedingly bad, and only barely justified by the difficulty of the thing. If I don't burn it you may see it.

And now that all that unpleasantly efficient bit of gossip is disposed of, there is time to grow emotional about your summer and verbose about my books. I shall spare you the former.

I am glad that you didn't find Russell completely piffle; it seems to me that what he analyzes is quite distinctly mind and not brain; that, by a few magisterial but unconvincing waves of his hand, he dismisses that "subconscious mind" as a going hypothesis, and that he excludes all truly reflex phenomena and such from his consideration; but yet he seems to have quite a valid point in insisting that what distinguishes mental phenomena, and particularly the more complex operations, is not consciousness, but rather the belief feeling or the Mneme.[c] Now I disagree with him. And being naturally pugnacious, I also disagree with your objection. Not that I like his suggestion that subconscious phenomena are naturally subconscious. It seems to me that here he is confusing unconscious with subconscious, and that he hopes, by that confusion, to refute the psychoanalytic hypotheses. These, I think, have such an ample a posteriori justification that they have, for the present, at least, all the value of any scientific theory. But, as you say, more later.

How do you like Katherine Mansfield? And please, we must see each other later on. And my best regards to Mrs. Smith.

I'm sorry that this is such a garrulous, scatterbrained note. But answer it in kind, if you can.

As ever—

Bob

a. Alfred H. Joy was an astronomer at the Mount Wilson Observatory near the newly established California Institute of Technology.

b. Inez Pollak remembers several visits to Cambridge in this period accompanied by her brother or sister. The Sachs estate, Shady Hill, was the home of the Pollaks' uncle, Paul Sachs, associate professor of fine arts at Harvard; interview with Inez Pollak by Alice Kimball Smith, April 20, 1976.

c. Bertrand Russell's *Analysis of Mind* was published in 1921.

Consulted in 1976 about the purchase of the ramshackle cottage on Cape Ann, Frederick Bernheim replied that it never materialized and that, as far as he was concerned, the huge cliffs of yellow granite belong to a mythological landscape. However, Cape Ann was a favorite weekend objective. He and Robert, joined on occasion by William Boyd, would drive to Gloucester in Bernheim's Willys Overland and spend Saturday night at an inn at Folly Cove where the food was exceptionally good. In those days before through roads and route signs, they often got lost in the streets and squares of suburban Boston. Finally Robert, who did not yet drive, learned to face backward in order to read the signs on the rear end of trolleys going in the opposite direction to find where they had come from.[14]

10 | TO HERBERT W. SMITH

Cambridge, Mass.
May 2, 1923.

Dear Mr. Smith,

Here are the masterpieces. But first of all, and very emphatically this time, may I have the other story about the mine? I shall probably use that one for Jackson, for it is the kind that is least likely to get a bad grade. If you can't find the silly thing, you might let me know and I shall concoct another equally innocuous.

And here, too, is the apologia that ought to accompany the four things I am sending:

Please don't read *Conquest* until the last; I am certain you will dislike it, and accuse me of morbidity and neuroticism. Also bad taste and poor writing. But there is one thing which you dare not imply; if you do say that this is a lot of sentimental drivel our metaphysical and literary intercourse will come to an abrupt conclusion. I shall seek death.

The other stories you will probably object to merely on aesthetic grounds. But I feel that you will be able to lacerate them more efficiently if I announce

that "It's Silly" is not meant for poetry,

that the Elysée is in New York, not Paris,

and that, as you also undoubtedly know, Conrad's *Youth* is a beautiful novelette on the futility of youthful courage and idealism.

All this sounds as though I were sending you at least a copy of "War and Peace" and the Iliad. But it is merely my trepidation that makes me thus apologize at such length in advance. Strangely enough, tho, Francis seemed to like the three he has seen.

I have had several piteous little notes from Mrs. Page. She seems to be

25

having a perfectly rotten time of it. Is there anything besides letters and promiscuous solicitude that I can give or do?

Moreover, I must thank you again for your Hewes plan. It really may work. I went to see Hewes, who agreed with me, and suggested that his word would be more effective if it came as an answer to a letter from the folks. So I wrote, telling them how much I wanted to be with them for some part of the summer, and generally exhausting all arguments but the one of health. It was very thorough. Then I suggested that, if they were really in doubt about the health question, they should ask someone whom they trusted, e.g., Hewes.[a] I promised to abide by his dictum.

And in the mean while, how are your plans? Francis has not yet heard from Erna [Fergusson]. And has Mrs. Page any maidens? Wouldn't Helen Weil do, in a pinch, for the Los Pinos party?[b] Well, that is for you.

Scatterbrainedly but sincerely—

Bob

a. Hewes may have been Henry Fox Hewes, M.D., of Marlborough Street, Boston, instructor of medicine at Harvard Medical School.

b. Helen Weil, a classmate of Robert's at Ethical Culture School, was later singled out by Herbert Smith as "the only person . . . [Robert] ever suggested as worthy to be included in the Chaves menage"; Smith to Alice Kimball Smith, July 9, 1975.

If Robert had any daring venture in mind for the summer, it did not come off. His vacation included a laboratory job in New Jersey, a month at Bay Shore, and a motor trip with his parents. Robert's health obviously continued to be a matter of concern to them. It was not a problem that dominates the recollections of his contemporaries, though Bernheim thought of him as something of a hypochondriac. Robert used to go to bed with an electric pad. One night when it overheated he put the smoking pad in the bathroom and went back to sleep. There was considerable local damage.[15]

THERE IS NO EVIDENCE that any of Robert's fiction was published, or survived in manuscript, or indeed left a lasting impression upon its readers. George Stevens, later a successful publisher, author, and critic, does not recall reading anything Robert wrote at Harvard.[16]

D 12 Standish
Cambridge, Mass.
May 15, 1923.

Dear Mr. Smith,

I hasten to thank you very vigorously indeed for your long and tolerant letter; hasten even more because, after my last supremely unlovely note, your answer is a gleaming token of a forgiving soul. I suppose that it is useless to apologize for the increased surliness of the note; but I must assure you that it was written in one of those spells of colitic insolence and misanthropy from which you have already suffered so often.

With most of what you have to say about my filthy stories I agree quite absolutely. I think, though, that what, in Conquest, you so magnanimously consider carelessness, is in reality ineptitude; for I thought it necessary to show enough of the antecedent circumstances to explain how the situation came about, but did not want to elaborate the old fisherman's motives; which, I tried to make it obvious, were very strictly pecuniary. And I have to admit, moreover, with the same shamefaced feeling with which I announced my mid-year grades, that I can discover no terminus a quo for the judge simile. I was almost flattered by your incredulity, for I had to preserve that passage against the attacks of Fred and George Stevens, who happened to be here when I wrote it.

Your diagnosis of the troubles with my other things delighted me. For I think that it is these, rather than any "conscious imitation of Katherine Mansfield" or artificiality of emotional situation that account for their utter failure. You see, I was no more conscious of imitating anyone in those than in any others; and I should not have the hardihood to write a story that was not based upon a very real emotional experience. But my things so reek with crudity, with unreliable detail and unreinforced implication, that the mere mechanics are likely to invalidate anything that I might have to say. Half the tragedy, you see, of Le Monde, is that Elisabeth could see in the grey sea a cosmic gutter.

So much for that. When I come down, I may have a few other things to show you, if that will not bore you too much. And thanks again.

Your letter was so spectacularly altruistic that you said nothing at all about what you were doing; and really, I should like to know. I have heard nothing about the magazine you were working for since I last saw you, and I should like to see your article in it. And how is the unsteady brat for next summer?

Your suggestion about dislodging the folks from Bayshore, is slowly and uncertainly being carried into effect. In father's letter this morning—"Your invitation to go west is very tempting. Perhaps we can all manage [it]"—So you see.

When I see you I shall say more of the comparatively Elysian life I have led here of late. And then we shall talk again with the free garrulity of midnight at Ouray—

And now a most grateful Adios.

Bob

Scurlock detonated again. R

SOMETHING MORE IMPORTANT than writing and course work took place that first year. Robert discovered Widener Library. He talked about this experience in 1963: "I have a book—I saw it yesterday—which is salt-encrusted; it's Jeans' *Electricity and Magnetism* and it's clear that I studied that when I went sailing in the summer . . . My guess is that it was the arrival at Harvard, the free availability of the whole library—which happened very soon—that suddenly got me reading very widely . . . I must have started reading physics in a major way. I don't believe [that] I audited a course, I don't believe that I went to any seminars in physics that first, freshman year, but I petitioned the physics department for graduate standing."[17]

Graduate standing, which did not imply candidacy for an advanced degree, would permit Oppenheimer to take graduate courses. He submitted his request through a junior member of the department, Edwin C. Kemble, then engaged in research on molecular spectra in gases. Kemble had received the Ph.D. from Harvard in 1917 and was a member of its physics department from 1919 until he retired in 1957.

12 | TO EDWIN C. KEMBLE

D 12 Standish
May 24 1923

Dear Sir:

I write to apply for permission to take Physics 6a next year, without first completing Physics C. In support of this application, let me mention the work that I have done which might prepare me for your course.

In preparatory school I took a full laboratory course in Physics, in which I received the grade of A. In addition to the regular work, I performed several experiments in mechanics, heat, and light; furthermore, I read rather widely in elementary books on optics, the theory of heat, and the physics of the molecule. I presented Physics as a subject for entrance, and received a 96 on the examination of the College Board.

This year I have taken Chemistry 2, in which I received a grade of A; Chemistry 3, in which my grade, up to the present, has been A; and mathematics with Professor [Julian L.] Coolidge, in which I have been receiving an A. On the advice of Professor Coolidge and Professor [William F.] Osgood I am going to take Mathematics 5 next year. During this time I have read several works on Thermodynamics and related subjects. A partial list follows:

Ramsay; Lewis: Vol. 1, Kinetic Theory.
          Vol. 2, Thermodynamics and Statistical Mechanics.
          Vol. 3, Quantum Theory.
Lewis and Randall: Thermodynamics.
Crowther (of Thomson's laboratory): Molecular Physics.
Poincaré: La Physique Moderne.
Walker: Physical Chemistry.
Ostwald: Solutions.
Gibbs: On the Equilibria of Heterogeneous Systems.
Jeans: The Dynamical Theory of Gases. (part)
Poincaré: Thermodynamique (part)
Nernst: Thermodynamics and Chemistry.
          (part of) Theoretische Chemie.
Sommerfeld: Atombau u. Spectral-linien (part)
Mac Dougall: Thermodynamics and Chemistry.

Whatever reading or work you may advise, I shall be glad to do; for I very sincerely hope that my petition may be granted.

Very truly,

                                        J Robert Oppenheimer

An entry in the minutes of a physics department meeting on June 6 was originally typed as follows: "It was *voted* to allow Mr. J. R. Oppenheimer to take Physics *6a* without taking Physics C. It appeared that Mr. Oppenheimer, according to his own statement had done considerable reading and study in Physics." Pencilled emendations changed the entry to "had read rather widely in Physics, for one of his age." Two days later Professor Theodore Lyman, the department chairman, informed Robert that his petition was granted.[18]

Recalling this episode in 1963, Oppenheimer added: "It may be apocryphal, but years later I was told that when the faculty met to consider this request, George Washington Pierce . . . said, 'Obviously if he says he's read these books he's a liar, but he should get a Ph.D. for knowing their titles.' "[19]

The reading list suggests a facility with languages other than English which Oppenheimer acquired early and retained. "I had had some French, but I didn't know the literature well and I couldn't write it fluently . . . I learned . . . something of how it sounded from a governess at one point. I had studied [German]. We didn't talk it at home; my mother didn't talk it well, my father didn't believe in talking it. But I had been to Europe . . . I never went back to studying Greek but I continued to read it. Latin I only got to read again much later; it's an old man's language . . . Scientific things I would read in whatever they came in, but literary things I would be reading in French and a little in Italian. One of the courses I audited was on *Vita Nuova*."[20]

FINAL EXAMINATIONS OVER, Robert left for New York in time to keep a date to see the *Devil's Disciple* with Smith. In due course he learned that his grade in freshman English was B, in all other courses A.[21]

13 | TO HERBERT W. SMITH

D 12 Standish
Cambridge, Mass.
May 30, 1923.

My dear Mr. Smith,

A hasty note to acknowledge the return of the illbehaved story and to confirm our date for the thirteenth. I shall probably be in to school to see you and decide where to meet; if not I shall call.

You know well enough what a futile and "ungemütlich" time this is: I shall not trouble you more with the degenerate dribblings of my Corona. The only news is that I shall probably get a C in English because I cut the last three classes.

Adios

Bob

FROM NEW YORK, though on Harvard stationery, Robert wrote Francis Fergusson the first of a series of letters through which they attempted to keep in touch during two years of separation.

[New York City]
June 14 1923.

Dear Francis,

Yesterday evening Smith and I saw the Devil's Disciple. He seemed comparatively cheerful, overflowed with the "hullo Bob" sort of thing, and regained with surprising ease the orbit of condescension from which I had so arrogantly jarred him. What, I think, was his worst trouble during the winter, and what accounts for his fits of misanthropy, is the series of Kowtowings he had to perform for the skinflint Jews whose infant he is to chaperone. But it is all settled now, and he has returned to his normal abnormality.

His irritation at my stories is not hard to explain, either. It seems that Kitty Pollak has recently started writing too, and he is much annoyed at having failed to detect and coddle even such puny ability when he could. But alas, it is not only that: he said, and if my typewriter were not incapacitated, I should print this in crimson—he said that he thought that the sort of thing we were trying to write was incapable of standing on its own feet, that, even with the great, it was scarcely successful, and with us hopeless. He excepted your Ralph story and mine about Jane—Alas . . .

One other thing and my official report will be complete: he thinks that you are not *Frank* enough with him—hear my Mephistophelian chortles— he suspects you of not telling either of us your real opinions—he hopes to get more out of you next summer. So you had better think up a platoon of plausible platitudes to sell as secrets, or your plans may not work so well. I hope that you understand the appropriate modesty with which I submit this resume, for it would be vain for me to dogmatize to you, my revered master and tutor in the science of Smithology; but I am so used to handing over my soul to you that I grow uneasy when I discover a few still undelivered fragments.

The Russian is coming: I am now at the stage where I can discuss vertebrates in the present tense with seeming erudition. As yet no news from Paul [Horgan]; and I wait with pronouncing my plans until my campaign advances a few more millimicrons.

Your books are on their way. Poincaré is out of print in English and unavailable in French, but you will be able to get him when you are in Europe. You know how glad I should be to hear from you, even if you descend to so trivial and selfcentered a note as this.

A bientot.

[no signature]

31

Rereading this letter in 1976, Fergusson was puzzled by the references to Smith since he cannot remember a time when he did not hold him in high regard and affection. "But of course it's Robert's style," he reflected. "Everything he takes up, he exaggerates." Smith himself made a similar comment in another connection, and Horgan too noted Robert's "baroque tendency to exaggerate."[22] In any case, the temporary rebellion against Smith in his quasiparental role did not last.

AN EFFORT to introduce variety into Oppenheimer vacations was not successful. New Mexico was apparently out of the question, and a proposed family expedition to the Selkirk Mountains in British Columbia was abandoned. Robert spent a few weeks in a dull laboratory job in New Jersey, which he left shortly after writing to Fergusson on July 17.

15 | TO FRANCIS FERGUSSON

> The Brittan
> 1025 East Jersey
> Elizabeth, New Jersey
> July 17, 1923.

Dear Francis,

This new and vicious George of yours must really be a very magnificent person,[a] and I realize well enough that it is not a bit proper or even natural for me not to be jealous of him. For not only has he captured the love and adulation of Los Pinos; but he is endowed with all those enticing traits which I find most ghastly in man. He is what the world was to me in earlier adolescence. And yet, damnabile dictu, I find in my unmanly soul no trace of that jealousy, and do not even grudge him the honor of having reduced your Bayshore modicum of twelve hours of sleep to three.

But oh, beloved, how I envy you! Three hours sleep; witty; charming; the soul and supporter of Los Pinos; the all but gastronomic consoler to the Pecos' host—successful; doing a little intellectual work on the side; blessed with enormous activity—Mon Dieu—Francis, you choke me with anguish and despair; all I can do is to admit to my hierarchy of physico-chemical immutabilities the Chaucerian "Amour vincit omnia."

It was in search of a similarly satisfying adventure that I wandered here. I have a job as laboratorian or chemist or something like that, and have searched the plant and the hotel for possible persons. Only one wretch have I found, and he penniless and dissipated; but he is six foot seven, has fine black moustachios, is a Bostonian via Oxford, is properly pessimistic and boasts cleverly about the right sort of thing, has read, and well, writes, and is a bit of a scientist. He works at a different plant and lives in a different city, but has come over for an evening a couple of times. But he has lost his job, and is going to South America. He is not a Jew.

Outre cela, rien. The job and people are bourgeois and lazy and dead; there is little work and nothing to puzzle at; and the establishment has among it less than one sixteenth of a sense of humour. So soon I am going home again, where, I find, I can read much and write a little. Later we are going on a trip, probably to the Selkirks in British Columbia.

Nothing I can write could be interesting, now. But I hope to cheat you into sending me another of your gloating letters. I feel almost as though I could say, naively and petulantly, of course, that it was so good to hear from you youngsters now and then. But I am not yet even as resigned as Smith— whom, by the way—you are now caricaturing quite as grotesquely through superiority as you once did in admiration—and I still squirm. That, I am afraid, is a sight to make not only Gods but grammarians weep, for my moans are always non sequiturs.

Boyd tells me that he is maintaining his program of selfintellectualization with appalling rigor. Smith's letters have grown affectionate again. Perhaps, now that he has seen you, he has decided that I did well to keep as sane as I am in your presence. All the rest is groans—and sailing and novels and mathematical physics.

Please, I almost whimper it, please write again.

[no signature]

a. George was one of Katherine Page's paying guests at Los Pinos.

Boyd was William Clouser Boyd, usually called "Clowser" by Robert, who consistently misspelled the name. With Bernheim, Boyd helped to fill the gap left by Fergusson's departure for Oxford. He and Robert had met as freshmen in Chem 3, the qualitative analysis course. Boyd had studied chemistry in high school in St. Joseph, Missouri, and Robert used to bring his tests on his unknowns to him for verification. Another member of the class asked Boyd, "Who is this guy Oppenheimer who keeps coming to you? I think he's a pest." Boyd reminisced: "Well, I didn't think he was a pest. It was obvious . . . that he was a very talented person, very able and very sensitive, and we had lots of interests in common aside from science. We both tried to write and we wrote poetry, sometimes in French, and we wrote stories in imitation of Chekhov . . . and he did a little painting which I have done since . . . The chief thing . . . we did not have in common was a love of music. I was very fond of music . . . but once a year he would go to an opera, with me and Bernheim usually, and he'd

33

leave after the first act. He just couldn't take any more. Totally amusical, I thought then. I tested him once, and he was not tone deaf."[23]

In view of Robert's later intense enjoyment of music, his indifference to it at this period is interesting. As a child he had shown a precocious ability to recognize themes in classical music but he was bored by piano lessons. He once had an illness with flu-like symptoms so severe as to suggest that he might have polio. When his mother asked him how he felt, Robert reportedly answered, "The way I do when I have to practice." The lessons were discontinued.[24] Herbert Smith, remarking that Robert's reliable memory failed him only under some sort of inhibition, recalled the following conversation. Said Smith to Robert, "You're the only physicist I've ever known who wasn't also musical, and I never heard you refer to music." "I don't know," Robert replied, "something must have happened because I used to be devoted to it. I just don't know what happened."[25]

ROBERT SOON LEFT the laboratory job and was at the shore with his family when he wrote Francis again in mid–August. Once he had experienced New Mexico's vast panorama of deserts and mountains and its casual social life, the conventional summer house on Long Island seemed a place of confinement, despite easy access to the sea and sailing, which he loved. Nevertheless, in 1923 Bay Shore was still an important part of the Oppenheimer way of life and gave pleasure to many people, sometimes even to Robert.

To Fred Bernheim, a New Yorker, it was "just an ordinary kind of house." The boys from Missouri and New Mexico were more impressed. William Boyd remembers it as elegant, Paul Horgan as "well staffed with maids and people on the grounds . . . a very comfortably spacious estate . . . It was my first taste as a resident of rather excessive luxury and grandeur and comfort on that scale. I enjoyed it enormously."[26]

Frank too has clear and happy memories of Bay Shore. At the pier below the house were moored the family's forty-foot sailing yacht, *Lorelei,* with auxiliary motor and other amenities, and the *Trimethy,* the twenty-eight foot sloop used by Robert and Frank, its name shortened from trimethylamine (C_3H_9N), a colorless liquid which smelled like pickled herring. "It was lovely on that bay," recalls Frank, "seven acres . . . a big vegetable garden and lots and lots of flowers." It was a place to share with friends and celebrate family festivals. On Frank's birthday and his mother's, which fell in summer, others in the family went out early to pick flowers with which they covered the breakfast table and even the seats of chairs.[27]

Bayshore N Y
August 16, 1923.

Dear Francis,

At last I see an opportunity for one of those longwinded, tapestried apologies whose prospect always delights me. Think of the august and pompous genuflections with which I might open this letter; consider the glittering array of explanations, the platoons of excuses, the phalanxes of apologetics that I might marshal to salute you. Racine himself could have conceived no more melodramatic a situation, nor one more prolific of potential sonorous verbalisms: —It is ten days since your letter arrived. — Thus long have I delayed answer, thus brazenly have I neglected to thank you—Hélas.

And that in the face of your perfect Pecos panorama, which leaves me, even now, with a disconcerting image of "George" and Smith and Katy [Katherine Page] mingling oaths and tears and ocote; in the face of your promise of Harvard and Los Pinos sagas, prospect which would have moved to action anyone less degenerate and callous than I. But really, maestro, I am terribly—yes, terribly, eager to see your things, and would even burn my new Jean's Electromagnetics for a glimpse of the Pecos one. I can't tell you how I admire the calm intensity with which you say "I shall do a big story about that—later on." Quelle patience inattendue et inhumaine! voir Herrick.

But I can keep the news from you no longer, even at the cost of sacrificing a more extended salutation: le jour de gloire est arrivé: Paul has been with me for the past three weeks. Of course I have been happy.

It all happened in a most perfectly well managed way. I was just on the point of leaving my job in Chrome permanently—for it was too boring even for my ascetic soul, and I had written all I wanted at the time—when a tornado and cymbal letter came from Paul, effervescing in the most considerate way with apology and cordiality and excitement. So we have been spending a most civilized and unexciting time down here, writing, reading enormously, travelling to town from time to time for books and exhibits and plays, and sallying every evening in tuxedoes, pathetically to ransack Bayshore or Islip for a vestige of adventure. Paul has even been tactful enough to sing extended paeans to Katherine Mansfield[a] and to conquer his fear of the sea often enough to permit him an occasional panegyric on sailing. He sketches with mother, goes riding with father and me, acts for Frank, praises my stories, and even brings himself, reluctantly enough, to examine Jeans and Poincaré. Ce n'est pas* un homme, c'est un monstre. And our expeditions to the city—*voir Herrick.

35

Later on we are motoring to Niagara with him, and then on to Quebec. N.M. was quite impossible, this year, I think. I fear that if I transported father and mother to the midst of the desert and dropped them, I should jeopardize my puny inheritance; and to chaperone them to Los Pinos would insure a new nervous breakdown. All that Smith and Mrs. Page write confirms your dismal account.

Perhaps, when you come through in the fall, I can arrange to see you. At any rate, you must call on mother and get your pictures and address; and you must let me see your stories, if you can possibly spare them. I shall return them without the Gargantuan promptings which were needed to extract them from Smith.

I have written eight or nine stories, but have worked on only a few. One of them satisfies me far better than anything else I have done, and I should be only too delighted to let you see it. As soon as I begin to know enough I shall not need to resort to these things; but that seems farther off now than ever, and this psychic celibacy is too stern a regimen. So I write my stories, and send you these notes of drivel. I am back at my moaning again, you see, in spite of the plaster of Paris fresco beginning. You must write, anyway, and forgive me these reams of tardy and inconsequential twaddle.

K.M.'s new book "Dove's Nest" is heartrending. There are several exquisite stories, and many lovely fragments. But there is so much that is incomplete, that is either unfinished or unpolished or fragmentary or insignificant, that it is a cruel thing to read—as disappointing as if the Hermes of Praxiteles were suddenly to develop viscera. You've probably seen it by now, anyway.

My corona is dying, too—Adiós.

[no signature]

Paul's still on The Press.

a. Mrs. Oppenheimer admired Mansfield's writing.

Horgan looks back upon those weeks in Bay Shore with the same untarnished delight with which Robert so many years ago announced *le jour de gloire* of his arrival. "We would go out on the sloop, the *Trimethy* . . . not every day, because some days we did go riding and exploring. Sometimes we'd go in to New York . . . He took me to see Jeanne Eagles in "Rain." I'd never seen that particular play with that wonderful actress. That was a great excitement. But we would go out on the boat—he was a very good sailor, good navigator—and anchor out in the shallow part of Great South Bay, off Bay Shore, and I would be up on the forward deck, working at a typewriter, writing desperately bad imitations of Chekhov and other short story writers, and Robert would be in the cockpit, sprawled over a book on thermodynamics and chuckling with great connoisseurship over it. It always impressed me very much. And I'll never forget one day when we were out. We sailed too close to the Fire Island Inlet, when the tide was going out, and we were carried with it. We could see enormous breakers just at the mouth of the inlet. It had been a great storm, and this was the aftermath, and that little sloop would have had a bad time against the breakers. Well, in three minutes we went down the inlet with this very great rush of tide, a distance which took us about two hours to recover coming back. He tacked magnificently, back and forth, and back and forth, finally got us clear of the inlet again, and back into the bay. But that was long after we were due to be back, and the family was frantic . . . We headed back toward the house . . . across the bay and were going very slowly. It was after dark, and . . . toward eleven o'clock at night we sighted the big yacht looking for us . . . We were rescued and brought on board and fed and cosseted . . . but it was a very exciting day. Robert was a heroic mariner, but he simply miscalculated on this tremendous rush of tide. It could have been extremely serious. And as a strange footnote to this, in an early novel of mine [*No Quarter Given*] I had an episode which recalls this . . . in which, through a kind of stream of consciousness passage, life is leaving the central character. And the image I used was being carried out to sea."[28]

William Boyd, too, remembers Robert as an excellent sailor, but he was not a cautious one, and Fred Bernheim, caught in a squall with Robert at the helm, had doubts about his seamanship.[29] Again, perhaps the New Yorker had more exacting standards than the inlanders.

HORGAN REMEMBERS no tension on the trip to Buffalo which Robert described in his next letter to Fergusson. "The parents were extremely kind to me and very gentle and solicitous about me as a youngster . . . and apparently very happy in our friendship . . . but what I did to bring this on must have been insufferable."[30]

17 | TO FRANCIS FERGUSSON

Bayshore N.Y.
September 16, 1923.

My dear Francis,

You really could not blame me for taking over a week to recover from the satiric ravages of your last note. Your attack was cruel enough anyway; and at the time it was delivered, particularly cruel because it nearly blighted a dinky novelette, a new branch of the calculus, and some half dozen charcoals which were getting themselves delivered from the foetal stage. And your less shrouded opinion of my Harvard oscillations I hope to find in your saga, when you so sketch Otto [Koenig] and me at the Athens, performing for you the most blatant of the superb series of misunderstandings which you propose to exploit.[a]

But in spite of my wounds I can not wait any longer, lest I be too late to urge you again not to neglect me in passing. At least you must write to tell me what your plans are; and if it is at all possible, I beg you to allow me to receive you in Cambridge.

I think I told you that we were to motor Paul to Buffalo on our way to Quebec. We did. And toward the end there developed such an intricate panorama of complications that I was regaled with a daily scene. Toward the end, you see, mother and father grew a little jealous of Paul, and a little irritated at the ease with which he disregarded obstacles whose conquests formed the central jewels in the Oppenheimer crown. The matter was further embellished by two luscious complexes, oozing ich or: mother's and father's, which tried to apologize for being Jews; the Horgan's, which whinnied and shied clumsily about richesse and poverty. Moreover, Paul was, because of "circumstances I am not at liberty to divulge" particularly sensitive about his painting and writing. I am sure that you will picture the results of this explosive agglomeration without more empiric advices.

On the way down from Quebec we stopped at Cambridge over night. This year, I think, I shall be somewhat more comfortable, with an Oriental rug, a few little oils and some rather better etchings, an old silver tea urn, and a well fenced garden— Still, when I make my alpine way from Wolcott Gibbs [Laboratory] thru the dank blackness of five o'clock Cambridge to those positively stinking squash courts, and thence to the equally fragrant Georgian [Restaurant], I shall think enviously of you; see you exploring London, or closeted with your tutor, or sketching the Gulf of Taranto—"I shall sit there, serving tea to friends". And I hope you will come to be the first to receive the tea from the sacred urn.

This week I shall be in town, chaperoning Boyd and getting an oculist to rehabilitate (I hear you snicker) my eyes, which have balked at a too rapid alternation of the Trimethylamine and Thermodynamics— And I shall cherch Smith; I am curious to see the wreck that you and Los Pinos have wrought of that gallant little band who went forth so gaily last June, Herbert W. Smith.

If you will pardon this redundancy, I shall ask you again to try to see me on your way through. And when you meet Paul, I wish you would hint to him, in your most Smithian way, that my parents are particularly finicky about thank-you letters.

And finally, to conclude these imprecations, will you remember me most earnestly to your mother and sister?

A Cantabrigia.

[no signature]

a. Frederick Otto Koenig, son of the director of the summer camp which Robert attended in 1918, was a graduate student at Harvard in 1923. The Athens Olympia in Boston was a favorite restaurant of Robert's.

ROBERT WAS BACK at Harvard, which opened on September 24, when Fergusson came through New York on his way to Oxford, but he sent a nightletter on September 28 to the *S.S. Albania*.

18 | TO FRANCIS FERGUSSON

Western Union Telegram
Cambridge Mass Sept 28

ONE LAST WAVE OF ULULATION APPLAUSE REGRET IT WOULD DELIGHT ME TO HEAR FROM TIME TO TIME OF YOUR ACHIEVEMENTS I ADMIT WHAT I EXPECT THEM TO BE SORRY MY LETTER MISSED YOU JEFFRIES TOO SEND GREETINGS DIOS TE GUARDE

Robert

Jeffries Wyman, Harvard '23, was starting graduate work in biology. He and Robert were closer friends than the Harvard letters indicate. Wyman surmises that their different backgrounds, old Boston Yankee and new New York Jewish, drew them together, each eager to be less parochial. Fergusson had commended Robert to Wyman as brilliant and precocious. "Indeed he was," says Wyman. "The first impression he made was that he was a little precious, and perhaps a little arrogant, but very interesting, full of ideas. We had a very good time together and talked about many things other than science." Like Boyd and Smith, Wyman noted a lacuna. "He was completely blind to music. In fact he told me that music was positively painful to him."[31]

Wyman and Robert saw much of each other in 1923–24 as Robert moved into graduate-level courses. They studied thermodynamics together and talked about interrelated problems in physics and biology. At first, Wyman found Robert enthusiastic and somewhat naive, despite his good school background, but "he was very quickly getting a much better picture of physics and mastering the basic mathematics of physics and becoming more sophisticated all the time." Wyman also joined some of the expeditions on which these serious young men let off steam; he remembers particularly days spent on Plum Island off Newburyport.[32]

THREE LETTERS that Robert wrote to Paul Horgan in the autumn of 1923 are among the few that survive of a copious correspondence, most of which was destroyed when a flood damaged Horgan's home in Roswell, New Mexico.

"Rody," to whom Robert refers in the first of these letters, was Paul's sister Rosemary, by all accounts a beautiful young woman, blue-eyed, dark-haired, delicate, and sensitive, who later developed a serious emotional illness. Robert was much attracted to her in these happier days. In fact, as a young man he was more moved by her than by anyone, thinks his brother Frank, an impression surely based upon Robert's later confidence, not on the direct observation of eleven-year-old Frank. Horgan and others agree about the strength of this attachment.[33] Rosemary later married Alan Grant.

Horgan himself, not yet settled in his career as a writer, was studying singing at the Eastman School of Music in Rochester, New York. In need of a job to support his studies, he had "crassly volunteered," as he put it, to become scenic designer of the school's newly formed Rochester American Opera Company. What had most impressed Horgan at their first meeting was Robert's extraordinary vocabulary. "This awakened something in me," he later recalled, "[We were enchanted] with the notion of great enrichment of language so that we often conversed in a baroque lingo . . . [indulging in] harmless fancies of curlicued language but all with humor." Francis Fergusson too was drawn into this game with words.[34]

19 | TO PAUL HORGAN

> 60 Mt Auburn Street,
> Cambridge, Mass.
> Sept 28, 1923.

My dear Paul,

Once more I am demolished by a wave of envy for your tactics. Simply, quietly, in the most natural and charming way in the world, you have corrected me for my untutored presumptuousness; you have shown me the naivete of my former ideas, and taught me that a letter from you is something to be awaited, hoped, prized, loved, treasured; something to be read and reread, lingeringly, with fondness; something even, perhaps, to be enshrined; but never, alas, anticipated or expected— If I could paint for you my weeks of anxious longing, sinking gradually into despair, if I could but paint you that, and then reveal the dissipation of my sorrows as I threaded through the intricate mosaic of your cliches and compliments, I am certain that you would never thus torture me again.

Most seriously and earnestly, though, I want to thank you for sending your sketches. I cannot help feeling, ingenuously, I suppose, that even the three things you sent me, which certainly are not so pretentious and laborious, say, as the Lodge murals, show a good deal more care and inspiration in their design than the Van Dyke and Giotto things you defend— I like immensely your abstract, particularly, I think, for its obvious but skillful repetition of color and texture, and the corresponding dramatic rapidity. Best of all, though, I like the nude, in spite of its technical scraggliness; your design in blue and rose, intricate curves and shadows over the faint spectral drop, is very good indeed, I think. Your landscape, for me, fails through one thing, and that probably as much the fault of the medium: your design isn't echoed at all in textural differences, and it seems a bit too primitive and static to succeed without that in two dimensions— I know that [I] ought to return them all at once; but I trust that you will forgive me if I keep them a short while longer; and thank you again for letting me see them.

I wish you would send your story. Is it the "til human voices wake us and we drown"? —Since I left you I have done three more stories and finished my novelette; but I am still attacking them from time to time, and shall let you see them later. Also the charcoals, which, as yet, are too simple to be worth your time. I have spoken to Clowser Boyd about Windows, and he is investigating and coming to a decision.[a] I shall be extremely busy anyway this year, and unless someone can do the economics and filthy work I shall be unable to work on it at all. But I shall let you know.

Some time ago I wrote one of my stupid fresco letters to Rody; it will doubtless induce her to flee Buffalo at my next approach. But I hope that it did not dissuade you and her from the visit which you promised me this fall. I earnestly want you to come. Then you may see La Clavel, mistress of my chambers, Jeffries Wyman, Boyd, stories, books, sketches to satiety. Then too we could cogitate upon Windows— And I shall be positively insulted if Rody doesn't come.

I have heard twice from Francis, but he has delivered little news. Yesterday mother wired that he was sailing on the Albania today. Lorcks and away, hélas: baton des exiles, lampe des inventeurs! Smith too, gave a somewhat distorted account of his summer. I promise you another harangue soon, to accompany your pictures— But do write first to tell me that you both are coming.

Please remember me to your mother, and do your most charming bow for me to Rody. And may Rochester turn to gold under your fingers.

[no signature]

a. *Windows* was a stillborn avant-garde literary review. Boyd wrote in 1977, "Such projects usually lose money and I for one didn't have any money to lose. So I was glad when the project expired before it even breathed." His only regret was that he never met Horgan; Boyd to Alice Kimball Smith, March 19, 1977.

60 Mt Auburn,
Cambridge.
October 6, 1923.

My dear Paul,

This note, hélas, has got to be as short and unrhetorical as my inebriate soul and the explosive nature of my felicitations can conspire to make it. I mean, beloved, that I would like, if I had time and power, to answer your splendid epic with one not incomparable to it, and match the intricate pattern of your quotations, allusions, epigrams, poetics, and flattery in my reply. But it is a tragic and overwhelming truism that *my* paltry successes do not come without assiduity and labor; that the Artzibasheffs I conquer demand a pretentious pertinacity and patience;[a] that I am, quae cum ita sint, hysterically engaged in keeping soul and body from complete disintegration and decrepitude; and that, accordingly, I shall be unable to fabricate a masterpiece fit to stand beside, say, your "Now he is on your ocean."

But certain matters most imperatively demand attention: (atto primo) I am—well perhaps not surprised—but positively enraptured by your wizardly and alchemistic transformation of la belle Rochester. You seem to have stored within you an infinity of energetic and altogether desirable bits of genius, which you periodically regurgitate as expediency suggests. With one tiny department of one of the great fields of creative exploit you patronize you seem to have gained a benison of wealth, honor, stimulus, and friends. Quelle consummation inauditée et magnifique, quelle conquête facile, incomparable! And, though my knowledge of Artzibasheff's achievements had previously lacked much that a properly educated esthete's should have had, I now pronounce without hesitation that he is one of the most talented artists who have yet come to give their attention to the stage, but that there may be one or two, not more, who are able to rival him in inspiration and excellence—

And I fear that this gilt efflorescence, combined with Knopf's disconcerting callousness, will drive you further and further from the inglorious realms of writing. But to urge you to continue I shall beg you to send me some of your things and promise you, in return, a few of the creations I have committed here, steadfast despite the appalling incrustations of thermodynamic and epistomological erudition which are being deposited upon me.

(Atto secondo) I thank you very earnestly and simply for your sketches. A little ashamed of robbing of them, yet too weak to send them back— Thanks again— And since you demand to know, I must confess that neither mother nor I was ever properly irate for your taciturnity. But I admit that I wanted to be. But, my dear Paul, you are completely reinstated, I swear to you:

> Qui donne a penser que le diable
> Fait toujours bien tout ce qu'il fait.

That, I know, is gross flattery.

(atto terzo) Again allow me to press you and Rody to come. Even your insultingly tourist reflection cannot keep me still. I shall be flattered if you come hysterical and enchanted if you come demure, but suicide awaits me if you stay.

(atto quarto) The Francis has treated me quite as snarkily as he did you. The customary and lengthy letter, with its usual modicum of flattery, felicitation, farewell, even, perhaps, affection. He is having Frances Keeley send me his Harvard saga;[b] so I will send some of my stories? and write? and forgive him for not coming up? —and the tragedy is that I will, that it is his own peculiar genius to insult so simply and yet so well. —But out in his country, we don't do that sort of thing; it's all this Harvard tradition of study and indifference. That too is the fault of the Atlantic. It is an ocean which says with every sullen breaker and every undulation "It is not with us as with those whom small things can annoy." You owe it a bitterer grudge for that than for having come so near to drowning you.

(finale) Fred returns your greeting, perhaps intensified by several milligrams of not too proper envy.

And even I, after reflecting again on your letter, am forced to this final perversion of our overburdened refrain:

> O Satan, prends pitie de MA longue misère—[c]

Most cordial regards to your mother and Rody.

R

a. Boris Artzibasheff, later a well-known portrait painter and *Time* cover artist, was Horgan's competitor for the job of scenic designer with the opera company. Horgan submitted a few hastily done drawings and got the job; Horgan to Alice Kimball Smith, February 24, 1977.

b. Frances Keeley was a friend of Fergusson's.

c. The refrain which follows each of fifteen couplets in Charles Baudelaire's "Les Litanies de Satan." "We chanted it to each other in comic commentary on almost anything," recalled Horgan; Horgan to Alice Kimball Smith, February 24, 1977.

SIXTY MOUNT AUBURN STREET from which Robert now wrote was an old house opposite the *Crimson* office where he was settled with his oils, etchings, and tea urn. There for the next two years he and Fred Bernheim occupied large adjoining rooms, Fred's at the front, Robert's in back with the bath next door. They considered themselves roommates, but "in the evenings when we had to work we just shut the door," recalls Bernheim. The charcoal in Robert's samovar did not always burn, and he had to resort to Sterno, but the tea was Russian style, a characteristic affectation that Bernheim found tolerable because Robert was "really interested in doing it." Bernheim too found Robert a little bit precious in the way he quoted French poetry—Verlaine, Baudelaire—yet it was these broad interests and Robert's articulateness about them that had attracted Fred to him the previous year in Standish Hall. "He wasn't a comfortable person to be around, in a way," reflected Bernheim, "because he always gave the impression that he was thinking very deeply about things. When we roomed together he would spend evenings locked in his room, trying to do something with Planck's constant or something like that. I had visions of him suddenly bursting forth as a great physicist, and here I was just trying to get through Harvard."[35]

Oppenheimer's influence may have been decisive in changing Bernheim's objective from the practice of medicine to medical research. "I think that he did actually show me how to do science," Bernheim commented recently. "Not in any specific sense, but [in giving me] a feeling that it was an exciting thing to do, that it's something that you could give your life to. And . . . he was able to supply criteria . . . articles that came out in *Science* and other general magazines that were useful. [I was] inclined at that age to accept anything in print as gospel, and he was much more critical . . . I certainly wouldn't have had this career if it hadn't been for him," mused Bernheim, referring to his position as Professor of Pharmacology at the Duke University Medical School.[36]

In later life Robert enjoyed bringing congenial people together and sharing friendships. At this period he seems to have compartmentalized them. With Bernheim, who doubts that he ever met Fergusson, Robert displayed "a feeling that we should make a unit." They had little to do with other students living in the house. The only person who dropped in often at their pleasant suite was William Boyd, who sometimes went out to dinner with Robert and Fred or shared their weekend expeditions. Boyd was the only person Bernheim could invite more than once without rousing Robert's possessiveness. After all, Boyd was Robert's discovery, and in those days he displayed an antic quality that appealed to the playful side of Robert's nature.[37]

Although Boyd, like Robert and Fred, completed his undergraduate degree in three years, he considered himself a plodder compared to Robert, who could afford to waste time and never seemed to have to study. At least, says Boyd, "he was pretty careful not to let you catch him at it." Dinner at Locke-Ober's on a winter evening, followed by a leisurely walk back to Cambridge along the Charles, upset Boyd's schedule but made no difference to Robert. Boyd's impression that Robert, Bernheim, and he "were the closest friends any of us had" at Harvard seems borne out as far as Robert was concerned by the casual way they appear in his letters to those other good friends Fergusson and Smith.[38]

Before writing again to Horgan, Robert brought Herbert Smith up to date on the activities of their mutual friends and referred casually to the continuing six-course load that would enable him to graduate in three years. In the order in which they appear on his Harvard transcript and as described in the 1923–24 "Harvard Descriptive Catalogue" they were:

Chemistry 4, Quantitative Analysis, gravimetric and volumetric, a full-year course for graduates and undergraduates.

Chemistry 8, Elementary Theory and Physical Chemistry consisting of lectures and reading, spring semester.

Chemistry 22, Experimental Organic Chemistry, chiefly lab work, fall semester.

French 6, General View of French Literature, a full-year course.

Mathematics 5, Differential and Integral Calculus (advanced course, Part I), fall semester.

Mathematics 9, Probability, spring semester.

Philosophy 9c, Theory of Knowledge, a study of judgment, inference, truth, and allied topics, fall semester.

Physics 6a, Heat and Elementary Thermodynamics, lectures and occasional lab, fall semester.

Physics 6b, Advanced Thermodynamics, spring semester.

Physics 16a, Quantum Theory, with Applications to Series Spectra, Atomic Structure and the Kinetic Theory of Gases, spring semester.

By 1963 Oppenheimer could not reconstruct the sequence of his second and third year courses but he remembered starting thermodynamics with Kemble, the first course he took at Jefferson Physical Laboratory. The course in probability was "terrible"; he could not recall everything he audited.[39]

But if some courses proved disappointing there were other ways of learning for a highly motivated undergraduate with an insatiable appetite for knowledge. "I can't recall how it came over me that what I liked in chemistry was very close to physics; it's obvious that if you were reading physical chemistry and you began to run into thermodynamical and statistical mechanical ideas you'd want to find out about them . . . I can't emphasize strongly enough how *much* I read and more really just in exploration.

You see, it's a very odd picture; I never had an elementary course in physics except for a very elementary school course and to this day I get panicky when I think about a smoke ring or elastic vibrations. There's nothing there —just a little skin over a hole. In the same way my mathematical formation was, even for those days, very primitive, and this was more than evident in the way I went about some of the things I did later . . . It's going to be hard for me to be sure where I learned things, from what book, but I'd like to give a clear impression of a very quick, superficial, eager familiarization with some parts of physics with tremendous lacunae and often with a tremendous lack of practice and discipline, just because the time was limited. And although I liked to work, I spread myself very thin and got by with murder; I got A's in all these courses which I don't think I should have."[40]

Before immersing himself in the first semester's work, Robert wrote some gossip to Smith and some nonsense for Horgan.

21 | TO HERBERT W. SMITH

> 60 Mt. Auburn
> Cambridge, Mass.
> October 6, 1923.

Dear Mr. Smith,

Now that we are again within our normal range of a few hundred miles, I know that you will yield to a sufficiently violent bombardment and write me a letter. So, sans plus en parler, I begin the attack:

First, I suppose, it is meet that I ask you for more details about Francis. He swept by Paul and me with no other gregariousness than he could compress into four pages apiece of illtypewritten crowing and flattery. "So busy— folks at one end, Rhodes scholars at other, you know—just couldn't manage it—but we will write? And send your things—" He is having his Frances Keeley send me his Harvard saga. And then, after a bit of his customary twaddle about my hypothetical achievements, he left me to search in vain for his virtues in his friends and attack with new bitterness the grey battlements of knowledge.

And then, in return, I must tell you that I had another coy note from Jane, announcing the acquisition of a new sofa and the impending arrival of another Kayser. Outre cela, rien. Except that Paul has been made Art Director of the Eastman Opera Company in Buffalo, attaining that magnificence over the head of his rival, the famous Artzibasheff. However, it will doubtless console you to know that Knopf refused his book.

My labors this year promise to be positively overwhelming. There is an imposing little thing in Epistomology; and Physics grows daily grimmer. So I have done only one story—a fair one. I am very glad, for I suspect that my work, together with such sailing and riding as is necessary to keep me from positive physical decrepitude, will leave me little energy— But, if it doesn't bore you, I shall write later— Answer, or you get another.

Please remember me affectionately to Mrs. Smith. And write me one of those notes of yours which are such fun to read because they positively bristle with answers. Then I shall do better.

Adios,

Bob

22 | TO PAUL HORGAN

Cantabrigia.
[October 1923]

My dear Paul,

You will doubtless recognize these dismal enclosures as my desperate and puling attempts to rival the glittering spilth of your letters. Of course a few hours lucubration would keep me from this obscene disgorgement; but

a) I haven't a few hours to lucubrate, and

b) I think it so important that one should be sincere and uncalculating.

And so, maxima con magnanimity, you will allow me to proceed without more than this unprofessional apology. For I confess that this drivel is merely a diluent for the central ascetic doctrine of the thesis: WHAT do you expect me to answer to a family that writes me that Rody cannot come because you cannot come and that you can come. I see only one possible retort; I am delighted that you could both manage to get off; and I beg you most solicitously to apprise me of the hour of your arrival, that my cymbals may be reassembled and reburnished. Je vous demande donc grace.

Lacrimae Christi, 1645—And four wax candles in a darkened room[a]— Yes, as you can see, I am having a positively Mephistophelian time. Hélas, sans Marguerite.

[no signature]

a. Robert slightly misquoted T. S. Eliot's "Portrait of a Lady," the second poem of *Prufrock* (1917) and a favorite of Robert's and Paul's; Horgan to Alice Kimball Smith, February 24, 1977. The line reads: "And four wax candles in the darkened room."

[Oppenheimer's "dismal enclosures" follow.]

My dear Miss Limpet,

Your last letter was *so* beautiful, really. I was *deeply* interested in the beautiful sermon you quoted, so well planned, so moving. It was just too thoughtful of you. We get so few good sermons here nowadays; just long lectures on the details of behavior, nothing general and ennobling like John's old ones before he died. But fortunately I do not need such inspiration. I know your sermon was really not meant for *me*. Only the other night I told the truth as I saw it under most trying circumstances. She said she would never again speak to me if I didn't take it back, but I wasn't to be bribed.

And Berengaria has always been one of my favorite books; not one I like most, you understand, but one I admire because *everybody* can understand it. I often used to make John read me it he read so beautifully. And only the other night I asked my son Henley to read it and he did. Henley has grown to be quite a man now you have no idea how Harvard has changed him. I am afraid it is not for the good of his soul to study so hard. He says the most *terrible* things. Only the other night I was arguing with him and I said but you believe in God don't you? And he said I believe in the second law of thermodynamics, in Hamilton's Principle, in Bertrand Russell, and would you believe it Siegfried Freud. Think of it. My own son, my John, so help me God. After he read me Berengaria he said now here is something else I will read you and then he gave it to me. I am sending it to you, because I know how interested you are in my boy, having none of your own. I must confess I couldn't make much out of it but I think his descriptions are *so* lovely. And the words he uses, it's awful.

But that is not nearly so bad as one could find to tell if they had plenty of time. I am afraid he's getting his head turned by that Horgan hussey, Rodolanthe, or something like that. Only the other day I found him sitting there reading a letter from her, smiling all over as though he were being co (I'm loosing my mind no less these days and can't seem to write what I mean). He was saying over and over something I couldn't quite catch, because I didn't want to spy on him. Something about the Amazon I think.

But that isn't anything to the way he is when he gets a letter from that Paul person. I guess they're a nice family and that, but I don't know, and I don't like for him to be getting too *promiscuous, my son*. But when he gets a letter he just sits there for hours on end reading it back and forth. If I ask him what it is he says he says it's not what he says it's the way he says it. I don't think that young man was so very clever. He didn't seem very clever to me. I guess he flatters Henley a little. As you once wrote to me and I haven't forgotten there I've gone and spoilt it again—pride goes but vanity lingers. It's a great saying.

Well I hope to have you at Christmas my dear Miss Limpet, if God is willing. But Henley is planning to have those Horgan people if they will come which please God they won't though it would break his heart. I mean Thanksgiving. Anyway please write me another inspiring letter like the last and

remember me
very fondly
your beloved
Celia

This is Henley's Poem.

C.

Out of the Delphian clarity of the booth
projects a raw voice, childish,
cutting the viscid miasmal plexus of uncouth
and interwoven soot and smoke and steam and ululation:
"Leven ten—Nourn thirteen minits, see?"
Meticulous, solicitous, precise, epitome
of excellent advice: efficiency.

"I have an hour and thirteen minutes to squander,
youth, and the city, preening for debauch:
Like Polypheme insensate I shall wander
glimpsing in passion through the stolid night
each suspect tumbril and sardonic torch—
Three minutes I shall harbor for the flight."

Tonight she wears a sealskin cape
glistening black diamonds where the water swathes her thighs
and noxious glints conspire to surprise
a pulse condoning eagerness with rape.
Even the paste tiara she must wear
to crown the umbrian limbus of her hair
leers faintly, now, spending its blatancy
threading black mists and gleaming evilly
on the wet pavements, sleek and debonair.
Even the tuneless drone of eager wheels in polychrome
melts to submundane threnodies,
serenade of Mephistopheles,
Stygian palindrome—

49

What does it mean?-
>Decaying hag
>shrewish in the wilted sheen
>of a stoop; raucous stag
>boasting loot in flesh and waistcoat,
>pretty penny, Henley, Ascot,
>left em not a rag.
No, that is not what it means.

"Two hundred thousand sages say
that's what it is if you get gay."

But isn't there something more in this wet, quivering city,
in this assaulting phalanx of limousines,
in the high festoons of lights, whether they blare or not,
in the hag, rot or not,
in the unchaste and vaunting mezzanines,
than a plucked handful of words to pocket for your pity?

On the train there will be time for that;
too much.

Cambridge, October

23 | TO HERBERT W. SMITH

Lowell House
60 Mt. Auburn
Cambridge.
November 2, 1923.

My dear Mr. Smith,

In spite of the fact that silence seems to be the most effectual method of extracting epigrams from you, I have been promptly detonated by your last note (to any one not so beastly literal about figures I should have said "detonated into a new efflorescence") But I have only uninspired dribblings to offer in exchange. I wish that I could rival your list of editors, which has impressed me deeply. And on your Review, too, I must congratulate you; it has a way of getting itself between the Adelphi and the Nation and Athenaeum at the really charming book shops, and I have often had it urged upon me in a store up here as "one of the best thoroughly high-brow magazines." On second thought I have come to the conclusion that *often* is a trifle hyperbolic; but I'm sure you see what I mean, anyway.

At this point you must permit me an injudicious exultation: I have a pair of letters from Francis. It matters not that they say as nearly nothing as one can in three pages, or that they contain neither cliches nor diatribes; their illegibility proves them authentic and that, Gloria Sancta Dei, is sufficient.

I am enclosing one of my weekly exudations of bilge. About all these things I have the naive terror of hearing "Well, is he really like that?" And so I gaspingly assert that I am not, not like that or Litany or Conquest, and that, of course, it is just for that reason that I write. It is queer that one should feel such solicitude about exposing a self that every wretched bit of critical sense in one denies and condemns, that one should show such an appalling likeness to all these disreputable people one isn't. But I suppose that anyone really properly impregnated with even the rudiments of psychology would take all that without such blaring.

Fortunately I am not at all worried, and the infiltration of thermodynamics continues undisturbed. I am working very hard now, so hard that I fear your epithet of grind. But if you could see the careless way in which I neglect French 6 or Chem to complete a theory about identity in Tensor Calculus, or how I flee the entire melange for a weekend in a sailboat off Gloucester, you might forgive me. But then you would see my grades, and your accusing finger would return.

I shan't be down till Christmas. But at that time I shall journey out to see you, even if the expedition entails my speedy disinheritance. And if last fall's saccharine precedent doesn't prevent, I hope Mrs. Smith will be good enough to accompany you to town some evening.

Doesn't A Lost Lady remind you, vaguely and sentimentally, of Mrs. Page?[a] Or doesn't it? You will write, though, please?

And I think that when you have travelled with a person all summer you might desist from blaming the machine.

A Dios—

R

a. Willa Cather's A Lost Lady was published in 1923.

BAB, WHO GOT into the next letter through a typographical error in a missing letter to Smith, was Babette Oppenheimer (later Mrs. Walter Langsdorf), daughter of Robert's Uncle Emil. Robert's "disgraceful performance" involved taking her to an Ethical Culture event, then asking Smith to see her home. Mrs. Langsdorf remembered only a warm and lasting friendship with her slightly older cousin.[41]

Cambridge, Sunday.
[ca. November 1923]

My dear Mr. Smith,

This note is about to commit all the sins for which yours so neatly apologized. It is, first of all, to regret very much that you are going to have your throat cut, and, selfishly, but nearly as much, the corresponding curtailment of the active part of the holiday. It is, unconditionally, ecstatically, and very gratefully going to accept your invitation; it is to thank you for your forgiveness, and to announce that I ignore your succinct but cruel allusion to the hierarchy of colitic execrabilities. It is furthermore to announce that BAB is BOB, and that, ever since my disgraceful performance at graduation, my cousin has been most strenuously repressed from consciousness. And it is going to close most improperly and abruptly.

Really, I have many things I should like to talk to you about. But they are so eminently unsuited to pollute this note that I wait with them and trust that your larynx will not be completely incapacitated on the thirtieth. Your larynx, observe, not your ear. The trouble is that Francis's novel has at last arrived, and that, though I have nothing but admiration for the Harvey-esque slickness and totally unHarveyesque perspicacity of its opening chapters,[a] I am dismayed and rendered hysterical by the notes for its continuation.

When do you return to Orange?

Good luck

R

a. Harvey Fergusson was Francis's older brother.

Lowell House,
Cambridge
December 1, 1923.

My dear Mr. Smith,

I hope that you are now perfectly well again. But I must not forget to tell you how flattered I was when I heard that my verses were indistinguishable in effect from some millions of streptococci catarrhensae; it's really most consoling.

And, my dear Mr. Smith, I assure you that I need to be consoled: I might string you out a lengthy miserere, telling you with all the beastly and stupid details how Francis and I corresponded frantically past each other till we were both insulted;[a] how Jane has frozen, because it was rude to understand her dismal notes and unthinkable not to; how my letter to Mrs. Page was dictated by home; how the Horgans have spent the fall arguing about what I meant; how Jeffries and I miss each other with coy opacity; how my Janitress spends her evenings in my room, in tears; how I have come, lugubriously, to the conclusion that the two people at Wellesley and the dozen or so here that even pretend to pursue me are a sorry and worthless lot; how all this has driven me to whorls of stories and notes on the div grad of an electrical field and French and merely English verses; and how, in a final catastrophe, I projected said verses toward you. But you would be bored by the details even more than by the threat; only you must forbear, and remember that if you again cast aspersions on the scansion of a perfectly respectable sestet, it may be enough to complete my despair and project me into the Charles.

From your note I guess that you are very busy indeed; I hope you are enjoying your magazine and its glorious collection of supporters, and finding it quite as pleasant to teach garment makers that Keats and not Pope wrote the peak in Darien sonnet as to ram elepoquenci (alias eloquence) down Paul Kaufmann's recalcitrant gullet.[b] Perhaps you will tell me about it during the holidays. But I remember the results of a similar suggestion last fall: throughout the whole evening you maintained an esoteric but unilluminating silence about your own adventures, while you assiduously exhausted me of mine. So I shall beware.

Now that it is beginning to be too cold to go up to the Cape weekends, I shall try to be a little more virtuous about writing to you. I see you blink with laconic boredom. Well, then, I won't.

There are lots of stories and things lying around, and if you would at all like to see them, I shall be glad to give them to you at Christmas. But you are doubtless sick of the drivel; and in any case I shall dedicate a book to you some day, a real book, full of mathematics, by the grace of God and his Majesty, the King.

I have got to stop now and turn to insulting someone else.

Diós te guarde.

[no signature]

And where are those chapters of Francis? Frances Keeley blames you, I think. I have not laid eyes on the things.

a. Neither side of the autumn correspondence with Fergusson has survived.

b. Paul Kaufmann was a classmate at the Ethical Culture School, president of the Athletic Association and of the Student Council in their senior year; "Who's Who," *Inklings* [Ethical Culture School publication], February 1921, p. 29.

Cambridge
Sunday [winter 1923–24]

My dear Mr. Smith,

You already have my threat to fight my way through a phalanx of parents and emerge at Orange; and I now solemnly swear to execute it. I am not quite sure how much of the skimpy holiday I shall be in town; for mother and father, preparing for the day when "the Professor had to be hurried to his country estate to prevent a nervous breakdown" are planning to insulate and isolate me at the shore. If you could manage to spend a few days down there I should be appeased and everyone delighted. But if not we shall arrange for another Voisin party, and this time I shall grow hysterical if all of the guests do not appear.

I begin to believe in eternal passions, now, when I see that each note from you still sends me into a violent schoolgirl flutter of excitement. I am able, though, to assure myself that my delight at your last one was at least half due to your magnanimous notes on my verses. I think you are very right about them, though, perhaps, a trifle too kind. I detect in your "you write for the thrill" the old rebuke of the handshake allegory; but I think the real crime lies, not there, but in the shameless exhibitionism which lets me reveal the debauches. Of course, when I do scrawl, I am always able to justify my strained figures and racked words; and not infrequently by a puny etymological device: limbus—limbo (that's true)—borderland of hell; or even worse, palindrome—running both ways—repetition. You see? It's vile, I admit. Generously, you ask what I do. Aside from the activities exposed in last week's disgusting note, I labor, and write innumerable theses, notes, poems, stories, and junk; I go to the math lib and read and to the Phil lib and divide my time between Meinherr Russell and the contemplation of a most beautiful and lovely lady who is writing a thesis on Spinoza—charmingly ironic, at that, don't you think?; I make stenches in three different labs, listen to Allard gossip about Racine,[a] serve tea and talk learnedly to a few lost souls, go off for the weekend to distill the low grade energy into laughter and exhaustion, read Greek, commit faux pas, search my desk for letters, and wish I were dead. Voila.

Your letters make me feel that you are superhumanly busy. It's partly, of course, the references to attorneys and other such elite appendages; and then I can imagine you saying it, and feel myself on edge to hear it all before the arrival of the next coy mère. But you don't tell me what you do, in my shameless way; and so, I suppose, I must wait till I can extract it with an approximation, the nearest New York affords, to an alligator pear cocktail, tincta seraphicorum cum lacrimis.

Please remember me to Mrs. Smith, and be tolerant.

R

At last the "Bob" is wearing off!

a. Louis Allard, professor of French, was Robert's instructor in French 6, A General View of French Literature.

Called Bob in high school, Robert had been gradually replacing this signature in the Harvard letters by Robert or simply R. In later years to refer to Bob Oppenheimer was a sign of very old acquaintance indeed or a slight one. Tradition has it that he was christened Opje during a brief stay in Leiden in the winter of 1928–29 in recognition of his success in making a speech in Dutch. Usually Americanized to Oppie, this was how he was generally known at Los Alamos. By the end of the war word got around that he preferred to be called Robert, and thereafter many of his intimates or those who wished to be so considered, made the change. Some former students and old friends clung to the affectionate Oppie or Opje.

27 | TO FRANCIS FERGUSSON

Bayshore.
Christmas 1923.

My dear Francis,

For once you have forced me to abjure pomposities; your chapters are splendid. You know how hard it is for me to like any novel, and how it takes an *Une Vie* or *Crome* to extract very much enthusiasm; but I tell you quite frankly that I enjoyed the beginning of yours very much indeed, and that my only serious trepidation is lest I may not see the remainder. In the first place, of course, I am overwhelmed at the ease and directness and literary slickness of the thing. Your style is as simple and unstilted as your brother's, but it is supple enough to keep it from seeming grotesque when you want to say something unusually neat, or when you are concerned with a little modest lyricism. The crudities that struck me were appallingly scarce; in fact, the only one I can remember is the "red and brown body" place on the first page. And at times, as in your elaborate phalanx of thrusts against Emerson, you are nothing short of brilliant. But the thing which, though not so startling, delighted me most about the opus is your skill with the people. Your incidents are few enough, and casual enough, to have them

55

taken without change: but your results—I grow lyric myself—are marvellous. If I knew a little more about how you have done it, if I were not quite so neophytic in reaction, I might be able to give you a somewhat less nebulous panegyric. As it is I can only tell you the people I liked best; the mother, the doctor, Kline, Emerson, and D'Amanda. It is with hesitation that I omit the hero himself; though you have been very careful to make his intellectual and social outlook seem inevitable, though he never acts preposterously, yet I find it hard to swallow, in the same person, such naiveté and such sophistication. When it comes to people he seems to have no difficulty at all in giving a fairly sophisticated account, and most of the smart things you say are made to appear his own. No one unfamiliar with the Cambridge milieu could see Emerson as he does; and no one even in the slightest familiar therewith, so it seems to me, would try out for the register except to prove his advisers wrong, or would, for instance, consider the malformed and greasy outcasts of the Cafeteria as even a first approximation to jeunesse dorée. I think you verge upon impossibility when you try to telescope an education that took even you several years into a few days, and when you try to make the same person simultaneously react as you may have, your first year in the Bronx, and as you may have, on leaving Harvard. Perhaps, really, you are that sort of person; I have always suspected you of hierarchies of profundities stretching out grandly behind your most innocent facades. But since the final and important emotion of the thing is going to be that of your hero, anyway, I think it is particularly important that you don't impose upon credulity too much. And, by the way, I think the finest thing you have in the chapters you let me see is Emerson's "My father is a doctor —" and the whole marvellous scene, before and after. That sits not too awkwardly at the same bench as the immortal scene in Vanity Fair. So there.

I suppose it is never quite possible for us to understand each other's layers of naiveté. And it is that which keeps [me] from agreeing entirely with what you say about the junk I sent you. I think all the snarkiest things you say— and, by the way, thank you for troubling—are perfectly true. Even to me it is obvious that my women are gargoyles and my lyricism, either absent or buried. But what I can't understand, for instance, is that you should think the *Rain* thing sophisticated, or the hero, in *Litany,* unnatural. It is merely an indictment of my things that what I mean for the febrile disgust of unsatisfied eroticism should look like the senile ravings of a 1910 debauchee, or that the Litany situation should entirely miss. What I meant, you see, was that the hero was prevented, being not very intelligent in the first place, from detecting his trouble, or doing anything but maunder about it, by his utterly frivolous and vain and complacent preconceptions which he had so diligently constructed in times of other stress. It may be perfectly true that no rational man would act that way, and that, to you, a knowledge of thermodynamics and a dilettante dawdling in literature implies a divine intelligence in all things. That's not so. Always you used to insist that a person was either intelligent or not, and—perhaps I misunderstand—not that he might be intelligent here or there, and blind as a fool in everything else. I find these awful people in me from time to time, and their expulsion is the sole excuse for my writing. I have none of that mere glee in narration, the conteur's delight, which you and Chekhov and your brother seem to have. I write to get rid of an ideal and impossible system, and it is, as you so cleverly remark, not writing at all; and it is that which makes the things of so exclusively masturbatic a character. I am sorry to have bored you. But you didn't seem to mind.

And despite such explicit and irrefutable discouragement as that of your letter I continue to write. It is strange that it should make no difference to me that I know that the stuff is useless, and equally strange that I should make no improvements. But I have not the skill or the fortune to find enough people, and physics is a stern and uncompromising muse— I wish, though, that I could get along without it. And with such alluring creatures as your Weir, with an eternal round of opacifying and soothing teas and cigarettes, I am sure I should be consoled. As for your additional mite of energy (sic) you ought to know that there is no such thing as insatiable energy, and that what most closely resembles it is a boring and exhausting petty activity. I appreciate your attempts to spare my jealous self, though, and thank you.

Your poem has reached my cortex, well enough, but more, I fear, in virtue of your own cerebral potency and the loveliness of one line, than as a result of any very protracted or definite emotional reaction. I am not quite certain that I understand the mood at all; but, if I do, it is one of exhaustion, of a somewhat drab inanition and placid moroseness. But the mood that I mean is certainly not majestic, as your rhythm implies, nor can it possibly [be] considered clairvoyant. It is a mood of languor, regret, perhaps apathy. Is that what you mean? And the part, accordingly, that I like best is the perhaps extravagant but lovely part about your childhood

"And the somnolent opulence of its interminable afternoons."
For the rest, I am not very much moved, even by the Shakespearian figure of the last line. But I suspect that I have totally missed your point.

Next year I shall certainly be in England. I am not yet sure whether I shall go to study at Cambridge or not, but if I don't I shall spend the summer abroad. I have no illusions, I think, about finding anything wonderful in the way of supermen or scientific marvels. And I shall only go there if I find it impossible to return to Harvard with enough enthusiasm to carry me through. This year hasn't been bad, because there is lots of work, and just enough people to keep me from starving. Boyd, as you charitably predicted, has improved. He did not get the Rhodes. And so I am ever so much happier than last year. But when I approach 96 Prescott I still have a twinge of the old malady. So that I am not at all sure that I shall be able to resist the indiscretion of boring you when I go across. "Oh, no, I've never had any friendships like that". I can not forgive you for having wrung that from me, Mephistopheles.

I enclose a verse or two. And I'm having these things forwarded. To Italy, I suppose. Adiós

R

BACK AT HARVARD, Robert wrote in a very different tone to Herbert Smith. The letter is headed "Cambridge Tuesday," a simplified form of dating that Robert used all too frequently in the years before he acquired an office staff. Reference to the approach of five examinations, which commenced on Thursday, January 24, 1924, makes Tuesday, the twenty-second a likely date for this letter.

28 | TO HERBERT W. SMITH

Cambridge. Tuesday
[ca. January 22, 1924]

My dear Mr. Smith,

Immediately upon the arrival of your letter the temperature of Cambridge, which has maintained itself at a disgraceful distance below zero for the last week, rose suddenly; three hours later the first blade of grass re-emerged from its hibernal blanket; and by the middle of the afternoon the insidious and delightful manuscript had so far undermined my scholarly morale that I tore up two dozen thermodynamic equations and one hundred and seven unfinished differential equations, forgot the portentous approach of five examinations, extracted my typewriter from its berth beneath two feet of lyrics, and proceeded to answer:

There are always a lot of things on which you must be congratulated; and this time, I think, most of all for your escape from the Kelly-Thayer menace.[a] It doesn't seem to my unsophisticated sense that a job that made Europe impossible, attached you to the school by positively irrefragible bonds, swamped you with work, and separated you from almost all of what makes the thing you do so much more satisfactory than selling toothbrushes, would be any sort of blessing at all, despite the shekels. And I'm awfully glad that you feel that way too. I shall meet you and your charges for a week at Fécamp, next July —

And the other good fortune is the Marie eblouissement; I think her thing is very nice, though it doesn't seem to me so extraordinarily good a motif to compress into the classic symmetry of an impeccable sonnet.[b] But I'd forgive anything to the

An arch of storms and the slow wash of sleep.

Thanks ever so much for sending it up, for I never see such things unassisted.

It is very good of you to feel that way about Broad;[c] I should hate to have you too regard my obsession with a sadness untouched by at least a little sympathy. For you know I should never have ventured the loch alone— Your person seems to have been just a trace more unreliable than mine, for the *Yachting* hasn't as yet fought its way through the snow. I shall let you [know] immediately when it comes; and I shan't thank you now, so that I may have ample excuse for another letter, soon.

And you liked St. Joan! But I still cling to Broun, against you and Shaw, that makes it look a sickly battle.[d] But when the epilogue only repeated what the play had said, clearly and much more subtly and poignantly, for four magnificent acts, when anybody ten days out of his chrysalis could see what it was all about, and feel what it was all about, why that pedagogic flourish at the end, that Osgood dissertation for those whose chrysalis still clung? —Anyway, it is probably only a question of how soon you are saturated, aesthetically, and not an occasion for this dogmatic ranting at all.

No word, lately, from Francis or Jane or Inez or Mrs. Page. I met a fool poet who saw her in La Jolla earlier in the year, and mother had a card or two, but that is all.

You know Cambridge, and its peculiar examination atrophy. The terrible time will be over soon, and if I survive I shall be doing some better work next half year. I have found, so far, that twenty thousand words of thesis was enough to cripple my skimpy muse of prose completely, and when I am inspired I jot down verses. As you so neatly remarked, they aren't either meant or fit for anyone's perusal, and to force their masturbatic excesses on others is a crime. But I shall stuff them in a drawer for a while and, if you want to see them, send them on.

In other respects, tho, all is prosaic. There are a couple of places in town where we go a few evenings a week, and that helps. One is a sort of salon kept by the Carters up on Beacon Hill, where there are books, and food, and a fire. There is a bad artist from Paris and a tech student and a member of the London Fabian society, who, for the rest, is an incorrigible aesthete and bore. There is a ravishing creature who brings food and writes scenarios and verses, and whose charm is pretty largely responsible for my frequent ascents of the hill. And there are several New England women trying to live down a congenital primness and psychic sterility. —Then there is another place, kept by a boisterous Italian, who tells stories and calls Eva Le Gallienne and Joseph Hoffmann by their first names, and introduces you to Mrs. Morton Prince. — e

All this is necessary as an antidote to the serious business of life, which is growing wise. Even in the last stages of senile aphasia I will not say that education, in an academic sense, was only secondary when I was at college. I plow through about five or ten big scientific books a week, and pretend to research. Even if, in the end, I've got to satisfy myself with testing toothpaste, I don't want to know it till it has happened. The other night Fred and Clowser and I walked all night from Portsmouth to Newburyport. That will tell you how unstable it all is.

I must drag my equations back from the basket, now, or I could rant forever. I hear you sigh, and bless the exams. Well, you bring it on yourself, and, if ever again you should gather courage to write so altogether charming a letter, I warn you that you will get one quite as long and quite as boring as this in return—
Affectionately

R

a. Kelly and Thayer were members of the Ethical Culture School administration who, according to Smith, were inclined to interfere with his teaching; Smith to Alice Kimball Smith, July 28, 1976.

b. Marie Luhrs, a classmate of Robert's at the Ethical Culture School, also wrote poetry.

c. Charlie Dunbar Broad published *Scientific Thought* in 1923.

d. A review of the world premiere of Bernard Shaw's *Saint Joan* by Heywood Broun, leading New York theater critic, had included the following: "He has written an epilogue which is shockingly and painfully unnecessary. Several portions of the play are tedious. A little of it is cheap. There is a touch of the maudlin. And it is, in our judgment, the finest play written in the English language in our day"; Heywood Broun, "Shaw and Shakespeare," *Sitting on the World* (New York: G. P. Putnam's Sons, 1924), p. 195.

e. Mrs. Morton Prince was a central figure among Boston's social and intellectual leaders.

Apparently neither the ravishing creature nor the two people from Wellesley, nor the lovely lady writing a thesis on Spinoza mentioned earlier, occupied Robert's serious attention during his three years at Harvard. Bernheim, Boyd, and Wyman all say that they never knew Robert to take a girl out, nor did they have much to do with girls themselves. Says Wyman: "We were all too much in love with the problems of philosophy and science and the arts and general intellectual life to be thinking about girls . . . We were all going through a series of love affairs [with ideas] . . . but perhaps we lacked some of the more mundane forms of love affairs that make life easier."[42]

Boyd ("Clowser") recalls a cold winter's walk along the shore with

Robert and Bernheim when one dared the others to go swimming. They stripped, tossed clothes on a snowbank, and plunged into the icy water. Bernheim remembers no winter skinny dipping, but sometimes they went to North Station, took the first train out, got off when they felt like it, and walked most of the night. One of these walks began some twenty miles from Worcester where they arrived at 3 a.m., trudging through deep snow with strange dogs barking at their heels.[43]

THE REFERENCE to Smith's having captured "the superintency" seems to place the next letter in the late winter of 1924, when he was appointed principal of the Ethical Culture high school. Since the preceding one does not seem particularly "beastly" or to reflect unusual distress, one or more may be missing. In the 1920s a second-year college student who did not succumb shortly after Christmas vacation to at least a mild depression and the distaste for study known as sophomore slump risked being considered an insensitive clod. Robert's troubled times were more basic and more frequent. Looking back over the years, Jeffries Wyman tried to explain them: "He found social adjustment very difficult, and I think he was often very unhappy . . . I suppose he was lonely and felt he didn't fit in well with the human environment. We were good friends, and he had some other friends, but there was something that he lacked, perhaps some more personal and deep emotional contact with people than we were having, because our contacts were largely, I should say wholly, on an intellectual basis. We were young people falling in love with ideas right and left and interested in people who gave us ideas, but there wasn't the warmth of human companionship perhaps. I don't mean that we weren't good friends, but it wasn't perhaps the kind of intimate relation that people sometimes have. I don't really know why he was unhappy."[44]

In 1922, a few months before Robert entered college, President Lowell had recommended that Harvard adopt a quota for Jewish undergraduates.[45] With cognizance of ethnic background thus officially sanctioned, and in the light of Herbert Smith's conviction that Robert felt handicapped by being a Jew, it is natural to wonder whether anti-Semitism contributed to the unhappiness that Wyman remembered. Robert's letters shed no light on this question. On the contrary, like his later recollections, they represent his close friendships at Harvard as ethnically and socially diverse, formed on the basis of intellectual compatibility. Boyd, of Scotch-Irish and German ancestry, recalls Robert's offhand comment: "Well neither one of us came over on the Mayflower," as indicating a relaxed attitude toward his heritage.[46]

Cambridge,
Immediately.
[late winter 1924]

My very dear Mr. Smith,

Thank you a thousand times for your letter; it has almost made me glad
to be unhappy, that I might not miss the relief of your manifold and charming consolation. After I had sent my beastly letter I regretted it, and thought
sorrowfully of the frightful position into which I had thrust you; I was
afraid that you would not answer, and infinitely more afraid that you
would; for it was a subject on which it seemed, then, impossible for even
you to say anything nice— And what has soothed me most, I think, is that
you perceived in my distress a certain similarity to that from which you had
suffered; it had never occurred to me that the situation of anyone who now
appeared to me in all respects so impeccable and so enviable could be in any
way comparable with my own; and the charity of that admission of yours
would very largely have sufficed.

For you are overwhelmingly right, it seems to me, in emphasizing the
secondary, induced character of many of our cravings. I do not think that it
makes the cravings any the less real to recognize this; but it certainly makes
their frustration less bitter to discover their former existence in you. But
you must see that it is very hard to remain innocent and satisfied, when science and literature and the people you admire—not the inhabitants of Denver, but those of Los Pinos—all proclaim the beauty and wonder and emotional and aesthetic wealth of a host of benisons which you haven't got. If
we could remain in the patriarchal farmhouse forever, if we could escape
"Of Human Bondage" and "The Wind Blows" and "Caesar and Cleopa-
tra" and "I'm a Fool" and "Three Contributions . . .", if we could disregard what Mrs. Page wants and what Francis wants and what Shaw wants,
if we could limit introspection to the gluttonous reverie of the uncritical,
perhaps we should seem more reasonable in our complaints. Isn't that rather
what Francis means by swearing that he will bring *his son* up a fool? For me,
and, I suspect, for you, it was never the opinion merely of the multitude that
counted so much; it was the opinion and the conduct of the great—I don't
mean absolutely, but to us. Abstractly I feel that it is a terrible pity that there
should be so many good people I shall not know, so many joys missed. But
you are right. At least for me the desire is not a need; it is an impertinence.
Cependant, even now, I envy you the favor with which the fates have
received your impertinences. Do I hear you muttering *élan vital?* I shall
change the subject.

And I land at a far more pleasant one. You seem to have captured the superintency—that needs another syllable, I think—and since you have taken it gladly I suppose that we may consider it a blessing. I hope that it will not keep you from doing what you want, and that it will console you for the imposition of new labors by many dinners at the Voisin, many wicked extravagances, and the glories of a plutocratic life. But I beg you not to overwork.

If you continue to write so flatteringly about my verses I shall be altogether too conceited for words. And you know that even were you to pray that you might never see another I should soon be sending them again. I have a story which I should like you to see, but it is at present both illegible and unrevised, and I must wait till I have time to type.

I am sending you two short books on Relativity which I found clear and amusing. They may be insultingly elementary for you, but I hope you will enjoy them none the less.

Aeons and Quaternions of gratitude.

R

30 | TO HERBERT W. SMITH

Cambridge, Sunday.
[ca. March 1924?]

My dear Mr. Smith,

No, I have not been permanently silenced by your heresy; nor can I blame this scandalous delay entirely upon the pon⌐ ⌐rings you advise. As a matter of fact, I think that if I knew quite what you mean by "vicious" I should thoroughly agree with you. But you are too much of a Moliereste for me, alas. I cannot think "Le Misanthrope" a comedy at all.

The other morning I found Daisy Neumann lugubriously observing University Hall in a blizzard. After such civilities as the wind and hail would permit she told me that "your Mr. Smith" was actually to be seen, now, manipulating the reins in 404.[a] I didn't think that you would be commandeered so very soon; and I sincerely hope that you will cling to your old headquarters, too, for, stupidly, I cannot conceive of a friendly, gossipy and irrelevant conversation in your new ones . . .

The reason that I have not written is that I have been using all my spare moments of consciousness carrying out calculations and searching data for an idea that I had, a couple of weeks back. At present I am brought very nearly to a standstill, but I am going to have a long interview with Kemble tomorrow, and if possible shall continue. I have had no end of fun working on it, though, and even though, as it most certainly must, it gets itself thrown into the trash basket, I shall not regret the sleepless nights and the criminal neglect of such pleasant matters as classes and dinners and writing to you.

A couple of weeks ago I went down to Provincetown for a few days; and I can understand better now than ever your enthusiasm for the Cape. Provincetown itself, though I don't think it deserves your comparison with Santa Fe, is certainly a charming little place, and even though the Portuguese contribute little to the atmosphere but their dark and wonderful countenances and their splendid names and a little squalor and an occasional impuritan scarf, that seems to be enough. And the dunes are nothing less than magnificent. You must remember that here we have had several feet of snow all year; and to be able to trudge over the hills, and lie on the warm sand hills and the beaches, and go swimming in the ocean, and watch a few brigantines and fishing schooners glide along the horizon, to climb the highest dune for the broadest view, to board a shattered wreck, to sit in the lea of the lighthouses, all this was a treat I shan't soon forget. You must beware; I threaten to return. And for some reason or other, I solved just enough problems, and had just enough pleasantly ridiculous adventures to make my memories altogether delightful. I had not realized before, though, how arduous your court [sic] must have been. But even at that I know that I too should have found it difficult to stay in Cambridge and do differential equations!

Next Spring, before we come down to go to Europe and domesticity, Fred and Clowser and I want to sail for a few days (a l'insu, de par Dieu). We thought of taking a seaworthy enough little sloop at Gloucester, sailing down to Provincetown in one long stretch, then crossing to Plymouth, and then up back. We'd be willing to give it nearly a week. Do you reckon we could? And if we get back in time in the fall, perhaps we could arrange some such jaunt together. I'd like to, awfully.

There hasn't been any word from Francis. Did you tell him to spare me? Or has he just naturally gotten bored with me? It's a little more remarkable because I had sent him some stuff, and he isn't usually rude, at any rate. Perhaps he fears that I will pursue him into the haunts of the viscounts, next summer.

My most sincere regards to Mrs. Smith. And, both of you, take this. "No, I thought thet thet ministur who marrid them wasn't a Cape Codder; he had sort of a forin accent." —And the "sound of the surf at Truro."

R

a. Daisy Neumann, in the class behind Robert at the Ethical Culture School, entered Radcliffe in 1922. She remembers the train trip to Boston with Robert that fall but no encounters thereafter; Daisy Neumann Newman to Alice Kimball Smith, February 17, 1977.

Bernheim and Boyd agree that the spring cruise to Provincetown did not take place. Boyd remembers only a day's sail out of Gloucester in a rented boat on which they had to pay a big deposit because they looked so unreliable.[47]

31 | TO HERBERT W. SMITH

Cambridge, Thursday.
[ca. April 10, 1924]

My dear Mr. Smith,

Please don't suppose that this is to be a letter, or that I hope to atone for my tardiness by splendour. I am writing now only to thank you for your note, to congratulate you on your plans for the summer, and to beg you for a weekend this spring. I shall be down next Thursday, I trust; won't you come out for a highly informal and highly impromptu sail in the Trimethy over Saturday and Sunday?— As you know, the place is rented, and we shall be forced to forego the luxuries of the shore; but if the weather is fair, and you are not too busy with other matters, I think I can assure you a jolly cruise. I haven't yet told my parents, and shouldn't have written to you had I not been anxious to find you free.

At present I am forced to regard myself as an extremely bad contributor to your symposium, for I confess that I am unable to find very much, from my stunted point of view, that is wrong with the college. It seems to me that, at least on the whole, it allows everyone an appropriate activity; and I cannot conceive of an environment which could more skillfully and expeditiously immerse men in the milieu they deserve. But perhaps I shall be a little more amusingly heterodox later on. At present my only grievance is against examinations which fall so indecently late.

Maybe, if I am good, you will confide some of your draughts or proofs to me on our yacht; I should mightily like to see them. And now forgive me if I turn to the more menial but more pressing business of the criteria of Bernoulli, Lexis, and Poisson.

R

The year's work was, as usual, rewarded by As except for a B in the second semester math course in probability.[48] Bernheim well remembers Robert's A in the notoriously tough elementary thermodynamics course. According to Bernheim, when Kemble realized that he had given an A to a student taking six courses, he decided his course must be too easy and made it even stiffer the following year when Bernheim took it.[49]

The Harvard letters, revealing though they are of aspects of Robert Oppenheimer's personal development and of the interests and attitudes of a segment of young American intellectuals, give only hints of what was going on in his own mind about his most vital concern—a career in science. His friends of the period, when asked years later what they had thought his future was going to be, all say that they foresaw distinction of some sort. Those who knew him first at Harvard assumed it would be in science. A few were not sure how the balance of his interests in science, philosophical ideas, and literature would tip. Paul Horgan, knowing Robert in a nonacademic setting, initially saw him as a great humanist and artist and later recognized the attributes of both in his style as scientist and administrator. At one point, Francis Fergusson, too, expected Robert to become a writer but must have sensed how the wind was blowing when Robert commented, after a year at Harvard, that as soon as he knew enough he would not need to resort to writing stories.[50]

THE OPPENHEIMER FAMILY spent the summer of 1924 in Europe. "My brother came and went," recalled Frank Oppenheimer. "He was with us in Munich and in Zurich and then joined us again in the Swiss Upper Engadine. He and I walked in the mountains together remembering our walks in the Seibengebirge in 1921."[51]

The first semester of Robert's third and final year at Harvard was not far along when he reported to Smith on his summer travels and other matters, including the possibility of following his older friends, John Edsall and Jeffries Wyman, to the University of Cambridge for graduate study.

32 | TO HERBERT W. SMITH

Cambridge, Tuesday.
[ca. October 1924]

My dear Mr. Smith,

This is a very belated thank-you letter about a delightful present of yours, ordered so long ago that, doubtless, its problematical existence has long since ceased to distress you. Mother has just forwarded the yachting annual. Already I have searched it for gratifying confirmation of a certain empirical knowledge of shoals; and it promises to save me from my disastrous errors in the future. It is a close second to the classic confectionery bearing the Chaves coat of arms.[a]

I confess that I want very much to write you a long and amusing letter. But I have been so scandalously remiss all summer that I find no tentacular apostrophes to cling to, and feel reduced to a mere recapitulation of what are, im Ganzen, quite a dull lot of odds and ends. But I trust that one of them will strike you as deserving of some passing & scornful comment, and serve as occasion for one of your brief but cherished notes:

Last summer I saw neither Jane nor Francis, chiefly because of a shyness in such things which I neither understand nor condone. Jane, I hear, oscillates back and forth between Lausanne and Paris with an incredible frequency, and is quite happy. Francis writes pathetically; he says he is lonely— For myself, the summer was inglorious; I worked a lot, with scanty results, wrote a little, sailed on the Irish sea, at [illegible], and climbed a few mountains, icy and splendid,—on the Italian border, in the Bernina & Forno. It will doubtless sound to you trite and trivial,—so great is greatness—but very often I wished that you were there to climb too, with the full measure of vigor and ecstasy which the place deserved. Mostly there were lazy people, who breathed. My parents & I got along much better than I should have predicted.

Here I am very busy again, chiefly with the Math. Phys. & Meta. I am taking a course with Whitehead of Russell & Whitehead, Cambridge, on the Metaphysical presuppositions of science, after which I shall doubtless be fit to give battle to you about the lamentable Broad.[b] I have, by the intervention of strangely kindly Gods, been unbewusst admitted to Christ's, at Cambridge; but I cannot decide to leave this Puritanical hole, even for all the vacuity of my life here, if I can do research next year with Bridgman. I shall be glad to bore you with my final decision, when it is born—

Your book must by now be emerging discreetly from the press. Will you send me a copy, or is my investment necessary to the bank? I should appreciate a little poem, signed. Someday, if God is good, I shall do as much for you, poem and all, maybe.

And really, I should like to hear about your adventures, and Los Pinos, and the desert, and Mrs. Page, about all those things that gripe and make me notice how blue and sunny the sky is, and what an exquisite filigree the chrome and coral leaves make, against it. And if, personatim, you should be able to come up for a day or two, and would, out of that, grant me an hour at tea, I should be so happy that I should smile slobber on your photographs, and talk about Grass Mountain, and Ouray.

If I am not sending you anything I have done—I hear, through the clear autumn, a professorial sigh—it is only that the things are most emphatically too pathetic to repay defiguration; if I can get them fixed I shall show you some Hiréshu translated, later on.

Permit me to bow low before your gracious wife.

Robert

a. The classic confectionery was a magnificent cake decorated with the Chaves family coat of arms which was dispatched to New Mexico at considerable expense for Don Amado's seventieth birthday. Smith, who accompanied Robert to a lower Manhattan bakery to order the cake, cites the episode as characteristic both of Robert's thoughtfulness and his pleasure at being accepted by the Chaves circle; interview with Smith by Alice Kimball Smith, July 9, 1975.

b. Robert's course with Alfred North Whitehead was Philosophy 20h, described as a Seminary in Metaphysics: Philosophical Presuppositions of Science, offered in the fall semester. According to his transcript and the Harvard course catalogue for 1924–25, Robert's other third year courses were: Chemistry 14c, Colloid Chemistry, primarily for graduates, spring semester; History 12, History of England from 1688 to the Present Time, a full year course; Mathematics 8, Dynamics (second course), a full year course; Mathematics 10a, Introduction to the Theory of Potential Functions and Laplace's Equation, fall semester; Mathematics 10b, The Analytical Theory of Heat and Problems in Elastic Vibrations—Fourier's Series, Legendre's Polynomials, Bessel's Functions, spring semester; Physics 9, Mathematical Theory of Electricity and Magnetism, a full year course of lectures.

Three letters to Smith and one to Fergusson—the slender remains of Oppenheimer's third-year Harvard correspondence—show that his thoughts focused increasingly on the coming year of graduate study in England. Smith, still the object of affectionate banter and an outlet for occasional bouts of *sturm und drang,* no longer provided a major intellectual stimulus. For the past year this had come from courses in physics, principally the three taken for credit in 1923–24 with Kemble and Bridgman. Oppenheimer regularly attended ten courses during this third and final year, five for credit and, as reported to Smith in February, five as auditor. They left an indelible, if not always precise or favorable, imprint upon his memory, as is evident in his comment on the course taught by Nobel Laureate Theodore W. Richards: "It wasn't until my third year at Harvard that I did get to take physical chemistry and by then it was a great disappointment . . . a very meager hick course . . . which would not get by today anywhere. But I didn't know that until I got there . . . It was formal, and tentative and timid; Richards was afraid of even rudimentary mathematics and very timid about non-phenomenological descriptions of things. I remember it but that was not what was really going on by then."[52]

According to Oppenheimer in 1963, mathematics too was "mostly very poorly taught" when he was an undergraduate but, he recalled, "I had the very good luck not to take but to audit [a graduate seminar with George

D.] Birkhoff on Sturm-Liouville equations, because he'd been working on it and wanted to talk about it . . . He was a remarkable fellow. He would begin: 'Well, you know, walking across the Yard this morning it occurred to me—' . . . This is the only [mathematics course] that I remember with happiness."[53]

What was "really going on" during the latter half of Oppenheimer's undergraduate career had much to do with Professor Percy W. Bridgman, the distinguished experimental physicist in whose laboratory he spent many hours, beginning with the spring semester of 1924 when he took Bridgman's course in advanced thermodynamics. "I found Bridgman a wonderful teacher because he never really was quite reconciled to things being the way they were and he always thought them out; his exercises were a very good way to learn where the bones were in these two beautiful parts of physics. I think as far as science goes they were the great point of my time at Harvard . . . [Bridgman] didn't articulate a philosophic point of view, but he lived it, both in the way he worked in the laboratory, which, as you know, was very special, and in the way he taught. He was a man to whom one wanted to be an apprentice."[54]

Other influences in the classroom and laboratory left a more diffuse impression. "I regarded the courses in physics and some others, but very much the courses in physics, as, of course, a master-pupil relation, but as a very vivid relation. I enjoyed them; I probably participated, they were small classes. They were not the comradeship of people the same age and the same interests, but there was a lot of comradeship involved. My friends were the same age and they were people who were mostly going into biology, but they were just a few. I lived with . . . a biochemist [Bernheim], and we had a very close friend who was also a biochemist [Boyd] . . . I'm sure there were [physics] students whom I knew, but in some funny way, by this crazily abnormal curriculum, I was doing gas analysis in the chemistry department all this time. By never having the same underpinning in physics or in collateral preparatory courses I had no 'co-moving' coordinates;' there wasn't anyone else who was having the same lack of preoccupations and the same preoccupations, and I couldn't name with certainty anyone who was in Bridgman's class, for instance."[55]

Cambridge.
[ca. January 1925]

My dear Mr. Smith,

This is a business letter: as nearly, at least, a business letter as I can write to you. The Senior Tutor of Christ's has written to me asking for the admission fee, and for a certificate from my 'head-master' at school, which is you. The certificate should say that you have known me for -?- years and that you believe me to be of good moral character; that two assertions so contradictory in sense should be demanded in one certificate is additional proof, I think, of the proverbial irrationality of the British.

I am a little hesitant about writing for even such a trifling official duty; for Mother told me that you were working much too hard & much too conscientiously. If you do not look out you will have to spend all of next summer getting reacclimated, & wearing your academic & administrative knees far enough apart to straddle Lady. Or are you going to the Cape, to get another good taste of salt, and an honest look at the water? I should think the sea would be getting jealous of the desert, with her painted mountains & muddy Rio Grande.

Wherever you are I do hope I shall see something of you; tired evenings & the perilous garrulity of a house party are not enough; & if we can we must manage to sail or climb or ride together for a few days. Myself, I do not know where I shall be, except that there will be a week or so up here til Commencement, at lab; a few weeks at Bayshore, where I shall sail & work & take an affectionate & efficient farewell of my parents; & if possible a few walks in the Mountains, west. I shall sail, I think, about September 2 or so— The other night, after a year or so of lethe I dreamt of Mrs. Page. She was standing at the porch steps, in the sunlight, in the olive riding jacket she used to wear. And the doctor was saying to her "Don't look at me like that" & I wasn't there, & it was all lovely. So now I keep promising myself to go out there again next summer. But I guess I won't.

The work goes much as before: frantic, bad, and graded A. I have got to debate with Whitehead at the Seminar next week, & am already trembling, of course— There are a few books I have read, & some I hope you like. Do you?: A Story Teller's Story, Anna Karenina, The Brothers Kara—, The Mysterious Stranger, Daisy Miller. Doesn't *Daisy* remind you of Chekhov, & particularly the *Lady & Dog?*

What a business letter!: far worse, even, than I had imagined. But forgive me; and, having reminded yourself that you have known me — years, write me, generously, & tell me all.

R.

In 1962, congratulating Bertrand Russell on his ninetieth birthday, Oppenheimer wrote: "It is almost forty years ago that we worked through the Principia Mathematica with Whitehead at Harvard. He had largely forgotten, so that he was the perfect teacher, both master and student. I remember how often he would pause with a smile before a sequence of theorems and say to us, 'That was a point that Bertie always liked.' For all the years of my life, I have thought of this phrase whenever some high example of intelligence, some humanity, or some rare courage and nobility has come our way."[56]

Talking with Kuhn, Oppenheimer again stressed the pleasure of learning with Whitehead, who gave this particular seminar only "when people came along and asked him . . . We must have been the first . . . there were just two of us."[57]

THE TRIPOS, in which Robert predicted failure in the following letter to Smith, was the final examination for Cambridge undergraduates. Holders of the bachelor's degree from other institutions were often required to take the rigorous two-part mathematical Tripos before commencing graduate study in science, but we have found no evidence that Robert took this examination.[58]

34 | TO HERBERT W. SMITH

Cambridge, Mass.
February 25. [1925]

My dear Mr. Smith,

Hosanna for the son! And the heartiest of congratulatory greetings to Mrs. Smith, who is, I hope, very well, and very happy. To me it seems an unusually solemn & splendid affair, because, at least as far as their reasonableness & deportment goes, your children seem, like Minerva, to be born full grown. But perhaps I only think that because I do not see with the sensitive & hypercritical eyes of paternity.

Thank you very much for the note. Doubtless, when I am ploughed at the Tripos, you will be compromised more than you need have been. Have you ever seen one of the papers? They are perfectly grisly, really. Rayleigh is the only one who got more than a $\frac{2}{3}$ credit on the Part II, and that, I think, is his best title to his peerage.[a] Even to think of it makes me do a comfortably transatlantic shiver.

I am so glad that you are all going to the Cape next summer! (you may say that I am selfish, & jealous, but I am gladder than all of that). For I will wager that it will be good to play with such things as logs and waves, after a winter of duelling with Mr. Lewis—I am now going regularly to 10 courses, & doing my research, & I have started to learn Chinese, with Clowser. But my muse still craves blood, and I do not know what she will allow me, in the way of laziness, next summer. Only this I swear. She shall not deprive me of the pleasure of driving a nail into the grand-ducal pavilion you are building at Brewster to accommodate the new son— Yes, you are perfectly right, it is not the nails that I insist upon.

Salut!

R.

Fred sends congratulations.

a. Lord Rayleigh (John William Strutt), Nobel laureate in physics and director of the Cavendish Laboratory at the University of Cambridge from 1879 to 1884, had inherited his title.

COMMUNICATION with Francis Fergusson seems to have lagged at times since Robert had written him from Bay Shore at Christmas 1923, though perhaps not to the extent suggested by the hiatus in surviving letters. As Robert wrote on the last day of Harvard's 1925 spring vacation, again from Bay Shore, Francis was nearing the end of the second of his three years at Oxford, where he had abandoned biology and fully indulged his love for poetry and drama. As a Rhodes Scholar, possessing social graces that Robert envied and a mature intelligence that inspired confidence in his elders, Francis had access to sophisticated circles such as the one that flourished at the Oxfordshire country house of Lady Ottoline Morrell. It was doubtless there that Francis had—in Robert's mind at least—learned how to treat dukes.

35 | TO FRANCIS FERGUSSON

Bayshore
April 25. [1925]

Dear Francis,

It is good to be writing to you again; it will be better still to sit talking together. If I were not such an ascetic creature I should not have denied myself so long. You will believe me when I tell you that I was waiting, childishly, til I might write you a scintillating letter, radiating well being & splendour. I have given up hope, now, of attaining to such a state; & I promise you I shall not deny myself again.

I shall not be in England before the end of August or the beginning of September; but, even after the preliminary courtesy to Christ's & Cambridge, I shall have a few weeks before the term opens, which I want to spend in Wales, sailing and recuperating from America. Don't you suppose we could manage to go together, & ruminate conjointly on our sins? And you will tell me how to treat the tutors & the dukes, & I shall tremble— For my plans for next year are not much, & not at all precise. I have been doing a problem with Bridgman this year, and that brief excursion convinces me that my genre, whatever it is, is not experimental science. But even Harvard has failed to extinguish my passion for the purely useless. Can't you too simulate even a mild tepidity for new mathematics, for instance? Perhaps the Auerbach set a permanent blight on your mathematical flora.[a]

Have you seen Jeffries? I haven't, of course, heard from him; but Demos told me that he was doing very well, but thoroughly tired of laboratory work, despite that.[b] Paul is now in Canada playing Pinafore; he is "preparing a book of his poems for his Boston publishers."[c] Smith continues to proliferate progeny with unfailing prodigality and vigor. The newest one is called Harden, & has already learned to wash dishes & to discourse with his father on Freud & Santayana. Smith himself is getting bald; and he no longer enjoys his wife's iconoclasm.

It is cold here now, & dull, & outside there is mud, mud, mud. There is a cold wet wind, & when we go sailing the spray freezes, as it did two years ago. And when I think of the first sail, with Mrs. Page, it is pleasant to reflect that next Easter I shall not be here. It is not conceivable that anywhere else people can talk so incessantly without saying anything, ever, that is not altogether empty, devoid of meaning.

Now I have written, & you will be bored; but for God's sake write again, or I shall perish before I see you. Have you seen Miss Lowell's *Keats,* & the new Chekhov letters?

Robert

a. Matilda Auerbach, who taught mathematics at the Ethical Culture School, is generally remembered as a fine teacher.

b. Jeffries Wyman had gone to the University of Cambridge in September 1924 and transferred to the University of London a few months later. Raphael Demos was a young instructor at Harvard.

c. Paul Horgan was now production assistant with the Rochester American Opera Company and occasionally sang a role as on this Canadian tour of *Pinafore.*

There are no letters to Smith or Fergusson between spring vacation and commencement. Perhaps none was written in Robert's last busy weeks at Harvard. The previous November he had been elected to Phi Beta Kappa in the "Junior Eight," but for the first time his final grades included more than one B—in Whitehead's fall semester "Seminary" and in the full year mathematics course in Dynamics.[59]

In June Robert was recommended by the Division of Chemistry for a degree with distinction, and his transcript records the A.B. summa cum laude in chemistry received "at commencement 1925 as of 1926."[60] (He remained officially a member of the class of 1926.) With Boyd and Bernheim, who also graduated after three years, Robert chose not to attend commencement but to celebrate privately with laboratory alcohol in Bernheim's room. "Boyd and I got plastered," Bernheim recalls. "Robert, I think, only took one drink and retired."[61]

II | "Making myself for a career"
EUROPE AND AMERICA, 1925–1929

WHEN OPPENHEIMER GRADUATED from Harvard in June 1925 still officially a chemist, the real question was what kind of a physicist he would be. His comment to Fergusson in April that the work with Bridgman "convinces me that my genre, whatever it is, is not experimental science" suggests that part of the decision had been made. Had he stuck to it, he might have spared himself much anguish the following year as a student at the University of Cambridge, where the dominant influence in physics was Professor Sir Ernest Rutherford, director of the Cavendish Laboratory. Under this renowned experimentalist, the Cavendish had become a mecca for bright young physicists from around the world. For Oppenheimer, too, Rutherford was the chief attraction: "I don't know why I picked Cambridge . . . I know I talked to Bridgman about it . . . I wanted to go to Cambridge to work in Rutherford's laboratory, but Rutherford wouldn't have me. He didn't think much of Bridgman and my credentials were peculiar and not impressive, and certainly not impressive to a man with Rutherford's common sense. But then it was arranged, I think by Rutherford, that I could work in Thomson's lab . . . It didn't occur to me to go to Germany. It didn't occur to me to go to Copenhagen. I don't even know why I left Harvard, but I somehow felt that [Cambridge] was more near the center."[1]

Even for a Harvard summa cum laude, getting "near the center" was not easy at this period when Oxford and Cambridge customarily required that holders of degrees from other institutions register as undergraduates.

Although Robert had been admitted to Christ's College, his status as a degree candidate had yet to be settled. From Bay Shore he invoked the assistance of Professor Bridgman.

36 | TO PERCY W. BRIDGMAN

Bayshore, N.Y.
June 13, 1925

Dear Professor Bridgman,

Last January I wrote to Sir Ernest Rutherford for permission to work in the laboratory at Cambridge; and I have just received the answer, which I enclose. It seems that access to the laboratory is only granted to those who are far enough along to work on a problem of their own; and it is for this reason that some sort of recommendation is necessary.

I should very much appreciate it if you would let me know whether or not you can send the recommendation, as that will probably affect my plans.

Thank you again for your help during the last year.

Very sincerely,

J. R. Oppenheimer

Rutherford's delayed reply must have suggested the course of action that Robert followed in an undated letter to the secretary of the Cambridge University Board of Research Studies.

37 | TO R. E. PRIESTLEY (BOARD OF RESEARCH STUDIES)

Saxons' Road
Bay Shore, N.Y.
[ca. June 1925]

Dear Sir:

Next term I expect to start studying at Cambridge for a Ph.D. I have already been admitted to Christ's College; but I am not certain whether I should make a further application in order to be allowed to do research. I hope to read in Mathematics and Physics, and, if possible, to work at a problem in the theory of metallic conduction.

I have been advised to write to you of my preparation; and, if there are any details concerning the work I have done which would be of use, I should be glad to give them. This June I took a degree of B.A. summa cum laude at Harvard, for which I had studied chiefly in Chemistry, Mathematics, and Physics. During my last year I worked at a problem on the pressure effect on metallic conduction under Professor Bridgman. I should be glad to wait a term before beginning research, if this seems advisable. But I am writing now in order to find out if such a plan is at all possible, and I should very much appreciate it if you would let me know what application I ought to make.

Very sincerely,

J. Robert Oppenheimer

FROM HIS SUMMER HOME in New Hampshire, Bridgman complied with Robert's request for a recommendation by writing at length to Rutherford. He hoped that Oppenheimer might be admitted to the Cavendish Laboratory, though he confessed to some uncertainty about his future in physics. Emphasizing Robert's brilliant record at Harvard, Bridgman noted his "perfectly prodigious power of assimilation," his vast reading, and the advanced courses he had taken:

"His problems have in many cases shown a high degree of originality in treatment and much mathematical power. His weakness is on the experimental side. His type of mind is analytical, rather than physical, and he is not at home in the manipulations of the laboratory . . . During this last year he started with me a small research on the effect of pressure on the resistance of alloys, and was evidently much handicapped by his lack of familiarity with ordinary physical manipulations. However he stuck at it, and by the end of the year had learned much, and obtained some results of value, all without being of much trouble to me personally, but he picked up many of the tricks of manipulation which he needed from my mechanic."

"It appears to me that it is a bit of a gamble as to whether Oppenheimer will ever make any real contributions of an important character, but if he does make good at all, I believe that he will be a very unusual success, and if you are in a position to take a small gamble without too much trouble, I think you will seldom find a more interesting betting proposition."

Bridgman felt compelled to add a final paragraph in which, following the custom of the period in letters of recommendation, he referred to the candidate's Jewish background: "As appears from his name, Oppenheimer is a Jew, but entirely without the usual qualifications of his race. He is a tall, well set-up young man, with a rather engaging diffidence of manner, and I think you need have no hesitation whatever for any reason of this sort in considering his application."[2]

To Robert, Bridgman wrote that he had told Rutherford about Robert's "very unusual equipment for theoretical work." If he was not admitted to the Cavendish, Bridgman hoped he would find some other way of pursuing his studies abroad.[3] Acknowledging Bridgman's prompt assistance, Robert reported on the research with which he was supplementing the more frivolous diversions of summer at Bay Shore. He was exploring the change in electrical conductivity of rutile (titanium dioxide) when it is ignited.

38 | TO PERCY W. BRIDGMAN

Bayshore [New York]
June 29, 1925

Dear Professor Bridgman,

Thank you very much for your letter, and for making out so good a case for me, and for wishing me so well. Our letters may have to lie for another few months in Rutherford's mail box before I hear again; but when I do hear, I shall be glad, if I may, to let you know where I shall be working.

I have just started at the electrical properties of rutile: the phenomenon does not seem very complicated. Rutile is a good dielectric ($\epsilon = 130$). When it is heated to 750°–800° C in hydrogen, it turns black, loses 1.6%–1.7% of its weight, becomes somewhat soluble (up to 6–7%) in acids, is more easily reduced, and becomes a pyroelectric conductor of specific resistance of the order of .1 ohm. When the black form is heated above 750° C in the presence of oxygen, it gains 1.7% of its weight, & returns to the form of ordinary rutile. The change of weight increases with the temperature used for the conversion. It is always too low to be accounted for by a stoichiometric reduction, & too high to be due to impurities. This seems to suggest that, whereas the high metallic conductivity requires the participation of nearly all the atoms, the much lower conductivity of metallic oxides depends on the presence of some atoms only with metal-like electrons. That is all that I have been able to find out now; if I should happen to find anything that is relevant later on, I shall be glad to tell you of it.

Very sincerely,

J. R. Oppenheimer

FROM BAY SHORE Robert also wrote to Francis Fergusson proposing a September reunion. The letter, forwarded from Oxford to Heidelberg, finally caught up with Fergusson in Munich.

Bayshore
July 20. [1925]

Dear Francis,

It is a long time since I have heard from you; and I hope that it is only because one of our letters miscarried, and not that you have grown weary of our Cornish expedition. In any case I shall risk boring you with repetition:

I shall arrive in England about September 16th; I shall want about 10 days or 2 weeks at Cambridge, to see about laboratory facilities and such matters. During this time you can reach me at Christ's College. We might meet at Cambridge, or at London; or at Winchester, which is probably the most convenient for you. But unless I hear I shall expect you at Christ's.

During August I shall be in the mountains, very probably in the Pecos. But if you write to Bayshore, I shall get your letter on my return. Paul [Horgan] will be down this afternoon. He is to stay a few days. He is pretty much unchanged, I think, except for the slightly pontifical assurance which success has given him. Smith is at the Cape this summer. He is coming down here later, largely, I think, to discuss with father the most effective method of obtaining money for the new school. That is your Smith. You would not know him.

I am supposedly working at a problem in electronic conduction at a laboratory near here. But they are forever short of apparatus, and, as a result, I spend most of my time pretending to study, & indolently sailing the Trimethy over the Bay. I am anxious to get away, & more anxious than I can tell you to see you again.

It is impossible to write with any considerable lyricism a letter whose arrival is so improbable. But do write. Or I shall drown myself before I get to Southhampton.

Robert

BEFORE SAILING for England, Robert made his first visit to the Pecos Valley in New Mexico since his introduction to it by Herbert Smith in 1922. His parents, comfortably housed at Bishop's Lodge on the outskirts of Santa Fe, joined him for a few days at the Pages' ranch, Los Pinos.

Los Pinos, Saturday
[ca. August 8, 1925]

Dear Mr. Smith,

Part A: Business.

The negatives are delivered. It is reported that a few of them are missing, but that they are unimportant, and that you will be forgiven. Whereupon lament for you and Oateman, who are lost souls.

I have your eversharp, and shall give it to Frank to take to school. Meanwhile I have been using it for the construction of the three sets of verses I am sending to you. If any of them are useful, don't hesitate to maltreat them, or add others, or anything. I tried to choose really decent things, but things whose excellence was not too frightfully obvious. If you have any new ones, I should like to see them.

Part B: Gossip.

The menage here is a good deal simpler this year, but very nearly as delightful. Don Amado is, of course, not well. But he is very hearty physically, and quite as charming as ever. Consuelo [Chaves] is at the Fiesta, where, God willing, she will stay a few days more. There is a family called Swann, from Massachusetts by the tubercular Tucson-Colorado Springs route. Most excellent people, with two daughters, both immensely learned, and one ravishing. If you were here Katherine would be jealous; but as it is all is sweet. Tonight Mr Page is to bring Mother, Father, Erna [Fergusson], and several more "perfectly charming people" from La Jolla, up from Santa Fe. Mrs Page and I hope to induce Erna to take us on a höchst rapid and abbreviated trip to the Snake dance.[a] Meanwhile Mr Page would take Mother and Father to Taos, and Puye. The Parents are really quite pleased with the place, and are starting to ride a little. Curiously enough they enjoy the frivolous courtesy of the place, and all is well — Of more intimate gossip there is very little. Katherine is not well, and probably no more happy than before. But she seems to have dominated Page's jealousy, and chides him about it only a few times a day. They are absorbed, together, in the mechanics of the menage, which are at present strained to the elastic limit. Mrs Page looks well and rides superbly. Lady is lame, and most of the horses underfed.

We have done only a few expeditions. Pecos Baldy and over toward the Truchas; Lake Peak and the divide, which was superb; and a feeble attempt to penetrate the caves at the Pancuela. Your trail, a new mine and a great expedition to Lake Katherine, and then the Brazos, for the next days. I do hope that we shall be able to do Walpi. As we now plan it, we could make it between Sunday evening and Thursday morning, with the dream mesas thrown in.

Francis is presenting a paper on America's place in literature to a learned society at Heidelberg—

Adios. They are calling for a walk. But more some other time.

R

a. The 1925 Santa Fe Fiesta was held from August 2 to 6; *El Palacio,* nos. 2 and 3 (August 1, 1925): 31–32, information provided by Orlando Romero, New Mexico State Library. Erna Fergusson, Francis' sister, was an authority on Indian dances. A snake dance, the culmination of sixteen-day Hopi ceremonies, was performed in the village of Walpi in odd-numbered years.

At Los Pinos, while Mrs. Page took the boys on long rides, Mrs. Oppenheimer sat on the porch and did beautiful petit point despite the awkwardness of her artificial hand.[4] Oral tradition credits Robert and his riding companions with the finding of an unmapped lake on the east side of Santa Fe Baldy, which they named in honor of Katherine Page. As Lake Katherine, it eventually appeared on the survey map of the area. This reference suggests that the lake was named on Robert's earlier visit to the area with Smith.

Paul Horgan recollects vividly everything except the date of a memorable expedition with Robert, which could have taken place on this 1925 visit since the Oppenheimers apparently did not yet own horses. Horgan recalls that in Santa Fe "we hired two horses with high pommel saddles and took a lunch . . . and I had a paint box full of tubes of paint and equipment for work because I was certain that somewhere along the line I would toss off a landscape. We started up the Lake Peak trail . . . to cross the Sangre de Cristos to Cowles. It turned out to be a day-long venture, full of merriment and nonsense as we rode. Presently I had a collapse of my paint box. It was tied to my pommel with a thong, which broke . . . and everything was precipitated on the ground. And idiotically I had to ride the rest of the way with it under my arm which was sort of superb. Then we hit the divide at the very top of that mountain in a tremendous thunderstorm . . . immense, huge, pounding rain. We sat under our horses for lunch and ate oranges, [and] were drenched . . . I was looking at Robert . . . and all of a sudden I noticed his hair was standing straight up . . . responding to the static. Marvelous. Then presently we were able to remount and go down the other side and we got to Cowles about seven at night, after dark, and Katy Page's windows were lighted. It was a very welcome sight. She received us, and we had a beautiful time for several days there. She referred to us always then and afterward as her slaves. 'Here come my slaves.' "[5]

THE REPLIES from Rutherford and from the Board of Research Studies that awaited Robert's return from New Mexico prompted three letters written before he sailed for England. The first two concerned arrangements for his study in England and the third was a report to Bridgman on the results of his summer research.

41 | TO PERCY W. BRIDGMAN

Bay Shore, New York
August 29, 1925

Dear Professor Bridgman,

Rutherford wrote to me that he already had so many "excellent applicants" that he could not take me, at least for a time. But the registrar for graduate studies wrote to me that he could get me admitted a little later in the year. But for that he insists upon recommendation. He is particularly interested to know whether the applicant has done any original work, experimental or theoretical; and whether he has shown any aptitude for this, or any originality in his attack upon assigned work. I am very sorry to have to bother you with this; I think that I can promise that it will be the last time. I am enclosing an envelope.

I did a few quantitative experiments on the resistance of rutile; the conductibility is not proportional to the number of reduced atoms, altho these are distributed at random; but approximately to the sixth power of this number. This certainly is not an agreement with a free electron theory. If you would like, at any time, a more detailed report, I shall be glad to send it.

Very sincerely,

J. R. Oppenheimer

42 | TO R. E. PRIESTLEY

Saxons' Road
Bayshore, N.Y.
August 30, 1925

Dear Sir:

Thank you for your letter of August 10th, and for the enclosed copy of the Regulations concerning the admission of students for research.

Since I expect, in any case, to study at Christ's College next term, I should like to be admitted to the University as a research student as soon as possible; but if admission cannot be granted at once, I should be quite willing to wait a term. I expect to be in Cambridge shortly; and I shall then submit my formal application.

Very sincerely,

J. R. Oppenheimer

43 | TO PERCY W. BRIDGMAN

Bayshore, N.Y.
September 5, 1925.

Dear Professor Bridgman,

Thank you for your note, and for the letter of recommendation. It is far better than anything for which I had hoped; and I feel sure that it will satisfy even the jealous guards of the Cavendish laboratory.

I am sending some of the details of the work I have done this summer. If I can get better samples, I shall make this work considerably more precise:

1) The reduction which rutile undergoes upon ignition in hydrogen does not change the external crystal form of the oxide . . .

2) The reduction is not a surface reduction . . .

3) The only considerable experimental difficulty is that of obtaining uniform samples . . .

4) A conversion of 4% means that the oxide is about 40% Ti_2O_3, and that, roughly, $\frac{2}{3}$ of the titanium atoms have valence electrons. If a large part of the conduction were done by the dissociation and migration of these electrons, then the conductibility would be roughly proportional to the loss of weight; if the curve were not a straight line, we should expect it to be concave downward. But if the valence electrons travelled along the atoms themselves, then the chance that an electron could travel, undisturbed, for n atoms would be, if the loss of weight w were small enough, proportional to w^n. For larger w I cannot compute this chance without knowing the mechanism of transfer; but, for fixed n, it would not vary as rapidly as w^n . . .

5) There is another thing, which, in this connection, seems very puzzling to me. If the conducting electrons are to travel along the atoms, it seems probable that they will follow quantum orbits. Yet, by a direct computation, from the Ham-Jac. [Hamilton-Jacob] solution for the Stark effect, I found that the maximum distance of an electron from its nucleus, in a hydrogen like atom, and an electric field, only changes by 10^{-7} of itself per volt. I did the calculation twice, and could not find the mistake; but I don't think that the result looks very encouraging.

I hope that you will pardon me the length and the garrulity of this note; and that, perhaps, some of it will be interesting to you.

Very sincerely,

J R Oppenheimer

WHEN ROBERT SAILED for England early in September, Frank and the captain of the Oppenheimer's yacht *Lorelei* sailed out to wave goodbye as the ship passed the Fire Island light. The Atlantic crossing, which took a week or more in 1925, gave Robert time to prepare a summary of his academic preparation as stipulated in the regulations of the Board of Research Studies. Before joining Francis Fergusson for the trip to Cornwall, he paused long enough in Cambridge to establish a connection with Christ's College and to make formal application for graduate standing.

44 | TO R. E. PRIESTLEY

Christ's College
Cambridge
September 16, 1925

Dear Sir:

I should like to apply for admission to the University as a graduate student. I hope, at the end of three years, to take a degree of Doctor of Philosophy at the University. In preparation for this I should like to continue reading in Physics, in Analysis, and in Physical Chemistry; and I should like, as soon as it seems advisable, to undertake a research problem in Physics. I am particularly interested in the theory of electronic conduction; the original experimental problems which I have worked at were both concerned with this theory; and I should be very glad of an opportunity for further experimental work, and, if possible, for critical advice in the corresponding theoretical problems. I am most interested in those aspects of the theory of conduction which can give an indication of the laws of force to which the motion of electrons are subject.

Almost all of the formal work which I have done in preparation was done at Harvard College. A part of this work I did for courses regularly given at the College; and I am submitting a list of these courses, omitting those required for elementary preparation, and those in other fields.

I took "for credit" the following courses:

Analysis (third year).

Calculus of Probabilities.

Potential Theory.

Problems in the flow of heat, hydrodynamics, etc. Introduction to the use of Bessel's functions, ellipsoidal harmonics, Legendre polynomials [etc.].

Capillary Chemistry (a course covering, approximately, Freundlich's "Kapillarchemie").

Physical Chemistry.

Thermodynamics (two courses).

Mathematical Theory of Electricity and Magnetism.

Introduction to Statistical Mechanics and the Quantum Theory.

Seminary on the Presuppositions of Science (Dr. A. N. Whitehead).

Organic Chemistry.

Analytical Dynamics (Advanced Course).

I attended the exercises, and recorded the lectures, in the following courses:

Problems in the dynamics of the quantum theory.

Mathematical theory of Relativity.

Electromagnetic theory of light.

Sturm-Liouville Methods in Linear Differential Equations.

The Theory of Complete Electrolytic Dissociation (Professor Debye).

In addition to this Professor Bridgman allowed me to work at a problem in the pressure coefficient of the electrical conductivity of alloys. The object of these measurements, which were carried to fifteen thousand atmospheres, was to [determine] whether the pressure coefficient was a function of the composition similar to the temperature coefficient. I succeeded in taking measurements on only two types of alloys. This summer, moreover, I was allowed to study the conductibility of the mineral rutile. It had previously been observed that, upon violent ignition, particularly in a reducing atmosphere, rutile became conductive. The object of the experiments was to explain this change, and to discover, if possible, the mechanism which it involved.

The other work I have done consists largely of reading, and of the preparation of the theses required in four of the courses mentioned above. It was not necessary that these theses solve new problems; but the treatment was supposed to be original.

In support of this application I am submitting my degree, my grade cards, and a few letters from the men with whom I have worked. If any more definite information is required, I shall be glad to try to give it.

I am twenty-one years old.

Very sincerely,

J. R. Oppenheimer

[Note appended to letter]:

Sir Joseph Thomson has expressed his willingness to take me as a research student, but advised me to take a course in laboratory manipulation during the first term.

J. Robert Oppenheimer

AFTER A TWO-YEAR SEPARATION, Robert and Francis Fergusson had much to talk about. For a week or ten days, Fergusson recalled, "we walked along the cliffs and talked, of course, about everything under the sun, and that was very pleasant. We always enjoyed that sort of thing." Later that year, after he realized how emotionally upset Robert had become, Fergusson wondered if these talks were partly responsible, for he had not only given a "rather Russian account" of what it was like to be an American student in Europe but had expounded theories and described adventures— social, intellectual, and psychological—about which he had perforce kept silent during a summer of travel with his mother.[6]

Perhaps Francis's qualms were partially induced by a letter he received that autumn from Herbert Smith. "How is Robert doing?" Smith enquired. "Is frigid England hellish socially and climatically, as you found it? Or does he enjoy its exoticism? I've a notion, by the way, that your ability to show him about should be exercised with great tact, rather than in royal profusion. Your [two] years' start and social adaptivity are likely to make him despair. And instead of flying at your throat—as I remember your being ready to do for George What's-his-name . . . when you were similarly awed by him—I'm afraid he'd merely cease to think his own life worth living.— Forgive the grandfatherliness, please."[7]

45 | TO FRANCIS FERGUSSON

Cambridge, [England]
Nov 1. [1925]

Dear Francis,

I am sending you some of the Karmeliten peppermints. Woodson wrote that I should soon be getting some pinones.[a] As soon as they come I shall send some on.

There is far too much to tell you in a letter. I do not think that Cambridge can be quite so bad as Oxford. But its excellences are just as fantastically inaccessible, and there are vast, sloppy strata where there is nothing, absolutely nothing, to be found. By next term, I think, I may have some people to shew you. There are a great many Americans, but they are not as universally wretched here as at Oxford. There are quite a lot from Harvard: Edsall, Fried, Haile, Castle, Fred [Bernheim], Sterling Dow, Mc Gill.[b] Did you know any of them? Jeff [Wyman] is up here this week end. Most of the scientists are frightful. There is one who shows hope. But all of them are uncommonly skillful at blowing glass and solving differential equations, and the academic standard here would depeople Harvard over night. The men here seem to have a great respect for American scientists. But they have nothing but contempt for the Germans.

I do not think that I shall be able to come to Oxford this term, but I am very anxious to see you, and I hope that it will be possible for us to meet very early in the vac.

I am having a pretty bad time. The lab work is a terrible bore, and I am so bad at it that it is impossible to feel that I am learning anything. I have just heard that Thomson is my supervisor, but I have not been to see him yet. The lectures are vile. And you know the rest.

Has Jean been to Oxford?[c]

Robert

a. Woodson was an Albuquerque lawyer friend of Katherine Page's.

b. John T. Edsall, A.B. 1923, A.M. 1924, beginning his second year of graduate study in biology at Cambridge; Walter Jay Fried, A.B. 1924; Henry P. Haile, A.M. 1925; Edward S. Castle, A.B. 1925; Frederick Bernheim, A.B. 1925; Sterling Dow, A.B. 1925; and Frederick T. McGill, A.B. 1925. *Harvard Alumni Directory*, 1926, Harvard University Archives, Pusey Library, Cambridge, Mass.

c. Jean de Menasce was a friend of Fergusson's whom Robert met some time during this year.

Robert seemed more sanguine when he next wrote Fergusson.

46 | TO FRANCIS FERGUSSON

Cam[bridge, England]
Nov 15. [1925]

Dear Francis,

Thanks for the George. It has a lot of magnificent things in it; but I have not found, yet, a tract comparable with the Gezeiten in your book. It is not quite so formidable syntactically either, and can mostly be read without the help of philologic treatises.

I shall have quite a lot to tell you. For the place is very rich, and has plenty of luscious treasures; and although I am altogether unable to take advantage of them, yet I have a chance to see many people, and a few good ones. There are certainly some good physicists here—the young ones, I mean; and they are very different from the Thomson Larmor generation,[a] and even more different from the Rutherford one. I have been taken to all sorts of meetings: High Maths at Trinity, a secret pacifist meeting, a Zionist club, and several rather pallid science clubs. But I have seen no one here who is of any use who is not doing science. This applies particularly to the Americans. There is a great mass of American English students. Most of them want to teach. They are a terribly poor lot, and are literally dying off under the rigors of disregard, climate, and Yorkshire pudding. When you come here next term you must let me take you to a colloquium, or something of that sort. It is very neat and precise; there is, really, a new generation, and for the first time in seventy years they have got people here who do both experiment and theory.

I am working with Thomson now. He thought my experiments quite good, but didn't help much otherwise. Of him too later.

There are some terrible complications with Fred, and an awful evening, two weeks ago, in the moon. I have not seen him since, and blush when I think of him. And a Dostoievskian confession from him. I have not been to a dance with a French Swiss.

Thanks for the book, again. And I hope that you will write. Let me know when I can see you, at any rate. I can't leave here now.

Robert

a. Sir Joseph Larmor, an almost exact contemporary of J. J. Thomson, was Lucasian Professor of Mathematics at Cambridge.

Oppenheimer later described what he had in mind when he worked with Thomson. "It was not a good idea, but I was puzzled by the conductivity business and I thought I would like to study what happened with beams of electrons and thin films of metal. This was not electron diffraction; it would, if properly done, presumably [have] led to it . . . ."

"As far as I remember I was introduced to Thomson, and he and [Ebenezer] Everett worked in one corner of this large basement room and I worked in the diagonally opposite corner . . . I did make some beryllium films which, I think, [James] Chadwick used for other purposes . . . [I remember] the miseries of evaporating beryllium onto collodion and then getting rid of the collodion, and so on. I did some studying . . . I don't remember any formal courses in physics . . . "

"The business in the laboratory was really quite a sham but it got me into the laboratory where I heard talk and found out a good deal of what people were interested in. I still had the feeling that I should be able to understand what was going on in metals, but, of course, I didn't, and even [Erwin] Schrödinger's paper, which might have given one ideas, didn't connect with this problem for me . . . "

"I was living in a miserable hole . . . Then in the spring I moved out to a place along the river half way to Grantchester which was less miserable. I dined in college."[8]

The "terrible complications with Fred," of which Robert wrote Fergusson, related in some way to the fact that his friendship with Frederick Bernheim had not withstood transplanting from one Cambridge to the other. Bernheim found this very natural. He and Robert were attached to different colleges, lived in different lodgings, and worked in different laboratories. Bernheim soon met a young woman in the biochemistry lab, his future wife, and spent many evenings with her. He found a certain relief in less constant exposure to Robert's intensity and drive, and he thought that Robert too was enjoying new contacts and experiences. In the coming months Robert himself would be making some rather startling confessions of dubious accuracy and may have overdramatized this November confrontation. Bernheim's memory focuses rather on an occasion in the spring of 1926 when Robert invited him to his digs for a strawberry and Devonshire cream tea and demanded a kind of showdown as to whether their friendship was to be revived or ended. At the time Bernheim did not realize that Robert's emotional balance was more precarious than usual. He recalls only one more meeting, an uneventful one when Robert visited him and his new wife in Munich in 1927.[9]

BEFORE CHRISTMAS Robert wrote to Herbert Smith. This letter is the last surviving item in the Oppenheimer–Smith correspondence until August 1945.

47 | TO HERBERT W. SMITH

[Cambridge, England]
Dec 11 [1925]

Dear Mr Smith,

Your conscience, I suspect, can not have been quite at ease about our mutual epistolatory obligations; for not long ago I heard from Father that he had seen you, & that you had confessed that you owed me a letter. But I appreciate your magnanimity all the same; and if it will encourage you in the construction of another such charming letter, I shall be glad to have you impute to me any sin, up to & including manslaughter. And in the interests of pure science I ought to add that epistolatory simultaneity must be measured, not in terms of the velocity of light, but by the more solemn progress of the U. S. Mails.

Nor are you quite right in supposing that it was any such technicality that kept me from writing to you: in such things I always feel so fully head over heels in debt to you, that a gross of letters could not make much difference. Nor, finally, is it because I have been busy, as you so charitably put it, making a career for myself. (If I seem to be spending all my faculties in contradicting you, you must remember that that is the subtlest form of flattery). Really I have been engaged in the far more difficult business of making myself for a career. And I have not written, simply because I have lacked the comfortable conviction & assurance which are necessary to an adequately splendid letter. You see that I have not forgotten how to protract & ornament my apologies.

Francis is going to be in New York next winter, & he will give you a much more coherent account of himself than I can. He has changed a great deal. Exempli gratia, he is happy. And he is now able to devote his scant energies, not, as before, to the precarious maintenance of his intellectual bulwarks, but to more adventurous speculations. And you must not pity him. He knows everyone at Oxford; he goes to tea with Lady Ottoline Morrell, the high priestess of civilized society, & the patroness of [T.S.] Eliot & Berty [Bertrand Russell]; & he is a member of a congress of littérateurs who meet every summer at Pontigny to talk about 'Mysticism & Literature' & other such modest things. You will see for yourself.

Your irony is perhaps a little too nice to be charitable. Betty Thomas is teaching school, & I, who was for long years in love with her shadow, am not to care a tinker's damn! —the only gossip I have is that Jane expects another infant about the New Year.[a]

Later I am surely coming back to America to live. But now I am too busy here for that. I hope to see you, though, next Spring, for I have much to tell & a good deal to ask. It is far too much to write; and perhaps when I see you my incoherence & garrulity will be somewhat mitigated by my very obvious desire to confide in you.

I shall miss our Xmas party this year. Please give my best greetings to Mrs Smith, & have a very jolly time. And do write again, if only a little.
Your

Robert

a. Betty Thomas had been a classmate of Robert's at the Ethical Culture School. Jane Didisheim Kayser was living in Paris, where Robert visited her and her husband Jacques while he was in Cambridge.

ROBERT'S DESIRE to confide in Smith was not compelling, for the ornate phrases in which he customarily addressed his former English teacher told almost nothing of his life in Cambridge or of his state of mind. Robert can hardly have realized how arduous the business of making himself for a career was to become in the next few months. Although he was indeed making new acquaintances among Cambridge scientists, none had yet become close friends. Soon after arriving in Cambridge, Robert had dropped in on John Edsall at St. John's College, and this friendship, begun three years earlier at Harvard, became stronger as the year progressed. Jeffries Wyman often spent weekends in Cambridge, and during the Christmas holidays Robert joined Francis Fergusson in Paris.

To Edsall, a biochemist, Robert tried that autumn to convey his tremendous excitement over new developments in physics and to explain their meaning. Edsall was impressed by Robert's eagerness to become involved with, and to contribute to, the new physics and sensed his disappointment that he was not two or three years older and ready to participate on an advanced level. However, not until after the New Year did Edsall appreciate the extent of Robert's frustration.[10]

Francis Fergusson was alerted to Robert's abnormal emotional condition by a bizarre incident during their holiday reunion in Paris. In the course of one of their customary exchanges about intellectual and personal matters, Robert suddenly leapt upon Fergusson with the clear intention of strangling him. As tall as Robert and more solidly built, Francis had easily warded off the attack, but this uncharacteristic display of violence, combined with Robert's despair over his inept performance in the laboratory and confidences about unsatisfactory sexual ventures, convinced Francis that his friend was seriously troubled.[11] Robert was immediately contrite, and on his return to Cambridge he tried to account for his strange behavior.

48 | TO FRANCIS FERGUSSON

Cambridge, [England]
Jan 23. [1926]

Dear Francis,

You should have, not a letter, but a pilgrimage to Oxford, made in a hair shirt, with much fasting and snow and prayer. But I will keep my remorse and gratitude, and the shame I feel for my inadequacy to you, until I can do something rather less useless for you. I do not understand your forbearance nor your charity, but you must know that I will not forget them.

I am doing physics now, pretty badly; and I shall, I think, stay on at least this year. But I am not well, and I am afraid to come to see you now for fear something melodramatic might happen. Perhaps we can see each other a day or two next vac. Anyway, if I may, I will pay you a visit early in the Easter term. I have a little to tell you, and a great deal to ask. And if you will come here I shall shew what I have found.

Please, if it is all right, tell Frances Keeley greetings from me.

I am sending you a can of pinons and a noisy poem which I just wrote. I have left out, and that is probably where the fun came in, just as I did in Paris, the awful fact of excellence; but as you know, it is that fact now, combined with my inability to solder two copper wires together, which is probably succeeding in getting me crazy.

Will you drop me a note, with the news?

Love

Robert

John Edsall noted a change in Robert after the holidays and, though not the recipient of as intimate revelations as Fergusson, he recognized a severe psychological crisis. "It was obvious," said Edsall of the ensuing weeks, that "there was a tremendous inner turmoil, in spite of which . . . he kept on doing a tremendous amount of work, thinking, reading, discussing things, but obviously with a sense of great inner anxiety and alarm . . . [It] certainly was partly mixed up with this terrific intensity of activity . . . [and with] frustrations going back into the past." Edsall did not observe any self-destructive tendency in Robert's behavior, but Robert did express a fear that he might have a mental breakdown and be unable to work. He told Edsall of periodic visits to a Cambridge psychiatrist.[12]

Meanwhile, Robert wrote calmly to Fergusson about plans for the long spring holiday.

49 | TO FRANCIS FERGUSSON

Cambridge, [England]
Mar 7. [1926]

Dear Francis,

Thanks for your letter. My regret at not having strangled you is now intellectual rather than emotional. If you want to come here before you go to Italy, it will be perfectly safe, & I shall be very glad to see you. If not, will you tell me where you will be in Italy? Probably I shall have to stay here during the vac, but if I can I will go with Jeff [Wyman] & Edsall to Corsica, & in that case would come back by Leghorn.

It is impossible to write. But I would like to see you before you go back.

Robert

In the absence of further correspondence, the principal events of that troubled spring must be reconstructed from the recollections of friends. Robert did make the projected trip to Corsica with Edsall and Wyman. For ten days they walked in the mountains, stayed at small inns, and enjoyed French food and wines. Occasionally Robert spoke of feeling depressed, but mainly they laughed at minor incidents of travel or talked about serious topics including the broad range of French and Russian literature, especially Dostoevsky, to which Robert had been introducing Edsall during the previous months of growing intimacy. Edsall remembers Robert's comment during one of these conversations about people who had achieved great things in literature and science: "The kind of person that I admire most would be one who becomes extraordinarily good at doing a lot of things but still maintains a tear-stained countenance."[13]

The three friends planned to go on to Sardinia, but at dinner the last evening in Corsica the waiter came to Robert with information he had requested about return boats to Nice. Edsall and Wyman were totally surprised by this sudden change. Robert, quite agitated, said he could not go to Sardinia; he must return to Cambridge at once. They recall that as he relaxed over wine he gave a most improbable explanation: he had left a poisoned apple on the desk of Patrick (P. M. S.) Blackett, an experimental physicist at the Cavendish Laboratory, and must make sure Blackett was all right. To this day Edsall and Wyman are not sure about the poisoned apple story; at the time they assumed it was an hallucination on Robert's part. They did not think it necessary to change their own plans. As Fergusson and Edsall both note of this period, in most contexts Robert was functioning quite normally. So he went back to England alone.[14]

Edsall does not recall following up the apple episode when he returned to Cambridge in mid-April. Fifty years later he and Wyman both told the story as an instance of Robert's aberrant behavior that spring. Metaphoric interpretations, which would have been characteristic of Robert in normal moods, should not be excluded. Perhaps the apple symbolized a scientific paper containing a suddenly recognized error or merely an unfinished piece of research. In any event, in Cambridge Edsall found Robert working harder than ever on elaborate numerical calculations relating to quantum mechanical energy levels. At Robert's request, Edsall spent hours one Sunday checking these figures, although as a biochemist he understood little of what they meant. Meanwhile, at lunch in one of the colleges Robert casually introduced him to Blackett. Edsall believes that while Robert may have been a bit jealous of Blackett's skill as both experimenter and theoretician and of his easy social manner, he admired him tremendously.[15]

No one of Robert's friends seems to have been privy to all that happened during these difficult months. There is a general impression that someone in authority in the laboratory or at Christ's wrote to Robert's parents, and that a visit they made to Cambridge that spring, natural enough in view of their frequent trips to Europe, was largely to straighten out problems arising from Robert's depressed and erratic behavior. When Francis Fergusson saw them, he did not mention the strangling episode. Robert's mother was terribly worried. His father was worried but tried to say that everything would be all right. They insisted that Robert see a new psychiatrist, but the results were no more satisfactory than earlier treatment.[16]

In June Robert told John Edsall that he had dementia praecox and that his psychiatrist had dismissed him because in a case like this further analysis would do more harm than good. Fergusson has a different, though not necessarily conflicting, version of the termination of treatment. In the late spring or early summer of 1926, shortly before Fergusson returned to the United States from his three years at Oxford, he met Robert by prearrangement in London outside the office of a Harley Street psychiatrist. The occasion made a lasting impression on Fergusson: "I [saw him] standing on the corner, waiting for me, with his hat on one side of his head, looking absolutely weird. I joined him . . . and he walked with terrific speed; when he walked his feet turned out . . . and he sort of leaned forward, traveled at a terrific clip. I asked him how it had been. He said . . . that the guy was too stupid to follow him and that he knew more about his troubles than the [doctor] did, which was probably true."

Fergusson, who had seen Robert in some grim moods in the five years of their friendship and who was to be close to him during less private crises still far in the future, regarded this moment on a London street as highly significant. "There's no doubt about it," he said. "Robert had this ability to bring himself up, to figure out what his trouble was, and to deal with it."[17]

A FRAGMENT of correspondence which does not in any way reflect these trials opens the engaging series of sixteen surviving letters written by Robert to his brother Frank over the next ten years in which, with tact and tenderness and apparently with increasing affection, he proffered advice on personal and professional matters. Although the first section is missing and the letter does not bear a full date, the enthusiastic recommendation of Corsica suggests 1926, and the comment on congratulations, a possible reference to

Robert's twenty-second birthday in April. Frank was approaching his fourteenth birthday on August 14.

50 | TO FRANK OPPENHEIMER

[Cambridge, England,
ca. late spring 1926]

. . . but you can get a much more complete list from Dr. Kelly. Skillful staining will greatly increase the amount you can learn from microscopic work, and it is probably pretty good fun to learn. I remember that I once borrowed an oil immersion objective from school for a term. It about quadruples the resolution you can get with your present high power, and still gives a reasonable illumination. Perhaps that would interest you. If you want an oil immersion you can have it for your birthday, or for any equally plausible time you can think of from me. But you had better not be too optimistic about the profundity of what you are learning. I don't think that even expert cytologists have established any very obvious connections between the form of a cell and its ultimate function; and I'm quite sure that you haven't. And as for the chemical analyses, they wouldn't be any use to you at all. You might as well hope to find out about the nature of a cheese cake by finding how much carbon and nitrogen it contained. If you want some notion of the complexity of organic things, you might read a simple little book by L J Henderson called Fitness of the Environment.[a] But don't take it too seriously; for I'm told by biochemists that it's not all right.

Mr Klock told me that he was enjoying his work with you.

And still more advice: I don't think you would enjoy reading about relativity very much until you have studied a little geometry, a little mechanics, a little electrodynamics. But if you want to try, Eddington's book is the best to start on. I remember that five years ago you were dressed up to act like Albert Einstein; in a few years, it seems, they won't need to disguise you. And you'll be able to write your own speech. And now a final word of advice: try to understand really, to your own satisfaction, thoroughly and honestly, the few things in which you are most interested; because it is only when you have learnt to do that, when you realize how hard and how very satisfying it is, that you will appreciate fully the more spectacular things like relativity and mechanistic biology. If you think I'm wrong please don't hesitate to tell me so. I'm only talking from my own very small experience.

Some day you must come with me to Corsica. It's a great place, with every virtue from wine to glaciers, and from langouste to brigantines. Perhaps the summer between school and college.

Do you still see Dr Kenworthy?[b] What is she like? Does she understand your scientific adventures?

I hope Micky is better.[c] If he is, give him my greetings, please. And do write again, soon, much, and wild.

Thanks for your congratulations. I feel about as manly as a tadpole or a cauliflower.

Love

R

a. Lawrence J. Henderson was a Harvard physiologist known for his wide-ranging intellectual interests. His *The Fitness of the Environment* (New York, 1913) was "an inquiry into the biological significance of the properties of matter."

b. Dr. Marion E. Kenworthy was a psychoanalyst.

c. Micky was a medical student who tutored Frank one summer. The illness was a fatal case of blood poisoning.

DESPITE HIS FRUSTRATION with the experimental work in the laboratory, Oppenheimer began to develop his own taste in physics. He heard papers presented at the Cavendish colloquium, read avidly in contemporary journals, and went to meetings of the Kapitza Club, an informal physics discussion group founded by the young Russian physicist Peter Kapitza, a long-term visitor at the Cavendish Laboratory. From these sources Robert heard about the new quantum mechanics and, as he later recalled, "in a rudimentary way I began to get pretty interested. [Someone] who was extraordinarily . . . kind and helpful was Ray [Ralph] Fowler, who had that gift of helping young people."[18]

Another stimulus to Robert's interest in the new physics was the constant flow of visitors to the Cavendish. "Through Rutherford I met [Niels] Bohr and at that point I forgot about beryllium and films and decided to try to learn the trade of being a theoretical physicist. By that time I was fully aware that it was an unusual time, that great things were afoot . . . When Rutherford introduced me to Bohr he asked me what I was working on. I told him [it was the two-body problem] and he said, 'How is it going?' I said, 'I'm in difficulties.' He said, 'Are the difficulties mathematical or physical?' I said, 'I don't know.' He said, 'That's bad.' "[19]

Robert also met Paul (P. A. M.) Dirac, an important contributor to the development of quantum theory. Dirac's work, said Oppenheimer later, "was not easily understood [and he was] not concerned to be understood. I thought he was absolutely grand." By spring Robert and Dirac regarded each other as friends.[20]

Blackett introduced Robert to Paul Ehrenfest, professor of physics at the University of Leiden. "[He] came to Cambridge and we went out on the river and talked about collision problems, Coulomb's law . . . and so on."

Ehrenfest was "extraordinarily warm and friendly." Later in the spring Robert joined other American physicists for a week at the University of Leiden, where he met Ehrenfest's assistant, George Uhlenbeck, who recalls, "We got along very well immediately . . . [Robert] was a very warm person . . . and . . . was so involved in physics . . . [that it was] as if we were old friends because [we] had so many things in common." Robert's memory of Leiden was that "it was wonderful and I realized then that some of the troubles of the winter had been exacerbated by the English customs."[21]

Another visitor to the Cavendish that spring was Max Born, director of the Institute of Theoretical Physics at the University of Göttingen. Robert was interested in the problem of continuous spectra and accepted Born's invitation to continue his work in Göttingen.

To Oppenheimer looking back, this year represented his "coming into physics." "When I got to Cambridge, I was faced with the problem of looking at a question to which no one knew the answer but I wasn't willing to face it. When I left Cambridge I didn't know how to face it very well but I understood that this was my job; this was the change that occurred that year. I owe a great deal just to the existence of the place and the people who were there; specifically I owe a great deal to Fowler's sense and kindness. . . . [By the time I decided to go to Göttingen] I had very great misgivings about myself on all fronts, but I clearly was going to do theoretical physics if I could . . . It didn't seem to me like foreclosing anything; it just seemed to me like the next order of business. I felt completely relieved of the responsibility to go back into a laboratory. I hadn't been good, I hadn't done anybody any good, and I hadn't had any fun whatever; and here was something I felt just driven to try."[22]

The fulfillment of that passionate urge to contribute to the new physics that Edsall had so astutely observed in Oppenheimer helped him to resolve his personal and professional dilemmas. From that miserable year in Cambridge Oppenheimer emerged a theoretical physicist as well as his own best therapist.

By 1963 when Oppenheimer reminisced, the tentative nature of the move to Göttingen had seemingly been forgotten. At any rate, he did not burn his bridges when he notified the Board of Research Studies that he was leaving Cambridge.

Cambridge, [England]
August 18, 1926

Dear Sir:

I should like to apply to the Board of Research Studies for permission to spend two or three terms next year in Goettingen. My supervisor, Prof. Sir Joseph Thomson is not at present in Cambridge. But Prof. Sir Ernest Rutherford has kindly told me that he would be willing to assure you that my work here had been satisfactory, and that the work which I intended to do at Goettingen was an extension of that which I have started here. He also advised me to tell you that I would, at Goettingen, be under the supervision of Prof. Dr. Max Born, and that Prof. Born was particularly interested in the problems at which I hoped to work. It is now my intention to return to Cambridge immediately on the conclusion of my work in Goettingen.

Yours very sincerely,

J. R. Oppenheimer

THE YEAR 1926–27 spent at the University of Göttingen was as important to Oppenheimer's personal and professional growth as any comparable period in his young manhood. He shed the depression of the previous winter and obtained the Ph. D. and a postdoctoral fellowship for the year to follow. More important, his standing in the world of physics was transformed by day-to-day discussion with major participants in the development of new theoretical concepts and by his own contributions to this work.

Long after the details had faded he remembered the stimulation of the Göttingen experience: "In the sense which had not been true in Cambridge and certainly not at Harvard, I was part of a little community of people who had some common interests and tastes and many common interests in physics. I remember this more than I do lectures or seminars. I think it quite probable that I attended some of Born's lectures, but I don't remember. I'm sure I gave a seminar or two, but I don't remember. I met [Richard] Courant . . . I met [Werner] Heisenberg who came there and I had not met him before; [I also met Gregor] Wentzel, and [Wolfgang] Pauli in Hamburg or in Göttingen so that something which for me more than most people is important began to take place; namely I began to have some conversations. Gradually, I guess, they gave me some sense and perhaps more gradually, some taste in physics, something that I probably would not have ever gotten to . . . if I'd been locked up in a room."[23]

Göttingen was at the crossroads of continental physics and burgeoned with new ideas. Oppenheimer, along with other young American and European students and visitors, was challenged by the possibility that the new quantum theory would account for certain physical phenomena that had not been satisfactorily explained by the old quantum theory.

The older theory was a way of describing atomic motion which took into account experimental evidence that energy was absorbed and emitted by atoms in discrete units of electromagnetic radiation known as quanta. This mathematical description of discontinuities was enormously successful, but it was fraught with difficulties.

Between 1924 and 1926, a swift succession of brilliant papers by physicists at several European centers gave rise to a bold new reformulation of quantum theory. The new theory, known as quantum mechanics, opened a floodgate of solutions to difficult problems by accounting for the behavior of atoms and radiation under specific conditions as observed by experiment.

What did it mean to be a theorist during this exciting stage in the development of physics? Oppenheimer and others were searching for more precise and successful applications of the new theoretical framework, whose boundaries were not fully known. Many of the physicists who grappled with the implications and applications of quantum mechanics in the late 1920s and early 1930s were struggling to match their intuition to their mathematics so they could formulate concepts in a way that was internally consistent while describing the essential things scientists wanted to know about the physical world.

The process was a collaborative one, with scientists from many countries sharing their tentative ideas, insights, and calculations. As Oppenheimer later described the period, "It was a time of earnest correspondence and hurried conferences, of debate, criticism, and brilliant mathematical improvisation."[24]

Oppenheimer's own surviving correspondence with other physicists during this period provides only a sporadic view of his day-to-day efforts to make physics comprehensible. Individual letters describe fragments of his work and these are difficult to understand and place in perspective today, even by his students. Some of the ideas he soon abandoned because they were wrong or because they did not lead to greater understanding; others emerged as publications in the scientific journals. Even much of the work that survived to the publication stage is now obsolete. Like most of the scientific literature more than a decade old, it has been superceded by new experimental discoveries and new theoretical formulations. As Robert Serber, one of Oppenheimer's students and close collaborators, recently reflected, "Things that are obvious now were not for the people doing it then. It all falls out once you know the answer. The problems they struggled through do not appear today. But there are other problems now."[25]

When Oppenheimer discussed physics in his letters from 1926 on, he frequently did so in mathematical terms, whether expressed in words or equations. Mathematics was, and still is, the language of theoretical physics. In later years Oppenheimer was known as an outstanding, and sometimes poetic, interpreter of theoretical physics to nonscientific audiences. But he was aware of the limitations of ordinary language. In the Reith Lectures in 1953 he noted: "One could go much farther in describing this discipline, even without mathematics; but the words would before long become cumbersome and unfamiliar and almost a misinterpretation of what in mathematical terms can be said with beauty and simplicity."[26]

Two letters written in November described physics in Göttingen and Oppenheimer's reaction to it in the different languages appropriate to the recipients. The one to Francis Fergusson in New York was general and had the mildly cynical tone of their usual discourse. Notably absent, however, was that note of incompatibility with his surroundings which had often appeared in letters to Fergusson from Harvard, Bay Shore, or Cambridge.

52 | TO FRANCIS FERGUSSON

Göttingen
Nov 14. [1926]

Dear Francis,

Mother wrote that you had found a job with a producer; but she did not send any details. Will you write?

You would like Göttingen, I think. Like Cambridge, it is almost exclusively scientific, & such philosophers as are here are pretty largely interested in epistemological paradoxes & tricks. The science is much better than at Cambridge, & on the whole, probably the best to be found. They are working very hard here, & combining a fantastically impregnable metaphysical disingenuousness with the gogetting habits of a wall paper manufacturer. The result is that the work done here has an almost demoniac[?] lack of plausibility to it, & is highly successful. Everyone else seems to be concerned about trying to make Germany a practically successful & sane country. Neuroticism is very severely frowned upon. So are Jews, Prussians & French. We must return from Van Gogh to Jan Steen. They have an enormous respect for America, for Ford & Compton & the bogus realism of Sinclair Lewis.[a] There are about 20 American physicists & such here. Most of them are over thirty, Professors at Princeton or California or some such place, married, respectable. They are mostly pretty good at physics, but completely uneducated & unspoiled. They envy the Germans their intellectual adroitness & organization, & want physics to come to America.

I don't know whether I shall go back to Cambridge before going home again or not. I'll probably get a degree here in March. I find the work hard, thank God, & almost pleasant.

Of course there are lurid stories, but they are bad for our morals.

Have you read Claudel's 'Jeune Fille Violaine', Holderlin, Stefan Zweig's 'Untergang eines Herzens', Chekhov's 'Ivanov', Fitzgerald's two stories 'The Sensible Thing' & 'Winter Dreams', Paul de Lagarde? Did you like Hopkins?

Catherine Swann's address is 47 Barrow Street.

Will you write, please. Yours

Robert

a. Arthur Holly Compton, professor of physics at the University of Chicago, had created a stir in physics circles in 1922 with his experiments on the interaction of x-rays and electrons.

THE LETTER to Professor Kemble of Harvard a fortnight later shows how thoroughly involved Oppenheimer had become in two months time in specific problems then occupying the attention of scientists in Göttingen. This and subsequent letters to other physicists demonstrate growing famil- iarity with the mathematical language of quantum mechanics and the range of Oppenheimer's interest in it. They also provide vivid glimpses of the in- formal communication patterns of scientists as they gossiped and as they proposed solutions to the problems that concerned them.

53 | TO EDWIN C. KEMBLE

Göttingen
Physikalisches Institut
Nov 27. [1926]

Dear Dr Kemble,

Many thanks for your kind letter. As I shall not see Mr. Fowler for some time, I have taken the liberty of quoting a paragraph from your letter in a note I sent him.

This term I am spending at Göttingen. It is a very nice place, and I think that you will surely like it. Even now there are quite a few American physi- cists here, and some will be staying on until the Spring. I expect to be here until March, & then go back to Cambridge; and I hope that I shall have the opportunity of seeing you either here or there.

Almost all of the theorists seem to be working on q-mechanics. Professor

Born is publishing a paper on the Adiabatic Theorem, & Heisenberg on "Schwankungen [fluctuations]." Perhaps the most important idea is one of Pauli's, who suggests that the usual Schroedinger ψ-functions are only special cases, & only in special cases—the spectroscopic ones—give the physical information we want.[a] He considers the ψ-solutions when any set of canonical variables is chosen as independent. But of all this you probably know more than I do. People here are also very anxious to apply the q-mechanics to molecules; but so far the only attempt, Alexandrow's paper on the H_2^+ —ion, seems to be completely wrong.

I have been working for some time on the quantum theory of aperiodic phenomena. It is possible to get the intensity distribution in continuous spectra on the new theory—and without any special assumption. And in fact the theory gives, when applied to a simple Coulomb model, a very good approximation to the X-ray absorption law. For K electrons, for instance, the absorption *per* electron is of the form $\lambda^\alpha Z^3$, where α lies, except just near the limit, between 2.5 and 3.1.

Another problem on which Prof. Born and I are working is the law of deflection of, say, an α-particle by a nucleus. We have not made very much progress with this, but I think we shall soon have it. Certainly the theory will not be so simple, when it is done, as the old one based on corpuscular dynamics.

Please remember me to Professor Bridgman. And thank you again for your letter.

J R Oppenheimer

a. The ψ (psi), or wave, function is a term which appears in Schrödinger's mathematical formulation of quantum theory. Physicists of the period debated whether a corresponding entity really existed or whether psi was simply an abstraction from the probability that certain sorts of events would occur.

ALTHOUGH AT THE END of November Oppenheimer had not yet eliminated the possibility of returning to the Cavendish Laboratory, the collaboration with Born was so satisfying and productive that he soon decided to complete his doctorate in Göttingen. As indicated in the letter to Kemble, Oppenheimer was continuing work started in England on the application of quantum theory to transitions in the continuous spectrum, in which radiation occurs at all frequencies. This research was embodied in the dissertation [1927a] for which he received the Ph. D. degree from the University of Göttingen in the spring of 1927. Meanwhile, he also employed quantum mechanics to explain scattering, the changes that occur in the path and velocity of two or more atomic particles or systems when they collide. An important contribution to theoretical physics was a joint paper with Born [1927d] on the quantum theory of molecules. The "Born-Oppenheimer approximation" remains in use today.

Born's favorable view of Oppenheimer is recorded in a letter of February 1927 to S. W. Stratton, president of the Massachusetts Institute of Technology. "We have here a number of Americans, five of them working with me. One man is quite excellent, Mr. Oppenheimer, who studied at Harvard and in Cambridge—England. The other men did not surpass the average, but I hope, that not only Oppenheimer, but also some of the other fellows will get their doctor's degree during the next term."[27]

Oppenheimer looked back with mixed feelings upon aspects of the Göttingen experience other than physics: "Although this society was extremely rich and warm and helpful to me, it was parked there in a very miserable German mood . . . bitter, sullen, and, I would say, discontent and angry and with all those ingredients which were later to produce a major disaster. And this I felt very much."[28]

Resentment over Germany's plight in the years following World War I was apparent in the household in which Oppenheimer lived. German universities did not provide dormitories. Students and visiting scholars lived in the town, usually with families occupying a full floor of a three-story apartment house. Oppenheimer's landlord was Dr. Cario, a Göttingen physician, and the house was a single-family one. His son, Günther, an experimental physicist, was an assistant in the university's Institute of Experimental Physics headed by James Franck. The Carios, Oppenheimer recalled, "had been very well off and the inflation had ruined them and they had the typical bitterness on which the Nazi movement rested. This is not for a moment to say that they were Nazi; I have no knowledge of that. But they had a very large house not far from the center of Göttingen, an enormous house and a garden . . . surrounded by a wall, and no money; so they took in . . . visitors . . . This was only a few minutes walk from the Institute and it was very near the wall around which Dirac and I used to walk."[29]

Paul Dirac also lived at the Carios' from February to June 1927. Daily association plus occasional long Sunday walks together cemented their friendship begun in Cambridge the previous year.[30]

When Karl T. Compton, professor of physics at Princeton, his wife Margaret, and their small daughter Jean stayed at the Carios' for two months before Christmas, Robert was the only lodger. Mrs. Compton's recollections round out his own. Frau Cario, the proverbial keys jingling at her waist, ran the house. The dinner conversation, directed by Dr. Cario, was usually about science. Karl Compton was single-minded in his pursuit of physics and found Robert's versatility slightly intimidating. Mrs. Compton could not join the talk about science, but Robert's gentleness, courtesy, and humor kept her from feeling excluded. When he saw two-year old Jean pretending to read a small red volume and found that its subject was birth control, he looked at her pregnant mother and commented: "A little late." He was so enthusiastic about Corsica that the Comptons went there for the Christmas holidays.[31]

The physicists by whom Robert was most influenced did not display the bitterness that he noted elsewhere. James Franck, he reflected, "was not a man to have any resentment and at that time I think he had no foreknowledge of what was to come. I think he took a very sunny view . . . Born of course was never a sunny man, but I think he was driven by an ambition to do good physics and was very self-confident in this year when I was there; I think perhaps he put off some of the Americans by how sure he was that his way was the right way."[32]

By February Oppenheimer was sufficiently at home with quantum mechanics to advise Bridgman on its application.

54 | TO PERCY W. BRIDGMAN

> Institut für Theoretische Physik
> Göttingen
> February 12 [1927]

Dear Professor Bridgman,

You may remember that when I was at Harvard two years ago I was very much interested in your theory of metallic conduction. Recently, in the course of some work in quantum mechanics, an idea has turned up which seems to offer a certain support to your theory. I think it will be some time before a complete quantum theory of conduction is possible, but perhaps I may tell you briefly of this one point.

On the classical quantum theory, an electron in one of two regions of low potential which were separated by a region of high potential, could not cross to the other without receiving enough energy to clear the "impediment." On the new theory that is no longer true: the electron will spend part of its time in one region, & part in the other. If the impediment is not very high, the electron will jump back and forth between the two regions quite often; if the impediment is higher, it will do so more seldom; but if one waits long enough, one can be sure of finding it, at some time, in each of the two regions.

Mathematically the simplest problem of this kind is that of a hydrogen atom in an homogeneous electric field. If one solves this problem—not by the Epstein-Schrödinger-Wentzel perturbation method, but completely— he finds that the field, no matter how weak it be, & provided only that it extend indefinitely, will in the course of time ionize the atom. One can compute how long this ionization is likely to take. For large fields it occurs more rapidly, but it will occur eventually even for small ones.

From the former of these considerations it follows that a valence electron in a metal is not to be thought of as associated with any one ion; it wanders about from atom to atom, never spending much time in the interstices, where the potential is high. In this sense the electron is free. Further, if one puts on an electric field, the electrons will tend to be in the part of the metal where the potential is lower; eventually they will be sure to get there; & the rate at which they wander is great when the potential between two ions is not too high, & falls when this rises. Is this not just your "gap" theory?

On one point the new mechanics suggests a change, however: the electrons, which are "free" in the sense defined above, are not "free" in the sense that they are carriers of equipartition thermal energy. In order to account for the Wiedemann-Franz law one might have to adopt the suggestion, due, I think, to Professor Bohr, that when an electron jumps from one atom to another the two atoms may exchange momentum.

With best greetings,

Yours

J R Oppenheimer

Just as Robert's letter to Bridgman displayed a new assurance, so Bridgman's reply of April 3 indicated that the doubts expressed earlier to Rutherford about an erratically brilliant pupil had been resolved. Robert's communication had prompted fruitful discussions with Bridgman's colleagues and might indeed prove relevant to his own research. After enquiring about future plans, Bridgman added: "From what I hear I judge that you may have your doctor's degree already. I saw Fowler in Oxford last August, and he gave the most glowing account of the work you had been doing with him. Had you thought of applying for a National Research Fellowship for next year in case you are getting your degree? If this appeals to you at all I am sure that we would all be very glad indeed to have you at Harvard again, and together with Kemble and [John] Slater you ought to make a team that would get some significant theoretical work done."[33]

By the time Bridgman's invitation reached Göttingen, Oppenheimer had already indicated his intention to spend the coming year in Pasadena. Years later he recalled that in the spring of 1927 he had received a letter asking if he would like one of the postdoctoral fellowships funded by the Rockefeller Foundation and awarded by the National Research Council to promising young chemists and physicists.[34] By the time he returned to the United States, Oppenheimer had decided to spend the fall term at Harvard before proceeding to Pasadena.

AMONG OPPENHEIMER'S on-going conversations about physics begun during the Cambridge–Göttingen period was a dialogue with George Uhlenbeck that was to continue for many years. The two had become good friends since their meeting in Leiden, and they easily shared ideas as they struggled through the intricacies of the new theory.

55 | TO GEORGE UHLENBECK

Göttingen
March 12. [1927]

Dear Uhlenbeck,

Many thanks for your good letter. It was a very great pleasure for me to meet Dr. Wiersma;[a] and everyone here, I think, was delighted by his visit.

I should be very much interested to hear more of your work on statistics & quantum mechanics, & I hope that you will write to me of it. My own feeling is that, whereas it is often correct to regard ψ as a probability amplitude, this interpretation is not the most fundamental one. It seems to me that the problem has entered a new stage now, & essentially because of Dirac's last paper. As you know, one can obtain all the previous "probability theory" from this, if one makes the single assumption that, for every dynamical system, & for *some* set of variables, the probability of all values of the momenta (& the time) is equal, if the values of the coördinates (& the Energy) are given. It seems to me that this assumption is (at least in the non-relativistic case) certainly justified, if one chooses the action variables as coordinates, observes that the angle variables increase uniformly with the time, & remarks, finally, that by "equally probable" one means "corresponding to equal intervals of time." Of course the relativistic problem is still unsolved, & so is the choice of "range" for a dynamical variable. But I feel that these difficulties are not critical, & I should very much like to know whether you share this opinion.

Recently I have been working a little on the Q.M. [quantum mechanics] of such effects as the polarization & depolarization of mercury resonance lines & impact radiation. As you surely know, all these things can be treated very simply & unambiguously on the quantum theory; but the results explain the observed facts so well that I have written a little paper [1927b] about it. Of course I will send you some when they come out.

Dr Wiersma told me that you were going to Ann Arbor next year, & I am very glad. I shall be going to America (Pasadena) next July, & if you think of going at the same time, & have no better plans, perhaps we might arrange to go together.

Please give my best greetings to Prof. Ehrenfest. I hope to see him again before I leave for America.

Yours

J R Oppenheimer

a. E. C. Wiersma was an experimental physicist working at the University of Leiden.

When Edwin Kemble visited Göttingen in June he was able to report to his colleague Theodore Lyman that Harvard's odd duckling was looking more and more like a swan. "Oppenheimer is turning out to be even more brilliant than we thought when we had him at Harvard. He is turning out new work very rapidly and is able to hold his own with any of the galaxy of young mathematical physicists here. Unfortunately Born tells me that he has the same difficulty about expressing himself clearly in writing which we observed at Harvard."[35]

AT THE END of June Oppenheimer and Dirac went to Leiden, where they had been invited to visit Ehrenfest's institute. Oppenheimer sailed for the United States from Liverpool in mid-July.[36] Uhlenbeck did not accept Oppenheimer's suggestion that they travel together, for in August he married Else Ophorst. In September they arrived in New York on the *S. S. Baltic,* accompanied by the physicists Charlotte Riefenstahl and Samuel Goudsmit, Uhlenbeck's collaborator in the recent important discovery of electron spin. Uhlenbeck and Goudsmit were on their way to join the faculty of the University of Michigan. Oppenheimer was at the dock, with his father's car and uniformed chauffeur, to welcome them. He took the Uhlenbecks to their hotel—the Brevoort on lower Fifth Avenue, because he thought they would like its European atmosphere—and to dinner at a hotel in Brooklyn from which they could see the lighted Manhattan skyline. Robert persuaded the Uhlenbecks to delay their departure for Ann Arbor in order to meet his parents at tea the next day. Having encountered one novelty in the form of New York stoplights, Else Uhlenbeck had another surprise when they reached the Oppenheimer's Riverside Drive apartment. "What a very large house," she thought as they went up in the elevator, for tall apartment houses were unknown in Holland. Because her English was still poor, her impressions of this first, but by no means last, experience of Oppenheimer hospitality were largely visual—the beautifully furnished living room, the Van Gogh and other paintings, Mrs. Oppenheimer's quiet graciousness, and Frank, just turned fifteen, standing shy and a bit awkward at the door.[37]

The Bay Shore house had been sold the previous winter, but the *Trimethy* was still moored there, and before Robert left for Harvard he and Frank had a last sail along the shore of Long Island. They then joined their parents on Nantucket. "My brother and I spent most of the days," recalled Frank, "painting with oils on canvas the dunes and grassy hills."[38]

From Harvard, where Oppenheimer worked until Christmas, he wrote to congratulate Dirac on becoming a Fellow of St. John's College, Cambridge, and to give his own version of the extraordinary productivity about which Professor Kemble had reported the previous June. Oppenheimer referred to a wide range of issues of interest to him and further demonstrated that at the age of twenty-three he had mastered the highly developed language of the new quantum mechanics.

56 | TO PAUL DIRAC

Jefferson Physical Laboratory
Cambridge, Mass.
Nov. 28. [1927]

Dear Dirac,

I have just heard that you received the fellowship. My very best felicitations.

There has been no direct news of what you have been doing for a long time. Did you keep your promise to stop quantum mechanics over the summer? I should very much appreciate it if you would let me know what you have got.

Here there is very little to report. Slater is working still at the wave functions for Helium. I have done quite a lot of little things, but nothing at all important. Last summer I sent in a paper [1928a], which is to appear in the Jan. Phys. Rev., in which I gave, I think, a simple and general treatment of continuous spectra, and showed how stationary solutions of the wave equation may be interpreted in aperiodic phenomena. Also I gave a condition for the validity of classical formulae in an aperiodic case, and applied it to show that for the two body problem the classical formulae hold both when the initial relative velocity is very large and when it is very small. I also worked out the theory of transitions between almost orthogonal states, giving the necessary second order correction. When this is applied to the ionization of atoms in a field it gives a period of ionization for H in a field of 1 V/cm equal to $10^{10^{10}}$ sec. Also I sent Ehrenfest a paper on the Ramsauer effect.[a] I don't know where this will appear. It is easy to show that, as the electron collides with the atom, the atom jumps up and down between its stationary states. Further one can show that there is a Rams[auer]. Eff[ect] for all atoms and

108

molecules for electron velocity low enough; if the molecule has no dipole moment in its normal state one gets the Rayleigh v^4 law for the intensity, and the electrons are uniformly scattered over all angles. Then I did a very short paper [1927e], in which the diffraction of the electron beam, and the resonance of the colliding electron with those in the atom, are taken more completely into account to explain Skinner's results on the polarization of impact radiation.[b] Just now I have worked out the capture of electrons by α-particles. One gets formulae for the probability very much like Fowler's, but which give a free path for capture proportional to v^6, and appear to agree well with the experiments. I have been trying for a long time to reduce the choice between Pauli and Einstein statistics to a difference in the experiments one can make on quanta and on $\left\{ \begin{array}{c} \text{electrons} \\ \text{protons} \end{array} \right\}$. That doesn't work. Nor does the fact that neutral systems are Einsteinian, and charged ones Paulian, follow from any simple experimental conditions. Do you understand how one must derive this result?

Please remember me to Sugiura.[c] I hope to see him at Pasadena when he passes through; and I shall be out there after the New Year. And give my greetings to Mr. Fowler, when you see him, and to anyone else at the laboratory who remembers me.

I hope that you will write. With best wishes

J R Oppenheimer

a. The manuscript sent to Ehrenfest contained some errors in interpretation and calculation. On Ehrenfest's advice, Oppenheimer revised it and submitted it for publication a few months later [1928c].

b. H. W. B. Skinner's paper on polarized light was published in October 1926 when he was doing postdoctoral research at the Cavendish.

c. Yoshikazu Sugiura, a Japanese physicist, was at the University of Copenhagen from 1926 to 1928.

Except for the slightly condescending "here there is very little to report," Oppenheimer does not comment on how he felt about his return to Harvard with a Göttingen Ph. D. and firsthand knowledge of the latest developments in European physics. The reaction of his former teachers was demonstrated by the job offer they made him the following spring. To someone meeting Oppenheimer for the first time, eccentricity still predominated. One of Princeton's bright graduate students in physics, Philip M. Morse, gave a colloquium on molecular vibrations at Harvard that fall. Years later Morse recalled meeting "a thin high-strung postdoctoral fellow by the name of Oppenheimer, who gave me a bad case of inferiority by talking mysteriously about Dirac electrons and quaternions. I didn't know what he was talking about and his talk didn't enlighten me. Oppie always affected me that way; I never could figure out whether his sibylline declarations were just a form of one-upmanship or whether he really did see a lot more in a theory than I did. Some of both, I finally decided."[39]

While producing a steady stream of technical papers, Oppenheimer found time to see John Edsall, who had returned to Harvard Medical School for a final year before receiving the M. D. degree, and William Boyd, working for the Ph.D. in biochemistry at Boston University Medical School. Boyd and Oppenheimer reestablished something of their former intimacy. As before, Boyd found Robert good company—sensitive, generous, and superbly intelligent. Robert spoke freely about the miseries of his year in Cambridge. As they talked Boyd was confirmed in the feeling he had had from the beginning of their friendship that along with serious problems of temperament Robert possessed the ability to deal with them.[40]

Oppenheimer also renewed the interest in poetry which he shared with Boyd, at least to the extent of submitting a short poem, "Crossing," to the avant-garde literary magazine *Hound and Horn,* which began publication in September 1927. This nostalgic piece, which appeared the following June, was Oppenheimer's only contribution to *Hound and Horn* in the seven years of its existence.

CROSSING

It was evening when we came to the river
with a low moon over the desert
that we had lost in the mountains, forgotten,
what with the cold and the sweating
and the ranges barring the sky.
And when we found it again,
in the dry hills down by the river,
half withered, we had
the hot winds against us.

There were two palms by the landing;
the yuccas were flowering; there was
a light on the far shore, and tamarisks.
We waited a long time, in silence.
Then we heard the oars creaking
and afterwards, I remember,
the boatman called to us.
We did not look back at the mountains.

J. R. Oppenheimer[41]

AFTER THE CHRISTMAS HOLIDAYS Oppenheimer moved to the California Institute of Technology. Robert A. Millikan, a commanding figure in American physics, had been president of Caltech since its founding in 1921. Oppenheimer observed the rich experimental work in progress there while keeping abreast of new developments in quantum theory and continuing his own explorations in that field. The research at Caltech and the opportunity to meet visiting physicists from the United States and Europe impressed Oppenheimer and influenced the outcome when he had to decide among several job offers that spring.

When Oppenheimer wrote Professor Kemble in February, he was seemingly acting as talent scout for the Harvard physics department. He also wrote about Dirac's latest contribution, which provided a powerful generalization of Schrödinger's equation and incorporated relativity.

57 | TO EDWIN C. KEMBLE

Pasadena
Feb 16. [1928]

Dear Dr Kemble,

Thank you very much for your good letter. You might have upbraided me, and with justice, for the Ramsauer fiasco. I worried a long time about the theory, and have now, I think, found the correct answer. The full paper is not done yet, as it is very heavy algebraically; but I am sending you a short note which Epstein sent in to the PNAS [1928c], and which indicates the essentials of the work.[a] It is not diffraction, but resonance, that does it.

I have asked a few people here about Houston. Everyone has thought a great deal of him, and recommended him personally and physically; he seems to be very much the man you want. You may have a little trouble getting him, as they are very fond of him here. Badger, who is going abroad this Spring, is a brilliant experimentalist, and an excellent man. He has been working recently in the extreme infra red, on the rotation spectrum of ammonia. Perhaps, too, you would be interested in Goetz, from Goettingen; but not, of course, for bands. He has been doing difficult and wonderful things with thermionics and photoelectrics, and would, I am certain, be a joy for Dr Bridgman.[b]

Langevin, who was expected this term, has not turned up; and Franck will be here, to everyone's relief, next week. Russell is here now and Laporte came through.[c] Dirac wrote to me that he had "explained" the spin . . . Pauling is starting a 'systematik' of non polar bonds.[d] Epstein has offered to do some of the refinements of the theory of continuous absorption spectra. Very fortunately Millikan and his people have just verified the

111

theoretical equation for the autoelectronic emission; and I am writing up a short account [1928e] of the quantitative agreement, which is not bad. There are a great many people here interested in thermionics and crystals and metallic conduction; we have talked a good deal, but I have no results that are specific enough to interest Bridgman. I hope that he has not grown weary of my infinite procrastination.

I was glad to hear that the rotational distortion comes out so nicely. Did Van Vleck use your model?[e] I should also be greatly interested, if you should have time to write, to hear of the progress in the work with the two atoms in resonance. Perhaps that will be connected with Pauling's 'systematik'.

The NRC [National Research Council] has written to tell me that, if I want the fellowship for next year, I must ask my professor to write them a note. I am sorry to keep bothering you with these things; and I hope that it will be no great trouble.

Please give my respects to Mrs Kemble, and to the Slaters, and to Dr Bridgman. I miss Harvard very much, and even the admirable Pasadena climate is not altogether an adequate compensation.

With best wishes

J R Oppenheimer

a. Paul Epstein was professor of mathematical physics at Caltech.

b. William V. Houston was assistant professor of physics at Caltech. Richard M. Badger, a physical chemist, and Alexander Goetz, an experimental physicist, were fellows at Caltech; both joined the Caltech faculty in 1929.

c. Paul Langevin was professor of physics at the Sorbonne. Henry Norris Russell was research professor of astronomy and director of the observatory at Princeton. Otto Laporte, a German theoretical physicist, was assistant professor at the University of Michigan.

d. Linus Pauling was assistant professor of theoretical chemistry at Caltech. That spring Robert gave him the mineral collection which had been the center of his own boyhood interest in science. He later recalled that Pauling "was then still stuck with crystals—inorganic crystals—so that he not only used them but he was very pleased [with] these enormous calcites," interview with JRO, November 18, 1963, p. 1.

e. John H. Van Vleck was professor of theoretical physics at the University of Minnesota.

THE SECOND LETTER among those preserved by Robert's brother, Frank, was written from Pasadena in the spring of 1928 shortly before their parents' wedding anniversary on March 23. As with the first letter to Frank, the opening section is missing, but the topic under discussion is obvious.

[Pasadena
March 1928]

. . . profession to make you waste your time with her; it is your profession
to keep clear. But the whole thing is only important for people who have
time to waste. For you, and for me, it isn't. And for the last rule: Don't
worry about girls, and don't make love to girls, unless you have to: DON'T
DO IT AS A DUTY. Try to find out, by watching yourself, what you
really want; if you approve of it, try to get it; if you disapprove of it, try to
get over it.—This has all been very dogmatic, and I hope you will forget
most of it; but some of it may possibly be of use to you, as the fruit and
outcome of my erotic labours. You are very young, but much more mature
than I was.

Mother and Father have been well and happy, and lazy beyond description; I think it has set them both up. They are going north to San Francisco
tomorrow, and we will meet near the Mexican border to celebrate their anniversary. Your Jensen thing is lovely. They ought to be delighted.

I have had trouble getting time to work, for Pasadena is a pleasant place,
and hundreds of pleasant people are continually suggesting pleasant things
to do. I am trying to decide whether to take a professorship at the University of California next year, or go abroad.

Will you write me your plans for the summer? If you are out here we
might knock around for a fortnight on the desert. And I hope you will write
soon.

> your
>
> r

Some of the pleasant people whom Oppenheimer found so distracting
included colleagues at Caltech. Others were congenial young people who
gravitated to lively hostesses like Maggie Lang, wife of a Caltech economist,
and Undine Bradley, whose daughter Natalie Raymond would become one
of Oppenheimer's close friends. At one of Mrs. Bradley's Saturday afternoon "at homes" he met Helen Campbell, a Vassar friend of his Ethical
Culture School classmate Inez Pollak. Helen was engaged to Berkeley physics instructor Samuel K. Allison, whom she would marry at the end of May;
that spring in Pasadena Oppenheimer took her out to dinner and read Baudelaire aloud. On canyon walks they discussed psychoanalysis and New
Mexico, where Helen had recently explored abandoned pueblos. In the fall
of 1929 their paths would cross again in Berkeley, where Samuel Allison
remained for another year before joining the physics faculty at Chicago.[42]

IN THE SPRING of 1928, as Oppenheimer later explained, "I . . . had many invitations to university positions, one or two in Europe, and perhaps ten in the United States." One of the offers came from Harvard. In a letter of April 10, Professor Theodore Lyman, director of the department of physics, offered him a position as instructor and tutor at a salary of $3,000 with responsibility for lectures and individual instruction not to exceed the equivalent of two courses. "Though we are not now in a position to make a definite promise for the future," wrote Lyman, "yet I hope and believe that after the first year you would receive the rank of Assistant Professor and a permanent place in the Department." Lyman was aware that other institutions might offer higher rank and a better starting salary but in the long run the advantages and opportunities of a Harvard appointment might be equal to any.[43]

Oppenheimer did not reply immediately to this first, though by no means last, gratifying offer from his alma mater, for he was weighing the advantages of two other tempting proposals: "I visited Berkeley and I thought I'd like to go to Berkeley because it was a desert. There was no theoretical physics and I thought it would be nice to try to start something. I also thought it would be dangerous because I'd be too far out of touch so I kept the connection with Caltech . . . I liked it enough to want to come back and enough to feel that it was a place where I would be checked if I got too far off base and where I would learn of things that might not be adequately reflected in the published literature."[44] While concluding arrangements for the double appointments at the University of California and at Caltech, he asked Lyman for time to consider Harvard's offer and in the end refused it.

59 | TO THEODORE LYMAN

Pasadena
April 21, 1928.

Dear Professor Lyman,

Thank you for your letter. I appreciate very much your invitation to come to Harvard for next year; and I should like to be able to accept. I had, however, planned to spend next year in Europe, and I am not quite certain that I should abandon this plan. Perhaps you will give me another week to make my decision.

I hope that this delay will not be inconvenient to you.

Yours faithfully,

J R Oppenheimer

Pasadena
May 7. [1928]

Dear Professor Lyman,

You will perhaps have learnt from my telegram that I am unable to accept
the instructorship for next year. I am sorry that I shall not be able to come;
and I trust that the delay in my decision has not interfered in any way with
your plans.

This delay was largely induced by my desire to accept your offer; I should
very much have liked to come. But I had previously refused positions for
next year both here and at Berkeley, on the ground that I wanted to go to
Europe; and I had promised that, if I should be granted a fellowship abroad,
and if the two Universities should agree to it, that for the following year I
would divide my time between them. The fellowship was granted, and the
people here seemed satisfied with the plan; and I was thus not at liberty to
accept your offer.

I hope that it will be possible for me to visit Harvard occasionally. I appreciate very much the kindness you have shewn me in the past.

Yours faithfully,

J R Oppenheimer

There remained the more difficult task of acknowledging Bridgman's
part in the Harvard offer.

61 | TO PERCY W. BRIDGMAN

Pasadena
May 16. [1928]

Dear Professor Bridgman,

Thank you for your good letter, and for the off prints. I have waited an
unconscionable time with answering; I hope that you will excuse me. For it
was hard to make the decision and harder still to write to you of it. I should
have liked above all to come to Harvard; and it would have been to me
some consolation for the fact that I should never be a physicist like you, that
I could work a little in the same department. I could not come because I had
made arrangements for the next years which proved to be irreversible. Next

year I am to go to Europe, and the year after to divide the time between Berkeley and here.

Your opinion of Sommerfeld's theory I more or less share . . .[a]

Perhaps it will be possible for me to visit Harvard again, either on my way to Europe, or after I have returned. And if I may, I should like to write to you when I have the metal theory in a less foetal state.

Thank you again for your kindness in writing to me.

Yours faithfully

J R Oppenheimer

a. Arnold Sommerfeld, a leading theoretical physicist, held a professorship at the University of Munich.

ONE OF THE ADVANTAGES of the Berkeley–Caltech arrangement was that it could be postponed until the 1929–30 academic year, giving Oppenheimer another postdoctoral year and further contacts with European centers of theoretical physics. Although his father could no doubt have financed an additional year of travel and research, in 1928 there was not the competition for fellowship support that shortly developed under the combined impact of the Depression and growing interest in the physical sciences. Oppenheimer therefore requested and received a renewal of his fellowship, but because it would be used in Europe, he now became responsible to the International Education Board in New York City, whose postdoctoral fellowships, like those of the National Research Council, were funded by the Rockefeller Foundation. However, the NRC screened physics applicants for the IEB.

Oppenheimer spent the first part of the summer of 1928 in Ann Arbor, where he participated in the annual summer school for theoretical physics, established in 1927 by Harrison Randall, chairman of the physics department at the University of Michigan. The summer sessions were held throughout the 1930s, and physicists from all parts of the United States and from Europe enthusiastically attended them as lecturers or participants. From Ann Arbor Oppenheimer notified the IEB of a change in his plans.

Ann Arbor
Aug 2. [1928]

Gentlemen,

On the recommendation of the National Research Fellowship Board in Physics you have granted my application for a fellowship in Physics for study in Europe in 1928–29. I had planned to sail early in September, and to go at once to Leiden. But it now seems possible that I shall have to abandon this plan, and postpone taking my fellowship until later in the year. The reason for this is that I have tuberculosis, and that several doctors have told me that it would not be very wise to go abroad until I am better. May I therefore ask you to allow me to postpone taking the fellowship, and to communicate with you as soon as I can set a definite date for sailing. I have had assurance from Professor Ehrenfest that he will be glad to have me with him, and shall accordingly retain my original plan of going first to Leiden.
   Yours faithfully,

J R Oppenheimer

This word was passed on to the National Research Council in Washington, which informed Oppenheimer in a letter of August 16 that his fellowship had been withdrawn but that he might reapply when his health permitted. Meantime, puzzled staff members at the NRC and the International Education Board corresponded in an attempt to discover why his formal acceptance of the fellowship, dated June 2, had been mailed without comment from Colorado Springs on August 12.[45]

After two weeks in the mountains Oppenheimer was feeling much better—his brother Frank is not sure that the diagnosis of tuberculosis was ever confirmed—and, oblivious to the administrative turmoil he had created, he addressed the following letter to the NRC's Fellowship Board in Physics.

[Cowles, New Mexico?]
August 25, 1928

Gentlemen:

Thank you for your letter of August 16. It now seems certain that I shall be able to take the fellowship of the International Education Board, and highly probable that I shall be able to sail before the middle of September, as originally planned. I therefore very much hope that the withdrawal of the fellowship will not prove permanent; and that it will involve no serious delay in my sailing. I plan to call at the office of the Board in New York as soon as I can get East, but I should appreciate it if you would advise me whether I shall have difficulty with the fellowship, if I can obtain the proper medical certificate.

Professor Epstein left Pasadena this summer, and I accepted Professor Randall's invitation to the summer school in theoretical physics at Ann Arbor. I remained there working until the second week in August, when it became necessary for me to leave. I expect to return to work as soon as I am permitted to do so.

Yours faithfully

J. R. Oppenheimer

Fortunately Oppenheimer did not have to wait for the fellowship check before buying his steamship ticket, for it was not until October 10 that the NRC's fellowship board voted to recommend Dr. J. Robert Oppenheimer to the International Education Board "for financial support to enable him to pursue his studies on 'Problems in Quantum Mechanics' with Professor R. H. Fowler at the University of Cambridge, England, and either at the University of Copenhagen, Copenhagen, Denmark, with Professor Niels Bohr, or at the University of Leiden, Leiden, Holland, with Professor D. [sic] Ehrenfest; such an appointment to be for the period of nine months, only, beginning on or about November 1, 1928."[46]

BETWEEN AUGUST 2, when Oppenheimer wrote the International Education Board from Ann Arbor, and his departure for Europe, he went to Colorado, New Mexico, and California. Frank Oppenheimer went to a camp in Colorado the summer of 1928 and then joined Robert in the Pecos Valley in New Mexico. Together they picked out land with a cabin on it, a mile or so from Katherine Page's guest ranch at Cowles, on which their father obtained a lease the following winter. From the Pecos Robert and Frank went to Colorado Springs, where they joined their parents at the Broadmoor Hotel and took driving lessons. Then they set out for Pasadena. Somewhere along the way, with Frank at the wheel, their car turned over, and Robert's arm was broken.[47]

In addition to Frank's theme mentioned in the following letter, Herbert Smith recalls another in which Frank said he was going to be a scientist. He knew it was a hard career. It was like climbing a mountain in a tunnel: you wouldn't know whether you were going to come out above the valley or whether you were ever going to come out at all.[48]

The 1928 visit to the Pecos was the first of the holidays there with Frank which were to mean so much to Robert in the next few years. The great closeness that was developing with his sixteen-year-old brother is reflected in a letter written from Utrecht just after Christmas.

64 | TO FRANK OPPENHEIMER

Utrecht
Dec 30 [1928]

Dear Frank,

Thanks for your good letters and the theme. By now I trust that you understand the five-four plus one—it was merely an indication that the reproductions were to come in two consignments; and only your surprisingly hypersensitive conscience could have transmuted it into a reproach for not writing. I am hardly in a position to blame anyone for that, for I owe innumerable letters. And I think that it is one's business to make others want to write, and not their obligation to do so against all inclination.

The difficulty of getting down to work after a summer of such miscellaneous debauch I fully appreciate, and share. I am glad that you are over the worst of it; I can see by your letter that you are. I cannot say as much for myself. And I would give a great deal, now, to have kept to my original plans, and never to have gone to the Springs.

Your theme I am returning, as you suggested. With much of what you say I agree—and especially with the thesis that "I like it" is not an artistic judgment. I think that you show a lamentable ignorance of history in the matter, but that is almost irrelevant: For in insisting upon the universality and objectivity of artistic standards you have found a very important, if extremely difficult, point;—one in which I deeply agree, and yet where I should be unable to elucidate. For the difficulty lies in this, that appreciation of art is in fact neither universal nor objective, that it depends on education, experience, taste; that, in its critical aspects, it is defined only by the " I like

119

its" of the sensitive and the initiated. A painter is rather an inarticulate person; more even than the poet, he knows what to do, but knows nothing of the reason; one has little warrant that the ex post facto interpretation of the critic is either relevant or true. Thus many generations admired the Joconde for her "inscrutable smile", which was presumed to express the subtleties of the woman qua mother; in recent times one will hear that the line of the mouth is used for purposes of design purely, that it has no "literary" significance, but only a plastic one. Leonardo is not to be questioned; but I doubt whether, even if he were, his answer would help much. To assert, therefore, that the excellence, the beauty, is in the picture, is not relative to the observer, is false to observation, because there is no such impersonal, absolute view of the picture in fact, least of all, perhaps, that of the artist. And yet I believe that you are completely right; and my own view is that the value of a picture is best defined as relative, not to the person, but to what one may vaguely call the civilization: the public, traditional culture and experience of the civilization for which it was painted.

I think that your suggestion that a painting expresses something, or the statement that what one gets from a picture could be gotten from reading — that these are misleading and in the strict sense false. They suggest that a picture communicates a truth, a statement, a knowledge; that it is expository in purpose. I do not believe this. What should the Mt St Victoire or the Gezicht op Delft express? It is true that in many pictures the ideational, literary element is important; that is so for Rembrandt and sometimes Van Gogh and Greco, and preponderantly so for Daumier. But it appears to be an accessory phenomenon, and not essential. And I should think that a better word than express would be create, or discover, or show: A picture — and this is true also of a poem, does not express something beside itself, more abstract than itself; it expresses itself, it IS the thing, the something, that it shows. It is not the exemplification of a truth, nor a commentary on the world; it is something new in the world, which was not there before, and which, for some reason — that it is for the critic to discover — is important. It is something deliberately put into the world by the artist. It has no "educational" value, except as art; it does not teach us anything, except to look at pictures, or, perhaps, to make them. It is neither so important nor so "intellectual" as you pretend, and it is purer.

I can't say more now, or I shall bore you. But borrow from Hirschland's, and read seriously, R Fry's "Transformations";[a] and don't be deceived by his dogmatic manner; he has often changed his mind himself. Your theme reveals your ignorance of Italian and Dutch painters. You might try to see and study them. The customary appreciations are confused, and to my mind often wrong; you will have to decide for yourself.

Please write again. I haven't answered everything you wrote, nor given you any brotherly advice. That is because it seems to me that you are on the right track, and because I think you know pretty well what I should say: discipline, work, honesty, and, toward other people, a solicitude for their welfare and as complete an indifference as possible to their good opinion. —I wrote M and F that I thought it quite wise for you to be left more or less alone when they come across.

Salut

[no signature]

a. Franz and Beulah Hirschland lived in the same Riverside Drive apartment house as the Oppenheimers. The American edition of Roger Fry's *Transformations: Critical and Speculative Essays on Art* was published in 1927.

OPPENHEIMER SPENT his second postdoctoral year at three European centers of physics, though not the three approved in October by the International Education Board. As he later explained: "Ehrenfest wanted me to come to Leiden. He was sort of short of people and I was a Fellow but I was also to act in part as his assistant . . . I gave a seminar or two in Dutch; I don't think it was very good Dutch but it was [appreciated]. I didn't do any instruction . . . I was a very great admirer of [Ehrenfest]. I thought of him, and I think not wholly inappropriately, in semi-Socratic terms, and I thought I would learn something from him and indeed certainly did . . . [but] I don't think that I [fully] appreciated [Ehrenfest's grasp of the new physics] until somewhat later. I think that his interest in simplicity and clarity was really a very great thing but I probably still had a fascination with formalism and complication so that the large part of what had me stuck or engaged was not his dish . . . There was not a great deal of life in the physics in Leiden at the time. I think Ehrenfest was depressed; I don't think that I was of great interest to him then. I don't think he told me what was on his mind and I have a recollection of quiet and gloom."

Because he felt that the situation he found in Leiden "spoiled this period from the point of view of physics," Oppenheimer went to Utrecht for a month to work with Hendrik (H. A.) Kramers, who at that time held the chair of theoretical physics at the University. Oppenheimer had then planned to go to Copenhagen to work with Bohr, but was deflected, as he put it, by two considerations: the persistent cough that made a drier climate desirable, and "Ehrenfest's certainty that Bohr with his largeness and vagueness was not the medicine I needed but that I needed someone who was a professional calculating physicist and that Pauli would be right for me . . . He thought in other words that I needed more discipline and more schooling . . . I did see a copy of the letter he wrote Pauli . . . [and] it was clear that he was sending me there to be fixed up."[49] In 1928 Pauli had become a professor of theoretical physics at the Eidgenössische Technische Hochschule in Zurich, so Oppenheimer requested permission from the IEB's Paris office to alter his plans once more.

65 | TO INTERNATIONAL EDUCATION BOARD

Leiden
January 3, 1929

Gentlemen:

I should like to ask for your permission to go to Zuerich to work with Pauli. This is not in accordance with my original application to the Board, which was for permission to work at Leiden, Cambridge, and Copenhagen. The modification in my plans is made at the suggestion of Ehrenfest and of Kramers; I should like to work at Zuerich until Easter, and go then to Professor Bohr in Copenhagen. I have, of course, written to Pauli for his consent.

I hope that it will be possible for you to grant this permission without waiting for the discretion of the American Board; for I should like to leave Leiden in the next weeks. I should be much indebted to you if you would communicate to [me] your decision.

Yours faithfully,

J R Oppenheimer

The note of January 12, 1929, with which Ehrenfest supported Oppenheimer's request is preserved in rough translation: "Dr. Oppenheimer . . . has been in Leiden up to the present time (and has been constantly exchanging ideas with our young people during his stay here; he is a very ingenious physicist). We discussed where he had better go now. I advised him to go to Zurich with Pauli. That seems to be in accordance with his views. I also believe that—so long as he keeps that obstinate cough which has not been in order since his arrival in Holland—it is better that he perhaps remains where the climate is more favourable than it is here. Please put this charming, fine—but whose health is questionable—young man under medical control, but without letting him know that I wrote you about it."[50]

The institutional link between the International Education Board and the Rockefeller Foundation placed Oppenheimer's affairs under the kindly supervision of Dr. W. J. Robbins of the Foundation's Paris office. Their subsequent correspondence is informative on a number of points.

Zuerich
Jan 23, 1929.

Dear Dr Robbins,

In accordance with Dr Tisdale's letter of January seventh, I am sending you Professor Pauli's note. Professor Ehrenfest said that he would write directly to you. I am now accordingly beginning work in Zuerich. I plan to stay on here until my return to America; but I should like to make, either in the Spring vacation, or in the latter part of June, a visit of a fortnight to Professor Bohr in Copenhagen.

I made the trip here at my own expense. I do not know whether the Board pays such travelling expenses; the fare was about fifteen dollars; and shipping the boxes cost twenty-nine.

I hope that my movements have been of no inconvenience to you, and that you have, or shortly will have, Professor Ehrenfest's letter.

Yours faithfully,

J R Oppenheimer

Zuerich
Feb 4, 1929.

Dear Dr Robbins,

Thank you for your letter. I did not, of course, leave Holland until I had assurance from Professor Pauli that I might work with him; but I had no letter which I could submit to the Board to indicate his consent.

I am enclosing the account of my expenses in travelling here from Leiden. The luggage was frightfully expensive, because of the weight of the books and offprints. I can see no reason, a priori, why the Board should pay for this.

I should be very glad indeed if you could arrange to visit us. There is to be a conference on X-rays here during the Summer term; and that might possibly prove of interest to you.

Yours faithfully,

J R Oppenheimer

SOON AFTER MOVING to Zurich, Oppenheimer wrote to Robert Millikan, whom he had met the previous spring in Pasadena. Millikan was deeply involved in experiments designed to yield information on the high-energy radiation coming to earth from outer space, to which he had given the name "cosmic rays." In 1929 the origin of cosmic rays and the nature of their interaction with matter constituted an active field of physics research and one to which Oppenheimer himself would contribute significantly in the next decade.

Absorption curves measured the slowing down of cosmic rays as they passed through increasing thicknesses of absorbing material. "Hard radiation" could penetrate to greater depths of matter than less energetic radiation. The prevailing view in 1929 was that cosmic rays were made up of photons (gamma rays) which lost energy when they collided with electrons in the surrounding medium. In 1922 Arthur Compton had demonstrated that in such collisions the photon rebounds at an angle and continues to move but at a lower energy, while the electron recoils in a different direction. This phenomenon became known as the Compton effect, and in 1926 P. A. M. Dirac proposed a theory which helped in the computation of the effect. A more accurate theory was developed by Oskar Klein and Yoshio Nishina in 1929, and it was their work that Oppenheimer conveyed to Millikan.

68 | TO ROBERT A. MILLIKAN

Physikalisches Institut
Polytechnicum
Zuerich
February 12, 1929

Dear Professor Millikan,

Last year, when you were working on the interpretation of the absorption curves of the cosmic radiation, you asked me with what certainty the formulae of Dirac could be accepted. I answered, I think, that they could be taken as reliable, and that they could not be appreciably altered except by a fundamental change in the equations of physics. As you surely know, I was wrong to insist upon this reliability; the fundamental equations of the theory have in fact been altered; and there is a corresponding change for the absorption coefficient of hard radiation. The new formulae have been worked out by Klein and Nishina, and shewn, in the region in which you are interested, to give an absorption differing by as much as fifty percent from that calculated on the older basis. The work refers, still, to scattering by free electrons.

My chief purpose in writing—apart from that of confessing an error—is to say that, from a theoretical point of view, the new formula is by no means certain. For the equations from which it is derived give a number of definite predictions in flagrant contradiction with experiment, and are certainly in large part incorrect. Many people have tried to remedy the defects in the equations; it has not yet been possible to do this; and the current opinion is that it will be necessary to wait for new experimental evidence—e.g. from the nuclei—before an advance will be possible.

At present two things seem of particular importance: to try to decide, in the region of the hardest gamma rays, which of the Compton formulae is the more correct; and to determine definitely whether the absorption of the cosmic rays is to be ascribed entirely to the extranuclear electrons. If the nuclei play an appreciable part in the absorption, the coefficient per extranuclear electron should be different, for example, when computed from the absorption in lead and when computed from the absorption in air. I believe that you found no such difference. I might mention also that the grounds adduced by Cassen for an increased probability of collisions in which many protons take part are invalid.

Here we have been working systematically on the problem of supraconductivity. As yet we have not solved it.

Please give my respects to Mrs Millikan, and to the men at the Institute. Yours faithfully,

J R Oppenheimer

Oppenheimer quickly became involved in the work underway at Zurich. "When I got to Zurich Pauli told me a little of his work with Heisenberg and I showed, I guess, more than a little interest in it. It was in a ghastly state and we did, off and on, work together on that; the part of it I got into was something . . . [we] at first thought the three of us should publish together; then Pauli thought he might publish it with me and then it seemed better to make some reference to it in their paper and let this be a separate publication. But Pauli said, 'You really made a terrible mess of the continuous spectra and you have a duty to clean it up, and besides, if you clean it up you may please the astronomers.' So that's how I got into that . . ."

"But I was then very much interested in field theory, and of course quite interested because [Felix] Bloch, apparently from a wholly different point of view than anything I had thought about, had got into the conduction problem and we talked quite a lot. I think [Rudolf] Peierls came later that year. [I. I.] Rabi was there; we were friends but I don't remember what he was doing. I think he was rounding out his education. It was a very use-

125

ful time. I got to be not only extremely respectful but also extremely fond of Pauli and I learned a lot from him. The time with Ehrenfest had seemed terribly inadequate to what was really in Ehrenfest and the time with Kramers had seemed good but not very substantial — very good personally, very close, but not very substantial. The time with Pauli seemed just very, very good indeed."[51]

BIRTHDAYS in the Oppenheimer family could no longer be celebrated with flower-strewn chairs as at Bay Shore, but they were not forgotten, and soon after he turned twenty-five on April 22, Robert wrote to thank Frank for his present and to advise and plan for the summer.

69 | TO FRANK OPPENHEIMER

Zurich
May 6. [1929]

Dear Frank,

Many thanks for the birthday note and for the delightful book of Degas; I am so glad to have it. I can easily understand that you should not care to write very much; we shall try to make up for that by word of mouth. I don't write to anyone. You may if you please be disgusted at my negligence; but I don't want you to be offended.

Now I am going to interfere with you again; and zwar about your operations for the summer. It is so.

A. The place in the Pecos — house and six acres and stream — are ours for four years. There is an allowance of three hundred dollars to be spent for restoration. Katherine Page goes out in May.

B. Mother and Father ought to [be] back by May twentyfifth. They will want a few weeks in or near New York.

C. I shall be back about the middle of July. I must be in Pasadena by August tenth, as I have to drive up to Berkeley, find diggings, and begin work on the fifteenth.

D. You will undoubtedly want to be near Mother and Father for most of the summer; also you will doubtless be a little weary and low in morale after the close of school.

E. Cependant, you should not, in my opinion, let the summer float over you.

ERGO, Suggestion: About the middle of June you should take M and F West. At first they should stay at the Lodge or some such place; later, when F is acclimatized, they should visit Los Pinos from time to time. You and a suitable friend should try to open up the place, get horses, learn to cook, make the hacienda as nearly habitable as you can, and see the country. You could stop for a time with Katherine, as she is mostly empty early in the year. You must choose the boy—or there could be two, but not more—carefully, as you will be living with him for a good part of the time. I will come straight out to the Pecos, and have about three weeks there. You can leave the canyon in the rainy season—after the middle of August—if you want.

Let me know your plans. As far as I am concerned, I am determined not to spend more than a week or so in the East in any case.

It has probably been sort of a hard winter for you. You will perhaps be glad of it later; but yours is, and may be for a few years yet, a bad age. I wish that I could be with you. You had better come to college in California.

With best love, Frank,

your

R

THE COUGH that had worried Ehrenfest at Christmas did not yield to the more salubrious climate of Switzerland. Years later Oppenheimer recalled that he had taken a month off that spring for reasons of health.[52] After a visit to Zurich, Dr. Robbins of the Rockefeller Foundation wrote to Oppenheimer: "First and foremost is the question of your health. Permit me again to recommend that you should not hesitate to get in touch with us at the Paris office at any time . . . We are personally interested in our fellows, and are only too anxious to assist them in every way we can. We consider that we represent their friends and relatives during the period while they are in Europe."[53] A Berkeley entry in the travel log of Dr. Tisdale of the International Education Board in September explains why, although Oppenheimer's health continued to concern others, there is so little reference to it in his own letters: "J. R. Oppenheimer—just returned from Zurich as R. F. [Rockefeller Foundation] fellow—is not too well, and expresses the opinion that rather than take care of the cough, etc. he prefers to live while he is alive."[54]

Robbins' April letter assured Oppenheimer that it would be appropriate to terminate his fellowship a month early in order to prepare for the autumn's teaching in Berkeley, then went on to say that he had been much interested in Oppenheimer's comments about the difficulties faced by Americans studying in Europe and hoped he would suggest solutions.[55] Oppenheimer's reply shows that he already had some perspective on his Cambridge–Göttingen experience.

Zuerich
May 14. [1929]

Dear Dr Robbins,

Thank you very much for your good letter of April thirtieth. It was most kind of you to write.

By now I am fairly certain that I shall be able to continue with the work until July. In the latter half of June I hope to visit Professor Bohr at Copenhagen for a fortnight; but I must write to him before I can advise you definitely of the details.

You have asked me to write a little of the complications which afflict Americans in Europe. Unfortunately I can not speak from experience except of physicists and a few chemists, but perhaps they may be taken as typical. The difficulties are not universal, but seem to be sufficiently frequent to deserve attention. They are most acute in men who combine a certain weakness, timidity, hesitancy of character with a quite robust vanity—or, perhaps more accurately—with an urgent desire for excellence. In Europe they are removed from their friends, from the pampering of an American university, and from a language which they can control; in many cases they are relieved of the main part of their work, of instruction or work in the laboratory; they are introduced to the more critical, more disciplined, more professional science of Europe. All this is no doubt excellent; but too often it induces in the victim a state of surrender, and a false metaphysical melancholy which replaces, and makes impossible, an active participation in the European scheme, and an honest attempt to learn from it. The melancholy is presumably unpleasant; it is usually dissipated by return to America, and the consequent renewal of the pampering. But it acts as a protective coating for the American against that which he was sent to Europe to learn; almost always it is a sterile melancholy. It is the melancholy of the little boy who will not play because he has been snubbed.

There is little by way of remedy that you do not already know. The presence of other Americans has the advantage that it tends to sustain the tonus, the morale; it provides an 'outside world' which cannot quite be ignored; and in acute cases that more than compensates the dilution in the European setting. But I think that the most useful preventive would be to let the men know a little better what their situation will be, and to warn them of the collapse, so that they may be on their guard against it, and may make a conscious and specific effort to avert it. Except in cases of preternatural pusilanimity, that should, I think, suffice.

I hope that you will excuse me for writing at such length of this business.

I think that you would find others to corroborate what I have said; it is pretty obvious.

With the very best wishes,

J R Oppenheimer

I have refrained from posting this in the hope of speaking to you here. I might add the suggestion that future candidates for fellowships be asked to consult a returned fellow.

J R Oppenheimer

III | "Physics and the excellences of the life it brings"

BERKELEY AND PASADENA, 1929–1941

ROBERT OPPENHEIMER arrived at the University of California in Berkeley in the summer of 1929. He was twenty-five years old, fresh from the leading centers of theoretical physics in Europe and a recognized participant in the quantum theory revolution.

Berkeley had a distinguished science faculty, but its physics department, like those in most American universities at the time, was weak in theoretical physics and had no one familiar with the new quantum mechanics. It was there that Oppenheimer did the major portion of his teaching. His reasons for accepting the concurrent appointment at Caltech were different. Although only eight years old, Caltech's faculty had both theorists and experimentalists. Oppenheimer found it a lively place and thought that "I would learn, there would be criticism, and that would be much better for me."[1] His teaching arrangement with Caltech was more flexible than that with Berkeley.

In the decade that followed, the physics departments at Berkeley and Caltech were both noted for outstanding discoveries and technical achievements. At Berkeley, Ernest Orlando Lawrence, who had joined the faculty in 1928 as an associate professor, invented and with his students developed the cyclotron, a machine that accelerated atomic particles to high energies and used them to bombard nuclei. At Caltech, nuclear disintegrations were achieved with another type of particle accelerator, important research was done on cosmic rays, and two new subatomic particles were discovered.

The new data provided constant challenges for theorists like Oppenheimer. He had a close working relationship with experimentalists, which was characteristic of American universities, where all physics was in a single department; in most European institutions, theoretical and experimental physics were generally done in separate institutes.

Oppenheimer later reflected on the transition from student to teacher and leader of a major school of theoretical physics:

"I think that the whole thing has a certain simplicity. I found myself entirely in Berkeley and almost entirely at Caltech as the only one who understood what this was all about, and the gift which my high school teacher of English had noted for explaining technical things came into action. I didn't start to make a school; I didn't start to look for students. I started really as a propagator of the theory which I loved, about which I continued to learn more, and which was not well understood and which was very rich. The pattern was not that of someone who takes on a course and teaches students preparing for a variety of careers but of explaining first to faculty, staff, and colleagues and then to anyone who would listen, what this was about, what had been learned, what the unsolved problems were."

"I think from all I hear [that] I was a very difficult lecturer, I started as a lecturer who made things very difficult. I had some help; I remember Pauling's advice, almost certainly in '28. He said, 'When you want to give a seminar or lecture, decide what it is you want to talk about and then find some agreeable subject of contemplation not remotely related to your lecture and then interrupt that from time to time to say a few words.' So you can see how bad it must have been. In Pasadena I taught all right, but it was never an important part of the Caltech curriculum except conceivably that first year in the spring of '30 when I was there a long time and where I probably gave a pretty good 'course of sprouts' in quantum theory."

"In Berkeley I gave what was normally a graduate course and in practice usually a second year graduate course which had not been given before on quantum theory and quantum mechanics and which varied in content but was always all right for someone who had had some background in classical physics and preferably at least a qualitative introduction to atomic theory, though it didn't too much matter. I usually gave a seminar on one other aspect of theoretical physics, typically statistical mechanics and relativity, both things that I loved very much. But these were all with people who didn't have to learn these things [but] wanted to . . . [It] was very rarely and only in quite different contexts that I ever worked with undergraduates. I think they didn't think I'd be any good for them and it didn't occur to me to ask to teach freshman physics or anything like that."

"You live in the department and if it's a growing and active department as Berkeley got to be and as Caltech was, there are problems that arise because people are doing experiments. I found this a very great source of stimulation and pleasure and I think actually the beginnings of collaboration with graduate students came very early, but the students weren't very good and I picked rather exotic problems. It wasn't really until the positron [in 1932] and more or less the full shape of the relativistic débacle, [when] the clues of cosmic rays came into the picture, that the collaboration with students began to take a more effective turn."[2]

BEFORE COMMENCING his new career as university teacher, Oppenheimer and his brother Frank had their first holiday together at the newly acquired ranch in the upper Pecos Valley in New Mexico. Following Robert's advice, Frank arrived at Cowles early in the summer accompanied by two Ethical Culture School friends, a Scots boy, Ian Martin, and Roger Lewis. Roger became an indispensable member of the establishment. They stayed with Katherine Page while waiting for beds and equipment from Sears Roebuck, did some work on the cabin, and moved in shortly before Robert's arrival. The ranch had become Perro Caliente, which was Katherine Page's more mellifluous version of the "hot dog!" with which Robert had greeted her news that it could be leased.[3]

71 | TO FRANK OPPENHEIMER

Berkeley
Sept. 7. [1929]

Dear Frank,

Many thanks for the delightful letter. It made me a little envious and pleased me awfully to hear of gay times at Perro Caliente. And I can think how let down you will feel now that it is so nearly time to close up. I hope the business of it won't be a bore. And what can you do for the horses? It would be a pity to have to sell them, I think.

Your tales of a burro were immensely entertaining—so entertaining in fact that I showed them to one or two friends. I hope you don't mind that. I think that if you could preserve some of the freshness and authenticity of your letter in writing themes, that you would find very little trouble with the formal difficulties of composition; and that, if you will make it a rule never to write of anything which does not immediately and factually concern you—which has not, that is, played a real part in your experience or thought or feeling, that you will write very well, and enjoy it, and develop in time a technique fully adequate to what you have to say. And what you said, for instance, about Truchas and Ojo Caliente at night was much more convincing and honest and in the end communicative of emotion than your bits of purple writing about miscellaneous sunsets of the past.

132

Mother wrote that you were a wonderful haciendero, and had blazed a trail, and had been—for which thanks also from me—awfully good both to M and F and to K [Katherine Page]. In some ways you will find it hell to have to stop the Perro Caliente life just as it seems to be fullest and most satisfactory, and perhaps Fieldston will seem by comparison something of a bore.[a] But I think that you will on the whole find it easier to return to work now than after a summer of greater tameness and indolence. I hope that you will like chemistry and the bits of calculus; and especially I hope that you won't find your friendship with the boys and girls so inadequate as you did before. Will you get Carl for next summer?[b]

I have been pretty busy, preparing lectures and giving miscellaneous counsel and working and getting to know people. The undergraduate college here seems not to be worth much, or I should suggest that you come here next year. For it is a beautiful place, and the people are pleasant. I think that I am going to keep my room at the Faculty Club, but go sometimes to live with some boys who have rented a beautiful cabin on the hill, with a view and great stone fireplace and balconies and so on. Tomorrow I have promised to cook Nasi Goreng on a camp fire, and I have a provision of spices that would make Ian squirm.

I sent you a wrist watch. They say it is a good one; and I hope that it keeps very good time. If it doesn't, have it regulated. The works have an extra celluloid case to keep dust out; and the chief trouble I have with my watch is that it gets gritty from time to time.

Please write to me very soon. Say good bye for me to the Pecos, and write to K from time to time, gratuitously.

greetings to Ian and Roger. and God be with you.

r

a. Fieldston School was the Ethical Culture high school division which had moved to Riverdale in 1928. It later included lower grades.

b. Carl Blumenthal was an Ethical Culture School friend of Frank's.

There are many stories about Oppenheimer's eating habits in this period—Spartan indifference to what and how much he ate, which sometimes left his guests hungry, punctuated by a gourmet's delight in special dishes. Comments on his culinary skills, which he exercised chiefly on special occasions, focus on excessively hot seasoning, especially red pepper. Else Uhlenbeck, who probably introduced Oppenheimer to her native Indonesian *nasi goreng,* later learned that young people in Berkeley called his version "nasty gory" and avoided it if possible.[4]

OPPENHEIMER HAD MET the Tolmans, whose visit to Perro Caliente is mentioned in the next letter, in Pasadena in the spring of 1928. Richard Tolman was professor of physical chemistry and mathematical physics and dean of the Graduate School at Caltech, where he had been a faculty member since 1922. "He was rightly very highly respected," Oppenheimer later commented. "His wisdom and broad interests, broad in physics and broad throughout, his civility, his extremely intelligent and quite lovely wife, all made a sweet island in the Southern California [locale?] . . . a friendship developed which became very close." Ruth Tolman was a clinical psychologist completing her graduate training at the University of California. The Tolmans' friendship quickly extended to Oppenheimer's family, and Frank remembered their first visit to Perro Caliente only as part of "one lovely, lovely record."[5]

72 | TO FRANK OPPENHEIMER

Faculty Club
University of California
Oct. 14. [1929]

Dear Frank,

Many thanks for your last long good letter. I should have written to you before this; but I have been very busy; and you are not one of those to whom I can write in odd moments. I have also to thank you for your report on the summer, and the expenses and storage. Have you sent an account of the repairs to Harvey?[a] If not I shall swear out an affidavit for him. As for the orders for next summer, I shall make them later in the year; we can correspond about that when the time comes. Do you approve of the plan of an outside stair? Of course none of the improvements are really essential.

Let us plan definitely to spend at least a month together on the Pecos next summer. I do not think that I shall go to Ann Arbor, and that will leave me free at least from mid June to mid August. When should you be able to come? The examinations will keep you until July, I should think; and for God's sake do not flunk them, or the summer will be spoiled. I think too that it would be good to be alone together for the month; if you want friends you can ask them for after August; and if I want people, which I rather doubt, I will have them early in the year. The Tolmans, by the way, spoke very warmly of their visit, and asked me to send you again their thanks, and their greetings—I think that I must miss Perro Caliente—and it is in this connection a very bad name and you were right to avoid it—nearly as much as you do. But we shall plan on another vacation next summer, and try to make it just as rich and perhaps a little more industrious and thoughtful than the last.

What you write about your feeling for the horses is very curious. I cannot think that your sehnsucht for them is either very abnormal or at all terrible really; I can't think that it would be terrible of me to say—and it is occasionally true—that I need physics more than friends; and the two assertions seem analogous. As for your abuse of horses, that you must know yourself; and if the tendency to browbeat them is real, I think that you are right in saying that the desire should be watched and disciplined. But it is not easy— at least it is not easy for me—to be quite free of the desire to browbeat somebody or something; and perhaps it is because, in your relations with other people, you do, and infinitely commendably, in my opinion, so little brow beating; that it should frighten you so to discover in yourself too the traces of that beastliness.

I do not have much time for diversions; but I ride about once a week. There are good horses, and lovely country among the hills overlooking San Francisco bay, and there is pleasant company. And from time to time I take out the Chrysler, and scare one of my friends out of all sanity by wheeling corners at seventy. The car will do seventy five without a tremor. I am and shall be a vile driver— Work is coming on the whole pretty well. I don't get enough done, because I am busy and lazy, and have not the strength to let other things go to the devil when I should.

Such counsel as I should give you about the refractory problem of the jeunes filles Newyorkaises would probably be unwelcome. I should say that you were wrong to let the creatures worry you; and that, if you felt ill at ease with them, it meant a) that they were much more important to you than you to them, and b) that they were important to you for indeterminate and unavowed reasons, and that it was because of this ambiguity of purpose that you could come to no understanding. I should say that you should not associate with them unless it is for you a genuine pleasure; and that you should have truck only with those girls who not only pleased you, but who were pleased, and who put you at your ease. The obligation is always on the girl for making a go of conversation: if she does not accept the obligation, nothing that you can do will make the negotiations pleasant. You have, in any case, other business just now; and you should not let yourself be interrupted in that unless the interruption promises you a real charm and a real negotiation. But I do not want to pretend that the matter is altogether trivial. Everyone wants rather to be pleasing to women; and that desire is not altogether, though it is very largely, a manifestation of vanity. But one cannot aim to be pleasing to women, any more than one can aim to have taste, or beauty of expression, or happiness; for these things are not specific aims which one may learn to attain; they are descriptions of the adequacy of

135

one's living. To try to be happy is to try to build a machine with no other specification than that it shall run noiselessly.

I am glad that the work at school is so pleasant; I can remember how much I enjoyed [Herbert W.] Smith and Muzzey when I was a senior.[b] Did you know that one could define the sine of an angle A by the infinite sum

$$\sin A = x - \frac{x^3}{3 \cdot 2} + \frac{x^5}{5 \cdot 4 \cdot 3 \cdot 2} - \frac{x^7}{7 \cdot 6 \cdot 5 \cdot 4 \cdot 3 \cdot 2}$$
$$+ \frac{x^9}{9 \cdot 8 \cdot 7 \cdot 6 \cdot 5 \cdot 4 \cdot 3 \cdot 2} \text{ and so on with } x = \frac{\pi A}{180}$$

Please do write again. I wish that we had some more satisfactory method of communicating. I do not know whether it would be good for you; but for me it would be delightful if you could go to school out here.

your

r

a. The Harveys owned the ranch leased by the Oppenheimers.

b. David Saville Muzzey, professor of history at Columbia University and the author of widely-used American history texts, had taught parttime at the Ethical Culture School since 1900.

Frank, like Robert, was interested in science. To the classmates with whom he would graduate the following June, his destiny seemed clear. The 1930 class prophesy, entitled "Talks with the Great . . . 1955," included the following: "I next paid a visit to Dr. Frank Oppenheimer, the noted physicist, who is doing some experimental work on the structure of the electron. I was unfortunately unable to get any statement from him, as he had to leave in a great hurry to see about some dynamite that he had left on the stove."[6]

THE BERKELEY academic year started in August; first semester classes were over before Christmas, and the second semester ended in April. Oppenheimer taught at Berkeley through the fall of 1929, then made what was to become for the next decade his annual migration to Pasadena, though the date of it varied. His parents visited him in Pasadena as they had done two years before when he was there as a postdoctoral fellow. The following letter is one of two from Julius Oppenheimer to Frank which are included in this volume because they provide glimpses of Robert's life in Pasadena and of family relationships. Within the family Robert was customarily called "brother."

Robert Oppenheimer, 1926 or 1927. (Courtesy of Frank Oppenheimer.)

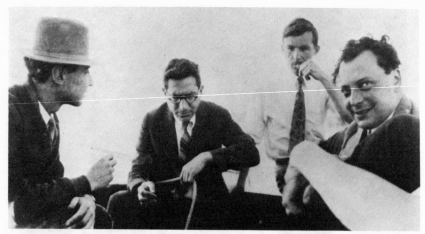

Robert Oppenheimer, I. I. Rabi, H. M. Mott-Smith, and Wolfgang Pauli, sailing on Lake Zurich, 1929. (Photograph by Rudolf Peierls; courtesy of A.I.P. Niels Bohr Library.)

Robert Oppenheimer, Enrico Fermi, and Ernest O. Lawrence, mid-1930s. (Courtesy of Lawrence Berkeley Laboratory.)

Dear Ernest,

There is a good deal to tell you, & I wish that I might run in to see you in the radiation labs, instead of writing.

I am sending Melba today an outline of the calculations & plots I have made for the deuteron transmutation functions. The analysis turned out pretty complicated, & I have spent most of the nights of this week with slide rule & graph paper. The results are not very different from the earlier ones, & altogether credible, but they need to be checked carefully & perhaps extended; I hope H. will do that soon. For $I = 2.2 \times 10^6$, $z = 13$, the curve I get is a fine straight line, cutting the axis (when extrapolated) at 1.49×10^6 volts. This is probably a little too high. If your extrapolated ticksona is q, then the best value to take for I is $\sim q/_{m}$. Unless I have made bad mistakes that should be right to better than 10%, I think. But you must give H time to work it over. I did not replot the in curve but it will be little altered. Nye came over Friday, & he & Charlie, Anderson & I had quite a good talk. His absorption measurements seem

my love to Molly, & my Father's affectionate greetings to you both. I wish I could be at journal club tomorrow night

Robert

love to Posadena.

Oppenheimer to Ernest O. Lawrence, spring 1935. (Letter 97.)

The cabin on the Oppenheimers' ranch, Perro Caliente, at Cowles, New Mexico, 1934. (Courtesy of Else Uhlenbeck.)

Robert Oppenheimer and Ernest O. Lawrence at Perro Caliente, before 1932. (Courtesy of Molly B. Lawrence.)

Pasadena, Calif.
March 11, 1930

Dear Frank,

We received your letters from Thursday and Saturday, and I know you do not like undue praise, but it would be most ungracious to refrain from telling you how very much we enjoyed your letters, —both the style and, of course, most, of what you have told us was most delightful. Your little chat with Dr. [Felix] Adler must have been indeed a fine experience, and if anything really puzzles you, I am sure he would be glad to see you again.

As long as we are on that subject, will you let us know how you are getting on with your history, and all the other studies, and have you arranged that your gym work is regular? While it is irksome to you, it would be really silly to make a fuss about it, and have it stand against you.

I must confess, that I miss seeing our paintings around us, but I am so glad that you can enjoy them over and over again. Have any of our friends come up to see them? The Toscanini concert must have been a rare treat. The Beethoven Eroica is, of course, one of the great masterpieces of music, and to have it conducted in so fine a way is a treat for a lifetime. You give us a poser when you ask what gives the appeal to music. I believe it is one of the primitive capacities, and through the ages, has developed into a fine art, and for some, into a fine understanding, a great emotion, and wonderful satisfaction to the various moods.

This is not much of a scientific explanation, but it is my own feeling.

You are right, your little experience, and your description of it, of the taxi kiss, did amuse us. Most I enjoyed your footnote, —that you will get the fragrance of the powder whenever you think of the evening. You must have that from me. Now that you know what this whole desire means, I presume you will be most careful not to repeat.

To have Roger [Lewis] with you is certainly fine, and pleasant for both of you.

Let me tell you a little about our doings. We like it very much at the Flintridge; it is very beautifully situated, and so far, we have had one evening alone. I do not know whether Mother wrote you that we had a delightful evening with the Tolmans. Tomorrow afternoon we are going there for tea and shall meet a number of the professors and some other of Robert's friends, and on Friday we are going with Mrs. Tolman to Los Angeles to hear the Tchaikovsky concert.

Brother is very busy with conferences, lectures, and his own work, but we manage to see him a short time daily. He has been a bit tired, but there will be vacation soon, which will come in handy for him. I doubt whether we shall go away, because it is so very pleasant here.

The reconstructed Chrysler emitted all sorts of groans, and I thought it very unwise for brother to continue driving it. We therefore bought a new one against severe protest on the part of brother. They allowed us $750 on the old one, which I thought was very wonderful. Now that brother has it, he is most delighted with it, and he has reduced his speed about 50% from what he used to drive, so we hope no further accidents will occur. I am certain you will get a letter very soon.

We have seen the Goldsmits a great deal, and we are giving a little party to them at the Flintridge this evening.[a] They always want to know about you, and send love.

Mother is anxious to know regarding your vacation, and also whether you have managed to see Dr. Poll. Do let us hear soon again, for it is a real joy.

Lots of love.

Father

a. Mrs. Oppenheimer's sister Clara Goldsmit and her husband lived in Pittsburgh.

Oppenheimer's fast driving was legendary. On one occasion in the early 1930s he crashed the car while racing the coast train near Los Angeles. His passenger was Natalie Raymond, whom Oppenheimer had met at her mother's parties in Pasadena in 1928. Though not seriously injured, she was knocked unconscious, and Oppenheimer thought at first that she was dead. Mr. Oppenheimer gave her a Cezanne drawing and a small Vlaminck painting by way of apology.[7]

ROBERT ALSO RESPONDED to the two letters Frank had written to their parents. His reply reveals an interest in music which contrasts sharply with the indifference bordering on dislike recalled by friends of the Harvard years.

Pasadena
March 12. [1930]

Dear Frank,

You make it rather hard for me to write to you by assuring me with such confidence that I shall be writing to someone I have never known. But it is not easy to believe that the Frank I knew is completely vanished; and I should be very very sorry if that were so. It has always seemed to me one of the inordinate inadequacies of letters—of letters which are not to serve some specific purpose, but are more or less gratuitous—that they necessarily give a pretty partial account of the writer, an account at once trivial and misleading. And for that reason I cannot be so desperate about our inability to keep flourishing a correspondence. The only letters which I can write with any conviction are technical ones, telling of physics, discursive and wholly ideational letters, love letters, and informative letters, which give geography and chronology and the major external data. It seems to me intrinsic to the act of living seriously that one should not be able to detach oneself enough to give a simple reflective account of what it is all about; the ability to do that comes only after the events are over, after one has ceased to be involved, when, that is, one is no longer the same person— Nevertheless I think that you do overestimate the inconstancy and incoherence of personal life; for I believe that throughout the variations—and they are wild enough, God knows—there is, there should be, and in mature people there comes more and more to be a certain unity, which makes it possible to recognize a man in his most diverse operations, a kind of specific personal stamp, which characterizes not so much the what as the how of a man's business. And this stamp is borne also by the letters, and is to be found, not in the contents of the letter, which may refer to a brief mood or a manic spell of action, but in the overtones of the attitude that the writer takes toward what he is writing— And you must so excuse me for not sending you a character sketch, or asking you for one; neither of us, I think, could furnish one adequately. For purposes of recognition it will suffice for you to know that I am six feet tall, have black hair, blue eyes, and at present a split lip, and that I answer to the call of Robert.

Mother showed me your last two letters. They interested me very much indeed, for they were completely charming letters. It is impossible not to observe the revolution in diction and style which the last months have made for you; and I should take this as evidence of a heightened sensibility and a more reflective temper. But what pleased me particularly in the letters was your surprising gift for digging up cardinal and leading questions, for reducing a specific and rather complex situation to its central irreducible 'Fragestellung.'

You are right in observing that music is unlike literature or plastic art in being essentially nonrepresentative, in being pretty purely evocative. I don't think that this very much aggravates the difficulty of understanding its power, because it shares with other art both a great formal complexity and a high symbolic power; and these appear to be the essential conditions for the development of art, and the representative—or in your terms perhaps reminiscent—virtue of some art seems to be only a special kind of fortification of the symbolic vigour; in music this vigour derives from a more sensuous and probably less cortical response. Even in plastic art there are very wide variations in the relative importance of the sensual and the representative; for Courbet or Rubens or Monet there is very little importance in the representation, and that is eminently true of Cezanne; for Rembrandt and Theotopoulos and Van Gogh there is a definitely literary and non sensuous association which is essential to an understanding of the picture. Only in music it is always, or always with the great and puzzling exceptions of Bach and Fauré and a few of the things of Debussy—inferior music which is highly representative. Think of Tristan and Scheherezade, and cf with Haydn symph in G maj or Debussy's quartet in G min. —I was grieved, obiter, to learn of your desertion of the flute.

Two other questions in your letters interested me: In how far is it possible to formulate ethical rules from which the proper conduct in specific cases may be deduced? —and— In how far is it wise to respond to a mood? In particular may one take the responsibility of affecting others by that mood? The former question I should rather like to talk of to you; it is too hard to write about, and in my opinion of high importance. For the second my own conviction is that one should use moods, but not be greatly deflected by them; thus one should try to use the gay times to do those things one wants to do which require gaiety, and the sober moods for the work one wants, and the low moods for giving oneself hell. I think that is about what you did, and that it was not your mood of amorous dalliance that made you make love, but rather that the mood enabled you to do graciously and simply what you had for a long time wanted to try. The reason why a bad philosophy leads to such hell is that it is what you think and want and treasure and foster in the times of preparation that determines what you do in the pinch, and that it takes an error to father a sin.

All the news you will have had from Mother and Father. I feel fairly certain that they are enjoying the visit here very much, liking the people and the place, and feeling well.

You have more or less committed yourself to answering this; and I cannot wholly suppress a malicious pleasure at the trouble you will have in doing it.

God be good to you; and don't you go and change too much, now; because I think you were pretty damn nice before.

r

THERE IS NO correspondence to document the quiet period with his brother in the Pecos that Oppenheimer had proposed for the summer of 1930, or to show what advice he may have offered Frank as a freshman at Johns Hopkins. When the letters resume, big-brotherly condescension was less evident. Robert and Frank were sharing their love of the outdoors and their interest in physics on a more equal basis. In the meantime their mother had developed leukemia. When Robert wrote to Frank from Berkeley in August 1931, he had been to the Pecos, to New York to see his parents, and to Ann Arbor, where he lectured at the theoretical physics summer session.

In Detroit he bought for Frank a secondhand Packard roadster, long and sleek and immediately christened Ichabod. Driving Wolfgang Pauli around Ann Arbor one evening, Robert lost his way. A police officer to whom he appealed for directions could scarcely believe that anyone had been in the town for three weeks, as claimed, without mastering its then simple geography. Oppenheimer further aroused the officer's suspicions when he was unable to open the special compartment for sporting equipment which the previous owner had installed. It was late by the time a legitimate relationship was established, and as the car drove up to the fraternity house occupied by summer school participants, a flat tire gave a final fillip to a typical Oppenheimer outing. Graduate students, hearing a loud crunch of rim on gravel, rushed out and changed the tire.[8]

A more familiar episode of the 1931 summer session took place during an Oppenheimer lecture which Pauli kept interrupting with comments. Finally H. A. Kramers shouted, "Shut up Pauli and let us hear what Oppenheimer has to say. You can explain how wrong it is afterward."[9]

Berkeley
August 10. [1931]

Dear Frank,

I have just had your marvellous letter on my return from a visit south. I hope that this will get to you before you leave; but I know the vagaries and vicissitudes of Pecos mail, and shall send you a wire, so that you may in any case have some word of me. I enjoyed your fine letter very much, and thank you for it, with all heart. And I thank you too for sending on the box of assorted linen and duderies; the box reminded me a little of those that we used to send at Christmas time to Elliott's poor.[a] I am a little curious too to know whether I owe the presents entirely to your own generosity; or is there some one else beyond you whom I must thank? The lighter is swell; and I put the bridge things away against a very very rainy day.

You will find Ichabod at the Packard place in A. A. I am afraid that the Uhlenbecks will be still away, but you might try (815 Arch Street), for they are awfully nice. The repair bill on I is paid, but you might check over it to see that the work is done. For two very minor things—adjusting the generator and keeping up the battery—you will have to pay. I hope that he will be a lamb for you.

Some time ago I wrote to father that we should want a new lease drawn up. His lawyer—Stern—will do it for us. But I do not know how to find Mrs Harvey. She was not at her San Gabriel Place. Did she tell you of her plans? It was good that you went at last to Tierra Amarilla; I doubt whether you will ever get your plane from the mine; but after our shameful negligence of last year we must make some atonement.

I am afraid that you will find mother pretty weak and miserable; the reports have not been very encouraging. I am glad that you will have a little time at home before school begins. Surely when you see mother and father so forlorn you will feel a little guilty to have had so marvellous a summer. But they will be happy in your happiness, in your strength and huskiness; not for the world would they have wanted anything else. I can trust you to do everything you can to cheer and comfort them. It might not be a bad idea to have F visit you for a few days in Baltimore or Washington, if you can persuade him to leave mother for so long. I think it pretty unlikely that M will be well enough to come west this winter; but if she can, I shall encourage her to come. Otherwise, and perhaps in any case, I shall be east at Christmas. I have a long vacation, and shall plan to spend most of it with her.

School should be fine this year; it is without much solicitude that I wish you a rich and deep and happy winter. I think perhaps that after this year you will want to leave Hopkins. And because your choice will to some extent commit your next years, I think that perhaps you will want soon to fix a little the virgin reaches of your future. I think that the world in which we shall live these next thirty years will be a pretty restless and tormented place; I do not think that there will be much of a compromise possible between being of it, and being not of it.

The nostalgia for New Mexico, for the life we have together there, has been acute and constant; your reticent notes about the nine day trip threw me into a fit of envy and dejection. I hope that you are planning to go back up next summer. There may be practical complications; but they will have to be great to keep me away. I have seen Val and the Tolmans and Nat, and they all send greetings. Lawrence and Lauritsen would both be glad to have you, next year, should you want to do experimental physics. Nat has gone east, having worn out the pacific coast; she will be in New York, probably at the Cornell medical school or the Rockefeller; probably you will see her.

Berkeley is good this year. The work is nice, the department honest and friendly. I enjoy chaperoning the boys and girls through the first problems in physics. I am learning sanskrit, enjoying it very much, and enjoying again the sweet luxury of being taught. I have a little house up on the hill, with a view of the cities and of the most beautiful harbor in the world. There is a sleeping porch; and I sleep under the Yaqui and the stars, and imagine I am on the porch at Perro Caliente. I feel well and strong, and have bought an alarm clock.

If you get this before you leave, give my love to Katherine [Page], and bless her winter for me. My greetings to Roger [Lewis]; and to you both my thanks, and an immoderate and sentimental salutation. I hope you have a fine trip east, with the horses and with Ichabod. What are you doing with Pal and Baldy? Are you going this time up to Huntsberger's place?[b] Write to me when you can. I shall answer.

[no signature]

a. John Lovejoy Elliott taught ethics classes at the Ethical Culture School and involved some of his students in settlement house activities and other good works.

b. The Huntsberger place was one of the ranches where Oppenheimer horses, currently Pal and Baldy, were wintered.

This letter introduces several close friends of Oppenheimer's Berkeley –Pasadena years. Ruth Valentine (Val), a psychologist in the Los Angeles school system, was a friend of the Tolmans. A gate connected their adjoining gardens. She was a sensitive person with a rare sense of humor.[10] "Nat" always refers to Natalie Raymond, a writer and editor. During Oppenheimer's first five or six years in Berkeley, Ernest Lawrence was his closest friend in the physics department. Charles C. Lauritsen, a native of Denmark, had joined the faculty of Caltech in 1930 after receiving the Ph.D. there the previous year. His presence in Pasadena was one of its attractions for Oppenheimer, as professional affinity rapidly developed into strong personal attachment.

BY EARLY AUTUMN Mrs. Oppenheimer's illness had progressed to a stage where Robert's presence was urgently required, in fact so urgently that he may have flown from California as implied in the first of two letters to Lawrence.

76 | TO ERNEST O. LAWRENCE

New York
October 12. [1931]

Dear Ernest,

It has not been easy to write to you before this; but I want you to have some little word from me. I know your understanding and your sympathy; and very deeply I appreciate it.

I found my mother terribly low, almost beyond hope. Every day since I have been here she has seemed a little stronger, a little more herself. She is in very great pain and piteously terribly weak; but there is a bare chance that she may have still a little period of remission. I have been able to talk with her a little; she is tired and sad, but without desperation; she is unbelievably sweet.

For my father alone I should have been glad to come. I think that it has been something of a comfort. He is brave and strong and gentle beyond all telling. He has promised to come out to me as soon as he can. My own departure is still not certain; it will not be surely before Saturday; I may stay a little longer; it will have to depend on how things go with Mother. You know that I shall come back as soon as I possibly can, and that, if I stay away so long, it is only because what I can do here seems incommensurate with the Berkeley duties.

The trip on was good enough. We had snow in Wyoming, and could not get through; that made me nearly a day late. I hardly think that I shall fly back.

I hope things are going well in Berkeley, that you are by now done wholly with the administrative horrors, and are having time for work and tennis and an occasional ride. I feel pretty awful to be away so long; you will do what you can for the fatherless theoretical children, won't you?

Affectionately

Robert

144

New York
October 16. [1931]

Dear Ernest,

Your sweet message, and the lovely roses, came last night, as my father and I were sitting together after dinner. Both of us were very much touched, Ernest, and grateful to you. My father asked me to tell you from him his appreciation and his thankfulness; several times during the evening he said "That was such a fine thing of Lawrence to do."

Things are pretty bad here, now. Mother, after a short respite, has been growing rapidly very much worse; she is comatose, now; and death is very near. We cannot help feeling now a little grateful that she should not have to suffer more, that she should not know the despair and misery of a long hopeless illness. She has been always hopeful and serene; and the last thing she said to me was "Yes—California." But even at that it is not very easy.

I shall try, I think, to get back to Berkeley a week from this next Sunday; but I shall not promise that, leaving it a little to time to decide. My father will come out as soon as he can get away; there are so many things that he must do before leaving. I do not think that I should wait for him. But when he comes, we shall do our best.

You must let me know if there is anything that I can do for you here; and if a word from me can be of any help to my deserted students, do not, please, hesitate to ask for it.

As a reminder of your promise of a visit next summer, I am sending you a snap of the new shack at Lake Katherine, 12,300 feet above sea.[a]

With every greeting, and again my thanks

Robert

a. Frank and Roger Lewis had built the shack secretly because it was in the National Forest. "The ranger discovered it just as we finished," recalled Frank, "but because it was for Katherine he just shook his head and let us get away with it"; communication from Frank Oppenheimer, June 1979.

Mrs. Oppenheimer died on October 17. Toward the end Herbert Smith spent an afternoon at the Oppenheimer apartment. Oppenheimer's despairing remark, "I am the loneliest man in the world," confirmed Smith's belief that Robert's attachment to his mother was exceptionally strong. Others who knew him as a boy share this impression. Seemingly there had been nothing for him to remember but gentleness and kindness, and for a sensitive son this must have been a very bad moment indeed. But the bond was not one that had broadened with time. Frank, too, observing

Robert's exceptional attentiveness to their mother over the years in the form of flowers and carefully selected presents, thought his brother must be closer to her than he. Years later he was surprised to hear Robert confess that he had had difficulty in finding things to talk about with his mother and that the attentions were what he supposed were expected from an affectionate son rather than a sign of deep understanding between them.[11]

WHATEVER THE EXTENT of the trauma produced by his mother's death, Oppenheimer soon successfully immersed himself in physics again, a therapy reinforced by the warmth and common interests outside science that enriched several of his close professional friendships. A note of late November to George Uhlenbeck demonstrates this point. It accompanied three pages of mathematical derivations that are omitted here.

78 | TO GEORGE UHLENBECK

Berkeley
Nov 29, 1931

Dear George,

This is no proper answer to your letter: only a note to go with the answers to your questions. I think the answer to your point 3) is complete; for 2) I can not do so well, but perhaps what I know will be enough to settle your doubts.

Some time ago there came the delightful Couperin's 'Arabesten'; & yesterday I found waiting for me a lovely heart warming bottle of sambal ikan merah. You must tell Else very many thanks for these, & my love, & the promise of a finite letter in finite time.

Do you plan to come to New Orleans at Christmas? It is a charming place; I am meeting my father & brother there ten days or so before the meeting; it would be most marvellous to see you.

Affectionately, & with every greeting

Robert

OPPENHEIMER, HIS FATHER, and Frank, then in his second year at Johns Hopkins, met in New Orleans as planned. Else Uhlenbeck noted the close rapport between Oppenheimer and Ernest Lawrence at the American Physical Society meetings on December 29 and 30. One animated conversation took place with Lawrence in an elevator and Oppenheimer outside.

After Lawrence had dashed in and out several times to make another point the operator called brusquely, "Break it up, sweethearts."[12]

As Oppenheimer and his father crossed Texas by train on their way to Pasadena, he commented to Lawrence about various aspects of the New Orleans meeting.

79 | TO ERNEST O. LAWRENCE

Texas
Sunday [January 3, 1932]

Dear Ernest,

This is an entirely gratuitous little note, written only to compensate for the brevity and sketchiness of our time together in New Orleans, and to thank you for certain very generous things to which in that time I did not do full justice. My brother was very happy at last to meet you, sorry only that the times had been so short. He asked me to tell you this, to send you his greetings, to tell you too with what eagerness he was looking to your visit next summer. We had a fine holiday together; and I think that it settled definitely Frank's vocation for physics. Seeing so together a good number of physicists, it is impossible not to conceive for them a great liking and respect, and for their work a great attraction. We went Thursday with Uhlenbeck and Thomas to a joint session of biochemistry and psychology;[a] it was enormously rowdy and very funny; and it discouraged an excessive faith in either of these sciences.

It was like you, Ernest, and very sweet, that you should whisper to me so comforting words about the Wednesday meeting. I was pretty much in need of them, feeling ashamed of my report [1932a], and distressed rather by Millikan's hostility and his lack of scruple.[b] Before I left I had with Swann a short pleasant talk; I think that he began to see why his arguments were not valid. I was glad to have a little time with him; he is very charming; and it was easy to understand your great affection.[c] New Year's day a reporter called me, saying that you had sent him. I did not give him anything; I hope that in that I did not offend your wishes.

The week end of the twenty second I shall spend in Berkeley. It is possible but not likely that I can get up the week end earlier. In any case I shall make the visit as long as possible; and if my father will come, I shall bring him. I have heard from Carlson and from Miss Phillips; both of them have been doing nicely. Miss Phillips wrote, but not very fully, of some new evidence on the degree of dissociation of potassium, which gives 10 times the number of molecules assumed by Ditchburn.[d] Her paper is nearly written up. About the more serious question of next year in Berkeley, I would not want to have you misled by Father's words: My decision, in so far as it can be purely mine, is made; if I can come to Berkeley for the whole of next year without complete rupture with Tech I shall come; otherwise I shall worry a little more before deciding. Father I think does not wholly approve; but then he knows Pasadena and not Berkeley.

I hope that in this week before term you will be able to get a good deal of work done. I suppose that it is too much to hope that by the beginning of term the big magnet will be ready; but perhaps by then your contractors will be done. If there are any minor theoretical problems to which you need urgently the answer, tell them to Carlson or Nedelsky; and if they are stumped let me have a try at them. When you see Sloan please give him my wishes for a good recovery; and to Berkeley my greetings.[e]

Thank you again for your fine Christmas present. Let things go well with you. à bientôt

Robert

a. This session was part of the annual meeting of the American Association for the Advancement of Science held in New Orleans at the same time as the meeting of the American Physical Society. Llewellyn (L. H.) Thomas was associate professor of physics at Ohio State University.

b. Millikan's hostility had probably been provoked by Oppenheimer's report suggesting that cosmic rays might be formed by a hypothetical particle proposed by Pauli. This theory was in conflict with Millikan's view that cosmic rays were bundles of photons. See Laurie M. Brown, "The Idea of the Neutrino," *Physics Today*, 31 (September 1978): 23–28; see also Oppenheimer papers 1931g and 1932a.

c. William F. Swann, under whom Lawrence had obtained his doctorate at Yale, was director of the Bartol Research Foundation of the Franklin Institute.

d. Robert W. Ditchburn was professor of natural and experimental philosophy at the University of Dublin.

e. Lawrence's big magnet was the central component of his cyclotron. It had to be designed to produce the appropriate magnetic fields, and Lawrence frequently made use of the computing skills of the theoreticians. David H. Sloan, an assistant physicist in Lawrence's lab, had serious back problems.

By 1932 Oppenheimer had attracted some talented graduate and postdoctoral students. Melba Phillips, his first doctoral student, came to Berkeley in 1930. She received her Ph.D. in 1933, was Oppenheimer's research associate in 1933–34, and held an instructorship in physics in 1934–35. J. Franklin Carlson, who received his Ph.D. with William H. Williams at Berkeley in 1932, was Oppenheimer's research associate in 1932–33, then became an instructor in physics. Each collaborated with Oppenheimer in publishing significant papers [1931g, 1932b, 1935e, 1937a].

Leo Nedelsky had commenced graduate work in physics in 1928 under Samuel Allison. After Allison moved to Chicago in 1930, Nedelsky became Oppenheimer's graduate student, seduced, as he described it, by a course in quantum mechanics of which he understood almost nothing. However, all the students were in the same boat and consoled each other after class. Oppenheimer's tendency to stammer as he lectured soon disappeared, but his blackboard manners were unorthodox. Questioned about a particular equation, which he had cited with a gesture toward the blackboard, Oppenheimer said, "No, not that one; the one underneath." "But there isn't one underneath," the students exclaimed. "Not below," said Oppenheimer, "underneath. I have written over it." In his first years at Berkeley Oppenheimer's real influence was exerted outside the classroom. "When you took questions to him," recalled Nedelsky, "he would spend hours—until midnight perhaps—exploring every angle with you. At that personal level he was an excellent teacher although he always overestimated what others knew or could learn."[13]

When Oppenheimer went to Pasadena during the Berkeley term, at the last moment he sometimes asked Nedelsky to lecture for him. "It won't be any trouble," said Oppenheimer on one such occasion, "it's all in a book." Finding that the book was in Dutch, which he could not read, Nedelsky demurred. "But it's such easy Dutch," said Oppenheimer.[14]

Wendell Furry, a postdoctoral fellow at Berkeley from 1932 to 1934, later recalled that Oppenheimer expressed himself "somewhat obscurely and very quickly with flashes of insight which we couldn't follow." Elegant language and highbrow allusions made his lectures even more incomprehensible. Nevertheless, students responded with exclamations of "Excellent! Fine! How illuminating!" But it was direct contact that really counted. "He praised all of our efforts even when we weren't so hot," says Furry. Sometimes he seemed impatient with questions but then showed his appreciation by asking the questioner to collaborate on the problem.[15]

Graduate students and postdoctoral fellows began to note a serious effort on Oppenheimer's part to improve his classroom technique.[16] In 1967 Robert Serber reflected upon the qualities that marked Oppenheimer's style. "By this time [the autumn of 1934] Oppenheimer's course in quantum mechanics was well established. Oppie (as he was known to his Berkeley students) was quick, impatient, and had a sharp tongue. In the earliest days of his teaching he was reputed to have terrorized the students. Now, after five years of experience, he had mellowed—if his earlier students were to be believed. His course was an inspirational, as well as educational, achievement. He transmitted . . . a feeling of the beauty of the logical structure of physics and an excitement in the development of the science. Almost everyone listened to the course more than once, and Oppie occasionally had difficulty in dissuading students from coming a third or fourth time . . ."

"Oppie's way of working with his research students was also original. His group would consist of eight or ten graduate students and about a half dozen postdoctoral fellows. He would meet the group once a day in his office. A little before the appointed time its members would straggle in and dispose themselves on the tables and about the walls. Oppie would come in and discuss with one after another the status of the student's research problem, while the others listened and offered comments. All were exposed to a broad range of topics. Oppenheimer was interested in everything, and one subject after another was introduced and coexisted with all the others. In an afternoon we might discuss electrodynamics, cosmic rays, astrophysics and nuclear physics . . ."

"Many facets of Oppenheimer's character contributed to his greatness as a teacher: his great capacity as a physicist, his wide intellectual interests, his astonishing quickness of mind, his great gift for expression, his sensitive perception, his social presence, which made him the center of every gathering. His students emulated him as best they could. They copied his gestures, his mannerisms, his intonations. He truly influenced their lives."[17]

Four years before he died Oppenheimer had given Thomas Kuhn his own version of the change that took place in his attitude toward physics and toward teaching in the early 1930s. "I would think that the transition was . . . from that of a person who had been learning and also explaining in European centers and in Harvard and Caltech to someone who couldn't much any longer learn from masters but could learn from the literature and from what he did himself, and who had a lot of explaining to do because there was no one else. I think it was not such a sudden transition. Living a life in which you lecture three hours a week and have a seminar [or] another lecture two hours a week leaves you a lot of time for physics and for lots of other things and I wasn't an altered character. I was still primarily a student in terms of what I spent time on . . ."

"[Lecturing] took energy, a great deal of energy, but I didn't have to look much up in the book and it was more a question of keeping the presentation fresh and making it sharper and richer. I would think that the big change was that I wasn't an apprentice any longer and I had decided where to make my bed . . . In a certain sense I had not grown up but had grown up a little, and I think if circumstances had been such that I had had to teach to make a living earlier it probably would have been better for me. I don't think it would have derailed my interest in physics but I think it would perhaps first of all have made it necessary for me to learn what I wanted to know."[18]

OPPENHEIMER'S CONCERN for his father in the lonely years after his mother's death, combined with Mr. Oppenheimer's outgoing personality, made it possible for Julius to share his son's life and friends in Pasadena or Berkeley for weeks at a time. Some who had known Robert as an adolescent felt that he never overcame a sense of incompatibility with his father or ceased to be annoyed by Julius' tendency to boast about his son's accomplishments. Others, knowing only the more mature Oppenheimer, found his concern for his father far from perfunctory. Mr. Oppenheimer was in Pasadena in January 1932 when Robert wrote to Frank. The sharing of friends now extended to Frank's circle at Johns Hopkins.

80 | TO FRANK OPPENHEIMER

Pasadena
Sunday [ca. January 1932]

Dear Frank,

No one who learns anything at all from experience could hope that we should make for each other much of a correspondence. But there is perhaps no reason for a tradition of unconditional silence; and I would urge you with all heart to write to me whenever you find together leisure and inclination, and to nurse the inclination a little. I want very much to know how, now, after your return to school, you find yourself. I should like to think that you have found again some of the freshness of last year, the assurance and the certainty, and to some extent that delectatio contemplationis which is the reward and reason of our way of life. These things are not all important, as we both know, and one may not expect always to be visited by them. But for that reason we try to do everything to invite them, cultivating a little leisure, and a certain detached solitariness, and a quiet discipline which uses but transcends the discipline of our duties. Ergo, for you, not too hellishly many hours of school; and a mind open and hospitable to the angels, even Çiva's angels;[a] and once in a while for your humility a green vegetable.

We have the lease for Perro Caliente, giving us the summers through '36; the option is signed and on its way. Father has not committed himself yet in his summer plans; always in the next years we shall have for them a certain solicitude. But I look with confidence and intense nostalgia to many many perfect months together in the mountains.

We are established here in a little house. We had a hell of a time looking in this waste for two pleasant places near together; we did not find any; and F is very much pleased with this place, liking the cottage—which is in fact excruciatingly ugly—and not I think sorry to have me under the same roof. F looks well, better than in months. The days are necessarily a bit empty; but he is studying French—with God knows what ineptitude for any study; he is to start driving tomorrow; I have been with him every day for lunch, and we have had the evenings together, often with people. There are concerts and stammtisches and even a seminar on International affairs; and on the whole I think it will be better for him here than we had hoped. The great

151

problem of breakfast was solved by Ruth Tolman's Moline, who every morning gets breakfast and fixes; and after I am gone listens with enchanting patience to F's reports on high finance.

The cigarette rolling prospers; it recalls a most marvellous holiday.

Greetings to Roger, the Boas', Dieke, Mac,[b] Ichabod. God keep you; and write when you can.

R

a. Çiva (Siva or Shiva) is a Hindu god who destroys life in order that reproduction can take place; he is also associated with asceticism.

b. Frank's friends at Johns Hopkins were: Roger Lewis, who had been in part responsible for Frank's decision to go to Hopkins rather than Harvard; George Boas, associate professor of philosophy, and his sculptress wife, Simone; Gerhardt Dieke, a spectroscopist; and Donald Macfarlane, a psychiatrist.

UNLIKE HIS SON, Julius Oppenheimer always meticulously headed letters with address and full date. The "Stammtisch" to which he and Robert both referred (literally "table reserved for regular guests") was a weekly dinner meeting at Caltech, an elite affair attended by people in various departments. Someone made a presentation, and stimulating talk followed. According to Frank, his brother's periodic efforts to steer him toward biology stemmed in part from the exciting new work in genetics discussed at these Stammtisches.[19]

81 | JULIUS OPPENHEIMER TO FRANK OPPENHEIMER

Pasadena, California
January 18th 1932

Dear Frank,

The letters have been a bit delayed and we received your first letter on Friday. We also heard from Aunt Clara [Goldsmit] that she had seen you during the week and that you were well. She inferred that you were going to visit her this weekend. Have you the time for so long a journey? I hope you will enjoy the visit.

Don't forget to take sufficient funds along.

We here continue to enjoy our little home. I study a bit of French every morning, making slow progress, as it is over forty-five years that I have not touched a French book. I also have taken a few lessons driving a car and I believe I am getting on quite nicely. I should not want to try it down Park Avenue as yet.

152

I have been to two Stammtisch Meetings. They are very good fun. We have also been at Ruth Valentine's for an evening meal. Robert fixed the odds and ends, and we had a most delightful evening. Clark Millikan and his wife, Robert and I entertained going to a theater with them and supper and tonight St. Clair and Elizabeth are going to dine with us,[a] so you see I am meeting lots of Robert's friends and yet I believe that I have not interfered with his activities. He is always busy and has had a couple of short talks with Einstein. Cal Tech impresses me as being very active just now. This weekend we may go to Berkeley and meet Lawrence and Ryder.[b] Robert wants me to come along and I may decide to do so. I am trying to give you as near as possible a bit of the doings for I know you want to be informed.

Ruth Tolman told us that Mrs. Boas received prices on two of her works. When you see her will you remember me and tell her I was so glad to hear this.[c]

I trust you will continue to enjoy your work and if it gets too much that you will drop something so as not to over-burden yourself.[d] Take good care of your health and let us hear from you very soon again. Lots of love, from brother and

Father

a. Clark Millikan was the eldest son of Robert A. Millikan. St. Clair and Elizabeth were Sinclair Smith, a Caltech astronomer, and his wife.

b. Arthur W. Ryder was the professor of Sanskrit at Berkeley with whom Oppenheimer was reading.

c. In regard to Mrs. Boas' sculpture, Mr. Oppenheimer apparently meant "prizes," not "prices." "Julius was one of the kindest men I ever knew," commented Boas. "The first time we had lunch with him in New York in his apartment with its two Van Goghs, its head by Despiau, and the other exquisite works of art, not many but very choice, we knew at once that he was a very rare person"; George Boas to Alice Kimball Smith, November 28, 1976.

d. Frank, like his brother before him, was taking the extra courses that would enable him to graduate from college in three years.

AS JULIUS OPPENHEIMER prepared to return to New York, Robert discussed with Frank how their father should spend the summer, suggesting that Julius' youngest sister Hedwig Stern should come from Germany for a visit and that Josephine, the family's devoted maid, look after them. Oppenheimer did not go to Europe in 1933. In fact, he did not go again until the summer of 1948, nineteen years after he returned from the postgraduate year in Leiden and Zurich.

Robert's advice to Frank about the advantages of studying biology before deciding to go on in physics was part of a continuing discussion between them about Frank's education. Frank recalled that in the spring of

1930 he wrote to his brother saying he would like to come west and study under him instead of going to college, but Robert did not think it was a good idea. Frank went to Johns Hopkins, where he found the biology courses unsatisfactory. He took his brother's advice seriously but "the physics and math were so very good at Hopkins (as were philosophy, French, and many other things) that I was seduced by it. In addition, I attended the spring American Physical Society meetings in Washington with my brother and Hopkins faculty and was captivated by what was happening."[20]

82 | TO FRANK OPPENHEIMER

Pasadena
March 12 [1932]

Dear Frank,

When, within the fortnight, you again see father, he will tell you that for days and days I have been making little initial gestures in the act of writing to you; he will tell you too, I think, a charitable story of the vicissitudes which have delayed the letter. For truly I have wanted to write, have carried with me the substance of many long hours of talk with you. Your last letters have been marvellous; the reading of them made a deep quiet happiness, a suggestion surely of the high moments. I have never been more eager for the summer.

You will find father well, I think, and pretty fit: at least he is so now. It would be good for him to have a little more time here; but he wants to be back with his affairs again, and is taking advantage of an offer from a friend to keep him company east. He is completely restored now from the operation,[a] and better than for many months; but he tires still very easily, and you must be prepared to keep him from discouragement if his first efforts in New York should exhaust him. He has had I think a genuinely pleasant time; I feel that he has had here about all that he could under the circumstances use; and it is with a pretty good conscience that I let him return. I have urged him very strongly not to go to Europe alone this summer, recommending that he have Hedwig come, and that he keep house with her and Josephine near town, perhaps in Westchester, where he could be near friends. Only if things should break unexpectedly well: e.g. should he find a very good person to travel with, ought he, or will he, go abroad. I have said too that next summer I should consider going myself, that in that case we could at least cross both ways together. For me this summer is definitely out, as I am planning to go to Berkeley in August, and do not get through here til some time in June. That time is for Perro Caliente; and neither of us would want to deplete it.

If you have not written to Father of your precise plans for meeting him, will you wire? It will comfort him to know. Will you too let me know about when you can get out to the mountains? I think that I can arrange to be there nearly as early as you; but I should have to know in advance.

It would seem then that you were not to be distracted from physics. I had thought that you might find in the biological sciences things to whet your appetite and curiosity, that might, for the time perhaps, call to you. I know very well surely that physics has a beauty which no other science can match, a rigor and austerity and depth. Only I must urge two precautions: Has the biology which you have had been typical enough, has it been good enough, to warrant a judgement? There are parts of physiology which seem to me, though pretty young, essentially sound: muscle and nerve physiology, embryology. Genetics certainly involves a rigorous technique, and a constructive and complicated theory which goes quite a way in enabling us to predict. I have a feeling that an elementary course in biology might miss entirely the good things; that except from a very good man you would get no idea of them. I would urge you not to dismiss this possibility. The other point is a simple one: I am sure that you are right in preferring physics as a science to study and learn; but should you prefer it as a science at which to work, a vocation? By all means, and with my whole blessing, learn physics, all there is of it, so that you understand it, and can use it and contemplate it, and, if you should want, teach it; but do not plan yet to 'do' it: to adopt physical research as a vocation. For that decision you should know something more of the other sciences, and a good deal more of physics.

Have you decided what to do next year? Could you spend another year at Hopkins with some fruitfulness? Could you take your B A there a year from June? (Do they give such things?) It would be in many ways an advantage to you to come to your next place as a graduate student: Harvard, Europe, Pasadena, to some extent even Berkeley would be much better so. But to Berkeley, though not here, you could come as an undergraduate. I doubt whether my plans can have any relevance: but I am arranging to spend the year in Berkeley, until Easter, and then to come down here, for Bohr's visit, until June.

You put a hard question on the virtue of discipline. What you say is true: I do value it—and I think that you do too—more than for its earthly fruit, proficiency. I think that one can give only a metaphysical ground for this evaluation; but the variety of metaphysics which gave an answer to your question has been very great, the metaphysics themselves very disparate: the bhagavad gita, Ecclesiastes, the Stoa, the beginning of the Laws, Hugo of St Victor, St Thomas, John of the Cross, Spinoza. This very great disparity suggests that the fact that discipline is good for the soul is more fundamental than any of the grounds given for its goodness. I believe that through discipline, though not through discipline alone, we can achieve serenity, and a certain small but precious measure of freedom from the accidents of incarnation, and charity, and that detachment which preserves the world which it renounces. I believe that through discipline we learn to preserve what is essential to our happiness in more and more adverse circumstances, and to abandon with simplicity what would else have seemed to us indispensable; that we come a little to see the world without the gross distortion of personal desire, and in seeing it so, accept more easily our earthly privation and its earthly horror— But because I believe that the reward of discipline is greater than its immediate objective, I would not have you think that discipline without objective is possible: in its nature discipline involves the subjection of the soul to some perhaps minor end; and that end must be real, if the discipline is not to be factitious. Therefore I think that all things which evoke discipline: study, and our duties to men and to the commonwealth, war, and personal hardship, and even the need for subsistence, ought to be greeted by us with profound gratitude; for only through them can we attain to the least detachment; and only so can we know peace.

Are there any Rameau things which would be suitable for a violin and piano? Ruth Tolman and Mrs Morgan play together;[b] and they would appreciate it very much if you could get for them anything that they could use. They would have I suppose to be pretty recent scores; and perhaps nothing suitable exists. But if it does, will you send it on to me?

You might like to try your spanish on Unamuno: Del sentimiento trágico de la vida. And Jane Austen; do you know her six marvellous novels?

con cariño

Robert

a. Mr. Oppenheimer had minor surgery.
b. Mrs. Morgan was a Pasadena friend of Ruth Tolman's.

OPPENHEIMER JOINED his brother in the Pecos in June as planned and stayed until close to mid-August, when he was due back in Berkeley. On August 14 from Topock, Arizona, where U.S. 66 crosses the Colorado River, he mailed a picture postcard of Needles Peaks with the message: "For our first trip into the delectable mountains, con cariño"—a reminder of their journey as novice drivers when Robert's arm was broken, but also of long talks, shared adventures, and wonderful country.[21] In Berkeley on a Sunday some weeks later he typed a long letter to Frank, now in his third and final year at Johns Hopkins.

Berkeley
Sunday [ca. fall 1932]

Dear Frank,

There has never been so long a time which I have let pass without a letter; and never a time when so constantly I have enjoyed your company. Our common life last summer left in me a fine deposit which I have been tapping all these months, a great repository of your words and gestures and of the good hours which we shared. Even now, perhaps, with an answer to your marvellous letters so long overdue, I should not be writing to you if I had not the hope and project of another common holiday in mind. And that is Christmas. I have just written father an elaborate disquisition on the possibilities, and think that the ultimate decision rests with him. Roughly though it is so: if he wants to come out here, or will let himself be persuaded to want it, by the New Year, let us meet again about half way. If he is staying east til February, let me then, who have such a huge vacation (for my classes stop the first week of December and don't start again til the second in January) come east, and let us make what we can of Baltimore and New York and the Physical Society meeting and such excursions as we can devise. My suggestion for a half way meeting is perhaps foolish: but how would New Mexico do, that we have neither of us seen in winter, that would be friendly and not quite so far for you as this coast? The only certain point for me is that we should be together, and that we should make the time as pleasant and as right for father as we can.

Your courses sound swell; only I am distressed by this, that they are covering an area very much like the one I cover in my introduction to theoretical physics; for I have an arrogant and stubborn wish that you might be learning these beautiful things from me. I feel sure that your three courses would profit by union: that the reciprocal illumination which function theory, vector analysis, and potential theory give each other is indispensable to a profound understanding of any one of them. Maybe you can try to fill in the bridges for yourself; and I shall try to get you a set of notes for next summer that will help to anchor them. You know of course that I have pretty mixed feelings about this program of yours in which theoretical physics plays such a large part: it is the most delightful and rewarding study in the world, and I can be only glad that you are enjoying it, glad too that we shall always be able to share this treasure. It is only the implications of the course that trouble me: the possibility that you are more and more deeply committing yourself to a vocation which you will regret; the possibility that your motives in this choice—and I wish that I might dismiss this, but only you can—are not wholly in physics and your liking for it. I take it

157

that the biology at Hopkins is abominable—this from many sources: and that the only other academic study of any consequence, that of hard languages, leaves you pretty cold; that does not leave much but vectors and Cauchy's theorem for you to try. But let me urge you with every earnestness to keep an open mind: to cultivate a disinterested and catholic interest in every intellectual discipline, and in the non academic excellences of the world, so that you may not lose that freshness of mind from which alone the life of the mind derives, and that your choice, whatever it be, of work to do, may be a real choice, and one reasonably free. Just yesterday I was over in Marin, the country on the northern seaward arm of San Francisco bay; it was a grey day, with heavy fog blowing in from the sea; and the little lighthouses at all the perilous points cut off from the world by the mountains behind and the fog banks out to sea. I suppose that only very gifted and industrious lighthouse keepers get to live in such places; but their mere existence makes me wonder how any man of sense can ever adopt any other vocation.

I am glad you liked the strong box. I had myself quite a time finding it, but was pleased with this, though the locks were not what they might have been. Did you find the English flask? It was sent in memory of one perfect snifter, late one afternoon in the upper meadows of the Baca location, where we learned canonically to define man's superiority over beast by his use of flasks. [a]

Mac is fine: not perhaps the boyish creature that came first to Perro Caliente; graver and perhaps with the shadow of a chip on his shoulder; but full of vigor and lots wiser. [b] His job is I take it not perfect, but satisfactory. We went sailing once, on a fine gentle day in a bird boat, out the gate and up the coast; but the winds have dropped now and there will be no decent sailing until spring. He, and Ruth [Tolman] and Val [Ruth Valentine] and Lauritsen and Melber and Lawrence all send you greetings; and Melber, who was in a minor way accessory to my discovery of your strong box wants due credit for it. [c] Also, and this will please you less: two friends here recognized you when they were east: the chemist Gilbert Lewis spotted you in an audience, alarmed at first at my presence hostile to his reflections, comforted then by knowing you my brother. And Edward Tolman, Richard's brother, spotted you and Roger [Lewis] on the train from Chicago east, but did not speak to you, fearing 'it might seem impudent.' Poor laddie, the mark is on you.

I have ridden a little mare out in the hills toward Diablo, a little five gaited blooded mare with the unforgettable roguish temperament of Dixie; and roasted green chile over the fire and made the cocktails of lime and honey. And when the maid neglects my bed and I must make it myself, I am glad; and can almost hear Roger desperately calling me to the late breakfast. Did you leave Io with Katherine [Page]? [d] I had your letter too late to answer, and no great choice in the matter. And is she still in the mountains? There has been no breath of word from her; and I am curious to know how she is. Did you have, when you left, the feeling that there was peace between you? And had she forgiven us for whatever she had taken as our offence?

The work is fine: not fine in the fruits but the doing. There are lots of eager students, and we are busy studying nuclei and neutrons and disintegrations; trying to make some peace between the inadequate theory and the absurd revolutionary experiments. Lawrence's things are going very well; he has been disintegrating all manner of nuclei, apparently with anything at all that has an energy of a million volts. We have been running a nuclear seminar, in addition to the usual ones, trying to make some order out of the great chaos, not getting very far with that. We are supplementing the paper I wrote last summer [1932b] with a study of radiation in electron electron impacts, and worrying about the neutron and Anderson's positively charged electrons, and cleaning up a few residual problems in atomic physics. I take it that there will be a lull in the theory for a time; and that when the theory advances, it will be very wild and very wonderful indeed. —I am reading the Cakuntala with Ryder; and at our next meeting shall afflict you with clumsy translations of the superb poems.

I wish that I knew the answer to your solicitude about father. I have thought a great deal about him, his need of work, the limitations which health and his aptitudes and the times put on its fruition. If I knew of anything to do I should do it. But I don't; and I feel that about all that we can do is to make the life as it is not too forlorn for him, and to confirm the one essential purpose that it still has, which lies in us. I feel very openminded about any suggestions; and when we are again together we shall talk together of this, and see if together we can make more of it than either of us can alone.

Write to me pretty soon, if only to tell me what plans for the holidays you like best. God keep you; and let the days be rich and sweet.

Robert

a. The Baca Location was a large land grant which included much of the Valle Grande in the Jemez Mountains northwest of Santa Fe. Robert, Frank, and Roger Lewis were riding there one summer afternoon when deer flies viciously attacked riders and horses. "So we set the horses to a full wild run up the two-mile length of the Valle," recalled Frank, "overtaking each other over and over again to pass on the welcome flask after slowing down to take a swig"; communication from Frank Oppenheimer, June 1979.

b. Donald Macfarlane was on leave from Johns Hopkins. His departure from Perro Caliente after his first visit there made an indelible impression upon Frank: "As an ambulance driver in France during World War I, Mac had often driven at night with the headlights off. The night he left Perro Caliente he wanted to recreate that experience for himself and for us. We drove down the tortuous road cut into the side of the Pecos River Canyon on a very black night with the lights out. The wisps of cloud that persist after a mountain rain storm would periodically envelop us, even more hair-raisingly shrouding the road. My brother and I were thoroughly scared but we did not protest"; communication from Frank Oppenheimer, June 1979.

    c. "Melber" was the way her friends commonly pronounced the name of Melba Phillips.

    d. Dixie and Io were horses.

Oppenheimer's remark about "trying to make some peace between the inadequate theory and the absurd revolutionary experiments" should be viewed against a background of important achievements in 1932 that focused the attention of the physics community on nuclear and cosmic ray research. In January Harold C. Urey at Columbia University discovered a heavy isotope of hydrogen (deuterium). In February James Chadwick at the Cavendish Laboratory demonstrated the existence of the neutron, a new nuclear particle. In April John Cockcroft and E. T. S. Walton, also of the Cavendish, disintegrated the nuclei of light elements by bombarding them with artificially accelerated protons. In August, at Caltech, Carl D. Anderson's photographs of cosmic ray tracks showed the existence of the positron, the positively charged electron. Soon after, at Berkeley, Ernest Lawrence with his students Stanley Livingston and Milton White used their new particle accelerator, the cyclotron, to disintegrate nuclei. These discoveries and techniques provided theorists with exciting challenges and opportunities.[22]

THE EXACT DIVISION of Oppenheimer's time between Berkeley and Pasadena was negotiable. In his March 1933 letter to Millikan about arrangements for the coming year there is evident a growing absorption in the teaching at Berkeley as well as concern about the effect of the Depression upon academic financing.

84 | TO ROBERT A. MILLIKAN

Berkeley
March 5, 1933

Dear Dr Millikan,

    When last I was in Pasadena, I spoke to you of coming to the Institute for the better part of next year, and asked you whether you could find a job for me. Since then, I know, the financial situation has grown only worse; and I am sure that it has not been easy for you to find the money. Since then too I have learned how much the department here in Berkeley has counted on my staying here, and how unwilling they are to see me leave at Christmas. It has come to seem to me a little wanton, for me to throw over this job where the money is available, and where as the only theoretical physicist I have a certain usefulness, to come to Pasadena, where in some ways at least I should be a burden, and where many men can do as well and better the things which I can do.

But with the third, Spring, term, the situation is different; for I can have that in Pasadena, as we have planned it for this year, without interfering essentially with my work here. I should like if it is at all possible to come to the Institute for this third term next year. In this way I should not have to sever altogether a connection which seems very precious to me, and should be able to work each year for a little time with the Pasadena physicists, and give such courses or seminars as would be useful to them. There is no need for me to know at once whether this can be arranged for next year; but I do very much hope that it will be possible to arrange it.

With cordial and respectful greetings,

Robert Oppenheimer

OPPENHEIMER AND HIS STUDENTS spent time with Niels Bohr at Caltech when Bohr lectured there in the spring of 1933. After Bohr's return to Copenhagen, Oppenheimer reported on his own attempt to explain the physical process involved in the appearance and disappearance of pairs of electrons, one positive and the other negative, and also examined the self-consistency of the theory.

85 | TO NIELS BOHR

Pasadena
June 14. [1933]

Dear Professor Bohr,

I am sending to you a copy of the letter which Dr Plesset and I have written for the Physical Review [1933b].[a] As you will see, we have not made much progress since you left, and have had to leave a number of points quite undecided. Of these the most important still seems to me the question of the validity of our calculations for the cosmic rays. We think that we have found a method free of all doubtful approximations which will give us the answer to this question; but the problem is analytically quite hard for us; and it may be some time before we can tell you the answer. We want to postpone publishing the details of the calculations until we can clear up the doubtful points.

With regard to the general formulation of the theory, the situation is just what you had prepared us to expect: there is, it appears, a complete correspondence between the new formalism of the transformation theory, and the possibility of observing by necessarily classical experiments the positives and the pairs. Thus one can only hope by such experiments to detect the positives when one uses an experimental arrangement for which one may abstract from their creation and disappearance; and this corresponds exactly to the requirements of the transformation theory, according to which it is only in 'coordinate systems' corresponding to such experimental arrangements that one can give any direct physical interpretation of the wave functions of the Dirac theory. In the general case the functions can not be interpreted in the same simple way as in the Dirac Jordan transformation theory.

It seems now hardly likely that I shall be able to come to Ann Arbor. At least I can and shall send you an account of what we are doing; but for me that will be a very poor substitute. You must know how happy I was in your visit, and how grateful for the generous and fruitful hours which you gave to talking with us, and helping us to understand what we were talking about. I envy Plesset very much his year in Copenhagen.

Oppenheimer

a. Milton Plesset was a National Research Council fellow working with Oppenheimer at Caltech; he subsequently spent a year with Bohr in Copenhagen.

OPPENHEIMER DID NOT GO to Ann Arbor. Instead he spent much of the summer of 1933 at the ranch in the Pecos, continuing his work on the theory of the positive electron. In the fall he wrote to Frank, who, after receiving the B.S. degree from Johns Hopkins in June, followed his brother's footsteps and began graduate study at the University of Cambridge.

86 | TO FRANK OPPENHEIMER

Berkeley
October seventh [1933]

Dear Frank,

A good many hours and miles are between us now; and I write with that curious tentativeness which separation gives, with a sense of clumsiness, as though one were trying with a very long stick to make at an immense distance some very delicate adjustment. But I have had your good letter from Baltimore, and seen your last almost asymptotic one to father: and want you to have some word of me, and want very much to hear. You know how happy I was with your decision to go to Cambridge, and that I have very high hopes of the fruitfulness of the year there. I know that it was not an easy decision to make; and inevitably there will be hours when you will regret going; but I think that these will not be the predominant hours, and that in the changed and perhaps fundamentally more rigorous life you will find new interest and conviction and competence, learning again and perhaps more deeply the taste of work. And particularly I hope that in this and in the very simple program you had made you will not be troubled by the lateness of your decision, the inevitable and infuriating red tape. Fowler wrote that it would at this stage be not at all easy to enter a college; and I have forgotten how much depends on that: whether you can get a tutor without that, or take the tripos at all. You will know all about that now; and I want only to urge you not to stay on in Cambridge unless you can get really the simple things for which you went: work in the laboratory and some help and direction in the mathematics. I hardly think it worth staying in Cambridge for lectures. They are as I remember them abominable; nor for the seminars, which however diverting are surely not now what you most want. If Cambridge—and I hardly think this will be so—should be a washout, why then do you not write to Kramers and, if he can have you, go to work with him? The theoretical physics should be awfully good in Cambridge, with Dirac there and Born;[a] and I envy you your time there. But that will only be valuable to you if first you find the honest schooling which you want. And you will let me know?

Leaving by plane is no less a nostalgic leaving; and this year as always it was a very wistful leaving for me: perhaps even a little more wistful, because there could be less of that reassurance than before that we should meet again in the mountains by the summer. You must have had a hellish time getting camp closed on such notice. The whole incident with Art [Winsor] has seemed to me shameful and unhappy, and I cannot forgive the skipper [Postmaster Viles] for his absurd vindictiveness, nor ourselves for having delayed until it was too late getting Mrs Harvey's permission. She gave us a long story, which may have some truth in it, as how Art had once lived at their place, and as how they had had to go to law to get him out, and he still owed them lots of rent. I take it that you were in some measure able to soothe Art; and the fence was a grand idea. As to Viles buying the place, I think it unlikely enough, though K [Katherine Page] too wrote of it; but we have confirmed our option and have reminded Mrs Harvey of it; and when in the next fortnight I go south, I shall see her and find out whether she is planning to run out on us. Father thought that if the skipper did not have too long nor too inclusive a lease, and if we could get the property for about 4500, we ought to buy it. But that is still of course open. After I have seen Mrs Harvey I shall write to Art; and perhaps I may have something pleasant to tell him.[b] K wrote me a fine long letter, but there was little in it that will be new to you. She had then still no plans for the winter, and no more certain ones for the horses. She had been riding Io, and asked to keep him over the winter if she were in Santa Fe. I told her yes please of course, and asked her to have a look at Martinez' elusive sorrel, and, if he were unsatisfactory, to write to her cousin to look about. From Roger [Lewis] I have had a note or two, characteristically conscientious, but without reference to Johnson's mare. From Gloria not a word, though either Father or I might have expected it: Are we to put significance in that silence?[c] Next to your getting camp closed, Ichabod's faithfulness is the most astonishing item of the autumn; you must have had a grand trip.

Father has had a perfect visit here. He has been well and happy and just busy enough, finding as I had hoped the life in Berkeley immensely congenial; living very simply; and achieving an almost unheard of popularity in his short visit. He will be leaving in about a fortnight, perhaps coming south with me and leaving from there. Even if later he should plan to go to Europe, he would have so six weeks at least in New York; and he wants at least that. You will be sure won't you to make your plans for the Christmas holidays early enough so that he will know. If you are coming back then, he will surely not go abroad until later, if at all; if you are not coming, he might well join you for a fortnight on the continent. What I do, though in a much more minor way, may depend on this too. They have asked me to make a speech in Cambridge about the positive electron—Cambridge here, of course. And of course I will not go if you and F are both abroad; but if you are here and they will pay, as I think, my trip, then probably I should come. Father got me a new Gamaliel. He is called Garuda, after the mechanical bird which the carpenter made for his friend the weaver who loved a princess. He combines in an unbelievable way the simple faithfulness of Gamaliel and Ichabod's bulky splendour.[d]

The work with the pairs and the MNtory has gone along nicely; and we have answered now all the questions which were still obscure at Perro Caliente: confirming the result that the theory gives the wrong answer for the production of very high energy pairs; showing that to all orders Dirac's equation gives correct energy values for all static fields; showing that the wave functions of the pair theory can—by horrible determinants—be expressed in terms of a complete set of Dirac solutions for the same problem; showing that the theory gives a consistent interpretation of our inability to localize a particle by experiment within hc/E, and yet does allow us to determine exactly the charge density of a system with unknown number of particles: in general cleaning up the formalism. But quite recently we have run into convergence difficulties, not unconnected with the breakdown of the theory at high energies, and similar to those of the radiation theory, which very seriously limit its applicability. All this will have to get itself written and published soon. Of other news in physics the most striking is Lawrence's, who has definitely established the instability of the H2 nucleus. It decomposes upon collision into neutron and proton, to the tune of about six million volts.[e] That makes as far as I can see a hopeless obstacle to Heisenberg's pseudo qm of the nucleus. Born's letter to Nature I saw; but my hunch is that it is empty. If you get to hear more of this, will you let me know? Lawrence is going to the Solvay congress on nuclei, and I shall have double chores in his absence.[f]—I have been reading the Bhagavad Gita with Ryder and two (2) other sanskritists. It is very easy and quite marvellous. I have ridden twice but not enough; I get to be very bad tempered. Have you got yourself a bike with three speeds?

Let me know then how it is, and write to me what you will of your days and your self. This year within the limits of the space between us and of my procrastination let us keep a word or two between us. You will be lonely perhaps and despondent; you will not always feel like writing; the word between us will necessarily be partial only; but let us keep it.

con cariño

Robert

Val [Ruth Valentine] and Mac [Donald Macfarlane] and Nat [Natalie Raymond] and Ernest [Lawrence] send you greetings, and many others I have forgotten.

a. After Max Born was dismissed from his Göttingen professorship in April 1933 because he was a Jew, he held a temporary appointment as Stokes Lecturer in Cambridge.

b. The Oppenheimers had been caught up in a feud between two neighbors in Cowles over the pasturing of cattle. Mrs. Harvey eventually sold the ranch to the Oppenheimers.

c. Gloria Kauffman was a college friend of Frank Oppenheimer's.

d. Garuda was Oppenheimer's third car. Gamaliel, its predecessor, was the car bought by his father in March 1930, over his protests, to replace the ominously groaning Chrysler. Ichabod was Frank's Packard.

e. Lawrence's claim that the nucleus of heavy hydrogen (^{2}H), or the deuteron, disintegrated into a neutron and a proton was not in accord with theories of nuclear structure and was widely disputed. He later acknowledged that the observations and his interpretations were wrong.

f. A small group of leading scientists were invited to the Solvay Congress, held in Brussels every three years, to present papers on a current topic in physics. The choice of nuclear physics as the topic for 1933 and the invitation to Lawrence recognized the importance of the new field and his major role in its development.

The "almost unheard of popularity" with which Oppenheimer credited his father later impressed Ruth Uehling, whose husband Edwin was a postdoctoral fellow at Berkeley from 1934 to 1936. "We had a marvelous time together," recalls Mrs. Uehling of her friendship with Julius Oppenheimer, then some thirty years her senior and to her an elderly and delicate man. He stayed at the Hotel Durant, and two or three times a week she and two other university wives would join him for lunch and bridge. In the evening, if her husband and Robert were doing physics, Mr. Oppenheimer would take her out to dinner and sometimes to the theater. He had recently had a slight stroke and tired easily. When midway through the play she saw his head nod, she would ask, "Mr. Oppenheimer, do you like this play very much?" "I don't think it is very good," he would reply, obviously relieved to get back early to the Durant where, he said, the old ladies kept him up too late. Robert often spent evenings with his father. New friends like Mrs. Uehling thought the relationship easy and uncomplicated.[23]

The "work with the pairs and MNtory" refers to Oppenheimer's attempt to build a full field theory of negative and positive electrons which Dirac had so brilliantly begun. Oppenheimer used the letter N to designate the number of negatives and the letter M for the number of positives. The coined word "MNtory," which suggests an inventory of the particles, appears only in letters to his brother and not in published papers on the subject, though the papers are studded with Ms and Ns.

Oppenheimer's commitment to developing a consistent theory is clear in his letters to Frank and to George Uhlenbeck. The existing theory was adequate for a system with a fixed number of particles, but pairs of particles were continually appearing and disappearing. When positive and negative electrons meet, they annihilate each other, and their mass is changed into energy according to Einstein's relationship $E = mc^2$. This energy is radiated in the form of photons. To describe these complex interactions required a new relativistic quantum mechanics, which became known in general as quantum field theory. However, the mathematics of the theory broke down when applied to high energies. Instead of converging to produce a finite and usable numerical result, the calculations gave an infinite result that could not be interpreted. Oppenheimer was convinced that the problems were not mathematical and that the trouble was in the theory itself. He believed that there was a limit to the applicability of quantum mechanics as a description of natural phenomena.

Even when computation was possible there were other difficulties. Some of the data reported by experimentalists were tentative and some proved to be erroneous. In addition, the interpretation of data by experimentalists and theorists alike was based on the assumption that only electrons and positrons were being observed, whereas other, as yet unidentified, particles were also involved. Hence, the new theoretical explanations often appeared to disagree with the data. This was discouraging, and efforts to improve the calculations did not seem to help. During this period of his work, Oppenheimer was keenly aware of these discrepancies. As his student Robert Serber later commented: "His appreciation of experimental results and his close association with experimental physicists, a strength in other aspects of his work . . . may have been a weakness [in his early cosmic ray work]."[24]

87 | TO GEORGE UHLENBECK

[Berkeley
Fall 1933]

Dear George,

Thank you very much for your good letters, and for the manuscript of the note with Fermi.[a] With your results, even in detail, we are in complete agreement. Carlson, who during the summer went through the work, had found a different formula; but there was a simple mistake in what he did that we found without trouble. With your general conclusions we are also absolutely in agreement, in that we too can see no way of accounting for the hard scattered radiation. This point puzzled me very much last spring, and Plesset and I only wrote so conservatively of it [1933b] because we were not sure how relativistic calculations would fall out; we thought too of the possibility of initial recombination in the atom in which the positive was born; but this too failed to give a large enough result. Now just recently I have heard from Plesset that Jacobsen has repeated with Miss Meitner's strong source the experiments on lead, and that he finds sensibly no radiation scattered except that at about half a million volts: he finds neither the million volt nor the unmodified radiation.[b] I hope this result is right, because it would be very hard I think to understand any sensible intensity of high energy radiation.

During the summer and since my return we have been working at two things; they are both quite clear now, and perhaps I may write you a little of them; they are not yet written up; or I should send you a much more complete account. For one thing we have wanted to look again at the calculations of the absorption coefficient of very hard gamma rays, where our perturbation method appeared so dubious, and the results so definitely in disagreement with experiment. We have found a way of calculating this absorption which for large enough gamma ray energies appears to be completely justified; and the answer is definite. The method rests upon the fact that for very high energies the particles are ejected within a very narrow range of angles . . . The results are even more definitely in disagreement with experiment than those which Plesset and I got; for small enough Z [atomic number] we get just our old result; whereas for larger Z we get a larger result than before, and increasing more rapidly than Z^2. I think therefore that the methods of the radiation theory give completely wrong results when applied to wave lengths of the order of the electron radius. For radiation which is not too hard the theory presumably gives the right answer; and I understand that in Cambridge they are making more careful and laborious calculations just for this case.

The other points we have been looking at have to do with the development of a general formalism and its physical interpretation. The formalism has some resemblance to Schroedinger's earlier attempts . . . The theory seems very pretty to me, and is in every way consistent with the possibilities of measurement, as long as one neglects the atomicity of the charges themselves.

You must give my love to Else. We have so many charming benefactions of hers which I have never acknowledged; no finite apology will ever make that up: sambals, and books, and the Kopenhagen Faust,[c] and the most perfect letters. Do what you can for me, George, in this great fault; I have not the effrontery myself to ask for pardon.

Van Vleck has written me of the projected symposium at Christmas.[d] My father is with me here, and Frank is in Cambridge; and it is not very likely that I will be coming east. You will have then to do the theory all by yourself. I shall send you copies of the work we have been doing, if it ever gets written up; and we must start at that very soon.

I have just heard of Ehrenfest's death.[e] Knowing your deep affection for him, and the close bond there was between you, I know that this will be a sorrow, a curiously terrible sorrow, which will stay by you. All of us who knew him must feel this; but to you who were so especially his friend, a word of deep sympathy. None of us, who were his students, shall be quite free of guilt in this his desperation.

Robert

a. Enrico Fermi was at that time professor of theoretical physics at the University of Rome.

b. J. C. Jacobsen was on the staff of Niels Bohr's Institute for Theoretical Physics at the University of Copenhagen. Lise Meitner was head of the radioactive physics department of the Kaiser Wilhelm Institute for Chemistry in Berlin-Dahlem.

c. A humorous parody of Faust, emphasizing current dilemmas in physics, was written and performed by physicists in April 1932 at the annual conference at Bohr's Institute.

d. In 1933 John H. Van Vleck was professor of physics at the University of Wisconsin.

e. Paul Ehrenfest, with whom Uhlenbeck had studied at Leiden, committed suicide on September 25, 1933, at the age of fifty-three.

OPPENHEIMER TALKED ABOUT the positive electron at the December 28–30 Boston meeting of the American Physical Society. There he found George and Else Uhlenbeck and persuaded them to return to New York with him and spend a few days at the smaller Park Avenue apartment to which Mr. Oppenheimer had moved after his wife's death.

Something about the Boston meeting had annoyed Uhlenbeck and Oppenheimer, and Uhlenbeck's description of it as "abominable" launched a game of French adjectives which kept them amused for some part of the train trip to New York. After a long pause Oppenheimer triumphantly concluded the game with "zezayant" (a form of the verb "zezayer," to lisp, which is unfamiliar to lexicographers). This was the kind of simple intellectual fun, mused Else Uhlenbeck, that they enjoyed with Robert in those days. The time in New York was gay and busy. The small apartment was crowded with a steady flow of guests.[25]

Returning to California by train, Oppenheimer wrote Uhlenbeck a short note on January 6 "to establish my good heart in the matter of letters," and to say how much he and his father had enjoyed the holiday visit. He had found Flaubert's *Lettres à sa nièce Caroline*, would read them on the train and send them along. He reported long talks at Columbia and Princeton about the electron–positron pairs.[26]

Transcontinental train trips were useful for reading and correspondence. The following day as the train crossed the prairies, Oppenheimer wrote a long letter to Frank on the portable typewriter with which he usually traveled.

Iris, Ichabod, Montauk, and La Cueva, offered to Frank as anchors against the disorienting effect of Cambridge, were, respectively, horse, car, and places that Robert and Frank had enjoyed together. (Of Montauk, at the tip of Long Island, Frank later recalled: "It had a wildness that my brother and I both loved. He and I drove out there again in 1948 and had the finest and longest talk together of all those during the postwar years.")[27]

88 | TO FRANK OPPENHEIMER

Kansas.
Jan 7, [1934]

Dear Frank,

There has seldom been a time when I have missed you so as in these last days, and never I think a more pressing plenty of things to write to you. And as always the writing is made a little difficult by my great vagueness of your coordinates. From Lawrence I know that, at least to his uncritical eye, you were fine and busy and eager;[a] your sweet and master[ly] letters to

Father tell me only good; and the cables gave us a pleasant suggestion of Lourdes and olive trees and the south of France. From these fragments I must put you together, and I want very much some direct word of you, which shall confirm or disprove the construction. I take it that Cambridge has been right for you, and that physics has gotten now very much under your skin, physics and the obvious excellences of the life it brings; I take it that you have been working very hard, getting your hand in in the laboratory, and learning mathematics at close hand, and finding in this, and in the natural austerity of life in Cambridge, at last an adequate field for your unremitting need of discipline and order. And all this is marvellous, and just what together we had hoped of your crossing. What I want to hear is that Cambridge, and in particular the quiet and not always sound eclecticism of the jeunesse dorée, is not getting too much under your skin: is leaving you peaceful and with some resources of self assurance, and leaving intact your specifically American competences, Iris and Ichabod, Montauk and La Cueva— This letter I shall send on from Lamy, of which even the name will make for you a mixed nostalgia. I shall be stopping to see Katherine [Page]: only for a day, for the time of my prodigious holiday is nearly over. Perhaps she and I will go together to visit the horses at Moriarty, or, if the weather is very inviting, up the cañon, or to Truchas. Then I must go on to California.

Father, as you know, is planning to come to see you late in February. The holiday with him was very sweet, although necessarily so hectic and populous that it was not always good for his health. He was in very good spirits, content with you and me; less well I think than in Berkeley, but needing chiefly rest and quiet. He is going to the doc this week, and from that we shall know whether he needs to take even more terrific precautions than before. He wants of course to see the German people, and perhaps, against all reason, will even go to Germany. He is planning to come west again early in August, and to come out with me to Berkeley. I hope then that he will stay there a long time, because everything in the life there is good for him, its ease and simplicity and friendliness and cordial climate. But I hardly think that he will abandon his New York apartment before next year. As for the summer, it is too early yet for us to be sure of our plans; but I would like you to be thinking of it, and would like to hear of any certainties you have. Ernest Lawrence told me that you had been thinking seriously of staying abroad, and of course there will be some reason for doing that, though I rather hope that you will not. If it is irgendwie possible I shall open Perro Caliente, though probably, if you do not come, for not more than a month. They have asked me to come to Ann Arbor, and would be willing to have me come for as short a time as three weeks. And George and Else [Uhlenbeck] have looked with great favor, though as yet without certainty, on coming with me then to the mountains. I thought that that would be equally good whether you were coming or not, for I know how fond you are of them. Roger [Lewis] I saw too in New York, though not as much as I should have liked. He was happy in his work, sound and marvellous as always. He is probably going to the Hopkins medical school next year, and spoke with heartening hopefulness of his coming to camp this summer. But he is very much worried—and this you must hear from him and not from me—about his father, who is drinking constantly heavily abusively and disastrously. Roger is himself now a l'ombre des jeunes filles en fleur. But the jeunes filles are indescribably and mournfully dreadful little bitches. He had one along on the New Year's eve party we gave, with George and Else and Nat [Natalie Raymond] and the Ritters: a wild confused, very amusing party saddened by Roger's deplorable bonds. And from what Cherniss and Curtis Ritter told me, he has an even more ghastly lady in Baltimore.[b] But this has not spoiled him at all, only given him spells of depression so overwhelming that even the disciplined and stable Roger can not hide them. He still hates Gloria [Kauffman] with an intransigent hatred, but does not speak of her so much. She is apparently well and busy and not unhappy; I should have tried to see her if my time east had not been so insanely busy and rushed. Of course everyone sends you greetings and love, and we drank many toasts to you: Nat, George and Else, Cherniss, many physicisti, all the californiacs. George and Else stayed with us, crowding the tiny apartment, but perfectly welcome. In Boston we talked on the positive, and everyone liked the theory—the now quite overgrown NMtory of the mountains; and more technically I spoke at MIT, Columbia and Princeton. I made many efforts to get jobs, chiefly for Furry and Wolfe,[c] and there I think succeeded. But for the most part I was met with offers for myself, or requests to come to Berkeley. For all his sketchiness, and the highly questionable character of what he reports, Lawrence is a marvellous physicist. But I think that he is probably wrong about the disintegration of the deuton [deuteron].

The work went well all autumn. I sent Dirac a copy of a long discourse on MNtory [1934b] but even since the writing we have come on some new and simplifying things. I do not know how Dirac liked what we wrote; but if you see him you might warn him that we shall send more presently, in which, by extending the group of transformations under which positive and negative states could be defined, we can greatly shorten some of the proofs, treat the gauge invariance much more adequately, and take into account the nonobservability of the wave functions of the theory. This extension, while it is not absolutely necessary for making a sensible theory, seems to me very clarifying. It makes the nonobservability of the susceptibility of the pairs even more certain. We also worked a good deal on the specific pair production probabilities. The only ones with which we were quite satisfied when I left Berkeley were those which Leo [Nedelsky] and I published for the internal conversion. There is no doubt that the theory is quite wrong for cosmic ray energies, but it is a devil of a job to see just exactly what it gives. That Born approximation which gives the logarithm, we have had of course a long time; but it is not right. I had been doing Sanskrit and teaching, and this term too will read the Timaeus. The life in Berkeley is quiet and pleasant and there is always plenty to do. Garuda is a lamb. I have driven him ninety five without opening the throttle wide.

There is wine now everywhere, and the country has a better look. In San Francisco one can get for fifty cents a table d'hote vin y compris a discretion. The Napa valley vineyards have some lovely things, especially the Beaulieu vineyard at Rutherford: the dryest Chablis, and a fragrant heady Chateau Yquem, and an airy sparkling burgundy to wash down wild duck. Liqueurs are still expensive, but there is good whiskey. And an even greater change: Nat has learned to dress. She wears long graceful things in gold and blue and black, and delicate long earrings, and likes orchids, and even has a hat. To the vicissitudes and anguishes of fortune which have brought this change to her I need say nothing. —With books it is not so good, new ones. I have reread all Flaubert, with ever growing wonder and delight. We have about finished the Gita, and are going to try some more Kalidasa. There are each year an immense number of competent and worthy french novels, but none that I have seen to write home about. Leo tells me that some of the new Russian things are good, and I shall try them.

This is Kansas, and there is dirty snow on the ground and a dirty sky. But the ground is beginning to rise, and there are rolling hills, as we get nearer the mountains, and tomorrow before dawn I get to Lamy. I wish that you were here with me; and I know that if you can you will come next summer. Do not come unless you can come peacefully, the heart good about the work. If you feel like it, how would it be to have a week or so in Ann Arbor?

We do not need to buy Perro Caliente. I have seen Mrs Harvey several times, and she is not eager to sell, and would not, I think, even if opportunity offered, which it has not, sell to another. The skipper [Viles] has lost the post office to Winsor, and is correspondingly furious.

con cariño

[no signature]

a. Lawrence stopped in Cambridge on his way home from the Solvay Congress in October.

b. Curtis and Charles Ritter were friends of Frank Oppenheimer's at Johns Hopkins. Harold Cherniss, a classicist on the Cornell faculty since 1930, first met Oppenheimer in Berkeley in 1929 through his wife, Ruth Meyer, in whose grandmother's home Julius Oppenheimer stayed when he arrived in New York from Germany. The families had remained close friends; Ruth Meyer and the Oppenheimer boys grew up together. Interview with Harold Cherniss by Alice Kimball Smith, April 21, 1976, pp. 1–2. Interview with Ruth Meyer Cherniss by Alice Kimball Smith, November 10, 1976.

c. Wendell H. Furry and Hugh C. Wolfe were National Research Council fellows who worked with Oppenheimer, Furry from 1932 to 1934, Wolfe from 1929 to 1931.

IN THE MIDST of the exciting new developments in physics in the early 1930s, events were taking place in Europe that would have a profound effect on the international community of physicists. Hitler officially came to power on January 30, 1933, and by April Jewish university professors were being dismissed from their posts. Efforts to aid the displaced scholars were immediately made by their colleagues in other countries. A specific appeal for help in providing financial support and positions for dismissed German physicists was made by Eugene P. Wigner and Rudolf W. Ladenburg, both of whom had emigrated from Europe and joined the Princeton physics faculty before the Nazis came to power. In December 1933 they circulated a letter, in German, to a small group of physicists at American institutions who had either emigrated from Germany or been educated there. This group was asked to set aside two to four per cent of their income for two years to aid "former colleagues in our field" who had lost their posts in Germany and to suggest possible positions. Oppenheimer received the letter through Theodore von Karman of Caltech, who had emigrated in 1928. Sponsors of the project were reluctant to ask for help from the broader community of American physicists because of the scarcity of jobs and because native anti-Semitism was sometimes reflected in the hiring policies of American universities.[28]

89 | TO THEODORE VON KARMAN

Berkeley
Sunday [ca. March 1934]

Dear von Karman,

Thank you for your good letter, and for the enclosure from Wigner and Ladenburg. I shall be glad to contribute to the fund which is being raised, and think that I could promise three percent of my salary for the next two years. My salary is unfortunately not very large, but this would come to about a hundred dollars a year. I think that the committee has been wise in not asking for help from American physicists, and I appreciate the circuitous delicacy with which they have approached me.

Professor Franck[a] gave me a message for you. It was to remind you of a man called Tiersch, of whom you will already have heard. I believe that Franck thought that he might be of use to you in the Institute, and that he

173

thought that you would be more solicitous in seeing what could be done than would Millikan. He sent you also very warm greetings.

Before long I shall be again in Pasadena. I shall not in the interval write directly to Wigner until I have heard from him.

With all good wishes

R Oppenheimer

a. James Franck moved to the United States in 1935. After three years at Johns Hopkins he was appointed professor of physical chemistry at the University of Chicago.

WRITING TO UHLENBECK about their forthcoming reunion at the Ann Arbor physics summer school, Oppenheimer described his latest efforts to develop a consistent theory of electron–positron pairs. He was attempting to apply the test of "gauge invariance," a technique used by physicists to determine the internal consistency of any equation involving electromagnetic forces. The complicated formulas which Oppenheimer and his colleagues had developed in an effort to place Dirac's fruitful theory on a logically defensible basis were still not formally completely sound. These difficulties were to plague physicists for more than a decade.

90 | TO GEORGE UHLENBECK

Berkeley
Sunday [ca. March 1934]

Dear George,

Professor Randall will have had my wire and letter saying yes to the invitation. I did not tell him, and perhaps I hardly need to tell you, that the most urgent argument of all for my coming is that I should be taking you and Else away with me in July. It is marvellous that you will come, and I look to the summer with a vast and childish eagerness. Whether Frank will come home from England is not yet decided, but I think that he will find it hard to resist when he hears that you are to be in the mountains. The Lawrences speak of coming too for a short visit; but that will depend a little on how the Ann Arbor arrangements can be made. As you will have heard, he would much prefer to come in the early part of the summer, when we will be there: partly for that, and partly for practical reasons involving long transcontinental journeys. If it could be arranged for him to come the first part of the summer, that would be very nice. But I realize that that will destroy the symmetry of the summer session.

First I must write you a little about physics. I am sending you a copy of a letter we are adding to our paper [1934b, 1934e], just about these gauge questions. For when I returned after Christmas we went into these questions, and also the Lorentz invariance, with a gloomy and determined thoroughness, and found to our distress that in spite of our proofs even in the simplest cases we did not have the necessary invariance. We then with great care went through the Lorentz proof, formulating it in various ways, and convincing ourselves—and we would be prepared to present these arguments before any audience—that the formal proofs were right, and that they established all that formally one needs. At this point came a letter from Pauli. He told us that he had set Peierls to calculating the magnetic susceptibility, and that they had found what earlier we had—that it was not independent of gauge[a] . . . Then came a period of long and arduous searching, the details of which, and of our arguments, I must some day tell [you]. The search was absolutely sterile, and we are now persuaded, although not beyond conviction, that no classification of states can be found in which the number of particles can be given a gauge invariant definition. This, coupled with the fact that the difficulties appearing in our formulation are, as far as expectation values of physical quantities are concerned, all due to convergence difficulties and the failure of the theory for high energies, has brought us to the point of view formulated in the letter I send you. We are prepared to believe that the theory can be improved, but we are skeptical, and think that this will not be so on the basis of quantumtheoretic field methods. This point should be settled by summer; either Pauli or Dirac will have found the improvement, or they will have come with us to share the belief that it does not exist. If these points had been as clear to us as they are now, our paper would have been written rather differently, and we should have put a good deal less emphasis on our configuration space functions. Pauli had in general only very friendly things to say of the paper, except for these miseries of gauge; Bohr had only a cordial word to say, and the promise of a paper of his own on observability in relativistic theory. And from Dirac we have not had a murmur . . . Then there is the experimental evidence, and the depressing proclamations of Gray and Tarrant.[b] From a careful study we have decided that the points which they hold against the theory rest on experiments inadequately precise to indicate a real discrepancy. Only one thing it is hard to discount: the existence, in heavy elements, of a hard scattered component . . . So much for the accursed pairs. Of other physics there is an important clarification in Lawrence's results, in the recognition that the protons and neutrons observed by him may in almost every case be accounted for by the capture by the bombarded nucleus of neutron and proton respectively from the deuton [deuteron] . . . I have little doubt that all the experiments which he originally construed as deuton disintegrations are to be interpreted in this way. It is true that this does not explain the disintegration of deutons in the target by protons; but these experiments are not nearly so trustworthy, and are I should think wrong. Lawrence of course is very far from admitting any of this. As for other physics, we have been enjoying ourselves with Bohr's fine but very very difficult paper on field measurements, Fermi's charming if wild calculations of beta decay (in which Pauli again believes),[c] and Born's efforts, which seem to us full of very grave errors, useless in the quantum theoretic parts, and very very dubious in the classical electrodynamics.

There are other miseries. Harvard asked Furry at once; but they asked me too. I have already said no twice, with long explanations. But Bridgman continues to write to me, and has at least half persuaded me, God knows how, that it is my duty to go there. I do not want to go, but after Bridgman's most recent letters I live in a morass of vacillation. Van Vleck will be there, you know. He was here for a time, and we saw a good deal of each other. I like him immensely, and we talked good solid oldfashioned physics to our common edification. I have written again to Stern, asking him to take Wolfe; I have not heard whether he will. Weyl wrote that perhaps Dirac would come next year to their institute; he asked me to come, but could do nothing for our students; they are still mostly without prospects.[d] I console myself with the Meghadhuta and the Timaeus, reading them with a painful pedantry. Early in April I go to Pasadena.

This is far too long a letter; and there are no questions to assure an answer. I wish you would drop at least a tiny note, and tell me anything that you may have learned, thought or felt about the unhappy pairs. And a word too of how you are. The visit at Christmas with you and Else was so sweet, and I miss you both very much. Then I think of next summer, and of our promised weeks in the mountains, and am impatient for the year to pass. My love to you both. And please, a word.

Robert

a. Rudolf Peierls returned to Zurich as Pauli's assistant in 1929 after receiving his Ph.D. from the University of Leipzig. Peierls was out of Germany on a Rockefeller Foundation fellowship when the Nazis came to power and decided not to return; in 1934 he was an honorary research fellow at the University of Manchester.

b. L. H. Gray and G. T. P. Tarrant were physicists at Cambridge University.

c. Fermi's theory of beta decay explained how electrons could be ejected from radioactive nuclei (although electrons do not preexist within the nuclei).

d. Van Vleck went to Harvard as professor of physics in the fall of 1934. Otto Stern had emigrated from Germany in 1933; in 1934 he was a research professor of physics at Carnegie Institute of Technology. Wolfe accepted an instructorship at City College of New York in 1934. Hermann Weyl, a 1933 emigre from Germany, became professor of mathematics at the Institute for Advanced Study in Princeton.

Furry promptly accepted the Harvard instructorship. He later recalled: "The question was whether anybody would get a job . . . I got a telegram from Harvard . . . while Oppenheimer was away at an eastern meeting . . . and I telegraphed back right away that I would take the job. Oppenheimer came back and was a little miffed with me for having been so fast about it. He said, 'You might have gotten a little bit more if you had played coy.' But I didn't feel at all inclined to play coy—Job? Can I have it? Let's make it as definite as possible as quick as possible.—That was my attitude."[29]

Furry's reaction was far more characteristic of the period than Oppenheimer's "morass of vacillation," for in 1934 not many academics had the luxury of choice. However, in his recollections Oppenheimer did not dwell on the miseries of indecision but rather on the sense of fulfillment that tied him to Berkeley and Caltech. "The fact is . . . I hardly left California until the war; I went to New Mexico summers . . . I came east to Ann Arbor summer school a couple of times. I gave a lecture on the positron at the Physical Society. But . . . [I moved] very little; I had really made a bed that I was content to be in . . . The fact that I stayed in one place, that I was interested in spreading this part of physics and [was] really rather widely interested in physics as a whole . . . that I felt responsible to my colleagues and for such students as came, and a lot of luck and accident, made it flourish pretty well."[30]

OPPENHEIMER'S increasing interest in nuclear physics, stimulated by new experimental results, is clear in a brief note of April 1934 to Ernest Lawrence. Fermi and his co-workers in Rome, using natural radioactive sources, had recently demonstrated that when almost any element is bombarded with neutrons, some of the atoms in the target are made artificially radioactive. Oppenheimer wondered what could be done with Lawrence's cyclotron, a much more powerful source of neutrons.

91 | TO ERNEST O. LAWRENCE

Pasadena
Monday [April 30?, 1934]

Dear Ernest,

I have just heard with delight the news of your election to the academy: I send you the warmest congratulations.[a]

This Friday I shall be driving north with Nordsieck, leaving after my lecture at four, getting in either Friday midnight or Saturday noon.[b] Keep a little time over the week end for me, for we shall have so many things of which to talk: not melodramatic, on my part; but probably pretty exciting on yours. Have you done anything on Fermi's β-activity? That he should find it with such a source is marvellous, & it should be relatively easy for you. Charlie [Lauritsen] had looked with Li n's [neutrons] & Al, but not carefully; & he found nothing— How does what I sent Malcolm [Henderson] fit your F-data?[c]

My love to Molly [Lawrence], & greetings to the laboratory.

Robert

a. In April 1934 Lawrence was elected to the National Academy of Sciences.
b. Arnold T. Nordsieck was one of Oppenheimer's students; he received his Ph.D. from Berkeley in 1935.
c. Malcolm Henderson was an honorary research fellow in Lawrence's laboratory.

SINCE 1929 when Hugh Wolfe, a National Research Council postdoctoral fellow, had worked with him at Caltech, Oppenheimer's growing reputation had attracted several NRC recipients. In 1932 when Wendell Furry was applying for an NRC fellowship, he was advised that Oppenheimer and Gregory Breit, professor of physics at New York University, were the two outstanding theoretical physicists with whom to work. Of the seven fellows appointed for 1934–35, three chose to work with Oppenheimer in Berkeley. Robert Serber, who had received his Ph.D. at Wisconsin in June and was planning to use his fellowship at Princeton, changed his mind after hearing Oppenheimer lecture and talking with him at the Ann Arbor summer session. Edwin A. Uehling was steered to Oppenheimer by George Uhlenbeck, supervisor of his graduate work at the University of Michigan.[31] The third was Frederick W. Brown, who had received his Ph.D. at Illinois in 1933. In May Oppenheimer wrote a note of welcome to Uehling.

92 | TO EDWIN A. UEHLING

Pasadena
May 12. [1934]

Dear Dr Uehling,

Thank you for your very good letter. I am delighted to hear that you have been awarded a research fellowship, and very happy that you are planning to come to Berkeley. I shall look forward then to your coming, and we shall do all we can to make your year pleasant and fruitful.

I hope that you do not overestimate my wisdom in matters statistical and gaskinetic. I have heard a good deal of your work from Uhlenbeck, and read your papers with great interest. But I feel confident that I shall learn more from you in these matters than I can teach you; and perhaps at times I shall be guilty of trying to distract you with the growing solicitudes of nuclear physics. You will be glad to know that Bloch will be at Stanford next year, and that we have already arranged for common weekly seminars. I am expecting Brown from Ohio, and probably Lowen and Johnson, in addition to the theorists now in Berkeley;[a] and we ought to have a good year of it.

With cordial greetings,

J R Oppenheimer

The housing problem in Berkeley is not at all difficult, and you should have no trouble finding a pleasant place to live after your arrival.

a. Irving S. Lowen and Montgomery H. Johnson, Jr., did not come to Berkeley; both accepted instructorships at New York University.

Felix Bloch, whom Oppenheimer had known in Zurich in 1929, left Germany in 1933. In 1934 he went to Stanford as an associate professor and with Oppenheimer organized the "common weekly seminars" for their theoretical physics students. One week the seminar was held at Berkeley; the next week at Stanford. Former Oppenheimer students remember the beautiful drive to Stanford, the stimulation of the seminar, and the social evening afterward.[32]

ON JUNE 4, as Oppenheimer prepared to leave Berkeley for the 1934 Ann Arbor summer session, he wrote a long letter to his brother, who had decided to stay in Cambridge, England, for a portion of the coming year. In the physics part of the letter he suggested variations on Frank's attempts to measure energies from gamma rays given off by heavy radioactive nuclei. Just as in an earlier period the properties of atoms had been studied by the light they gave off, in this period the properties of nuclei were studied by the gamma rays they emitted.

Pasadena.
June 4 [1934]

Dear Frank,

Only a very long letter can make up for my great silence, and for the many sweet things for which I have to thank you, letters and benevolences stretching now over many months. Benevolences starting with the precious Meghaduta and rather too learned Veda, through the crescendo of the pomerancia to the delightful Petrarch and Dante and the coffee pump, superb in chromium and complication. The Meghaduta I read with Ryder, with delight, some ease, and great enchantment; the Veda lies on my shelf, a reproach to my indolence; the curacao once only graced a crepe suzette, and was thereafter reserved to solemn drinkings of your health and happiness. The little books shall go with me this summer; and the coffee machine has performed so splendidly on the available 110 volts—with great obscene gushings from its two spouts,—that I hesitate to expose it to the 160 for which its label clamours. And not one of the presents but has evoked your presence and your tastes, and deepened the nostalgia for you, and made a sweet gratitude.

The nostalgia is very deep indeed, and now, with the coming of summer, reaches saturation. Your reasons for staying in Cambridge are wise and good, and I must admire you and approve that you give ear to them. But I shall miss you very very much, and comfort myself only with the thought that next summer surely you will come back. The summer in Cambridge is pleasant and casual, and a fine time for work. I hope that your work will go very well, and the time pleasantly, rewarding you for your virtue, and that you will take time for one good holiday at least before the autumn term.

I have been entirely delighted by your reversion to experiment, and by the problems you have been on. Have you completely abandoned the work with Klemperer—the recoil electron range method for gamma ray energies? Just recently both Lawrence and Lauritsen have taken to it, in connection with the six million volt gamma rays emitted by F and Li under proton bombardment. These rays fall on the ascending branch (ascending because of pair production) of the absorption curves in Pb, and check the theoretical absorption very beautifully; but the curves are quite flat, and it is hard to compute the energy within a million volts by absorption measurements alone. The Li ray Cockroft could surely get at 600 kilovolts; would you want to try it? Use a light absorber for the gamma ray, to get a large ratio of Compton recoil electrons to pairs. As for the nuclear energy levels, I am pretty much in agreement with your estimate of the difficulty of interpreting them. But something at least can be learned by correlation of the alpha beta and gamma results, and angular momenta assigned to the levels. And it was a [long] time after the study of the He spectrum that one came to know about the exclusion principle, the spin, and exchange forces. By the way, the evidence of Gray and Tarrant for nuclear levels seems to me completely vile; in fact Lauritsen and I are just writing a paper [1934g], trying to show how one can understand all the discordant results on gamma ray scattering by taking into account only Compton effect, annihilation radiation, and the continuous Xray spectrum from the secondaries. Have you seen what Gamow has done about angular momentum quantum numbers for the levels of the radioactive series? It will be wrong in detail but right in principle.[a] My own labors have been largely devoted to disentangling the still existing miseries of positron theory; and Furry and I have just published another manifesto [1934f] after which I hope to be able to forget the subject for a time. All of us have been working quite hard, and if you were here I should have a good many minor things of which to tell you; but only in conversation could I do sufficiently casual justice to them. As you undoubtedly know, theoretical physics—what with the haunting ghosts of neutrinos, the Copenhagen conviction, against all evidence, that cosmic rays are protons, Born's absolutely unquantizable field theory, the divergence difficulties with the positron, and the utter impossibility of making a rigorous calculation of anything at all—is in a hell of a way.[b]

In a fortnight I shall be driving to Ann Arbor, to have three weeks there, exposing positrons. Gamow will be there, and Uhlenbeck, and it should be pleasant. They asked me next year to go to Princeton, where Dirac will be, and permanently to Harvard. But I turned down these seductions, thinking more highly of my present jobs, where it is a little less difficult for me to believe in my usefulness, and where the good California wine consoles for the hardness of physics and the poor powers of the human mind.

I shall be in Ann Arbor only three weeks, and then go to Perro Caliente. As I wrote you, George and Else [Uhlenbeck] have promised to come, but I still feel some doubts of whether they will. After Mr Lewis' death I wrote Roger, asking him to bring his mother to camp if she would like it, and spending as long there as he would. He has written that they will come, and probably Mike too; the dates are uncertain still, but he speaks of opening camp early in July, before I get there. Katherine [Page] is at Los Pinos now of course. She brought our horses up with hers, for the country was very dry, and the horses only in fair shape. Art [Winsor] has built himself a cabin in the meadow below camp where Vixen threw me. I had hoped to stop by with Katherine on my way east, but it looks pretty cramped in time for that. If she has not already found herself her horse, we shall surely do that this summer. We are going to miss you terribly, and it is with very mixed feelings that I shall return to the mountains without you. About new horses I shall let the possibilities determine me; but with George and Else, who have never ridden, Vixen and Dink will have their uses.

Perhaps I shall see Father when I am at Ann Arbor; but I rather hope that he will go to the shore again, as he did last year, and then join me either in New Mexico or Berkeley to spend the autumn months. His visit last year became him famously, and I hope that he will stay longer this year. All your friends here are well, and ask of you often: Ruth and Richard [Tolman], Val [Ruth Valentine], Mac [Donald Macfarlane], Lawrence, and all the people who have been to camp. Nat [Natalie Raymond] speaks of stopping by at camp next summer. Lauritsen too asks of you, though you do not, I think, know each other. But he hopes that you will some day come to work with him, listens with eagerness to what you write of your work, and with despair sister to mine of your neutron electron cross beam experiment. (White in Berkeley by the way is doing a million volt proton on proton scattering—and that should be illuminating.)[e] Tolman's book you will have seen by now. Furry has a job at Harvard for next year, and under the strain of worrying about positrons has developed a somewhat schizoid sense of humour. Finally Garuda does ninetyfive with an unopened throttle, and seventeen miles to the gallon. Unlike the lamented Gamaliel he indulges in no solitary orgies of gurgling. Robert Brode will be in England on a Guggenheim fellowship.[d] He is a good egg, and will look you up. Do I know any of the people whom you see in Cambridge? Where do you live? and eat? Do you hear music? How is the flute? Do you go often to London? And have you heard the Kunst der Fuge? Buhlig played his two piano arrangement, very good I thought, at a Bachfest here; in its way it is not incomparable with the B minor mass, and to me as moving.

There are so many other questions: Do you read? Have you learned Italian? And the mathematics? Like you I feel an overwhelming frustration at the distance, such a desire to see you and talk to you as makes me play with the notion of going to Europe instead of the mountains for the five weeks I have. It is inexcusable that I write so little, but perhaps you will understand that it is the nostalgia which makes the writing hard. I would give my vacation at Perro Caliente for one evening there with you.

Write to me at the Physics department in Ann Arbor, and later to Cowles. I will write back, just such immense disorderly letters as this; there won't be again silences of such an order of magnitude as this.

[no signature]

a. Otto Klemperer, a refugee physicist from Germany, was at the Cavendish Laboratory in 1934. George Gamow had left his post as professor of physics at the University of Leningrad in 1933. He came to the United States in 1934 and was temporarily at the University of Michigan.

b. "Neutrino" was the name given by Enrico Fermi to the as yet unobserved particle proposed in 1930 by Wolfgang Pauli as a solution to an apparent contradiction in the problem of conservation of energy in nuclear disintegrations. The "Copenhagen conviction," advanced by Niels Bohr, turned out to be justified; by 1940 it was shown that primary cosmic rays were comprised mostly of protons. Max Born's theory was "unquantizable" because it extended the classical field theory outside the form whose relation to quantum field theory was known.

    c. Milton White was a graduate student working with Lawrence in developing the cyclotron.

    d. Robert Brode was professor of experimental physics at Berkeley.

EXCEPT FOR Frank's absence, the 1934 holiday at Perro Caliente was just the sort Robert loved best. Frank's friend Roger Lewis, dependable and fondly regarded by everyone, was getting the cabin in order with the help of Natalie Raymond when Robert arrived from Ann Arbor, accompanied by the Uhlenbecks.

For Else Uhlenbeck the visit to New Mexico was a delightful and novel experience. Two themes run through her recollections: what fun it was to be with Robert at this period of his life and what crazy situations he could get into. "How do you manage to make things so complicated?" she once asked. "It's a gift," Robert replied succinctly. The gift was fully evident to the Uhlenbecks that hot, drought-ridden July as they made their first long cross-country drive from Ann Arbor to New Mexico in "Garuda." With the top down, Robert drove the big Chrysler at high speed, racing trains across the open prairie. The second day out he got something in his eye. A doctor in Hannibal, Missouri, removed a piece of foreign matter, but the eyeball was badly scratched, and Robert had to wear a patch and turn the driving over to George for the next few hundred miles. As the heat became unbearable, they slept during the day and drove all night. Whenever they stopped for coffee Robert urged toast and eggs; the nights seemed a succession of breakfasts. As they drove into a Colorado town at four a.m. looking for a place to wash and relax, Robert again demonstrated his talent for doing things the hard way. The Harvey House would be near the railroad, so he asked a policeman the way to the station. "But there isn't a train for hours," said the officer. "But I don't want the station," said Robert. "I want the Harvey House." They settled in the end for an all-night cafe where a woman in the next booth, already drunk, sent the tired travelers into a fit of giggles by taking a long drink from the catsup bottle.

The Uhlenbecks enjoyed their stay in the Pecos as much as their host enjoyed having them. Else and Roger did most of the cooking, with Else's Indonesian dishes adding variety to the menus. Surprisingly there was no talk of physics, but a game of tiddleywinks by the fire—Robert had invented a lethally complicated version—was a part of the ritual before everyone tucked into cots on the porches beneath piles of Indian blankets. Cooking arrangements and plumbing were primitive. Pipes laid on top of the ground produced hot water during the day when the sun shone; at night the stove heated the water in both cold and hot taps.

There were expeditions, usually on horseback. Most went smoothly; vagaries of mountain weather and minor mishaps made others memorable. On one occasion Else, George, Roger, and Robert camped overnight at a lake below the Truchas peaks. Arriving in the afternoon, the three men, though well acclimated, were seized with altitude sickness. It was very cold in their sleeping bags that night, and in the course of keeping a fire going, someone lost the axe. By morning two horses had disappeared, leaving two mounts and the packhorse for four riders. Undeterred by their recent indisposition or the prospect of a slow trip home, the men decided to climb Truchas, the highest and most exposed summit in the southern Sangre de Cristos; they reached the top in a thunderstorm and came down soaking wet. The ride back was indeed exhausting, but a drink at Katherine Page's induced such euphoria that Else Uhlenbeck remembers the trip as a high point of the summer. Vixen and Iris, the two runaways, reappeared next morning, and Robert, clad in pink pajamas, chased them into the corral.[33]

These recollections encompass much that Robert did not need to include in his midsummer letter to Frank, who could so readily visualize the cabin, its occupants, and the trails over which they rode.

94 | TO FRANK OPPENHEIMER

Cowles
July 31 [1934]

Dear Frank,

Here at Perro Caliente you have been present so perfectly that it would be almost profanation to say that we have missed you, desperately. And after the constant converse which inevitably I hold with you, every hour, over every ride and every incident, there must be a certain strangeness in writing. Only for you it can not have been so quite, and you will want at least a word, and shall have it for your birthday, if planes and boats are faithful. You too will be feeling now a little lonely for us and nostalgic; and for a special birthday wish I think most of this, that your next shall be here, and with us together. Of the general birthday wishes you know: that you may have all your heart wants and all I want for you: peace and beauty and a good life, with the world pure in your eyes and unaltered. And now too that physics may be going well for you, with the intervals between rewards not too long nor lean, and that Cambridge in summer may be sweet, friendly, rich in reflection and trust. Very soon now the labs will be closing, and you will be having your self something of a vacation. I send you this money only as a sort of material witness of my wishes for the vacation. Perhaps you would like to go to Georgia. The country is marvellous, I hear, wild with great mountains; and it should be a good time of year.

The local news, sehr sehr stark schematisiert, Roger has sent you: how the horses are fine, rolling in fat, well, free, delightful; how Ruth and Nat and Val and George and Else have been here, G and E for the summer. Katherine is superb, surer and finer than ever; and now Los Pinos is full beyond capacity. K has had minor griefs with teeth and back; they are gone now and she looks fine. On the twelfth we shall take Lady and Io to Jarosa. Camp runs like a charm. The chief innovations are kerosene lamps and stove, and two army cots, both to meet the better the somewhat fluctuating and exorbitant demands of the summer's hospitality. This week end I expect Paul Horgan, grown wise and gentle and disciplined, and a writer of something close to high comedy, and his enchanting sister Rosemary. Maybe Felix Bloch will come, but otherwise there will be only sporadic further company. George and Else ride competently though hardly macroscopically by now; and at the moment Roger is outwitting George at tiddleywinks. About horses we have not sold nor bought, partly because of the very short time I am to be here, partly because this summer more than ever we have been grateful for Vixen and Dink, who are fast, completely competent, full of spirit, and even of a good deal of sense. We met Patches, Martinez' famous sorrel, near the Pecos Baldy divide the other day. He is five, gentle, high bred, straight but well gaited. I think of buying him, for he would stand up very well, and is ridiculously cheap. But that will depend a little on when Martinez brings him, and how he seems on closer looking. K has Midnight now, and I should be glad to get rid of him and Blue if there were any takers. K does not want a horse. Her chief problem is again bread and business for the winter. Perhaps she will go to New York with Rosemary Horgan.

I flew to New York for a day to see father. He was well, very well indeed, in good spirits, unworried about money, and very very sweet. He is in Nantucket now, and will come to Berkeley about the middle of September, for a long stay I hope. G and E are driving out there with me. It will be a busy year, and I have a lot of research fellows coming out to work. Ann Arbor was hot, strenuous, sterile and pleasant. I send you a snapshot Franz [Hirschland] sent me, charming and just, I think, and which you may like.

What else? A great great deal, but mostly that I miss you like hell, and wish you were here, and will not easily again spend a summer on the Pecos without you. Write to me, when you are on your vacation, lots about physics, your physics specially. Shall we see each other at Christmas? I can hardly arrange to come to the International congress in October.

con cariño

R

George Roger Else send love. Actuellement.

AFTER SIX WEEKS at Perro Caliente, the Uhlenbecks went on to Berkeley. Dining with a member of the physics department, they naturally talked about the strenuous life they had been leading and about Oppenheimer's prowess as camper and outdoorsman. Their host commented tersely that he didn't know Oppenheimer could do those things. The Uhlenbecks later learned that he was not an Oppenheimer admirer and had in fact been advocating his removal from the faculty with the argument that he had a tendency to TB and was physically frail.[34]

Complementing the Uhlenbecks' memories of Perro Caliente are equally nostalgic recollections of what it was like to be part of the scarcely distinguishable professional and social circles in Berkeley and Pasadena of which Oppenheimer was the center. Robert and Charlotte Serber and Edwin and Ruth Uehling arrived in Berkeley in August 1934 and became his close friends.

Serber later described the unpredictable merging of physics and social life: an evening session in the laboratory might break suddenly for a movie; a seminar would adjourn for dinner at Jack's in San Francisco, where Oppenheimer quietly paid the bill, or at some obscure Bay Area restaurant. Wives often joined the group. "The world of good food and good wines and gracious living was far from the experience of many [students]," recalled Serber. "We acquired something of his tastes. We went to concerts together and listened to chamber music. Oppie and Arn Nordsieck read Plato in the original Greek. There were many evening parties where we drank and talked and danced until late."[35]

Oppenheimer's kindness and his flair for misadventure are recurrent themes in anecdotes of this period. The Uehlings' first social evening with him, shared also by his graduate student Glen Camp, Camp's wife Ilva, and Melba Phillips, was the Berkeley counterpart of the Uhlenbecks' eventful camping trip a few weeks earlier. There was a gracious beginning with mint juleps at Oppenheimer's apartment at 2665 Shasta Road, to which he had recently moved from the Faculty Club, then dinner at a small Mexican restaurant in Martinez, where they drank wine and listened to music until after midnight. On the drive back to Berkeley, as Oppenheimer's Chrysler, with Ruth Uehling and Melba Phillips as passengers, paused at a stop sign, two cars sped past and collided, one of them the Uehlings' Buick, the other a police car, its radio still blaring, "Pick up two convertible coupes going seventy miles an hour." No one was seriously hurt, but the hand of a policeman was slightly injured and the side of the police car was crushed. At headquarters, Oppenheimer was booked for speeding. Uehling's charge of careless driving was reduced to the less serious one of not observing due caution after the offenders showed courteous concern about the officer's injured hand. The Camps' certified check saved for emergencies paid Uehling's ninety dollar bail. Oppenheimer, assuming full responsibility for the unfortunate denouement of his party, was at the Uehling's door early next morning with an offer, which was refused, to pay Edwin's fine along with his own. Three court appearances were required to settle the case, which, thanks to cordial relations that developed between the physicists and the police, was not reported in the press. This was a great relief to all participants, who had in mind the publicity which Oppenheimer had achieved the previous year when he took Melba Phillips for a drive in the hills above Berkeley, got out for a short walk, and absent-mindedly returned to his room at the Faculty Club without her or his car.[36]

AFTER EHRENFEST'S DEATH in the fall of 1933, H. A. Kramers was invited to succeed him as professor of theoretical physics at the University of Leiden. In due course, George Uhlenbeck was asked to take Kramers' chair at Utrecht. It was a difficult decision for Uhlenbeck and his wife. They enjoyed life in Ann Arbor, and Uhlenbeck had become firmly established in the American physics community. He did, however, decide to accept the Utrecht post and remained there from 1935 to 1939.

95 | TO GEORGE UHLENBECK

Berkeley
Sunday [ca. fall 1934]

Dear George,

Else's good and welcome letter has just come; but it is not of that, but of the unwelcome word in your own note, that I must write. The Utrecht blow has fallen, now when we were almost persuaded that the danger of it was past. I know that you must be very unhappy over this decision; and although I have nothing to say that you will not know already, it is of that that I must write.

I think that you will find that you must go, George. I say this with sorrow: personal sorrow because it will mean that you are much farther away, that we shall see each other rarely, that the American part of you, which has grown so big, will gradually disappear; and with a less personal solicitude, shared I know by many others, because you have done so much to bring order and light and decency into physics in this country, because there will be a great hole when you go. I know too in how many ways life in this country has been good to you, and for Else even to the point of breaking her frailer allegiance to Holland. But for you it has not done that, and in this I think lies your obligation to go. You said to me that some day you would return to Holland, that it is there that you would grow old. America, for all its charm and all that you have taken from it and brought to it, will always be your colonial period. You have spoken of the obligation which your parents' wishes would put on you; I think that the obligations are even deeper than that: I think that if you were to stay here now, when you are wanted in Holland, needed perhaps, asked certainly, you would in a sense make an outcast of yourself, and in repudiating this responsibility lose the right to return to Holland later, to make it your home, to grow old there. These things are vague for me of course, but I have such a feeling about America; and I know that they are strong in you, and that by them ultimately your decision must be made. I think I know how in the end that decision must be, must be for all the nostalgia that you will have for America. And it is because I think that you can postpone perhaps but cannot with peace escape the decision, that I write to you so, urging you to do what I hope you will not do. Nostalgia for America you will have, and not only for the Truchas Peaks. But if the time has come now when you must leave, let us be thankful that before your going we had a summer together, that you have ridden the ranges, and slept on spruce boughs. And let us think, if you must leave now, that you will come back some time to America; that by accepting in full the responsibilities of being a Dutchman, you will have earned for yourself the right to be a little of an American too.

Gamow, as perhaps you know, has a job at George Washington University; Hall and Johnson are to be at NYU.[a] My brother Frank has been in Morocco. He will come to America at Christmas, and unless he has time to visit here, I shall go east to see him. My father will not come out til after the new year. Katherine Page is still in New Mexico, and her plans for the winter still open.

In physics we work hard, but with no spectacular fruit; Uehling, like Serber and Brown, spends much time learning, and seems very content, though the calculations go very slowly . . . I have been worrying much over the high energies, and have started to write down a little for a quiet careful paper on these matters. I cannot find any Ansatz which works in the quantum theoretical calculations of ionization, though the cut off works fine in the classical ones. But this makes it a little hard to know whether the cut off is really a sensible procedure, and gives one no chance for detailed quantitative calculations . . .

Will you let me know, George, when your decision is taken? When would you be going: in June, as you had planned, or earlier? Give my love to Else, and thank her for her dear letter.

Affectionately,

Robert

a. Harvey Hall received his Ph.D. from Berkeley in 1931 and was an instructor in physics at Columbia from 1931 to 1934.

FRANK OPPENHEIMER returned from England to spend the Christmas holiday of 1934 with his father and brother in New York. Returning to California, Robert wrote to Frank as the train crossed Nevada, starting with physics, then shifting to news of family and friends.

Frank's studies at Johns Hopkins, which had long been a center for spectroscopy, had influenced his choice of nuclear spectroscopy as a research topic at the Cavendish Laboratory. He was working with C. D. Ellis, developing techniques to measure the intensity of the radiation emitted from radioactive nuclei, either directly or indirectly through interaction of the radiation with objects in its path. The problem was to get consistent results no matter which way the measurements were made, and theory was needed as a guide. Robert was working on the theory and offered ideas and suggestions to his brother. Some of the calculations involved were also indirectly needed for Robert's study of the pair production process.

96 | TO FRANK OPPENHEIMER

Nevada
Jan. 11 [1935]

Dear Frank,

First of the physics: It seems that my memory of the discrepancy between theory (using Dirac equation, retardation, H-like wave functions) & experiment for the K photoelectric discontinuity was right. The theoretical values are about 20–25% too low for the heaviest elements. Rabi, Hall, & (most authoritatively) Stobbe confirmed this, & agreed with me that an error in the same sense & of comparable magnitude might be expected in the internal conversion. How this error will vary with Z & V is still not clear to me, but offhand I should expect it to be most important near the threshold. As soon as I get to Berkeley Melber & I will have a careful look at the calculations, & see whether we cannot give you a sound estimate of the correction. It may be quite difficult to do tidily. At the moment I feel that this discrepancy which you have found is not to be taken too seriously, & that it is likely that the greater part of it can be explained by the inadequacies of the theoretical model. What did Hulme say? It is hard for me to judge how important your proposed geiger counter calibration is. Gurney's values might well be off by 15–20%; could you do much better than that?[a]

Just now the most pressing problems suggested by your level scheme seem to me—this just repeats what we said before—these:
1) Where does the level which, according to you, lies just below the $j = 0$ upper level of the totally converted line really belong? Not, surely, where it is?

189

2) Can one accept Bacher's suggestion of separate normal states for the two systems?[b] One might then expect the very soft combination line $j = 0 \to j = 0$ to be wholly internally converted, but hardly by the k-electrons: Can one make anything of this?

3) Is it really impossible to devise a scheme—even involving more levels—in which one can see, in general at least—why the added levels give no alpha-particles? This point seems to me the saddest of all, & the strongest argument against the essential soundness of your scheme. Would it be worth looking for a weak α-line where according to you one has most to expect one? (high energy, low j). Or has all been done in this connection that can be?

Tant pour ça; you will hear of the internal conversion as soon as we have anything to tell you.

It was bad, having you go, & the hour of your going completely desolating. There have been far worse partings, though, with less behind them and far less ahead. I sent the books the next day; have they come? Father—very naturally—was a bit wearied by the emotion of your leaving; but since then, in the pretty busy days in town, on the trip, has been very well, serene, & rather touchingly cheerful to be on his way with me. It has occurred to me that the lost art of writing letters might fill for him the empty mornings, & lessen the separation from New York. Tuesday he & Franz [Hirschland] & I had lunch. Franz was really enchanted by our records—had played them all—the variations & the quartet for the first time.

I had a good day at Columbia, but was glad, after talking with him, that you were not committed to Dunning—not a bad egg, but you would not like him.[c] Bacher went down & back with me to Princeton, kept talking of the Picasso. Princeton is a madhouse: its solipsistic luminaries shining in separate & helpless desolation. Einstein is completely cuckoo; Dirac was still in Georgia. I could be of absolutely no use at such a place, but it took a lot of conversation & arm waving to get Weyl to take a *no*. George & Else I saw briefly but with the old intimacy & sweetness; & some sadness, at the unwelcome future. Their plans for the summer are still uncertain; & it is possible that they will be then in Cambridge. If so it is possible—though it is not to that that I look forward—that you will see them. George was interested & duly wretched over RaC'. He has found a cute thing: the Fermi β-decay distribution curves come much better if one takes the coupling proportional to the neutrino-momenta—i.e. the ψ-vector   ; this pulls the maximum back to lower energies for electron & positron decay distributions. He has also checked internal conversion (by pairs) & low energy pair production; with surprising agreement with published values. Else eradicated the excess of sambal with a lunch of chile verde con queso. Both of them just about cried over Perro Caliente.

The last days were impregnated with Nat [Natalie Raymond]; her always new & always moving miseries. We heard Samuel together: that helpless pathetic idiotic smirking & convulsive creature, like a frog's leg on some very celestial circuit, making—or rather having made through him—the most marvellous Bach I hope ever to hear. Later we sat in a rose & violet fog on top of radio city, drinking—o horror—champagne cocktails & not listening to the mascara-eyed violinist wailing Home on the Range & Liebestod. Nat & I in an undesperate mood decided to get Val [Ruth Valentine] a superior but reasonably transportable phonograph. Chick [Ritter] said—& by his enthusiasms—showed—that he would like to make us one. He was fine, but Curtis [Ritter] still a bit enrhumée. The phonograph you will profit by next year.

The Ronsard has stayed with me. And on the train, as an alternative to making lectures & playing a newly fantastic variation of Rummy with father—I have slaughtered it by translation. The hexameter of the original was too heavy in English. I send it to you, gruesome though it is—for your malicious content.

Marion, the shrewd eyed wench, said 'What happened to Frank on his trip: he was so changed.' But father noticed nothing. And I thought myself that you were pretty close to perfect.

The Napoleon is with me, & the Chartreuse. Within me battle concupiscence & a sense of desecration.

What a letter this has turned to be. But you must write to me. Our coordinates redefined by this meeting, I feel less helpless about letters. Watch it with the flying.

I have asked Nat to discourage Rosemary [Horgan]'s tropism for Perro Caliente. I shall think of your coming unless I am forced by cruel fact to abandon it.

R

a. Martin H. Stobbe, a German physicist, was a member of the Institute for Advanced Study in Princeton from 1934–1937; Henry R. Hulme and Ronald Gurney were physicists at the University of Cambridge.

b. Robert F. Bacher held a one-year appointment in 1934–35 as instructor in physics at Columbia before joining the Cornell faculty in the autumn.

c. John R. Dunning was an instructor in physics at Columbia.

Asked years later to comment on the description of Princeton and its solipsistic luminaries, Frank Oppenheimer smiled. "It's a kind of youthful cockiness," he said, "and some of it stayed with my brother a little longer than it should have."[37] Robert expressed a more considered view in a 1939 radio talk celebrating Einstein's sixtieth birthday, lauding his contributions to science and "those personal qualities that are the counterpart of great work: selflessness, humor, and a deep kindness."[38]

"The shrewd eyed wench" was Marion Cassidy, who had for some years been Julius Oppenheimer's secretary and continued to assist him with financial matters after he sold his textile business. In 1951, when she tried to return a contingency fund that Mr. Oppenheimer had deposited years earlier for her use, Robert wrote to her that the money was his father's, who regarded her as almost a member of the family, and should be accepted as "repayment from people who have much to thank you for."[39]

This is the last surviving letter to Frank until 1948. Soon after he returned to England in January, Frank left Cambridge for Florence, where he remained until he came back to the United States in September 1935 to work toward the Ph.D. in physics under his brother's good friend Charles Lauritsen at the California Institute of Technology.

DURING THE 1935 spring term at Caltech Oppenheimer wrote to Ernest Lawrence about the theoretical work he and Melba Phillips were doing to explain the results of the Berkeley cyclotron experiments in which elements were sometimes made radioactive by bombardment with deuterons. They found that this occurred when the deuteron, which consists of a neutron and a proton, gives up the neutron to the bombarded nucleus. The proton comes out of the reaction separately, and the nucleus which captures the neutron is transmuted into a new radioactive atom. The paper describing their work was submitted for publication in late June 1935 [1935e]. What has become known as the Oppenheimer–Phillips process is still recognized as an important contribution to the understanding of nuclear reactions.

Oppenheimer also reported the puzzling results of measurements of the absorption of cosmic rays by various materials. He and other theorists were interested in the fact that the rate at which showers occurred varied in different substances. The data were confusing to them because they were unaware that some of the effects were caused by a cosmic ray particle, the meson, whose existence was not firmly established until spring 1937.

Pasadena. Sunday
[ca. early spring 1935]

Dear Ernest,

There is a good deal to tell you, & I wish that I might run in to see you in the radiation lab, instead of writing.

I am sending Melba [Phillips] today an outline of the calculations & plots I have made for the deuteron transmutation functions. The analysis turned out pretty complicated, & I have spent most of the nights of this week with slide rule & graph paper. The results are not very different from the earlier ones, & altogether credible, but they need to be checked carefully & perhaps extended; I hope M. will do that soon. For $I = 2.2 \times 10^6$, $Z = 13$, the curve I get is a fine straight line, cutting the axis (when extrapolated) at 1.49×10^6 volts. This is probably a little too high. If your extrapolated threshold is y, then the best value to take for I is $3y/2$. Unless I have made bad mistakes that should be right to better than 10%, I think. But you must give M time to work it over. I did not replot the Cu curve but it will be little altered.

Nye came over Friday, & he & Charlie [Lauritsen], [Carl] Anderson & I had quite a good talk.[a] His absorption measurements seem right now; they give a μ_ϵ decreasing systematically but slightly with increasing Z, which will agree quite beautifully with Bloch's formula for energy loss to complex atoms if one chooses a reasonable energy 10^9–10^{10} volts. We all thought these results good, intelligible & quite satisfactory, & I gave Nye the reference to the theory.

Of the results on showers (off line counts) we were less sure. Nye himself distrusts his coal measurements, & only in the case of $BaSO_4$ do his data really indicate an increase in showers. Anderson says that C is definitely known not to give many showers; & except for Ba Nye's points are so scattered & the counts so few that no influence can be established.

With Ba there is an effect, & it is this which has troubled us. For Nye finds a large increase when he fills his bin from ½ full to full. But

1) Shower particles have a range of at most a few inches of $BaSO_4$;

2) In Pb the first few cm's increase the showers; but more Pb reduces them again, & after 10 cm there is practically no effect (a slight increase perhaps over no Pb, but far less than with 2 cm).

3) Nye's own experiment ⟍⟋° shows that showers produced in the upper part of the bin do not get through to the bottom.

Therefore, if Nye's results are right, they have in my opinion to be interpreted as showing that the Ba produces a fairly penetrating *shower-producing* radiation. This must be able to get through the greater part of the bin; surely all registered showers are formed in the bottom 10 inches. We considered also the possibility that the counts came from extranuclear high energy secondaries; but a simple estimate shows that these are far too infrequent. In view of the unexpected character of these results, & the great importance they would have if confirmed, we suggested urgently to Nye that he repeat his $BaSO_4$ off line measurements, & see whether the former shower-increase could still be detected. I rather doubt it myself; but he agreed to look . . .

I sent Fleming a wire Thursday, saying that I could not come.[b] Houston is going east (& perhaps to Copenhagen); I have taken one of his classes; & it seemed a long trip to take & a bad time to be away from here. But in a way I should have liked to go.

My love to Molly [Lawrence], & my Father's affectionate greetings to you both. I wish I could be at journal club tomorrow night.

Robert

a. Arthur W. Nye was conducting experiments on the absorption and shower producing effects of cosmic radiation in coal, water, barium sulphate, and other materials. Although he had been a professor of physics at the University of Southern California since 1907, he pursued graduate work at Berkeley, where he received his Ph.D. in 1935 under Lawrence.

b. John A. Fleming was director of the Carnegie Institution of Washington.

The Berkeley physics department Journal Club met every Monday night to hear preassigned reviews of recent articles in physics journals. The meetings were well attended and are remembered as exciting occasions because so many changes were occurring in the field.[40]

Throughout the 1930s Oppenheimer continued to divide his time between the University of California and Caltech. He spent occasional weekends in Pasadena in the fall and winter, but the formal move took place in April. As Robert Serber later recalled: "Many of his students made the annual trek with him. Some things were easier in those days. We thought nothing of giving up our houses or apartments in Berkeley, confident that we could find a garden cottage in Pasadena for twenty-five dollars a month. We didn't own more than could be packed in the back of a car. In Pasadena, in addition to being exposed to new information on physics, we led an active social life. The Tolmans were good friends, and we had very warm relations with Charlie Lauritsen and his group . . . We spent many evenings at the Mexican restaurants on Olvera Street and many nights partying in Charlie Lauritsen's garden."[41]

The Uehlings joined the migration the two years they were in Berkeley. Their first arrival coincided with a Tolman party for Oppenheimer's birthday, a dinner which began with avocados brimming with caviar and ended with apple pie topped by lighted candles.[42]

After Frank Oppenheimer came to Pasadena in the autumn of 1935, he too was swept into the warm and lively circle created by the Tolmans, Lauritsens, Ruth Valentine, and Robert's other friends. Across the street from the Caltech campus the Tolmans had built a one-storey Spanish-style house, white-walled inside and out, shaded and cool with tile floors and a large study at one end known as "Richard's folly." Across a small but lushly blooming garden was a one-room guest house and bath which Robert often occupied on his weekend visits and sometimes for longer periods. He and Tolman talked a lot, and together they went over the manuscript of a book Tolman was writing and had wonderful arguments about it. Ruth Tolman and Frank often played the flute together and once gave a concert for the benefit of the Spanish loyalists.[43]

NINETEEN THIRTY-SIX was an important year in Robert Oppenheimer's life, marked by a new interest in social and political questions. He later emphasized how little attention he had paid to current events prior to 1936, and friends of the period confirm his lack of interest in economics and politics.[44] Leo Nedelsky describes Oppenheimer as not so much naive about politics in those days as ignorant of it. He once said to Nedelsky, "Tell me, what has politics to do with truth, goodness and beauty?" Yet Nedelsky recalled that, at a time when overt expressions of patriotism were definitely out of fashion among American intellectuals, Oppenheimer never made a secret of his love for America.

Oppenheimer began to develop social and political concerns in part as a response to the Depression, the consolidation of fascism in Germany, and the Spanish Civil War. These concerns were shared by his brother and by many academic and professional friends and colleagues. Oppenheimer did not shy away from these discussions and interests of the late 1930s, which involved labor unions, Marxism, university politics, civil liberties, and international affairs. As in physics, his style was to move from idea to idea and person to person, contributing to the evolving discussions.

Very few letters have been found which document this shift in interests and the new associations with individuals that accompanied them. Frank, Robert's most intimate correspondent of the previous decade, was now in Pasadena. On September 15, 1936, Frank married Jacquenette Quann, who was studying in Berkeley. "The three of us saw each other a great deal in Pasadena, Berkeley, and Perro Caliente," recalled Frank, "and between my brother and me there was the continuing sharing of ideas, enterprises, and friends, and the continuing mutual influencing of each other that was gradually becoming more symmetric."[46] These frequent meetings removed the need for the long letters that had cemented their friendship.

Had there been occasion to write, letters to Frank would, in some measure at least, have reflected Robert's new interests. In the absence of this contemporary source, we turn to the information provided by Oppenheimer eighteen years later when he replied to the United States Atomic Energy Commission's charges that his activities and associations of the later 1930s disqualified him to continue as adviser on nuclear policy with access to official secrets. Oppenheimer's 1954 response, influenced by the circumstances under which it was given, reconstructed some aspects of his life during that period:

"I spent some weeks each summer with my brother Frank at our ranch in New Mexico. There was a strong bond of affection between us. After my mother's death, my father came often, mostly in Berkeley, to visit me; and we had an intimate and close association until his death."

"Beginning in late 1936, my interests began to change. These changes did not alter my earlier friendships, my relations to my students, or my devotion to physics; but they added something new. I can discern in retrospect more than one reason for these changes. I had had a continuing, smoldering fury about the treatment of Jews in Germany. I had relatives there, and was later to help in extricating them and bringing them to this country. I saw what the depression was doing to my students. Often they could get no jobs, or jobs which were wholly inadequate. And through them, I began to understand how deeply political and economic events could affect men's lives. I began to feel the need to participate more fully in the life of the community. But I had no framework of political conviction or experience to give me perspective in these matters."

"In the spring of 1936, I had been introduced by friends to Jean Tatlock, the daughter of a noted professor of English at the university; and in the autumn, I began to court her, and we grew close to each other. We were at least twice close enough to marriage to think of ourselves as engaged. Between 1939 and her death in 1944 I saw her very rarely. She told me about her Communist Party memberships; they were on again, off again affairs, and never seemed to provide for her what she was seeking. I do not believe that her interests were really political. She loved this country and its people and its life. She was, as it turned out, a friend of many fellow travelers and Communists, with a number of whom I was later to become acquainted."

"I should not give the impression that it was wholly because of Jean Tatlock that I made leftwing friends, or felt sympathy for causes which hitherto would have seemed so remote from me, like the Loyalist cause in Spain, and the organization of migratory workers. I have mentioned some of the other contributing causes. I liked the new sense of companionship, and at the time felt that I was coming to be part of the life of my time and country."

"In 1937, my father died; a little later, when I came into an inheritance, I made a will leaving this to the University of California for fellowships to graduate students."

"This was the era of what the Communists then called the United

Front, in which they joined with many non-Communist groups in support of humanitarian objectives. Many of these objectives engaged my interest. I contributed to the strike fund of one of the major strikes of Bridges' union; I subscribed to the People's World; I contributed to the various committees and organizations which were intended to help the Spanish Loyalist cause. I was invited to help establish the teacher's union, which included faculty and teaching assistants at the university, and school teachers of the East Bay. I was elected recording secretary. My connection with the teacher's union continued until some time in 1941, when we disbanded our chapter."

"During these same years, I also began to take part in the management of the physics department, the selection of courses, and the awarding of fellowships, and in the general affairs of the graduate school of the university, mostly through the graduate council, of which I was a member for some years . . ."

"The matter which most engaged my sympathies and interests was the war in Spain. This was not a matter of understanding and informed convictions. I had never been to Spain; I knew a little of its literature; I knew nothing of its history or politics or contemporary problems. But like a great many other Americans I was emotionally committed to the Loyalist cause. I contributed to various organizations for Spanish relief. I went to, and helped with, many parties, bazaars, and the like. Even when the war in Spain was manifestly lost, these activities continued. The end of the war and the defeat of the Loyalists caused me great sorrow."[47]

IN 1937 OPPENHEIMER and his associates were continuing to work on the theory of cosmic rays and their interaction with matter. In a letter to Millikan he attempted to relate the theory to data on the intensity of cosmic radiation at different latitudes as determined by the amount of ionization produced at different altitudes. The letter demonstrates that Oppenheimer thought the discrepancy between theory and data could be due to the existence of a new, as yet undetected, particle in cosmic rays. At a Caltech colloquium in November 1936 Carl Anderson and Seth Neddermeyer had presented evidence for the existence of such a particle.[48] Stimulated by these results Oppenheimer and Carlson had included this possibility in an important paper they wrote on cosmic ray showers in December 1936: "One can conclude, either that the theoretical estimates of the probability of these processes are inapplicable in the domain of cosmic-ray energies, or that the actual penetration of these rays has to be ascribed to the presence of a component other than electrons and photons. The second alternative is necessarily radical; for cloud chamber and counter experiments show that particles with the same charge as the negative electron belong to the penetrating component of radiation; and if these are not electrons, they are particles not previously known to physics."[49]

[Pasadena]
April 19, 1937

Dear Professor Millikan:

Bowen and Neher have shown me the beautiful data on the altitude–latitude ionization, and we have talked of the interpretation of these results.[a] Since some of the conclusions to which Bowen and Neher had come seem to me quite misleading, I should like to write to you briefly of how things stand at present.

(1) If one compares the latitude–difference curves with the curves given by Carlson and me with unaltered constants, the fit is quite good for depths up to 4 m. [meters of water equivalent]. Compared to the experimental curves, the theoretical ones are shifted a little (0.3 m) to greater depths, but this discrepancy is of just the sort to be expected from the approximations in the theoretical treatment, and can be almost eliminated by choosing a somewhat larger, and equally plausible value, for the ionization loss constant β.

(2) For depths greater than 4 m. the theoretical curves fall definitely below the experimental, and between 5 m. and sea level the theoretical absorption coefficient is about $2\frac{1}{2}$ times the experimental. This discrepancy is just like that which we found with Pfotzer's counter data, but we know now that no part of it can be ascribed to very high energy radiation. Can this very definite and large discrepancy be ascribed to any approximations in the formulae of Bethe and Heitler or of Carlson and me? One must be careful not to give too final an answer to such a question; yet a careful reconsideration of the whole question, and comparison with the work of Bhabha and Heitler has convinced me that the discrepancy cannot be traced to the inadequacy of the theoretical treatment of known processes, but points to the fact that our picture of the mechanisms involved is still incomplete, and that the discrepancy is worthy of serious attention.[b]

(3) The attempt of Bowen and Neher to save the situation by altering the fundamental constants seems to me for several reasons fruitless. For one thing these constants ought to be reliable to within 20%; for another, the assumption used by Bowen and Neher of a considerable reduction in the probability of radiation and pair production even for radiation of low energy (for it is the partially degraded radiation which determines the curve at great depths) seems to me peculiarly untenable theoretically. But the strongest argument is that it is not possible by any change of this sort to fit the absorption curve near sea level without spoiling completely the agreement near the top of the atmosphere, and pushing the theoretical maximum to depths 2–3 times those actually observed. The fact that Bowen and Neher did not find this rests upon a misunderstanding of some of our equa-

tions, and *no conclusions* whatever may legitimately be drawn from the apparent good agreement which they found. The good check on the observed and expected positions of the maxima suggests quite strongly that there is nothing seriously wrong with the theoretical formulae for pair production and radiation even at very high energies.

(4) It seems to me that the relatively high incidence of large showers at sea level, and the many anomalies observed in the cloud chamber, make one more ready to believe that the discrepancy is real, and comes from the existence of processes and types of radiation ignored in our simple treatment. It can perhaps not yet be decided whether these are associated with a nonelectronic primary radiation, or whether they are secondary radiations and processes induced by the electron–photon component; but the fact that according to Anderson the nuclear disintegrations increase in incidence with altitude roughly as do the electron–photon showers, makes me favor the second alternative, and suggests that the increased penetration of the radiation is closely connected with the production of less absorbable secondaries in these nuclear encounters. In any case, I think that if one takes the theoretical work at all seriously one *cannot* say that between 5 m. and sea level electrons and photons alone are enough to account for even the latitude sensitive part of the cosmic radiation.

With every respectful and cordial greeting,

Robert Oppenheimer

a. In April 1937 Ira S. Bowen was professor of physics at Caltech and H. Victor Neher was an instructor there.

b. George Pfotzer's curves of data relating ionization to altitude, published in 1936 while he was at the Technische Hochschule in Stuttgart, were widely used in cosmic ray research. Hans A. Bethe and Walter H. Heitler, physicists who had left Germany in 1933, were at the University of Bristol in 1934–35 and there developed the quantum theory of interaction processes most important at high energy. Homi J. Bhabha was at Cambridge University in 1936 when he published papers with Heitler on cosmic ray showers, parallel to the work of Carlson and Oppenheimer at about the same time.

Oppenheimer wrote more briefly to Lawrence about what he had found in Pasadena.

Pasadena
Sunday. [April 1937]

Dear Ernest,

Thank you for the Birge-money; I had stopped by at my landlady's to say goodbye & was sorry to miss you.[a]

Laslett & Van [Voorhis] came Friday night to our nuclear seminar,[b] & told me of the fine proton results with the Rochester cyclotron, & also, but not very explicitly, of the new Ir[?] developments; you know how eager I am to hear of these things when they are straightened out.

Charlie [Lauritsen]'s plans are still unsettled, & since Millikan has left they are likely to stay so. The only exciting physics is some beautiful cosmic ray work of Bowen & Neher, which shows just how far our shower work can explain the altitude-latitude curves, & suggests that new & probably nuclear effects play an important part, except in the first few meters in the atmosphere.

Come through here on your way if you possibly can. All greetings

Robert

a. Raymond T. Birge joined the Berkeley physics department in 1918 and became professor of physics in 1926. In 1933 he commenced what was to be a twenty-two year term as chairman.
b. L. Jackson Laslett was a doctoral candidate and S. N. Van Voorhis an NRC fellow at Berkeley; both worked with Lawrence.

Within a week after Oppenheimer's April 1937 letters to Millikan and Lawrence, the definitive evidence for the existence of a new particle in photographs of cosmic ray tracks was publicly announced. On the heels of the discovery Oppenheimer and Serber wrote a paper [1937c] connecting these results with the particle of mass intermediate between the electron and proton suggested by the Japanese theorist Hideki Yukawa in his theory of the forces between particles within the nucleus, published in February 1935. The new cosmic ray particle was first called the mesotron and later became known as the meson.

For about a decade physicists assumed that the mesotron was identical with the particle proposed by Yukawa. Only in the late 1940s was it definitely established, due to the discovery of yet another new particle, that the cosmic ray mesotron was not Yukawa's particle, but rather a product of its radioactive decay. As a result the mesotron or meson was renamed the muon or mu-meson to distinguish it from the pion or pi-meson, the true

Yukawa particle identified in cosmic rays in 1947. In the intervening years Oppenheimer and other physicists struggled with the problem of reconciling the observed mesotron with the role it should play in Yukawa's theory of nuclear forces. Nevertheless, the belief that they were observing Yukawa's mesons opened up a fruitful field of inquiry in cosmic ray physics and provided a viable theoretical framework that made experimental physics intelligible. As Oppenheimer wrote in 1966, "The imagined existence of these particles makes it for a time somewhat easier to describe important regularities that we do observe among particles known to exist."[50]

IN A LETTER to George Uhlenbeck, who was visiting the United States to participate in the Michigan summer school of theoretical physics, Oppenheimer suggested a reunion and shared some news of work on nuclear theory.

100 | TO GEORGE UHLENBECK

Cowles
June 29. [1937]

Dear George,

You & Else are in America again, near enough so that I would like to break the long silence, near enough so that I hope that soon we shall see each other. What most of all I hope is that when summer school is over you will come for a visit to California—it will I think be too late for the Pecos. But in August it will be fine in San Francisco: we shall be getting started in Berkeley, & Fermi & Bloch & Nordsieck will still be in Stanford;[a] it will be very beautiful; & it is with all heart that I ask you to come: not for work surely, but for a holiday & only a little friendly talk of physics. I have a fine house on the hill in Berkeley, where you & Else would probably be comfortable & surely so very welcome.

Ann Arbor tempted me very much, & the certainty of seeing you there. If still I felt that I should not come, it was because by the summer I was fairly well worn out with a long & in some ways a hard year, & thought that some weeks here in the mountains were more than ordinarily a good idea. I ought to be back in California not later than August first, & that would leave woefully little time for the trip east & a fortnight in Ann Arbor. But I do want so very much to see you. If you could get away before the end of July, perhaps you could have a few days here & then go west with us.

Of physics, I think I shall not try to write, but rather hope that our meeting will make that unnecessary. Bohr was in Berkeley for a month last spring, & Kalckar stayed on in Pasadena til June;[b] & we came so to go a little

201

more closely just into the questions of probabilities of formation & decomposition of compound nuclei, & into the conditions under which elementary statistical arguments can be applied to connect decay rates & collision cross sections . . . But I think that this will not be of a specially pressing interest to you, & we can talk it over later on.

For really the purpose of this letter is to get word from you of your plans, & to urge you as strongly as I can to include in them a visit west; to say welcome again to this country, & to say that we must not let this chance go by without seeing each other.

Affectionately

Robert

Roger [Lewis] & Frank [Oppenheimer] send you both all greetings.

a. Nordsieck was an NRC fellow at Stanford in 1937; Fermi lectured there that summer.
b. Bohr was accompanied to the United States by his wife Margrethe, one of his sons, Erik, and his young assistant, Fritz Kalckar.

JULIUS OPPENHEIMER died of a heart attack on September 20, 1937.[51] A few days later his youngest sister, Hedwig Stern, and other relatives emigrating from Germany arrived by boat. Mrs. Stern had planned to live with Julius in New York; she settled instead in Berkeley with her physician son Alfred and his wife Lotte. Oppenheimer established warm relations with the Stern family and was particularly devoted to his Aunt Hedwig. When Hedwig Stern died in 1966, her son Alfred wrote Oppenheimer about her active, purposeful life and added: "Your closeness has made it richer still. As long as she could think and feel, she was all for you."[52]

Oppenheimer reported on the family's progress to his cousin Louise Oppenheimer Singer, daughter of Julius Oppenheimer's brother Emil. Alfred Stern, like other physicians trained abroad, had to repeat his internship and residency in the United States.

Berkeley
October 21 [1937]

Dear Louise,

Thank you for your good wire.

Alfred & Lotte are making out well. Alfred's work is arranged: he is to start work tomorrow, as extern to one Berkeley & one Oakland hospital. Everyone has been friendly & helpful, & the work itself promises well. Alfred & Lotte have found a fine house up in the hills north of Berkeley, big, with a garden & a view of the bay; negotiations for it are not quite closed, but will be, I think, soon. Berkeley has been at its most beautiful, & I think they are not sorry now that it is to be their home.

Will you come to visit us again?

Affectionately

Robert

WHEN NIELS BOHR was in Berkeley in March 1937 to deliver the Hitchcock Lectures, he and Fritz Kalckar worked with Oppenheimer on several problems, including Bohr's theory of the compound nucleus. A letter Bohr wrote to Oppenheimer from Copenhagen the following December is an early example of the frequent exchange of news and of expressions of fond regard that took place between the two men over the next quarter century. On this occasion Bohr shared with Oppenheimer his sorrow over the recent death of Rutherford. Three weeks later, the sudden and untimely death of young Kalckar was to be the subject of another letter from Bohr.[53]

102 | NIELS BOHR TO ROBERT OPPENHEIMER

[Copenhagen]
December 20, 1937

Dear Oppenheimer,

With these lines I want to bring you my very best wishes for the New Year and the warmest thanks for all your kindness during our stay in Berkeley last spring. It was a very great pleasure to me indeed to get opportunity of coming into still closer connection with you and to feel how, in spite of all differences as regards points of approach, we sympathize with each other so thoroughly in physics as well as in many other things. I am also very grateful to you for your kindness and helpfulness towards Kalckar, for whom his stay in California, above all due to you, has been a most instructive and encouraging experience indeed.

Both my wife and I read with the greatest pleasure the books you gave us on our departure from San Francisco and they have given me much occasion to think of your fine judgement in art as well as in science. I would have written to you long before, but on account of accumulated duties I have had a very busy time ever since my return. First a few weeks ago I saw that the paper, in the translation of which you took so kind and helpful an interest, did actually appear in the July-number of "Philosophy of Science". I am sorry not to have any reprints and therefore not to be able to send you even such a small reminding of all your work with it. As a little greeting I enclose, however, a reprint of the article in "Science" with which you helped Kalckar so kindly, and the appearance of which as a remembrance of my stay in Berkeley has been a special pleasure to me.[a]

As I hope, you will already have received the general article of Kalckar and myself which under the circumstances we just let appear with a small addendum. We hope, however, soon to continue the work with a more detailed discussion of the experimental evidence which is so rapidly increasing. In the last weeks I have been occupied with the problem of the selectivity of the nuclear photo effects disclosed by the continuation of Bothe's beautiful researches.[b] I think it can be explained quite naturally by realizing that the excitation of the nucleus due to the absorption of the photon will for a short but appreciable interval not be distributed among the various modes of oscillation in the manner corresponding to a thermal equilibrium. I am preparing a little note about it and shall send you a copy of the manuscript as soon as it is finished.

Like anyone else who has had the privilege of coming into personal contact with Rutherford you will surely have been much affected by the sad news of his sudden death in the midst of his work. I remember so clearly the first time I met you, when as a quite young man you came into Rutherford's office in the Cavendish Laboratory, while I was sitting and talking with him there. When you went out, I remember, that Rutherford said some warmly appreciating words regarding his expectations about you. Life is poorer without him; but still every thought about him will be a lasting encouragement to us all.

Thinking of the future I hope very much that we here in Copenhagen shall keep up the close connection with your group in Berkeley and especially that we shall once have the pleasure of welcoming yourself here among us for a while.

With the very kindest regards from us all,

Yours,

Niels Bohr

a. As a result of their collaboration during this visit, Oppenheimer, Serber, and Kalckar published two joint papers [1937d, 1937e].

b. Walther Bothe was director of the Institute for Physics, Kaiser Wilhelm Institute for Medical Research in Heidelberg.

ONE OF THE nonscientific organizations that Oppenheimer joined in the latter half of the 1930s was Consumers Union, founded in 1936. "For perhaps a year," Oppenheimer later testified, "I was a member of the western council of the Consumers Union which was concerned with evaluating information on products of interest on the west coast." The following letter is part of a slender record of Oppenheimer's participation in Consumers Union activities which began, at least, on a practical level. The other two Oppenheimer letters in the Consumers Union files explain that he was too busy to attend council meetings.[54]

103 | TO MILDRED EDIE (WESTERN CONSUMERS UNION)

Pasadena
May 29 [1938]

Dear Boss,

Thank you for your good letter. If you will let me know where and when to find you, I'll call for you and have you meet Borsook, Emory Ellis who can probably take care of the milk testing, and anyone I can dig up on the poison oak and dark glasses. So far I've found no one for either of these. At least one buyer I think I have found you: Jane Muir. She said she would be very glad to do that work, has the time, and I believe the reliability. She is up north this weekend and you may have seen her. The market surveyor is beyond me.

The April issues came, and I thank you for them, and am putting them to work. The membership books did not come.

Please let me know when you want me. A phone message at the Norman Bridge Laboratory or the Athenaeum of C I T will get me.

Faithfully,

Robert Oppenheimer

IN THE SPRING of 1937 Oppenheimer had suggested that the newly discovered meson was radioactive. Referring to the paper that he and Serber published [1937c] linking the new particle with Yukawa's theory, Oppenheimer later explained: "We did not, as we originally intended, include evi-

205

dence of the radioactivity of the mesons, for Bohr persuaded us that that was a logically quite separable point, as indeed it was; but within a year Blackett published that, with better evidence than we had found." Serber recalls that Millikan had discouraged Oppenheimer from publishing the work in 1937 because it disagreed with Millikan's ideas on the subject. After Blackett's publication in December 1938, Millikan, apparently reversing his position, wanted Oppenheimer to get credit for the earlier discussion.[55] In response, Oppenheimer wrote a diplomatic note.

104 | TO ROBERT A. MILLIKAN

Berkeley
Jan 1 [1939]

Dear Dr Millikan,

Thank you for your good note. I shall be in Pasadena again by the eleventh, and shall come to see you right away.

You are right about the radioactivity of the mesotron; I have been thinking of it for two years now, and gave a seminar on it here while Bohr was with us. The only evidence we had at that time came from Rossi's work in Eritrea, which he has just recently interpreted in this sense in a letter to Nature.[a] We felt that the extension of your own earlier work on air and water absorption would provide a so much cleaner and less ambiguous test of the idea (which as you can guess rests on no very sure theoretical basis) that, perhaps mistakenly, we did not publish it, but just urged Bowen to get the air-water experiment done. I do hope that next summer that will be possible. It would put this whole subject on a much firmer foundation.

With all good greetings,

Robert Oppenheimer

a. Bruno B. Rossi had been professor of physics at the University of Padua. He left Italy in 1938 and after brief stays in Copenhagen and Manchester came to the United States in the spring of 1939. During the 1930s he made major contributions to cosmic ray research through his experiments and development of new instruments and techniques.

OPPENHEIMER'S CLOSE scientific and personal ties to the Caltech nuclear physics group were evident in letters written in the late 1930s to William Fowler. Fowler received his doctorate at Caltech in 1936, worked as a research fellow with Charles Lauritsen, and joined the faculty in 1939. Oppenheimer often wrote Fowler brief undated technical notes about the experiments on nuclear reactions at the Pasadena laboratory.[56]

The following letter to Fowler was written two days after Oppenheimer and the other Berkeley physicists learned of the discovery of nuclear fission. After the German chemists Otto Hahn and Fritz Strassmann had demonstrated in December 1938 that the nucleus of uranium, one of the heaviest of the elements, could be split into two or more parts, the news traveled rapidly throughout the world. Physicists familiar with nuclear reactions immediately attempted to confirm the experiment and extend and explore its implications. The response at Berkeley was later described by Glenn T. Seaborg, then an instructor in chemistry: "I remember . . . a seminar in January 1939 when new results . . . on the splitting of uranium with neutrons were excitedly discussed; I do not recall ever seeing Oppie so stimulated and so full of ideas."[57]

In his letter to Fowler, Oppenheimer reviewed the history of the discovery and the experiments undertaken at Berkeley in the few days since the arrival of the news. His interest in how many neutrons "come off during the splitting" was shared by scientists in several countries, who saw that if enough neutrons were produced, an energy producing chain reaction would be feasible.

105 | TO WILLIAM A. FOWLER

Berkeley, Saturday
January 28?, 1939]

Dear Willie,

. . . The U business is unbelievable. We first saw it in the papers, wired for more dope, and have had a lot of reports since. You know it started with Hahn's finding that what he had taken for Ra in one of the U activities fractionally crystallized with Ba. And then the recognition that the ekauranium series was chemically compatible with a series starting with Ma, running on through Rhe and Os and Pd. And then understanding suddenly why there were such long chains of beta decay, to get rid of the neutron excess with which half a U nucleus would start; and why one had 'isomeric' chains that were really isotopic; and then remembering how a drop when it is charged up elongates, becomes less and less stable to longitudinal oscillations, final[ly] ruptures. At that point there were a lot of experimental things done here: recording the pieces when U is slow neutron bombarded on a differential chamber; seeing them, with about 2 cm maximum range and unbelievable ionization, in a cloud chamber at reduced pressure, and only during the neutron bombardment; measuring their range by the activities left in foils behind the bombarded U; measuring their energy by collecting ions, with a maximum of about 60 mv, as one could expect from the Coulomb field;

207

showing that the 72 hr activity goes chemically with Te, leads to an X ray which is the K alpha and beta of Iodine, is followed by an Iodine activity. Many points are still unclear: where are the short lived high energy betas one would expect? Are there strong gammas as one would think from the big dipole moments of the pieces? In how many ways does the U come apart? At random, as one might guess, or only in certain ways? And most of all, are there many neutrons that come off during the splitting, or from the excited pieces? If there are then a 10 cm cube of U deuteride (one would need the D to slow them without capture) should be quite something. What do you think? It is I think exciting, not in the rare way of positrons and mesotrons, but in a good honest practical way.

The rest will keep. hasta luego

Robert

NEWS OF RESEARCH on nuclear fission and interest in the enormous amounts of energy that might be released were also the focus of a letter to Uhlenbeck, who had returned to the University of Michigan faculty in 1939.

At the same time, Oppenheimer was working on the application of general relativity and nuclear physics to theoretical astrophysics. The significance of his work on neutron stars and gravitational contraction [1938b, 1939a, 1939c] became evident in the 1960s and 1970s when the reality of neutron stars, pulsars, and black holes was established through new astronomical research techniques. This work and his continuing interest in the radioactivity of the mesotron is also mentioned in the letter.

106 | TO GEORGE UHLENBECK

Berkeley
Feb. 5 [1939]

Dear George,

I want to answer your fine long very welcome letter at once, partly to show how happy I was to have it, partly to say a word of my own personal celebration of your staying in America . . .

Here too there is further evidence for the bursting U. They have recorded the heavy tracks in a differential chamber, and seen them, very prominent over the haze of recoil protons and the faint alpha tracks, from a U foil bombarded by neutrons in a very low pressure cloud chamber. Also Abelson showed that the 72 hour period follows chemically Te, and emits an Xray which by differential critical absorption can be positively identified as the K alpha, and a little K beta, of Iodine.[a] The next activity after Te separates out with I chemically. We too of course have been thinking of the 10^{18} ergs per gram. It seems to me that the pieces after parturition must be highly excited, if only because of their anomalous charge distribution. Some of that must go into radiation, but one would expect neutrons too. So I think it really not too improbable that a ten cm cube of uranium deuteride (one should have something to slow the neutrons without capturing them) might very well blow itself to hell.

There would be much physics to tell, in exchange for your good account, perhaps too much for a letter . . . We have been working here too on static and nonstatic solutions for very heavy masses that have exhausted their nuclear energy sources: old stars perhaps which collapse to neutron cores. The results have been very odd, will be in part out so soon that I won't bother to write them here—I have gradually talked myself into believing the mesotron decay, although the evidence is not much better than it was two years ago when we first were thinking of it. The Pasadena people promise to do a really clean experiment with ionization chambers in lakes 4000 m apart next summer.

Two more points, and I shall write soon again. For the first, we have been hoping to get to Perro Caliente quite early in June this year. It is a very beautiful month there, without rain, but with snow on the peaks and very green. How is it: could you and Else come? Don't forget: not the time nor the place nor your welcome . . .

Say a warm greeting from me to Else, whose generosity reopened this long dormant correspondence; tell her to take good care of herself so she can ride a horsie next June.

hasta luegito

Robert

a. Philip H. Abelson, a doctoral candidate at Berkeley, was an assistant in the Radiation Lab. When the news of fission reached Berkeley, Abelson immediately saw that the research he was doing for his dissertation might have led to the discovery. As he later recalled, "I almost went numb as I realized that I had come close but had missed a great discovery"; Philip H. Abelson, "A Graduate Student with Ernest O. Lawrence," in *All in Our Time: The Reminiscences of Twelve Nuclear Pioneers,* ed. Jane Wilson (Chicago: Bulletin of the Atomic Scientists, 1975), pp. 28–29. Abelson's account provides further information on the Berkeley fission work.

OPPENHEIMER CONTINUED to share with his New York cousin a concern for the welfare of their Aunt Hedwig and her family in Berkeley. Hilde was the seven-year-old daughter of Alfred and Lotte Stern.

Berkeley
April 26 [1939]

Dear Louise,

Thank you for your dear warm birthday letter. It was good to have that word of you, & to know, as much from the feeling as from anything you said, how rich & serene your life has been.

Alfred is getting on wonderfully well: not that he has as yet anything like enough patients, but that he has some, & thinks that it is going to go. Hedwig has been well all winter, & you will need no telling to know how beautiful she is. And from Hilde every few days there comes one of those sharp gems of truth that only a few children can find.

Frank is really getting his degree this June. His plans for next year are not settled, but he may be at Stanford. We are going to New Mexico this summer, & if I come east it will be early in July.

My love, & every wish for you both

Robert

AFTER WRITING about Fowler's work on nuclear energy levels, Oppenheimer commented on the nonaggression pact between Nazi Germany and the U.S.S.R. which was signed in August 1939.

108 | TO WILLIAM A. FOWLER

Berkeley, Saturday
[September 9, 1939]

Dear Willie,

Thanks for your fine letter. The situation with N13 etc is not at all what I expected but what Frank tells me of your work and his is pretty convincing. How similar are the three positron spectra? Is that known at all? Can Tomlinson work on them?[a] I suppose that it is SURE that no one Fermi curve can fit them. It is theoretically a little strange that they should not be complex, as Wigner will have told you. Of course the intensity is a pretty sensitive function of the energy, and one can't make too good an estimate of where the higher levels in the daughter nucleus should lie. I feel that the conclusions you have reached are very critical, and that you should be sure to make your account of them public and convincing . . .

I'll be down next week end, the 16, and we can talk of all this. Berkeley is very crowded with physicists and there is a little gossip of physics that will keep.

I know Charlie [Lauritsen] will say a melancholy I told you so over the Nazisoviet pact, but I am not paying any bets yet on any aspect of the hocuspocus except maybe that the Germans are pretty well into Poland. Ça stink.

Til a few days then

Robert

a. Everett P. Tomlinson was a doctoral student at Caltech.

BY 1940 university jobs for physicists were somewhat more numerous than in the Depression years. Still, the placing of his students was a matter of deep concern to Oppenheimer, as shown in a letter to F. Wheeler Loomis, chairman of the physics department at the University of Illinois, on behalf of Sidney M. Dancoff. Dancoff obtained the one-year appointment and remained at Illinois.

109 | TO F. WHEELER LOOMIS

Pasadena
May 13, 1940

Dear Dr. Loomis,

Serber tells me that there will be a one year instructorship at Illinois next year, because Bartlett will be on leave of absence.[a] There is a man in Berkeley, Dr. Dancoff, whom I would very much like to see get that position. Serber knows him well, his work and character; but I thought that it might be helpful to have a word or two of recommendation from me. Dancoff took his degree in Berkeley last fall: this year he has had a research and teaching job in our department. Lawrence has suggested taking him on for the 'theoretical' staff of the Radiation Laboratory next year, but we are all agreed that that is not the ideal place for him, and would like to see him in a position where he could do more teaching and have greater responsibilities than are possible in Berkeley.

Dancoff's research will be known in part to you, and more fully to Serber: with Morrison (and he did surely his full share) he did the important work on internal conversion of gamma rays that has borne such good fruit in unscrambling isomeric and radioactive transitions.[b] He gave the most complete solution we have, going far beyond that of Pauli and of Bloch and

Nordsieck, on the quantum theory of the effect of radiation reaction in collisions, that was a difficult and expert piece of work. He has been much interested in spin orbit coupling; published a brief note on the He_5 doublet, and has now in press a long paper dealing exhaustively with this and related problems. He has made calculations on the stopping of cyclotron neutrons and gamma rays by the water tanks, that should be published in conjunction with the observations they confirm. It would be impossible to detail all the many questions into which he has looked, on which he has reported or toward which he has made helpful contributions: he is a good physicist, well trained and with good ideas and great technical facility in calculation.

During his years in Berkeley, with the exception of the time he held a University Fellowship, Dancoff has constantly been teaching elementary courses. He is a good teacher, clear, interesting, painstaking; I have heard only good reports of this phase of his work. His more advanced teaching (he has occasionally lectured in my course) and his seminars, are uniformly excellent. He has occasionally spoken to seminars at Stanford and Cal. Tech. as well, and has always done a fine job.

I have found, and I know that Serber will confirm this experience, that Dancoff was a very pleasant man to work with: modest, considerate, scrupulous and very friendly. I think he would fit in well in any department, and know of nothing that would make him unwelcome in any way. He is likeable, married for two years now, and happily.

You may wonder that so good a man is not already placed. Jobs for theorists are not too common, and he has had the competition of older men of greater reputation: Schiff, Schwinger, Snyder for instance in Berkeley, to meet.[c] There is a good chance that for the year after this an opening for him will be available at UCLA, but this is alas not sure. In any case I think that with the added opportunities of a year in Urbana he will probably have no great trouble finding a satisfactory place for the following year. Thus I think that you will not be incurring an essential responsibility by taking him on.

I hope that this note will help to supplement and confirm what Serber can tell you. If I can give you any other information that would be of use, either by mail or wire, please do not hesitate to ask me.

With all cordial good wishes to you and to Mrs. Loomis and to your thriving department.

Robert Oppenheimer

I ought to add, though it is a point more properly Serber's, that I think that Dancoff and Serber will make a very good team, and that from this point of view too it would be a good thing for them and for your department.

a. Serber was appointed assistant professor of physics at Illinois in 1938. James H. Bartlett was associate professor of theoretical physics there.

b. Philip Morrison, a graduate student of Oppenheimer's, received his Ph.D. from Berkeley in 1940.

c. Leonard I. Schiff was a research associate, Julian S. Schwinger an NRC fellow, and Hartland Snyder a doctoral candidate.

FROM JUNE 18 TO 21, 1940, Oppenheimer attended the American Physical Society meeting in Seattle. The afternoon session on June 20 consisted of an informal symposium on theoretical physics which Oppenheimer opened with a talk on "The Present Crisis in the Quantum Theory of Fields."[58]

The meeting took place the week France capitulated to the Germans, and the physicists gathered in Seattle, many of whom were already involved in war research, were especially concerned about the implications of this event. Oppenheimer's note acknowledging the Uehlings' hospitality, which he had shared with former Berkeley associate J. Franklin Carlson and his wife, was written from the Tolmans' address.

110 | TO RUTH AND EDWIN A. UEHLING

Pasadena
July 4 [1940]

Dear Ruth & Ed,

It is time now that I wrote a word to you of the sweet days together in your home. You will have come to Ann Arbor, with the confusion of packing & leaving, & the long drive, behind you. But I hope you will still have warm memories of a visit which was to your visitor so sweet. For it was not the fine house alone, nor the trip to Rainier, nor your friends, nor all your graciousness: but above all the sense of renewing & deepening, after some years, the affection & understanding between us. For that *thanks* is a poor word, but still I would use it.

Our trip south was very fine, the coast lovely & the company friendly & cheerful. For Wenonah [Nedelsky] too it was a rest & restoration. The day I left Berkeley she was talking to the red cross about a job: the other, housemothership in S.F., seemed not to be panning out.

About July 15 I think Frank & Jackie & Judith & I will go to Perro Caliente.[a] There is a very good chance camp will be open when you return: perhaps you can still arrange to come that way.

Have a sweet time & fruitful in Ann Arbor, & give my love to George & Else, & good greetings to Betty & Wendell & Willis & Melber & the

213

Serbers & Wigner & everyone else you think of.[b] And again, for the visit & all its goods, my hand in thanks.

Robert

a. Frank Oppenheimer was completing a two-year appointment as a research–teaching associate in physics with Felix Bloch at Stanford. Judith, his eldest child, was born in Berkeley, May 25, 1940.

b. Wendell Furry was now associate professor at Harvard. Willis Lamb, a former Oppenheimer student at Berkeley, was an instructor at Columbia. Melba Phillips was an instructor at Brooklyn College.

OPPENHEIMER SPENT much of the summer of 1940 at Perro Caliente with Frank, Jacquenette, and their baby daughter, Judith. Among the guests was Katherine Puening Harrison, wife of Stewart Harrison, an English physician engaged in cancer research at Caltech. Over the past year Oppenheimer and Katherine Harrison, always known as Kitty, had developed a deep attachment. Early in 1934 Kitty had interrupted undergraduate studies at the University of Wisconsin to marry Joe Dallet, a Communist Party organizer in Youngstown, Ohio. She also became a member, but her lack of enthusiasm for the cause was largely responsible for a separation from Dallet two years later. He joined the Loyalist forces in the Spanish Civil War, as one of the large contingent of American volunteers comprising the Abraham Lincoln Brigade. Still in love with Dallet, Kitty undertook to meet him in Spain and was in Paris in October 1937 waiting for instructions when she learned of his death. Kitty returned to the United States to complete her undergraduate work in biology at the University of Pennsylvania. Toward the end of 1938 she married Stewart Harrison, whom she had met in England a few years earlier. Shortly thereafter he returned to Pasadena; Kitty followed him when she received her bachelor's degree in June 1939.[59]

Before the first anniversary of her marriage to Harrison, Kitty and Robert Oppenheimer had fallen in love. In the autumn of 1940 she filed for a Nevada divorce. On November 1 she and Oppenheimer were married in Nevada and proceeded to Berkeley, where they were welcomed by Ernest and Molly Lawrence.[60] In Berkeley the Oppenheimers lived first in Robert's apartment on Shasta Road, then at 10 Kenilworth Court until August 1941, when they bought a house, 1 Eagle Hill, in the Berkeley hills.[61]

Two months after the Oppenheimers' marriage, in January 1941, John Edsall and his wife Margaret, who were spending the year in Pasadena, visited Berkeley and dined with them. The other guests were the physicist Ronald Gurney and his wife Natalie. The talk was mainly about science at Berkeley—Edsall recalled the admiration with which Oppenheimer spoke of Lawrence—and to some extent about the war in Europe. Edsall remembered the occasion for more personal reasons: "The house was up on a high hill, and it was a very stormy night, with a driving rain and high winds; it was quite dramatic, the feeling of the wind and rain all around us . . . [Oppenheimer was] quite outgoing and friendly; on the other hand, you felt that he was very deeply absorbed in his thoughts and what he was doing, so that I didn't feel a kind of close contact with him at that time that I had during that year we had been in Cambridge together. Which was not surprising. After all, we hadn't seen each other really for over a decade. I felt that he obviously was a far stronger person, that [the] inner crises that he had been through in those earlier years he had obviously worked out and achieved a great deal of inner resolution of them. I felt a sense of confidence and authority, although still tension and lack of inner ease in some respects, and yet this extraordinary power and sense of authority at the same time, and a feeling of such an extraordinarily brilliant and rapidly moving and scintillating mind that was beyond the power of most of us to follow. He could reach and see intuitively things that most people would be able to follow only very slowly and hesitatingly, if at all. This was not only in physics, but in other things as well."[62]

OPPENHEIMER'S SERIES of notes on physics to Fowler seems to have ended early in 1941 after Fowler obtained leave from Caltech to serve as assistant director of research for the National Defense Research Committee. The previous August he had married Ardiane Olmsted.

This letter to Fowler notes an impending investigation by a California state legislative committee on "un-American activities."

111 | TO WILLIAM A. FOWLER

Berkeley
Saturday [spring 1941]

Dear Willie,

We were so glad to have your good letter, to know that things were going pretty well with you—and now that Ardiane has come I expect more than pretty well—and that you'd thought friendly of us as we so often do of you. I expect that as time goes on you'll have more and more a feeling of confidence and conviction in the work you are doing; and I don't think you could ever have felt right about not going. I have a lot more misgivings even than you ever had about what will come of all this; but even so I think surely if I were asked to do a job I could do really well and that needed doing I'd not refuse. I'd worry a lot, perhaps more even than you. But we worry anyway . . .

Gamow asked me to the nuclear congress in Washington in April, on the elementary particles. I said I'd come, and shall, if the meeting is held and nothing too serious comes up; maybe Kitty will come too but we're not sure. It sure will be fine to see you again. I may be out of a job by then, because UC is going to be investigated next week for radicalism and the story is that the committee members are no gentlemen and that they don't like me. We'll do the best we can.

Kitty is fine, and she sends you her love, and she does remember the good time in Oregon. Our best to Ardiane and to you, and write us whenever you can.

Robert

DESPITE THE DISRUPTION that the war was causing in the physics departments at Pasadena and Berkeley by the spring of 1941, Oppenheimer, accompanied by his wife, made the usual move to Pasadena, where their son Peter was born on May 12.

112 | TO EDWIN A. AND RUTH UEHLING

Pasadena
May 17 [1941]

Dear Ed & Ruth,

It was fine to get your warm long good letter. If there has been a little delay in my answer, that is for 2 reasons: one good, one not so good. I've been sick, in Berkeley of pneumonia, & here of a miserable but not at all lethal disease called mononucleosis—

A week ago Kitty, unexpectedly & two months early, had us our baby: a very small little boy called Peter, who is doing fine. Kitty herself is getting along well, should be home in about a week now. We'll be staying here about a month after that, then going north—

I remember the wonderful visit of last June so warmly: it is easy to think of that as initiating this year, whose fortunes, so evil for the world, have been so good for me. It was such a sweet visit, & even now a year later I want to say thank you for it again.

Your desire for a spectroscopist at the University I'd heard about. You are going I think to find it pretty hard to get *any* decent physicist these days, with the demand suddenly exceeding the supply so violently . . . If you are ever interested in theoretical people, there will be some first rate ones coming up next year. This year's crop is pretty well spoken for already. The situation in Berkeley & here in Pasadena is in some ways very gloomy: here specially almost all the men active in physics have been taken away for war work. Those left are swamped in administrative & teaching duties & their own defense problems. The number of graduate students too is way down: the losses heaviest among the men about to finish, in nuclear physics, but noticeable all along the line. In Berkeley we've lost Alvarez, McMillan, 2/3 Lawrence, Brode, Loeb.[a] Only the last is not missed. I expect, unless there is a drastic change in policy on the part of the research boards, that physics in our sense will just about stop by next year.

Our own work—on all sorts of minor things—has gone well enough, & I am real hopeful about some relatively new "strong coupling" theories of the mesotron field, & the light they throw on 'Heisenberg' showers, proton isobars, scattering, & other such recondite matters. I'm supposed to be in Washington this week at the Nuclear Congress, but am having a conflict deciding whether or not to fly on—[b]

I felt the greatest sympathy with what you wrote of the war. My own views could, im Kleinem, hardly be gloomier, either for what will happen locally & nationally, or in the world. I think we'll go to war—that the Roosevelt faction will win over the Lindbergh. I don't think we'll get anywhere near the Nazis. Later I think the Hearst-Lindbergh side will kick the administration 'humanitarians' out. I see no good for a long time; & the only cheerful thing in these parts is the strength & toughness & political growth of organized labor.

Let us know when to expect you *both* in Berkeley—
Thanks again for your letter, from Kitty too—
Affectionately

Robert

a. Luis W. Alvarez and Edwin M. McMillan, both promoted to associate professor effective the next academic year, were on leave for war work on radar at the Radiation Laboratory at Massachusetts Institute of Technology. Lawrence was working for the recently formed National Defense Research Committee. Robert Brode was at the Applied Physics Laboratory at Johns Hopkins, and Leonard B. Loeb, professor of physics, was in the Naval Reserve.

b. The Seventh Annual Washington Conference on Theoretical Physics, May 22–24, 1941, was on the topic of the theory of elementary particles. The annual conferences were sponsored jointly by George Washington University and the Department of Terrestrial Magnetism of the Carnegie Institution of Washington. On May 22 Oppenheimer led the discussion on the theory of the meson. For a report of the conference see *Science,* 94 (July 25, 1941): 92–94.

OPPENHEIMER'S POLITICAL CONCERNS during this period are evident in his letter of protest to Senator F. R. Coudert, Jr., co-chairman of the State of New York Joint Legislative Committee to Investigate the Public Educational System. Since the beginning of 1941 the committee had been conducting a highly publicized probe into alleged subversive influence in the New York City college system, at a time when the Teachers' Union was making gains in its organizational efforts. The style, familiar to those who remember the subsequent techniques of Senator Joseph McCarthy, was characterized by public accusations or innuendos that various faculty members had communist ties or sympathies. The New York City Board of Higher Education set up "trial" committees which often recommended the dismissal of the accused. In one such case John Kenneth Ackley, registrar of City College, was dismissed in June 1941 "after being found guilty of conduct unbecoming a member of the college staff." An analysis of the case was made by Harlow Shapley and Donald Menzel of Harvard and Ernest M. Patterson of the University of Pennsylvania for the American Committee for Democracy and Intellectual Freedom (ACDIF), which condemned the motives and procedures of the investigating committees in a statement published in the *New York Times* on September 25. By that time, twenty-eight staff members had been dismissed at City College alone. Coudert responded by attacking the ACDIF, accusing them of communist ties and cooperation with the Teachers' Union, and his position was supported by a *New York Times* editorial.[63] Oppenheimer was a member of the teachers' union in California and of the ACDIF. His letter to Coudert clearly identified the fundamental issues at stake.

113 | TO F. R. COUDERT, JR.

Berkeley, California
October 13, 1941

Dear Senator Coudert:

Thank you for your letter of October 3, for the interesting clipping from the Times, and for your long reply.

As a remote and not very active member of the American Committee for Democracy and Intellectual Freedom, I should like to answer two points in your statement that seem, at this distance, not without interest.

1) It was, I suppose, the immediate purpose of your investigation to discover, expose, and force the dismissal from the school system of communists, and communist sympathizers. It will have been said, assuredly not without justice, that men have been dismissed because of the activities of your committee who do not in fact belong in that category; it will also have been said, and perhaps also with justice, that the purposes of your investigation went far beyond this avowed purpose. It is not with these points that I am concerned, but rather with your contention that this investigation was compatible in spirit as well as in letter with the Bill of Rights. You state that

218

your committee has not challenged the right of a teacher to any beliefs, however radical. But the Bill of Rights guarantees not the right to a belief, but the right to express that belief, in speech or in writing—and this right has been held to include (subject to restrictions having to do with libel) the right of anonymity. The Bill of Rights also guarantees (here with restrictions on the "clear and present danger") freedom of assembly. I think it a reasonable presumption—and one that no evidence of your committee that has come to my attention would disprove—that the activities of teachers who were communists or communist sympathizers consisted precisely in meeting, speaking their views, and publishing them (often anonymously), in engaging, that is, in practices specifically protected by the Bill of Rights. Under these circumstances your statement that the investigation committee denied to no teacher his freedom of belief seems to me of an extreme and vicious disingenuity.

2) The second point concerns the procedure of your committee, about which I have read grave and well substantiated charges, and the procedure at the "trial" of Ackley and others. The careful and, I assure you, quite disinterested studies of my colleagues Shapley and Menzel could hardly leave any doubt about the "trial" procedure; but it took your own statement, with its sanctimonious equivocations and its red baiting, to get me to believe that the stories of mixed cajolery, intimidation and arrogance on the part of the committee of which you are chairman, are in fact true.

Faithfully,

J. R. Oppenheimer

THE FOLLOWING NOTE to Lawrence refers to the American Association of Scientific Workers, established in 1938 on the model of an older British organization concerned with social relations of science in general and in particular with salaries, hours, and conditions of laboratory work.

In 1954 Oppenheimer testified at the hearing before the Personnel Security Board that "some time after we moved to Eagle Hill, possibly in the autumn of 1941, a group of people came to my house one afternoon to discuss whether or not it would be a good idea to set up a branch of the Association of Scientific Workers. We concluded negatively, and I know my own views were negative."[64]

With the exception of a few senior scientists, including Arthur H. Compton, members of the AASW were mostly young, and Berkeley was not the only place where its union-like claims were discouraged as war approached.

Berkeley
November 12, 1941

Dear Ernest,

I had hoped to see you before you left, but will write this to assure you that there will be no further difficulties at any time with the A.A.S.W. I think that your own feeling about the men working directly with you will have a good deal of weight also with those scientists whose defense efforts are not in the Radiation Laboratory, and I doubt very much whether anyone will want to start at this time an organization which could in any way embarrass, divide or interfere with the work we have in hand. I have not yet spoken to everyone involved, but all those to whom I have spoken agree with us; so you can forget it.

Have a good trip and come back soon!

Robert

I. I. Rabi, Dorothy McKibbin, Robert Oppenheimer, Victor Weisskopf at the Oppenheimers' home in Los Alamos, New Mexico, about 1944. (Courtesy of Los Alamos Scientific Laboratory.)

Robert Oppenheimer and Major W. A. Stevens on a trip to select a site for the first atomic bomb test, early May 1944. (Courtesy of Kenneth T. Bainbridge.)

Robert Oppenheimer and General Leslie R. Groves revisiting the Alamogordo, New Mexico, test site. They are at the base of the steel tower on which the atomic bomb had been mounted in July 1945. The blast had vaporized most of the tower and fused the surface of the surrounding sands into a jade green glass-like material. (United Press International Photo.)

IV | "These terrible years of war"
LOS ALAMOS, 1942–1945

THE SECRECY that shrouded Oppenheimer's wartime activities fostered the legend of an ivory-towered scientist and aesthete with leftwing political sympathies suddenly and miraculously transformed into an outstanding administrator and an influential member of the scientific establishment. The change did not happen overnight and was not a miracle. True, many who knew the prewar Oppenheimer would not have predicted it, but in the leader of the unprecedented undertaking they recognized familiar traits: the quick and omnicompetent intellect, the capacity for hard work, the personal charisma, the thoughtfulness for others. What had not always been obvious was the self-discipline that enabled Oppenheimer to apply these talents to the problems of a large and multifaceted project.

Writer Paul Horgan, in no way privy to Oppenheimer's wartime occupation, was not surprised to learn what role his old friend had played. "A true relation to the imaginative art," explains Horgan, "[involves] a sense of design and order in affairs . . . Robert was a first class manipulator of the imagination and interpreter of it. It doesn't amaze me at all—it didn't at the time—that he should create this immense organization and have it run to his wishes, to his design."[1]

Whatever the reaction of his friends, Oppenheimer emerged from the Los Alamos experience with a new self-image. Letters from the war period illustrate this, the most dramatic of several transitions in his life. These letters, which have been selected from a huge corpus of correspondence and memorandums, illustrate Oppenheimer's style as director: his determination to pick the best people, his persuasiveness as a recruiter, his involvement in the varied aspects of the enterprise, and his concern for the well-being of his oddly assorted charges. From the beginning Oppenheimer recognized that he was dealing in all areas with the highly unpredictable, though like others he failed to foresee the scale of operations and the size of the community needed to sustain them.

Although Oppenheimer eventually came to symbolize the scientific achievement represented by the atomic bomb, by the time he played a significant part in it the project had a complicated administrative and diplomatic history and much research had already been done in laboratories in Britain, France, and America.[2] Of the nearly one hundred papers on topics related to fission that appeared prior to the scientists' self-imposed ban on publication, none bears Oppenheimer's name, but he constantly engaged in theoretical speculation and discourse. In early 1941, when Ernest Lawrence began to develop the electromagnetic process for separating the uranium isotope 235, Oppenheimer and a group of theoretical physicists worked directly with him.

Since October 1939 a presidential Committee on Uranium had been trying to coordinate research directed to the separation of isotopes and to the achievement of a sustained chain reaction, but many scientists considered these efforts woefully inadequate in view of the probability that the Germans were working on an atomic weapon. Their concern led to major reorganization of the United States project in June 1941 through which the Committee on Uranium became the Section on Uranium (S-1) in the newly established Office of Scientific Research and Development (OSRD) headed by Vannevar Bush and his deputy James B. Conant. Oppenheimer was aware, as were many nuclear physicists and chemists, of the debate over which method of separating isotopes should be developed—gaseous diffusion, thermal diffusion, or Lawrence's electromagnetic process—and of the final decision that, in the interest of speed, pilot plants for all three, plus a graphite pile for the production of plutonium, must be built. It was well known, too, that Bush had delegated the building of these plants, which involved site acquisition and recruitment of personnel and equipment, to the Army.

Bush and his military counterparts were still trying to settle thorny questions relating to major plant construction when America's entry into war in December 1941 provided the incentive for more rigorous organization of the fission-related research under way in civilian laboratories. Arthur H. Compton was assigned the task of coordinating and expanding theoretical and experimental studies relating to fissionable materials and the production of a weapon. In January 1942 he organized the work in progress in Chicago under the code name of the Metallurgical Laboratory (or Met Lab) and recruited new staff. Compton also supervised work in laboratories across the country, including Fermi's slow neutron graphite pile at Columbia, later moved to Chicago, and research on fast neutron reactions for eventual application to explosives under way in several locations under the direction of Gregory Breit.

Robert Oppenheimer's direct participation in these critical developments began late and then only when Ernest Lawrence insisted that he be invited to a conference in Schenectady, New York, on October 21, 1941, to discuss fast neutron reactions. "Oppenheimer has important new ideas," Lawrence wired Compton on October 14, and in a follow-up letter, "I have a great deal of confidence in Oppenheimer." In Schenectady Oppenheimer offered his estimate of the amount of U^{235} required for a bomb. On December 8 he sent Compton some more figures and explained why these did not agree with Compton's.[3] In January 1942, as Compton reordered his sprawling command, he made Oppenheimer responsible for the fast neutron research at Berkeley. Soon thereafter Oppenheimer acquired regular secretarial help and began keeping a file of official correspondence, though some letters have a distinctly personal cast as do earlier ones primarily about physics.

OPPENHEIMER'S RESPONSIBILITIES as head of the fast neutron work in Berkeley, combined with the general dislocation in normal routines of teaching and research that had taken place since Pearl Harbor, prompted a letter to President Millikan at Caltech.

115 | TO ROBERT A. MILLIKAN

Berkeley
March 20. [1942]

Dear Dr Millikan,

The wholly altered character of our work, both in Pasadena and in Berkeley, during these war years, has made it seem wise for us to reconsider whether my customary visits to the Institute, and my work there during the Spring semester, might not with reason be abandoned. It is I think certain that the arguments that have in the past justified my work in Pasadena no longer apply, and that new and compelling reasons have arisen for my leaving Berkeley as little as possible. I have appreciated too deeply the opportunities for research and collaboration that my connection with the Institute has afforded to be willing to see that connection lightly or irreparably broken. Would it be possible for us to discuss this question, in Pasadena, at your convenience, at some not too distant time? It would be possible for me to be in Pasadena any Saturday. Would you let me have a note to say when you will be there, and when it will be most convenient for us to have a few minutes together?

With all cordial greetings

Robert Oppenheimer

Millikan replied that he and his associates would also be loathe to see the Caltech tie broken. "It is of course true," he continued, "that the emergency has thrown all of us here completely out of our normal orbits and thus changed very radically our activities and the theoretical needs of our jobs. Charley [Lauritsen]'s nuclear physics work has been dropped completely because he is so extraordinarily useful and effective in producing tangible results on short order war-time devices."[4] This exchange, plus whatever conversation followed, severed Oppenheimer's formal connection with Pasadena for the duration of the war.

In May, when Breit resigned as director of the fast neutron research being done under S–1 Committee auspices, Compton asked Oppenheimer to take his place. Oppenheimer's task was to coordinate theoretical calculations on basic nuclear reactions with experimental data in order to estimate both the critical mass of material needed for fission and the efficiency of the proposed weapon. Oppenheimer accepted the assignment on condition that an experimental physicist could assist him. Compton chose John H. Manley, professor of physics at the University of Illinois, who had joined the Metallurgical Laboratory the previous January. Manley had once met Oppenheimer casually and doubted that he could communicate at all with such a "high-powered and erudite theoretical physicist." However, Manley was persuaded to accept the appointment, and for the next nine months, until he joined Oppenheimer at Los Alamos on April 4, 1943, they were in constant touch through conferences and correspondence.[5]

Once Manley's assistance was assured, Oppenheimer began seeking advice from scientists who had done research in neutron physics, even though some were currently employed on other war projects. One of those consulted was Robert Bacher, since 1940 on leave from his professorship of physics at Cornell to work on development of radar at the M.I.T. Radiation Laboratory. The conference that prompted the following letter to consultants and research directors was one of several convened by Oppenheimer in the pre-Los Alamos period.[6]

224

[Chicago, Illinois]
June 10, 1942

Dear Dr. Bacher:

As a result of our discussion in Chicago last Saturday, it has I think become clear to all of us how very far we are from the solution of our essential problems; what I am writing about is to suggest some minor organizational steps which I hope will help to assure the two things that we most need: reliability and speed. I think that probably some trouble has arisen in the past because too much work has gone on without detailed consultation. It would seem to me that all directors of projects in this field should recognize the importance of communicating at once either with Dr. Manley, or with me, or with other authorized persons, if they run into a problem which worries them or which promises to delay their work. In the same way, I think that if other materials, if made available, would facilitate the work, project directors should communicate their needs at once to this office. In fact, if the difficulties in the work appear serious enough, there is no reason why we should not call a conference to discuss them either in the laboratory where the specific project is in progress, or here in Chicago. It seems certain that on some of the projects which are being pursued simultaneously along parallel lines in more than one laboratory, we shall want to get together the people involved for a critical discussion at not too infrequent intervals.

Dr. Manley will make his headquarters in this laboratory but he will be free when the need arises to come to any of the laboratories where our work is in progress. I would like to urge you to take advantage of the possibility of discussion and help which this will afford us. In general, the purpose of this letter is only to ask you not to count the inconveniences of communication, travel, and the time of Dr. Manley and myself as very valuable in comparison with the actual progress of the work. You will receive from Dr. Manley an outline of the work now in progress which may help to clarify what we are really after. Finally, both Dr. Manley and I should like copies of your fortnightly progress reports. In order to fix our responsibilities, Dr. Manley and I would appreciate it if all correspondence were addressed, either specifically to him, or specifically to me; but that in all cases copies be sent to both of us.

Cordially yours,

J. R. Oppenheimer

Meanwhile, Oppenheimer was organizing a summer session in Berkeley to explore the theoretical aspects of nuclear explosions for which he was directly responsible. One of his first recruits was John Van Vleck of Harvard, whose help he then sought in securing the presence of Hans Bethe. Bethe had moved to the United States in 1935 and joined the faculty at Cornell University, where he became professor of physics in 1937.

117 | TO JOHN H. VAN VLECK

[Berkeley, California]
June 10, 1942

Dear Van:

Compton talked yesterday to DuBridge;[a] apparently that end of it is quite clear. Bethe's contract is not with the Radiation Laboratory directly but at Cornell. He is at the Radiation Lab for a month only, to gain experience, and DuBridge indicated that it would be quite appropriate for him to spend the summer with us, if that is what seems to him the best way to put in his time. This means, therefore, that there are no formal difficulties and that the essential point is to enlist Bethe's interest, to impress on him the magnitude of the job we have to do, and thus the fact that a week's consultation would not be enough, and to try to convince him, too, that our present plans, the organization which we have set up, are the appropriate machinery. I know that you will be more successful in this than anyone else who could attempt it.

Mostly I am busy with the experimental side now, but every time I think about our problem a new headache appears. We shall certainly have our hands full. I should like to tell you again how glad I am that we are going to be working together.

Please do not hesitate to let me know if anything comes up where I can be of use or comfort.

Cordially,

[Robert Oppenheimer]

a. Lee A. DuBridge was director of the Radiation Laboratory at M.I.T., on leave from the chairmanship of the physics department at the University of Rochester.

Van Vleck met Bethe in an empty spot in Harvard Yard to obtain his consent, then sent word to Oppenheimer via a twenty-five cent "kiddygram" containing some prearranged code message such as "Brush your teeth."[7] Others who attended all or part of the Berkeley sessions were Edward Teller, nominally of George Washington University but temporarily at Columbia, Emil Konopinski of Indiana University, Felix Bloch of Stanford, and three of Oppenheimer's former students: Stanley S. Frankel, Eldred C. Nelson, and Robert Serber. All but Van Vleck would later join the Los Alamos staff.

While assembling what he described as the "luminaries," Oppenheimer replied to John Manley's reports with comments of his own. He questioned the value of two proposed pieces of research; one of the men suggested was reputedly difficult to work with. There were problems in several laboratories: equipment improperly designed, similar samples yielding conflicting data, delay in completion of a contract which in turn affected priorities in obtaining supplies. It was hard to settle such matters by correspondence, but Oppenheimer hoped to postpone a trip to Chicago until the end of July, when the theoretical group in Berkeley had completed its report. As for himself and Serber, "We are up to our ears in every kind of work," said Oppenheimer, noting especially the fission neutron yields obtained from uranium bombarded with neutrons of various energies. He worried about the effect of U^{238}.[8]

THE BERKELEY CONFERENCE absorbed Oppenheimer's attention during much of July. Reviewing the experimental data and the theoretical calculations available from British and American sources, the group concluded "that the development of the fission bomb would require a major scientific and technical effort."[9]

The Berkeley group also made theoretical calculations relating to a far more powerful explosion that might result from a thermonuclear reaction in deuterium, a possibility that had been discussed before the war. At a certain point in the Berkeley deliberations, when figures seemed to indicate that an atomic explosion might trigger an uncontrolled reaction in the atmosphere, Oppenheimer went to Chicago and pursued Compton to his cottage on a remote lake in northern Michigan to warn him that such an event seemed theoretically possible. They agreed that the Berkeley theorists must continue their calculations. If these failed to provide absolutely conclusive evidence that an atomic explosion could be contained, the bomb project must stop.[10]

Final results from Berkeley satisfied Compton and his associates, but one participant in the summer session continued to think about a more powerful, though controlled, device.

[Berkeley, California]
September 11, 1942

Dear Edward:

Your fine letter came yesterday. We are planning to leave here on the streamliner September 17. That brings us to Chicago September 19. I am so informing Kski.[a] Our plans are to spend five days to a week in Chicago and it is possible that I shall stay on longer myself.

Your worries certainly differed very much from ours over this past week and, in fact, the suggestions that you make have by now for us a pretty fantastic sound. We have been reexamining, especially Hans [Bethe] of course, the question of conductivity and the first result of this is that very high temperatures will be extremely hard to reach and that the edge of the deuterium will always be quite cool. At a half a million volts temperature the electron mean free path is 40 c.m.; the albedo really does not help much and therefore unless one has huge volumes, temperatures will certainly be limited to something under this value. Even if one does have huge receptacles the temperature near any body which can radiate effectively will be very much lower. For this reason, too, in addition to those we spoke of before, no other thermo-nuclear reactions will occur. We are satisfied, however, with the uranium.

Of course, this big conductivity further complicates the initial detonation and it seems likely that somewhat larger disks of 25 [uranium 235] and fairly careful wall design will really have to be used. We have some rough ideas on these subjects.

We spent one afternoon looking at the wedges and are willing to guarantee that they will be a lot of trouble and not worth it. The rest can wait until we get to Chicago, except all our cordial greetings and our good wishes to you both.

Robert Oppenheimer

a. "Kski" was the contraction generally employed by Emil Konopinski's friends.

OPPENHEIMER AND JOHN MANLEY exchanged frequent reports. They made a good team, but, in Manley's words, "it was really no way to run a program."[11] At the highest level of what had become the Development of Substitute Materials (or DSM) project, Bush and Conant were reaching the same conclusion. A June 1942 reorganization, designed to define lines of authority between OSRD and the Army, had not prevented arguments over contracts, priorities, and construction sites for the pilot plants to produce fissionable materials which would eventually make up the huge installations at Oak Ridge, Tennessee, and Hanford, Washington.

Progress in resolving these problems was speeded up immeasurably after September 17, when General Leslie R. Groves took charge of the Manhattan Engineer District (so-called because Groves' predecessor had operated out of a New York City office). To assure the continued influence of scientists, Bush proposed a military policy committee to work closely with Groves. This three-member committee began to function immediately. Bush represented OSRD, with Conant as his alternate; the other two were Army and Navy officers. Major decisions had yet to be made; policies, programs, and time tables were constantly revised. But from the time of Groves' appointment, he and the Military Policy Committee directed the multifarious activities of the Manhattan Project. Conant, backed by Bush, served as liaison in matters relating to scientific research and bomb development.

One of the first decisions made by Groves and the new committee was to centralize the work that Oppenheimer and Manley were supervising, for if the Allies were to win what was then assumed to be a race with Germany to develop a fission weapon, certain scientific and engineering problems had to be solved quickly. A new weapons laboratory might be attached to the Chicago Met Lab, but attention there was focusing on Fermi's experiments with slow neutron reactions in a graphite pile; besides, security was difficult to enforce in a large city. Another possible site was Oak Ridge, where research relating to production of fissionable materials was being concentrated, but Oppenheimer, among others, was opposed to making the weapons laboratory an appendage to the giant production plants.[12]

Plans were still tentative when he wrote Manley about the proposed changes. "Ed" was Edwin McMillan, on leave from the Berkeley physics department, first at the M.I.T. Radiation Laboratory, then briefly at the U.S. Navy Radio and Sound Laboratory in San Diego. In the autumn of 1942 he returned to Berkeley to help Oppenheimer plan the new laboratory.[13]

Oppenheimer also reported to Manley on a typical set of personnel problems and on the progress of certain research projects. Most of the scientists for whose work they were responsible were studying nuclear reactions. The investigators were using as targets a variety of substances which they bombarded with atomic "projectiles" accelerated to high energies in a cyclotron, a Van de Graaff (electrostatic) generator, or a Cockcroft–Walton accelerator. The results of the reaction were observed with one of several available counting devices and expressed numerically as cross-sections. (The cross-section represents the probability that a given type of reaction will occur and is obtained by dividing the observed number of events by the

229

number of incident particles and the number of target nuclei per square centimeter.) Oppenheimer and Manley were receiving a great deal of useful experimental data, but in assuring themselves that results obtained at different laboratories were truly consistent and accurate, they faced complicated logistics problems, including exchange of samples and procedural information. The difficulties in establishing the quantitative basis for the design of an atomic weapon became an important argument for a central laboratory.

Nuclear physicists employed a shorthand to indicate the substance used in a given experiment, the type of particle with which it was bombarded, and the type of particle resulting from the bombardment. In the following letter, Li (p, n) referred to an event in which lithium had absorbed a proton and emitted a neutron (or, more colloquially, proton in, neutron out). D-D indicated that deuterons had been bombarded with deuterons (producing high energy neutrons). Oppenheimer was not always meticulous in using the comma, the hyphen, and the parentheses, but his correspondents understood the type of reaction to which he referred.

The numbers 49, 25, and 23 were Project codes for certain fissionable isotopes and were formed by combining the last digits of the atomic number and of the atomic weight. For example, plutonium 239, atomic number 94, became 49; uranium 235, atomic number 92, became 25; uranium 233, atomic number 92, became 23.

When news of uranium fission broke in 1939, scientists began to speculate about other, as yet unidentified, elements that might be fissionable. In June 1940 Edwin McMillan and Philip Abelson (a visitor at Berkeley from the Carnegie Institution of Washington) published results of experiments which identified element 93 (neptunium) and indicated the presence of yet another transuranic element. When McMillan left to work on radar at M.I.T., Glenn Seaborg carried on McMillan's research. Using a Berkeley Radiation Laboratory cyclotron to bombard uranium 238 with neutrons, early in 1941 Seaborg's team produced measurable quantities of element 94, which they named plutonium. In April 1942 Seaborg moved to Chicago as a section chief at the Met Lab.

A contributor to the plutonium experiments was Emilio Segrè.[14] Segrè had come to the United States from Italy in 1938, and in 1941 held a research appointment at the Berkeley Radiation Laboratory. When the Los Alamos laboratory was organized in 1943 he became a group leader in the Experimental Physics Division.

[Berkeley, California]
October 12, 1942

Dear John:

I shall answer your fine letter at some length, in spite of the fact that I may be in Chicago about as soon as this answer. The reason for that is that I may want to sit in on a conference Thursday for the planning of our laboratory. I did see General Groves when he was here and we discussed the problem of the laboratory rather fully, and by this means managed to undo such certainty as had before been reached. I think that he was convinced of the necessity for proceeding immediately with the construction of the laboratory and the reorganization of our work, but I think that he was much less willing than he had been before to see it at the same site as the production. For this reason some rather far reaching geographical change in plans seems to be in the cards and I do not know to what extent this will bring jurisdictional changes with it; that is, I do not know whether plans for this laboratory will still be cleared through Chicago or whether we shall need some new machinery for these problems. In the former case I will probably come to Chicago for the Thursday meeting.

Because of these complications I am not quite sure who should do the approving and checking of our temporary plans, but I think that everything that you have done to get some sketches into the hands of Stone and Webster is to the good.[a] I think our plans are quite modest as far as space is concerned and Ed [McMillan] seems to share this view. If there is any revision in the number of rooms I think it should be a revision upward; from 38, say, to 50. I am afraid that if we postpone expansion for another year it will be much harder for us to get the buildings up.

Now for some of the other questions:

1. I was pleased to get Holloway's report and hope that he will make up his mind as to the relative virtues of Rochester and Yale. Probably by the time this gets to you, you will have settled it. I think that Rochester would have the advantage of being a little bit less far from Chicago and I have a little bit more confidence in the technical qualities of their cyclotron. Also, it is nearer Cornell. If the personnel problem can be solved, let us push for Rochester.[b]

2. Langer seems a good solution for Auger. In any case, we should start now on a policy of absolutely unscrupulous recruiting of anyone we can lay hands on. It will pay us well later.[c]

3. I have had no answer from Urey on the depleted carbon. You might check with Mrs. Tracy to see whether the letter ever got to him. If it did and we don't hear from him I will follow up with something more urgent.[d]

4. I have also discussed with Seaborg the desirability of testing the 49 and 23 but think that we should use Li(pn) and DD for this work. I am a little reluctant to turn over these materials to any of our outlying laboratories and wonder whether it could be arranged to make comparative runs with DD in Chicago. We have already arranged to investigate them with the Berkeley photo neutron sources. The evidence now is that 49 at least is appreciably better than 25.

5. I think that the problem of McKibben's fugacity will probably remain unsolved until Ed gets on the job. I should hate to see you spend your time there and think that it would on the whole be a greater loss than it would benefit. But I do think that if you could plan to run up there even a few hours a fortnight you might do a lot of good. Is it possible to establish contact also with Hanson? Is he a more steady, responsible fellow? I think it will do nothing but make trouble if Williams comes down there.[e]

6. The nD cross sections from Williams' runs seem quite reasonable to us, perhaps a bit on the low side. The errors still are too large. I think that we will have to be willing to use the theoretical n,p cross sections and as you know, we are preparing a report on them which will be something of an improvement over Kittell and Breit.[f] It is obvious that any really valid check on this theory would be very helpful and therefore my answer to your question about oxygen is that if Williams can do it in such a way that the measurement has any meaning it would be a fine thing. Is there a possibility of working with liquid oxygen? I don't see that it will do us any good to introduce a new uncertainty such as would arise in the work if we used an oxide. Also, I think that it will be of no use to us unless the oxygen cross section can be known to within 10 or 20 per cent, and even this I believe will involve an error greater than in the theory.

7. I am going down to Stanford Wednesday to see Bloch's set-up. He is delighted with the performance of his icebox and feels full of confidence that their work will go along rapidly and well. I need give you no report on developments here since Segrè is in Chicago and nothing new has arisen.

8. That leaves only one question unanswered: how to get you out of the mad house and to California. I think it will be easy to get you out of that mad house and that we will be doing that very soon now, but I am afraid that what you will be getting into will be a good deal worse; at least, a good deal grimmer.

How is Snell's experiment?[g] If I'm not coming on next week let me hear from you soon.

Good luck—

[Robert Oppenheimer]

a. Stone & Webster Engineering Corporation was a principal contractor for the DSM Project.

b. Marshall G. Holloway, a member of the Cornell physics department, worked with the cyclotron at the Purdue Research Foundation until he and his group went to Los Alamos in 1943.

c. Lawrence M. Langer, a physicist from Indiana University, went to Los Alamos in 1943 as an alternate group leader. Pierre Auger, a French experimental physicist, had been a research associate at the University of Chicago since 1941.

d. Harold Urey, professor of chemistry at Columbia and a member of the S-1 Executive Committee, was in charge of work on the gaseous diffusion method of separating uranium 235.

e. Joseph L. McKibben and Alfred O. Hanson were young physicists at the University of Wisconsin who went to Los Alamos in 1943. Oppenheimer's long-distance judgment about McKibben's volatility was not a final one. McKibben proved so reliable that he was entrusted with a critical last-minute task at the 1945 Alamogordo test. John H. Williams, associate professor of physics at the University of Minnesota, was an early arrival at Los Alamos. Initially a group leader in the Experimental Physics Division, he later held other responsible administrative positions.

f. Charles Kittel, Breit's collaborator, was a 1941 Ph.D. at Wisconsin.

g. Arthur H. Snell was chief of the cyclotron section of the Met Lab.

Neither the official history of the Manhattan Project nor that of the Los Alamos Laboratory (soon to be designated Site Y) assign a precise date to Oppenheimer's appointment as director of the new laboratory. Groves later stated that he first met Oppenheimer in Berkeley on October 8 and that, after careful consideration of all available candidates, he concluded that Oppenheimer was the best qualified although he lacked the administrative experience of other Manhattan Project leaders and the prestige of a Nobel prize.[15] If Oppenheimer's comments to Manley about the tentative state of planning reflect his own ambiguous position, this did not halt his vigilant watch over detail.

Meanwhile, the process of selecting a site for the new laboratory got under way, the principal consideration being isolation. Oppenheimer, no less than Groves, was concerned about security of information, but security from whom? Letters of the summer and autumn of 1942 show how many angles Oppenheimer had to keep in mind. In addition to the obvious threat of foreign spying, there were strict rules regarding compartmentalization of information within the Manhattan Project. And with Bush's concurrence, the Army had decreed that British scientists, who had provided so much information basic to the development of an atomic weapon, should not be given figures relating to energy release and demolition areas—no great problem, Oppenheimer confided to one of his correspondents, since these figures were not known anyway.[16] Still, the restriction, though temporary, enlarged the concept of "the enemy" from which the new laboratory had to be secured.

THE NEXT TWO LETTERS, one of them from Seaborg to Oppenheimer, relate to one of the most serious problems that arose in the course of developing an atomic weapon and give a sense of the complexity of the problems that regularly confronted Oppenheimer as director of the weapons project. Scientists in Berkeley and Chicago, as well as in Britain, were beginning to realize that alpha particles formed by the natural radioactive decay of plutonium would react with any traces of light elements present as impurities. Neutrons produced in such a reaction could in turn cause a low-level explosion before assembly of a bomb was complete. The problem was eventually solved less by development of chemical and metallurgical techniques that achieved the necessary extreme purity than by developing a wholly new and much faster method of assembling the critical mass of fissionable material, largely eliminating the predetonation problem.[17]

120 | GLENN T. SEABORG TO ROBERT OPPENHEIMER

[Chicago, Illinois]
November 3, 1942

Dear Robert:

There is one point that has been worrying me quite a good deal since the discussion that we had in Berkeley the early part of last month. This relates to the number of neutrons that it is permissible to have present in the final 49 product in order not to cause complications in its control. You have stated that it would be ideal if the spontaneous fission rate were as long as 10^{19} years. If this figure is a desirable limit, and if you can not get around it any other way, this creates a formidable chemical problem because of the possibility of forming neutrons from the α,n reaction on light element impurities. Since the alpha-emitting life of 49 is about 10^4 years, 10^{15} alphas must not produce an undesirable neutron. Assuming that an element like boron, for example, has a cross section for the α,n reaction of about 1 in 10^4, this would mean that boron must be absent in the final product to the extent of 1 part in 10^{11}.

You can see why I am disturbed if this calculation is correct and if you are actually limited by this requirement. Even if you can stand 10^5 times as many neutrons as this, making the limits of light impurities which are permissible one part in about a million, the final chemical purification is still a formidable problem. In fact, if these requirements are going to be placed upon our chemical procedures, I should like to know definitely about it as soon as possible since this will require a great deal of development work along lines which so far have never been attempted.

I have discussed this matter somewhat with Dr. Manley and Dr. Teller and I believe that they also consider it a rather serious problem.

With best regards,

Cordially,

Glenn T. Seaborg

121 | TO GLENN T. SEABORG

[Berkeley, California]
November 6, 1942

Dear Glenn:

Thanks for your fine letter. The problem you raise is not a new one, nor is it limited to the 49. I've thought about it a little in connection with the 25-24, and it is probably time to get possibilities clear.

With the 25 alone matters would not be so bad: a concentration of light impurities (B Be Al, C N) of 10^{-4} would give us the more than ideal 10^{19} years equivalent. If, as in our present set up, almost all the 24 goes along with the 25, then things are about 25 times worse. I believe that we can probably get along with 10^{17} years equivalent if we have to. Therefore I should say that the chemical problem with 24-25 mixture was hard but probably soluble. Do you agree in this?

With the 49, even allowing a factor 10 in your estimate of yield and a factor 100 in our requirements, it still comes to a purity of about 10^{-8}. Is this hopeless?

It would be a help to know what you think on these points fairly soon, since if your answers are in the negative it will mean not only rather radical and I am afraid rather inefficient redesign, but also the immediate prospect of some new production problems for other materials.

How bad is 23?

Thanks again for your letter, and let me know what your ideas re this chemistry are as soon as you can.

With all good greetings,

Robert Oppenheimer

235

WITH ISOLATION UPPERMOST in mind, Lt. Col. W. H. Dudley, to whom Groves assigned the preliminary survey of laboratory sites, narrowed the choice to the southern Rockies and finally to a site near the village of Jemez Springs on the western side of the Jemez Mountains northwest of Santa Fe, New Mexico. Presumably Oppenheimer's status as director had been clarified when he wrote Manley enthusiastically about the prospective location which he had visited on pack trips from the Pecos.[18]

This letter illustrates the importance to the bomb project of prewar research in nuclear physics and chemistry in laboratory facilities at universities throughout the United States. Joseph W. Kennedy, an instructor at Berkeley, collaborated with Seaborg in carrying to a conclusion the work that led to the discovery of plutonium. Kennedy became director of the Chemistry and Metallurgy Division at Los Alamos.

122 | TO JOHN H. MANLEY

[Berkeley, California]
November 6, 1942

Dear John:

I have still to thank you for your good letter and for the copy of the plans. Ed [McMillan] and I made no changes in these and they will be used as the basis for the actual drawings as soon as the question of terrain is settled.

Dudley and Groves were here and the question of site is well along toward settlement. It is a lovely spot and in every way satisfactory, and the only points which now have to be settled are whether the human and legal aspects of the necessary evacuations make insuperable difficulties. Ed and I plan to go down and have a look next week, and will probably spend a few days there getting some of the important questions settled. I know that you will be very pleased with the site if we can really get this one.

I have written to Conant requesting the immediate transfer to our work of Herb, Bacher and Kurie.[a] We thought that with this group, together with you and Ed and me, we could really get started. I have no idea what success Conant will have, or whether the men themselves will be fully cooperative, but I think that Conant will bring a very sympathetic attitude to our personnel problems and that we may find fewer difficulties in all this than we anticipated. Conant's wire, by the way, was effective and Ed is with us.

There are some developments locally. The most pleasing is that the direct calibration of Segrè and Kennedy raised their cross sections by about 40 per cent. This corresponds to a manganese-hydrogen ratio of 36 and on reexamining the literature we found no shred of support for the 26 that [Herbert] Anderson gave me. Their cross sections are now in reasonable ac-

236

cord with Heydenburg and with the results that McKibben has been sending.[b]

The second development is this. Ed and I went down to Stanford where they were just beginning to detect the fission neutrons. Ed made the very useful suggestion of reducing the fast neutron effects by a monitoring fast neutron chamber put on the grid of their first tube with an appropriate negative amplification. This will cut down very much the time they need to wait. Segrè and Kennedy went down there too, and are helping them set up an enriched fission chamber which they can use to measure directly their fast neutron densities. This not only has the advantage of rendering their spectrum absolute, but will throw some at present needed light on whether their hydrogen chamber is really performing as it should.

As for Minneapolis, the problem is rendered difficult because we are not yet sure how soon it will be appropriate to move people into the new laboratory. But there is one point it would be worth their looking at if they can do it in a reasonable time: that is to get an idea of the angular distribution of the n–D scattering at their higher energies. If you remember our program, we will be principally interested in energies of 5 Mev and above, and I thought it would be some time before the Minnesota results would be available there. The angular distribution work need not be very precise.

We have the curves for the n,p scattering and they are being reproduced now. They will be accompanied by a short explanatory article on the uncertainties and approximations. Actually, these curves are about the most certain thing we have in the whole work. I shall send you a few copies of these curves and might leave it to you to find out whether we need any further authorization before sending them around to the laboratories concerned.

Kamen has decided that it would be better to make our He^3 by devoting the cyclotron to D-D bombardment for a few days, and is doing that now.[c] We will have time to increase the amounts to what is needed before the Purdue people are ready.

I had to re-refer Simon's request to Bush since he was unwilling to have me invite Peierls.[d] I hope it will come out all right, but am quite worried.

I am not sending a copy of this to Compton since there are some parts of it that do not immediately concern him, but I should be glad to have you tell him anything about the developments in physics that you think he would like to hear. Don't tell him about our laboratory. We will leave that to other people.

I still don't know when I'll get East, but it certainly won't be after December 1, and may be much sooner.

Yours,

[Robert Oppenheimer]

a. Bacher joined the project; Raymond G. Herb of the University of Wisconsin and Franz N. D. Kurie, doing war research at Berkeley, did not.

b. The amount of fissile material which would have to be made for each weapon was very dependent on the values of these various nuclear cross sections being measured. Herbert L. Anderson was a graduate student at Columbia. Norman P. Heydenburg was making cross section measurements at the High Voltage Laboratory of the Carnegie Institution of Washington's Department of Terrestrial Magnetism.

c. The physical chemist Martin Kamen was at the Berkeley Radiation Laboratory.

d. Franz E. (Francis) Simon, professor of physics at Oxford, and Rudolf Peierls, professor of physics at Birmingham, were members of the British atomic weapons project's technical committee. At the time of Peierls' proposed visit Bush was engaged in delicate negotiations about exchange of atomic information with the British. For the context of these discussions, see pp. 266–267 below.

Oppenheimer and McMillan visited Jemez Springs with Colonel Dudley on November 16.[19] By the time Groves arrived in the afternoon, the two scientists had decided that the deep canyon, while certainly remote, was much too constricted for laboratories and housing and that boundary fences atop the steep rock walls could not be properly patrolled. Dudley was not convinced. "We were arguing about this when General Groves showed up," McMillan later recalled. "As soon as Groves saw the site he didn't like it; he said, 'This will never do,' and I never had a chance to make my fine arguments about it." At that point Oppenheimer remarked that on up the canyon, on the east side of the Jemez range, was a boys' school on a flat mesa; this might be a possible site. "So we all got into cars," continued McMillan, "we didn't ride horses, as some people have said (that's too far), and . . . went . . . to Los Alamos Ranch School . . . [It] was late in the afternoon. There was a slight snow falling . . . It was cold and there were the boys and their masters out on the playing fields in shorts . . . As soon as Groves saw it, he said, in effect, 'This is the place' . . . I think Oppenheimer privately wanted that site anyhow but he didn't put it forward until this occasion." It is McMillan's recollection that none of the party went inside the school that day, but Groves immediately instituted inquiries about acquisition. Oppenheimer and McMillan accompanied him to Washington for further discussion, but returned four days later (on November 20) for careful inspection of the site and buildings.[20]

The Los Alamos Ranch School occupied the broad mountain end of a two-mile long mesa. Steep canyons formed the north and south boundaries. Open places could be fenced or guarded. Nearby canyons and mesas offered seclusion for nuclear experiments and test explosions. The school buildings —a dining lodge, dormitory, houses for seven or eight married teachers and a dozen maintenance staff, plus miscellaneous workshops, sheds, and storehouses—provided a nucleus around which laboratories and housing could be built for the thirty or so scientists and their families that early plans envisioned.

The nearest railroad stop was some sixty miles away, and the bad roads which isolated the mesa also made it hard of access, but by the time the general's car had descended the ten-mile track to the Rio Grande, with its hairpin turns and precipitous drops, his engineer's eye had constructed a wider and safer road. (The new road would carry load after load of building supplies, gravel for roads, laboratory equipment, including the large Harvard cyclotron magnet, and furniture, not to mention cars filled with wide-eyed, sometimes frightened, women and children before it in turn gave way to a paved and more gently curving highway.)

As for the "necessary evacuations," enrollment at the Ranch School had declined from a high of forty-two boys as the war restricted travel, but the comforting rumor that it must soon have closed for lack of students is not repeated in published accounts of its history.[21] On December 7, 1942, the formal eviction notice was received from the War Department; in February 1943, a month before the first scientists arrived, the school closed.

OPPENHEIMER'S NOVEMBER 30 report to Conant reflected the swift accumulation of data, such as that relating to tolerable levels of impurities in plutonium, that was making the new laboratory essential. It also demonstrated Oppenheimer's place in the hierarchy of information gathering, evaluation, and decision making within the Manhattan Project.

As the complexity of engineering a weapon became apparent, recruitment of staff absorbed much of Oppenheimer's attention. He had already developed a certain toughness in rejecting unsuitable candidates: one was eliminated because he was slow to adopt new ideas. Now he became more aggressive in filling gaps in his new staff. Scouts were on the lookout for needed talent; Conant could arrange release from prior commitments, but it often took an interview with Oppenheimer, in which he cautiously but eloquently described a project that would end the war and have peacetime applications of untold benefit to mankind, to persuade a man to uproot his family and join the adventure in the New Mexico mountains.

Berkeley
November 30, 1942

Dear Dr. Conant:

Your letter reached me with some delay since I returned to Berkeley only a day or so ago. I should like to answer first your P.S. You are quite right that the purities listed in Groves' compulsory memo are a little misleading. The reason for this is that Groves defined a satisfactory bomb as one that had a 50 per cent chance of exceeding a 1,000-ton TNT equivalent. The absolute requirements are figured on this basis. It is, of course, my opinion that we should be wanton to strive for such a low goal, but I believe that some good was in fact done by indicating at that time that the purity requirements are not fantastic. The desirable requirements are equally undefined since the purer the material (up to a purity of about 100-fold that given) the less must we be worried about getting the maximum speed for the firing mechanism of the detonator; and this will make for simplicity and reliability in operation. In the Washington memo all impurities were listed on the assumption that not more than five elements would reach the tabulated values. I have, in the meantime, given a much more careful account of what the actual situation is to the committee. I met with them one day in Chicago, came out with them on the train, and have spent two days with them here in Berkeley, and we have had ample opportunity to discuss the purity question and many other aspects of our problem. The information which I have given them now is contained in a Chicago report on the feasibility of the 49 project and is as follows: If the concentrations by weight are as given in the accompanying table, then the chance of pre-detonation is 5 per cent, if only one element is present in the listed amount. If n elements are present in the listed amount the chance of pre-detonation is 5n per cent. The chance of a pre-detonation in which the energy release is less than 10,000 tons TNT equivalent is 0.5n per cent. In this range the effects of impurities are additive, and from the actual concentrations and figures listed one can figure out the probability of any given energy release. In any case, unless the firing mechanism fails completely the energy release will be more than sufficient to destroy the material and to make its recovery impossible. The figures given in the table are in part based on experimental values. In the case of O and C the figures represent highly conservative estimates based on the assumption that those isotopes which are dangerous will be as dangerous as the worst element, namely, Be.

Element Concentration by Weight

Be	10^{-7}	F	5×10^{-6}
Li	5×10^{-7}	Na	2×10^{-5}
B	2×10^{-7}	Mg	10^{-4}
C	2×10^{-5}	Al	2×10^{-5}
O	10^{-4}	Si	5×10^{-4}
		P	10^{-4}

(Some purity requirements on elements between P and Fe; none beyond Cu)

The only essential changes since the Washington memo are that we have sufficiently examined the experiments on elements between Na and P to be sure that we may relax the requirements somewhat; and that we have studied the case of N carefully enough to be positive that there are no purity requirements on that element. The committee was of the opinion that the purity requirements as they now stand could, with a very high probability, be met. In fact, the Chicago uranium is good enough except for C and O, and they have made no effort at all to solve this problem. If it were necessary it would be possible to work with depleted C and O and so considerably relax the chemical conditions on these elements. In fact, the committee was of the opinion that the major extraction processes which have to be handled automatically and the removal of traces of active material, coupled with the necessity for working in lots of less than 100 grams or of introducing suitable neutron absorbers as "safers," would present greater technical difficulties than the purification. Nevertheless, in our last discussions they seemed convinced that the helium-cooled graphite pile was a good bet.

Now to the second point, the main subject of your letter, where I feel myself on less secure ground. It is, of course, natural that the men we are after will leave a big hole. I may though, in this connection, remind you that when McMillan himself left the Radiation Laboratory for San Diego there were the same dire predictions of disastrous disruption. Nevertheless, the Radiation Laboratory has not only survived but has, as you know, flourished and expanded. In view of this and of the very large number of men of the first rank who are now working on that project, I am inclined not to take too seriously the absolute no's with which we shall be greeted. I believe that it is important to emphasize that we should in any case be willing to let these men have time enough in their old positions to try to minimize the disruption of their leaving. I also agree that a fundamental clarification on this personnel problem, which can hardly be complete without Dr. Bush's participation, will be necessary. The job we have to do will not be possible without personnel substantially greater than that which we now have available, and I should only be misleading you and all others concerned with the S-1 project if I were to promise to get the work done without this help.

The suggestion of Eckhardt as a substitute for Kurie is a welcome one and we shall arrange to talk with him on our next trip east.[a] There are, however, two reasons more substantial than prejudice why the limitation to men who are known to us is sound: 1) that the technical details of this work will in large part have to do with atomic physics so that any man whose experience has been in another field will necessarily be of more limited usefulness; Kurie, for instance, would have had as one of his responsibilities the installation and servicing of the cyclotron. The second reason is that in a tight isolated group such as we are now planning, some warmth and trust in personal relations is an indispensable prerequisite, and we are, of course, able to insure this only in the case of men whom we have known in the past. You will have had from me a note on possible alternatives to Kurie. If none of our suggestions seem practicable we shall see whether Dr. Eckhardt could fill the bill.

With all good wishes,

Very sincerely yours,

Robert Oppenheimer

a. Probably E. A. Eckhardt, a physicist who was vice president of Gulf Research and Development Company in 1942.

OPPENHEIMER'S PERSONAL RAID on the Rad Lab took place in mid-December, probably in conjunction with a conference in Washington with Groves on the fourteenth. In Cambridge he had a long talk with Hans Bethe and his wife Rose about the terms of employment and the living conditions that might entice Bethe and others away from rewarding Rad Lab research and the civilized life of Cambridge. On December 22 Bethe forwarded a list of questions. Rose Bethe offered to run an employment agency and information center until professional staff could be hired (an offer that brought her the thankless task of housing assignments for the first busy months). Bethe raised two additional points: to avoid delays, procurement should be independent of the Army and some effort should be made to equalize salaries. He had worked on recruiting two physicists on leave from Columbia: Norman R. Ramsey would come if Isidor (I. I.) Rabi came. Rabi, associate director of the Rad Lab, was wavering but not yet convinced.[22]

[Berkeley, California]
December 28, 1942

Dear Hans and Rose:

Thank you for your fine letters and documents. I would like to answer as many of the questions that you raise as I now can so that you may be informed about the present state of affairs. Some of the points have not yet been settled and one or two of them have not even been raised. I shall keep your lists as a reminder of what we shall have to do.

First, the points of your letter:

1. We are trying now to put the laboratory, as distinct from the town, on the basis of an OSRD contract with a dummy contracting agent, say Cal Tech or Harvard. This will give us the flexibility in salary and procurement that we all so much desire. I am, however, assured that the Army procurement procedure has quite recently been radically altered. It is no longer necessary to obtain the conventional three bids; procurement can be carried out by our agent in Pasadena without any authorization and on the unique basis of getting what we need as fast as possible. It is our plan to pay all civilians $\frac{18}{16}$ of their university salary and for the younger men to pay on the M.I.T. salary scale. It is not yet clear what we shall do about subsistence. We may pay it and charge for rent, utilities, schools, hospitals, etc. On the other hand we may not pay subsistence and provide housing, utilities and normal services in the town without charge. It seems to me that either of these schemes will be satisfactory. It is largely a question of whether we wish to keep some form of control on the services (how much electricity and fuel is used, for instance) which procedure we shall follow.

2. We looked into the question of Dana P. Mitchell and were unable to get anywhere with it. At present there is a good possibility that Allison will come to us from Chicago; in fact, he visited the school with me on my last trip.[a] I also understand that Kurie is very anxious to come and as soon as we have given Conant and Bush a chance to live up to their commitments we will look into this. In the meantime, McMillan, Kennedy and I will try to get the rudiments of the procurement problem outlined.

3. I do not think that I can at this time refer Ramsey's name to Conant because of my promise, but one of the reasons that I am so optimistic about our future is that if we really get the men promised us there will be many others who will want to come and that should immensely simplify the job of getting them released.

Now to Rose's questions. There will be a sort of city manager who will be distinct from Colonel Harmon.[b] Harmon was trying to find a man for this job and there is a man in New Mexico, a civilian, whom we could obtain if he is not successful. There will also be a city engineer and together they will take care of the problems outlined by you. We hope to persuade one of the teachers at the school to stay on to be our professional teacher. It is true that both Kay Manley and Elsie McMillan are professional school teachers and there will no doubt be others, but it seems to me unlikely that anyone with a very young child will be able to devote very much time to the community. There will be two hospitals, one in the town and one in the M.P. camp. The one in the town will be run by our doctor or doctors and she will be paid a regular salary so that she will be independent of our fees. I believe we shall have a group health plan of some kind but this is one of the questions that is tied up with how we handle subsistence.

Room is being provided for a laundry; each house will have its washtub; and we shall be able to send laundry to Santa Fe regularly. It may be necessary for us to provide the equipment for the group laundry since this is now frozen, but this is a point that is not yet settled.

We plan to have two eating places. There will be a regular mess for unmarried people which will be, when we are running at full capacity, just large enough to take care of these. The Army will take care of the help for this and I do not know whether the personnel will be Army or civilian. We will also arrange to have a cafe where married people can eat out. This will probably be able to handle about twenty people at a time and will be a little fancy, and may be by appointment only. We are trying to persuade one of the natives to operate this and we have a good building for it.

There will be a recreation officer who will make it his business to see that such things as libraries, pack trips, movies, and so on are taken care of, and he will no doubt welcome the help of as many of us as are willing. The bachelor apartments will be run by the Army and will be completely served. The store will be a so-called Post Exchange which is a combination of country store and mail order house. That is, there will be stocks on hand and the Exchange will be able to order for us what they do not carry. There will be a vet to inspect the meat and barbers and such like. There will also be a cantina where we can have beer and cokes and light lunches.

The employment agency is something which we have not made any official provision for although we have discussed it with Harmon. I think it would be fine if you planned to help out with this as soon as you get there, and provision will be made to pay you for that work.

I am a little reluctant to do too much writing about the details of our life there until people are actually on the job, but I agree with you that some rudimentary information about the nature of the life and possibilities of work should be made available to everyone. I am answering as well as I can your questionnaire on the enclosed sheet.

That will have to be all for the moment. But I would appreciate it if you would get in touch with me if any new problems arise which we ought to consider, or if you think any of the arrangements that we have made so far

are definitely unsatisfactory. Our best guarantee that they can be made satisfactory is in the great effort and generosity that Harmon and Groves have
both brought to setting up this odd community and in their evident desire
to make a real success of it. In general they are not interested in saving
money, but are interested in saving critical materials, in cutting down personnel, and in doing nothing which would attract Congressional attention
to our hi-jinks. I found that there were 1800 people working at the school to
get things built fast.

With all good greetings—

[Robert Oppenheimer]

QUESTION	ANSWER
I. Housing	
1. Type of house	2 and 4-family units; bachelor quarters
Number of rooms	3, 4, 6 rooms (1, 2, 3 bedrooms)
Size of rooms	Kitchen, 10 × 14; livingroom 14 × 18
2. Type of heat	Hot air—one furnace for unit; wood fuel
Hot water heater	One heater for unit; wood fuel
Type of stove	Insulated wood & coal range, electric plate
Electricity?	Yes
Phone?	No
3. What furniture will be furnished?	Shelves, kitchen table, beds, chairs . . .
Ice box	Electric refrigerator
Ironing boards	Probably
Fireplace	Yes
4. Rent?	Free for Army;? for civilians*
What price utilities?	" " " " " " *
5. Will there be servants available for occa- sional help, especially for heavy work?	Yes
6. Small garden?	Yes; water limited in Spring and Fall
II. Geography and clothing	
1. Will it be permissible to describe location in letter?	Altitude 7300; in Southwest
2. Mean temperatures	Monthly means from 27.1 in January to 66.7 in July
Rain and snow fall	Heavy rain in summer; light snow in winter; temperate summers.

3. Type of clothing needed	Warm clothing; informal
4. Shoes	Boots for occasional use; skis
III. Community Services	
1. Public laundry charge	Probably a small charge
2. Garbage collection	Yes
3. Carpenters and other crafts	Yes
4. Store	Army Post Exchange
5. Hospital	Run by doctor
6. Mess hall or cafeteria	Mess hall and cafe
7. City tax	Probably not

* For Army, most services free. For civilians, may be included in rent to make $150/mo. subsistence. Not yet decided.

a. Dana P. Mitchell was a physicist at Columbia University, where he had charge of purchases and lab service. Samuel Allison, at this time director of the Met Lab, did not come to Los Alamos until 1944.

b. Colonel J. M. Harmon was the first commanding officer of Post Administration which had charge of the construction and management of the town.

The prime contracting agent was not Caltech or Harvard but the University of California, which assumed responsibility early in 1943 and eventually opened a special office in Los Angeles for Los Alamos business. The proposal about salaries was generally followed. For married scientific and technical staff, rent was geared to salary regardless of whether the family occupied a former Ranch School house on Bath Tub Row (so christened by an envious apartment dweller who disliked showers), a three-bedroom apartment in the four-unit frame buildings in adjacent "Snob Hollow," a duplex for couples without children, or less desirable variants of instant shelter that went up as the population of the mesa climbed.

To comment adequately on the remainder of Oppenheimer's letter and the Bethes' questionnaire would be to write a domestic history of Los Alamos.[23] Wartime residents have their own vivid recollections of the mirror-image apartments, the acrid smoke that poured from ventilators at 5 a.m. as Spanish-American janitors, accustomed to piñon logs in adobe fireplaces, shoveled on the soft coal, of the communal laundry, of competition among working wives for maid service, of shopping and eating facilities that never quite kept pace with demand. The men and women employed in the heavily guarded Technical Area, especially those who bore major responsibility, will think of long hours, of six- and seven-day weeks, of prob-

lems unprecedented in magnitude and challenge, and of frontiers of technical competence and scientific knowledge crossed almost daily. They will
also remember mountains and canyons explored with old and new friends.
For most of its new residents, Los Alamos became, as it had been for hundreds of schoolboys, a magic place. If the magic sometimes vanished in the
construction and blowing dust of that first summer or the mud of the ensuing winter, to retrieve it one had only to walk eastward along the
piñon-covered promontory to look over the Pajarito Plateau and the Rio
Grande Valley to the Sangre de Cristos, or climb the old trails westward
toward the Valle Grande, or simply watch the sun set behind the Jemez skyline.

WHILE PLANNING an environment conducive to productive work and
compatible with a minimum standard of comfort for what was, at this
point, viewed as a small community of academic families, Oppenheimer
dealt with the more basic question of militarization of the new laboratory.
In his willingness to agree to Army commissions for himself and other senior scientists, he was a minority of one among the advisers and potential
colleagues he had recruited. In Washington on February 1, using the letter-
head of the National Defense Research Committee (which had become part
of the Office of Scientific Research and Development), he summarized for
the committee's chairman his interpretation of a conference they had
attended two days earlier at which Luis Alvarez of the M.I.T. Rad Lab had
joined other consultants.

125 | TO JAMES B. CONANT

Washington, D.C.
February 1, 1943

Dear Dr. Conant:

The discussions of which you were a witness in the early stages with
Rabi, McMillan, Bacher, and Alvarez continued all Saturday. Rabi, with the
full concurrence of the other three men, formulated the following indispensable conditions for the success of the project:

(1) That the Laboratory must demilitarize: the arguments here were first
that a divided personnel would inevitably lead to friction, and to a collapse
of Laboratory morale, complicated in our case by social cleavage, and, more
important, that in any issue in which we were instructed by our military
superiors, the whole Laboratory would be forced to follow their instructions and thus in effect lose its scientific autonomy. My efforts to persuade
the men that such a situation would not arise were unsuccessful.

247

(2) That the execution of the security and secrecy measures should be in the hands of the military, but that the decision as to what measures should be applied must be in the hands of the Laboratory. On this point I fully concur with the other men because I believe it is the only way to assure the cooperation and the unimpaired morale of the scientists.

(3) That we should be able to supplement Army procurement by OSRD contract procurement in order to expedite the solution of an intrinsically very serious problem.

(4) That in our limited but urgent personnel needs we should have a high priority; in particular, we need at the present time a procurement man of experience and real power. Dana Mitchell of Columbia is the only man we know adequate to this job. In the second place we need a man capable of organizing the mechanics of the Laboratory, and A. Allen of the Radiation Laboratory is the man suggested.[a] We need the services of these men most urgently in the immediate future, and it is possible that within six months, we should be adequately organized to survive without them. Our other personnel needs at the present time are modest.

The first two of these points I discussed with General Groves, making only casual reference to the last two. I believe that he realizes the seriousness of these requests, but I am not sure that he feels that they can be met. He will discuss these questions with you on his return to Washington Thursday. I also at your suggestion discussed these problems briefly with Dr. Bush. I should say that he agreed with all four points. He is, however, completely unwilling to take jurisdiction over these considerations since General Groves has been given the authority to deal with them. He, furthermore, is unwilling to ask for the release of any men for our project until these fundamentals have been clarified.

Dr. Rabi will be in town this week, and I have suggested that he come to discuss these matters with you. I shall be in Berkeley from Thursday on, and shall be glad to come back as soon as I can be helpful.

It seems to me that with some sacrifice and considerable delay we might have been able to make a Laboratory go, more or less, without fulfilling the conditions listed above. I believe that a real delay in our work would, however, have been inevitable. At the present time I believe that the solidarity of physicists is such that if these conditions are not met, we shall not only fail to have the men from M.I.T. with us, but that many men who have already planned to join the new Laboratory will reconsider their commitments or come with such misgivings as to reduce their usefulness. I therefore regard the fulfillment of these conditions as necessary if we are to carry on the work with anything like the speed that is required.

Very sincerely yours,

Robert Oppenheimer

a. Alexander Allen did not go to Los Alamos; Dana Mitchell did and made an invaluable contribution as head of procurement.

A solution to the militarization issue evolved as part of an organization plan for town and laboratory which was formally communicated to Oppenheimer in a letter of February 25, 1943, from Conant and Groves.[24] During the experimental stage of work, civilian administration of the laboratory would continue. When large-scale trials commenced, though not before January 1, 1944, at the earliest, members of the scientific and engineering staff would become commissioned officers and take their orders from military superiors. The shift never took place. Bacher, from the beginning a division leader and member of the Governing Board of the laboratory, believes that General Groves never raised the militarization question, nor did the Atomic Energy Commission's official historians find evidence that he did so.[25]

The overall administrative arrangements of which the Conant–Groves letter officially apprised Oppenheimer are summarized in the official history of Los Alamos as follows: "The Los Alamos site, together with a large surrounding area, was established as a military reservation. The community, fenced and guarded, was made an army post. The laboratory, in turn, was built within an inner fenced and guarded area, called the 'Technical Area.' Both the military and technical administrations were responsible to Major General L. R. Groves, who had over-all executive responsibility for the work. The Commanding Officer [of Post Administration] reported directly to General Groves; he was responsible for the conduct of military personnel, the maintenance of adequate living conditions, prevention of trespass, and special guarding. Oppenheimer, as Scientific Director, was also responsible to General Groves, who had as his technical adviser J. B. Conant. In addition to his technical responsibilities, the Director was made responsible for the policy and administration of security. This provision represented a guarantee that there would be no military control of the exchange of information among scientific staff members, and at the same time fixed responsibility for the maintenance of security under these conditions. In carrying out his responsibilities for security, the Director was to be given the assistance and advice of a Military Intelligence Officer."[26]

Knowing that some aspects of this plan would not appeal to those he was most eager to have as colleagues, Oppenheimer hastened to invoke the aid of Rabi, his most influential consultant and also one of the staunchest opponents of a militarized laboratory.

February 26, 1943

Dear Rabi:

I made in Washington a strong and extremely painful attempt to have our project transferred to O.S.R.D. under a special committee established for that purpose. I did not get to first base. The reasons which make this seem so difficult will in part be clear to you from the Groves-Conant letter to me, a copy of which should be in your hands by the time you get this. The set-up as we have it was established pretty directly under a Presidential directive by the Secretary of War, and Dr. Bush is reluctant to change it in our case, which is in some ways the heart of the project, not only for organizational reasons, but because he feels that the position of the O.S.R.D. is not at the present time strong enough for him to be willing to undertake that respon-sibility. I do not know whether the arrangements as now outlined will work, for that will take in the first instance the good will and cooperation of quite a few good physicists; but I did not draw out from my position, and I am willing to make a faithful effort to get things going. I think if I believed with you that this project was "the culmination of three centuries of phys-ics," I should take a different stand. To me it is primarily the development in time of war of a military weapon of some consequence. I do not think that the Nazis allow us the option of carrying out that development.[a]

I know that you have good personal reasons for not wanting to join the project, and I am not asking you to do so. Like Toscanini's violinist, you do not like music. I am asking two things of you, within the limits set by your own conscience.

(1) I hope that we can have a conference on the physics ahead of us in April, perhaps from the 10th to the 30th, at Los Alamos. The theoretical people I should like to have there at that time, and some of the experimental ones will be there too, though they may be busy with installation. I should like to have you come to that to talk over the physics, and to give us the benefit of your advice at a critical time. This is not a method of tricking you into the project, and it is not for the purpose of talking politics. It is just for the physics, and such relatively simple arrangements as we have to make at that time to see that the physics gets done.

(2) There are two men whom I should be more than reluctant not to have on the project: Bethe and Bacher. I think that you know the reasons in each case, and agree with them. You have a great deal of influence with these two men, and they in turn on many others who are involved in the project. I am asking that you use that influence to persuade them to come rather than to stay away.

I am sending a copy of this letter to Dr. Conant and General Groves to keep the record straight.

Yours,

Robert Oppenheimer

a. Oppenheimer's argument appears to require insertion of the word *not* in this sentence ("the option of [not] carrying out that development"), but the carbon copy reads as above. The editors have not located the original.

FROM ROOM 325, Le Conte Hall, the office of Edwin McMillan in the physics building on the Berkeley campus, which had become the organizing center for the new laboratory, Oppenheimer planned the April conference that was to launch Los Alamos.[27] One whose presence he was eager to secure was the Italian physicist Enrico Fermi. In December 1938 Fermi had used the trip to Stockholm to accept a Nobel prize as an excuse to emigrate from Italy, where racial laws posed a threat to his Jewish wife. With his family Fermi continued on to the United States and a professorship at Columbia University. With the Hungarian physicist Leo Szilard and their assistants, Fermi developed a graphite pile to produce a chain reaction using slow neutrons. In the spring of 1942 this work was moved to the Chicago Metallurgical Laboratory where, under Fermi's supervision, the first controlled nuclear chain reaction took place on December 2, 1942. Fermi's extraordinary competence as both theorist and experimentalist, as well as unique qualities of personal and intellectual leadership, made his participation in the new enterprise highly desirable.

127 | TO ENRICO FERMI

Berkeley, California
March 11, 1943

Dear Dr. Fermi:

We are planning to hold a three-week conference at Los Alamos, starting probably about April 15. The purpose of the conference is to discuss the scientific problems of the Los Alamos laboratory and to define its schedules and its detailed experimental program. The background of our work is so complicated, and information in the past has been so highly compartmentalized, that it seems that we shall have a good deal to gain from a leisurely and thorough discussion. My own view is that this is likely to contribute

251

essentially toward our carrying out our directive in the simplest and fastest way. I want very much to have you present at the conference, whether or not you will have moved permanently to the site by that time.

We are still a little vague on how complete the living arrangements at the site will be and how soon we can get things going there. For this reason it may be necessary to delay the conference a little. But I shall make every effort to have things comfortable enough so that we can meet and work effectively from the middle of April on. I will let you know at a later time just what the timing is. There will be some twenty people invited to this conference, of whom the majority will already be in residence at the site. If the pressure of other work makes it impossible for you to be there during the whole three weeks, will you nevertheless plan to come for as much of that time as possible. I should suggest that it would be better to come in the later rather than the earlier half.

Very sincerely yours,

Opje

Fermi attended the April conference and eventually moved to Los Alamos. Meanwhile, he visited the laboratory and was often consulted in Chicago.

On March 16 Oppenheimer and his wife took the train to Santa Fe, leaving two-year-old Peter with his nurse and Oppenheimer's secretary, Priscilla Greene, to follow a few days later. Working at the Berkeley Radiation Laboratory, Priscilla, for the past few months, had been "loaned" part-time to help Oppenheimer with the fast neutron project. His correspondence and ecstatic description of the new laboratory site so stirred her interest that, to Lawrence's dismay, she accepted Oppenheimer's offer of a job there. She remained one of his most valued assistants until the spring of 1945, having meanwhile met and married the chemist Robert Duffield. Because of her expert help, and later that of Shirley Barnett, wife of the Los Alamos pediatrician, the old Corona typewriter or its successor, on which so many letters in this volume were typed, no longer accompanied Oppenheimer on transcontinental journeys. Years later Priscilla Duffield was surprised to learn that he knew one key from another.[28]

Oppenheimer stayed a few days at La Fonda in Santa Fe to help recruit prospective staff members. Among them was Dorothy McKibbin, who soon took charge of the laboratory's Santa Fe office. It was one of Oppenheimer's inspired appointments. World-famous scientists and travel-weary families stopped for gate passes and directions at her tiny office in the shaded courtyard at 109 East Palace Avenue, then continued to their mysterious destination refreshed and reassured by her warmth and humor. A Smith graduate, widowed and with a young son to support, Mrs. McKibbin had previously worked for the Spanish and Indian Trading Company. She knew every pueblo and Spanish village, every artist, rancher, scenic wonder, and ancient ruin for miles around. Like Oppenheimer, she had first come to New Mexico for reasons of health. They became great friends. Throughout the war Dorothy McKibbin knew almost everything about Los Alamos except its exact purpose, but from the moment she met Robert Oppenheimer in the La Fonda lobby she felt that whatever he was doing must be worthwhile.[29]

The Oppenheimers moved to the laboratory site at Los Alamos as soon as the Ranch School headmaster's house was ready for them. It was a simple one-story log and stone building close to what would remain the center of wartime Los Alamos but on a quiet road, partly shielded by shrubbery and garden. They lived there until early November 1945.

THE APRIL GATHERING brought together the few scientists already living at the site, others temporarily housed with their families at ranches in the valley, and those who would soon join the laboratory. Consultants and members of a special reviewing committee appointed by Groves to evaluate progress also attended. Because most participants had at best a partial view of the project, the first order of business was a course of lectures by Robert Serber summarizing theoretical calculations and experimental data. Among the topics covered were energy release, chain reaction, critical size, cross sections, possible ways of assembling fissionable materials, the deuterium bomb or "super," and finally, damage.[30] A copy of Serber's lectures, known as the Los Alamos primer, continued to serve as an introductory manual for new recruits.

After Serber's briefing, conference members turned to the planning of programs for each of the divisions into which the laboratory was initially organized: theoretical physics, experimental physics, chemistry and metallurgy, and ordnance. Each division was subdivided into groups. The programs were examined by Groves' reviewing committee: the two least developed areas—chemistry and metallurgy, and ordnance development and engineering—should be emphasized and would require additional staff. The investigation of theoretical aspects of a thermonuclear bomb should continue, but the atomic weapon was to have priority. The committee strongly commended Oppenheimer's performance as director and suggested appointment of three assistants to lighten his load.[31]

The opening up of so many scientific and technical frontiers would alone have made the conference memorable. There was also an exhilarating sense of mission and of comradeship. One evening the Oppenheimers gave a party. Edward U. Condon picked up a copy of *The Tempest* and sat in a corner reading aloud passages appropriate to intellectuals in exotic isolation. As the days went by, Oppenheimer saw his new colleagues, most of them at any rate, succumb to the spell of his beloved New Mexico. In time some found the arid beauty of the landscape a stimulant, not a distraction, and claimed they could never have worked so hard and effectively in any other environment.

Robert Bacher's contributions to the April planning sessions made Oppenheimer more than ever anxious to lure him away from the radar project at M.I.T. Before Bacher returned to Cambridge, he received a statement of why his presence was essential and what his responsibilities would be. The ornate language of Oppenheimer's earlier (and later) correspondence is notably absent from his wartime memorandums, of which this one to Bacher is a typical example. The direct no-nonsense tone reflects his own total commitment as he turned from planning to implementation.

128 | MEMORANDUM TO ROBERT BACHER

Los Alamos
Santa Fe, New Mexico.
April 28, 1943

After our discussion of yesterday, I took up some of the points raised in your letter of April 26 with Wilson, Williams, Bloch, Segrè, Rabi, Tolman and Fermi, and I think that as a result of this I am in a position to make a few clear statements which may help to get your relations to the project better defined than they have been in the past.[a]

1. You know that I have been extremely eager to have your help in this work. I think perhaps that you have not fully realized how much I appreciate your administrative experience and obvious administrative wisdom, nor how aware I am of our need for just this in the present project. Perhaps too you do not evaluate highly enough the fact that you have worked so much in neutron physics and that you are so well informed about the last year's developments at M.I.T. These three qualifications make you, in my opinion, very nearly unique, and that is why I have pursued you with such diligence for so many months. In addition, I want to express in writing my own confidence in your stability and judgement, qualities on which this stormy enterprise puts a very high premium.

2. I should like to offer you the direction of the experimental physical work at Los Alamos. I think that you will find the men with whom you have to work and who are here now extremely cooperative. They are all well aware of the need for such direction and no one of them believes that he is able to provide it. I know that you will so organize the work that the leaders of projects who are now here will have a real sense of responsibility and a maximum freedom compatible with the effective coordination of the

work. You would be responsible, as director of experimental physical research, to the governing board of the laboratory, and to the director, but neither would interfere in any way with your freedom of action as long as you held the position.

3. The governing board of the laboratory does not yet exist, but I should like to start it by appointing you as a member.

4. You have my unqualified support in trying to develop an adequate physics-engineering group and in initiating at the earliest possible date the design and ordnance work which we both recognize to be our main problem. I should like to have your help in bringing here a group of men whom you would call physicist engineers, and would want to give you a good deal of freedom in selecting these men. I should also want your help, both in establishing contacts and in general organization to get the new work started in an effective and prompt way. I do not have any doubt that we shall have support for an expansion program roughly of the order of that which seems appropriate to us. The issue seems to me of enough importance so that I am willing to let my direction of the laboratory stand or fall on whether or not we get these things going in the near future.

5. I believe it is essential if you wish to undertake, under the conditions sketched above, work in this laboratory, that you accept without further delay. I know that you cannot leave M.I.T. before the middle of June at the earliest, and that in itself will be a disadvantage and will make some difficulties for the men who will be under your immediate direction. However, if they can be assured that you will accept this position, and if you can by consultation and correspondence, and by personnel work elsewhere, help to give some structure to this group, I believe that the problems when you arrive here later will not be as serious as they would be if you postponed acceptance for another two months. Furthermore, I think that a good deal of the work on supplementing our staff must be done in the near future and cannot be done here. I hope that your duties at M.I.T. would leave you some time for this, and that you and Rabi together will get to work on it at your earliest convenience. You will understand why, in our present disorganized state, it would be impossible for me to regard any long continuance of your indeterminate relations to the laboratory as healthy or constructive, and I am sure that the men with whom you will be working would share this view and feel even more strongly about it than I.

Robert Oppenheimer

a. Robert R. Wilson, an experimental physicist with a Ph.D. from Berkeley in 1940, had been in charge of the isotron development project at Princeton. At Los Alamos he was head of the cyclotron group, the youngest group leader there.

Bacher agreed to join the project, but he remained so strongly opposed to military control of the laboratory that his letter of acceptance stipulated that it was also his letter of resignation effective the day the Army took over. As already indicated, that day never came. Bacher stayed at Los Alamos through the war as one of Oppenheimer's most trusted associates, serving at times as scapegoat when policy decisions proved unpopular.

A note to General Groves touched upon one of the many topics discussed at the April meetings.

129 | MEMORANDUM TO LESLIE R. GROVES

Los Alamos
April 30, 1943

In accordance with our discussion of last week, I have given some thought to the question of a story about the Los Alamos Project which, if disseminated in the proper way, might serve somewhat to reduce the curiosity of the local population, and at least to delay the dissemination of the truth.

We propose that it be let known that the Los Alamos Project is working on a new type of rocket and that the detail be added that this is a largely electrical device. We feel that the story will have a certain credibility; that the loud noises which we will soon be making here will fit in with the subject; and that the fact, unfortunately not kept completely secret, that we are installing a good deal of electrical equipment, and the further fact that we have a large group of civilian specialists would fit in quite well. We further believe that the remoteness of the site for such a development and the secrecy which has surrounded the project would both be appropriate, and that the circumstance that a good deal of work is in fact being done on rockets, together with the appeal of the word, makes this story one which is both exciting and credible.

This question has been discussed with the governing board of the laboratory who approve it and who further recommend that the technical staff of the laboratory be specially warned neither to contradict nor to support a story of this kind if they should run into it.

J. R. Oppenheimer

At about this time John Manley and Charlotte Serber, the librarian of the laboratory, were authorized to visit a bar or two in Santa Fe "for the purpose of deliberately spilling something about an electromagnetic gun."[32] But no "official" story could stem local speculation as the project's growing and highly varied population searched Santa Fe stores for scarce items of food and clothing, visited museums and curio shops, and replaced peacetime tourists at Indian dances. WAC and Navy uniforms on the streets inspired the more imaginative explanations of activity at Los Alamos: a home for pregnant WACS or the building of a large submarine in the Ranch School pond. Dorothy McKibbin used her wide acquaintance to spread the word that gossip was out of order.

OPPENHEIMER EXPLORED another angle of the security problem with his former Zurich mentor, Wolfgang Pauli, who spent the years 1940 to 1945 at the Institute for Advanced Study in Princeton.

Victor F. Weisskopf had attended the April conference at Los Alamos and was appointed a group leader in the Theoretical Division, of which Hans Bethe was head. Weisskopf had been Pauli's assistant in Zurich from 1934 to 1937 before joining the physics faculty at the University of Rochester. Teller headed a group working on the "Super" in the Theoretical Division.

130 | TO WOLFGANG PAULI

[Los Alamos]
May 20, 1943

Dear Pauli:

Weisskopf was here not long ago and he spoke to us of your uncertainties as to whether you should or not go into research directly connected with the war. It is hard to give an answer to this question that has more than a temporary validity, but my feeling is that at the present time it would be a waste and an error for you to do that. You are just about the only physicist in the country who can help to keep those principles of science alive which do not seem immediately relevant to the war, and that is eminently worth doing.

In addition to this there is the practical argument that there have been and will be some men who because of legal complications cannot work on military problems and for whom your guidance is likely to be decisive. In this way one may hope that when the war is over there will be at least some people in the country who know what a mesotron is and who have a habit of study which is not directed toward a very immediate objective. This is only my personal opinion and I think that in time pressure may be brought to bear on you to help with a war problem, but certainly I should regard that as something not to be looked for but to be guarded against.

There is one suggestion that many of us have made from time to time and that I think deserves to be taken seriously, although I know that you will

257

laugh at it. One of the things that worries us is that none of the people in our field are publishing work in the Physical Review for the very good reason that they are not doing anything that can be published. It must be apparent to the enemy that we are finding good uses for our physicists and in some cases I think that this is in itself a piece of information on the nature of the work we are doing. We have often wondered whether your great talents for physics and for burlesque could not appropriately be put to use by your publishing some work in the names of a few of the men who are now engaged on things that they cannot publish. It would give you a chance to express in the most appropriate way possible your evaluation of their qualities and you would have a delicious opportunity to argue with yourself in the public press without any interference. I think that you should not undertake this without getting the permission of your victims, but I know that Bethe, Teller, Serber and I would be delighted to grant you that and I have no doubt that there would be many others. Do not dismiss this thought too lightly.

I am looking forward to seeing your report on Dirac and also the recent work on the process and the weak coupling. I have a feeling that this is too cheap a way out, but if it is right it will at least show that to get any further with the problem of the nature of the fundamental particles lies beyond not only our present theoretical ideas, but any present experimental evidence. Just that, namely the fact that nothing that we know about nuclei and little that we know about mesotrons helps to clarify the deeper questions, would be something of a disappointment to me. Will I have to believe it?

With the very warmest greetings to Franca and to you from Kitty too.

[Robert Oppenheimer]

Pauli's reply, like the earlier letter in this volume from Niels Bohr, documents an enduring professional and personal friendship. After Oppenheimer became director of the Institute for Advanced Study in 1947, Pauli, an always welcome visitor, had no reason to complain, as he did in this letter, of reluctant institute support.

Princeton, New Jersey
June 19, 1943

Dear Oppenheimer:

Many thanks for your letter of May 20th. I appreciate very much that you stressed the value of the continuation of a pure scientific work so much. While I heard a similar view also from other scientists, the non-scientists who give me the money (the Rockefeller Foundation and the Director of the Institute for Advanced Study) are becoming more and more, lets say, reluctant with it. This is a source of practical difficulties to carry out your proposal, that is to publish my papers under other names. Although I would be glad to be helpful in the suggested way, I am afraid I should publish the few things which I have at present to say with my own name to prove to the quoted money-givers that after all I am working something for their money, fearing their sense for burlesque to be rather undeveloped. Moreover I don't think that your proposal would really reach the purpose to make the enemy believe that the persons whose names figure as authors are not occupied beside some scientific work also with war problems—and the whole Don-Quichotery would be in vain.

I hope my report on Dirac's theory will appear soon while I am just going to write the paper on the λ-process and the weak coupling. I have no doubt that this can only be a preliminary stage of the whole problem. I consider it as logically very disturbing that in the case of the coincidence of two particles the order of the limiting processes $\lambda \to 0$ and $r \to 0$ (r being the distance of the two particles) is relevant. With Dirac's "hypothetical world" I was running into serious troubles (troubles of physics not of mathematics) in applying it to the problem of the emission of many low frequency photons (the problem treated by Bloch and Nordsieck). Whatever this may be, it is not satisfactory that in the meson theory one needs a vector-meson, which is not derived in the theory itself, besides the pseudo scalar meson to explain the nuclear forces. In a reasonable theory there should not be so many arbitrary assumptions and just this circumstance may justify the hope to clarify also some deeper questions with our empirical knowledge about mesotrons and nuclei even if the weak-coupling theory with the λ-process works to a certain extent.

Many greetings to Kitty and to you, also from Franca.

W. Pauli

INTO OPPENHEIMER'S new world of crucial decisions, formalities occasionally obtruded. Early in July he received a letter from President Roosevelt asking him to assure the scientists working with him that their efforts were appreciated. "I am sure we can rely on their continued wholehearted and unselfish labors," continued the President. "Whatever the enemy may be planning, American science will be equal to the challenge. With this thought in mind, I send this note of confidence and appreciation."[33] Oppenheimer read the letter at the colloquium held each Tuesday evening for the scientific staff, then he replied in kind.

132 | TO FRANKLIN D. ROOSEVELT

[Los Alamos]
July 9, 1943

Dear Mr. President:

Thank you for your generous letter of June 29th. You would be glad to know how greatly your good words of reassurance were appreciated by us. There will be many times in the months ahead when we shall remember them.

It is perhaps appropriate that I should in turn transmit to you the assurance that we as a group and as individual Americans are profoundly aware of our responsibility, for the security of our project as well as for its rapid and effective completion. It is a great source of encouragement to us that we have in this your support and understanding.

Very sincerely yours,

J. R. Oppenheimer

IT WAS A HAPPY COINCIDENCE for Oppenheimer that one of the Manhattan Project's top advisers was his good friend Richard C. Tolman of Caltech. As vice-chairman of the National Defense Research Committee, Tolman shared with its chairman, James Conant, supervision of scientific and technical aspects of bomb development. Among his many contributions to the work at Los Alamos was keeping its staff informed about ballistics research relating to the gun component of the bomb at laboratories with which security prevented direct contact.[34]

[Los Alamos]
July 23, 1943

Dear Richard:

General Groves has just sent me a copy of your letter of acceptance which formalizes the de facto help that you have been giving to this project. You will not need to be told, but I should like nevertheless to tell you, how pleased I am by this. I know that in the difficult days of scientific and practical development ahead your association with the project will be of the very greatest help, and that by accepting this responsibility you have really contributed to the probabilities of our timely success.

I know that your responsibilities go very much beyond the work at Los Alamos, but I would like to put in a special claim on your time because I think that the newness of our project and our isolation mean that we will have special need of your help. In particular, the state of our work now is such that I think a visit from you in the near future would prove profitable to us and perhaps not uninteresting to you, and I hope that before long we may expect you.

Cordially yours,

[Robert Oppenheimer]

As Oppenheimer turned felicitous phrases for the President and Tolman, he was undergoing a real crisis in self-confidence. The heady experience of creating a new laboratory and pulling together the disparate parts of the scientific work had been stimulating and euphoric. Then came a reaction. On several occasions in the early summer of 1943 Bacher found Oppenheimer depressed by the magnitude and complexity of the director's task. He told Bacher he could not go through with it, but Bacher's advice was simple: Oppenheimer had no alternative, for no one else could do the job.[35]

Launching the science and engineering was an intellectual challenge. Providing basic necessities for simple living amidst the beauties of New Mexico had the romance of Perro Caliente writ large, but Oppenheimer was highly vulnerable on the nontechnical side of administration. He had never even chaired a physics department, and there was no one person on the staff that first summer who was qualified to coordinate the support services that so quickly outstripped all projections in scale and variety. Oppenheimer found himself making decisions regarding housing, security, salaries, draft deferment, the business office, procurement of supplies, classified documents, health and safety, technical workshops, construction and maintenance of the plant, and a patent office. Others, including two philosophers from the University of California, developed unexpected competence in these areas, but not until January 1944, when a young New York lawyer, David Dow, became assistant director for nontechnical administration, was Oppenheimer's burden of day-to-day decision making substantially reduced.[36]

Meanwhile, external factors contributed to Oppenheimer's slump in morale. Following a trip to San Francisco in mid-June 1943, when he visited his former fiancee, Jean Tatlock, security officers began persistent questioning about his relations with suspected communists. In particular they wanted to know more details about the account he had volunteered of a conversation six months earlier with a friend in Berkeley who mentioned that a third party had offered to relay technical information to the Russians.[37] The questioning often took place at the end of exhausting travel or all-day meetings. Constantly faced with major decisions at Los Alamos, Oppenheimer failed to resolve the dilemma posed by this incident, which seemed minor to him, and gave inconsistent and sometimes evasive answers.

OPPENHEIMER WAS ALSO FINDING that among the mesas and mountains where he had once ridden and camped with carefree delight he had constructed for himself a kind of privileged prison. The following communication from General Groves made this quite clear.

134 | LESLIE R. GROVES TO ROBERT OPPENHEIMER

July 29, 1943

Dear Dr. Oppenheimer:

In view of the nature of the work on which you are engaged, the knowledge of it which is possessed by you and the dependence which rests upon you for its successful accomplishment, it seems necessary to ask you to take certain special precautions with respect to your personal safety.

It is requested that:

(a) You refrain from flying in airplanes of any description; the time saved is not worth the risk. (If emergency demands their use my prior consent should be requested.)

(b) You refrain from driving an automobile for any appreciable distance (above a few miles) and from being without suitable protection on any lonely road, such as the road from Los Alamos to Santa Fe. On such trips you should be accompanied by a competent, able bodied, armed guard. There is no objection to the guard serving as chauffeur.

(c) Your cars be driven with due regard to safety and that in driving about town a guard of some kind should be used, particularly during hours of darkness. The cost of such guard is a proper charge against the United States.

I realize that these precautions may be personally burdensome and that they may appear to you to be unduly restrictive but I am asking you to bear with them until our work is successfully completed.

Sincerely

L. R. Groves
Brigadier General, C. E.

The complexity of Oppenheimer's job did not lessen as work picked up momentum. Long known as a late sleeper, he was now at his desk before the eight o'clock whistle blew; he continued to work late. At the very time he was questioning his own ability, a signal capacity for leadership was becoming obvious to others. John Manley, who had watched from the beginning, says Oppenheimer grew with the job. He never observed the notorious Oppenheimer "put-down" at Los Alamos; he marveled rather at Oppenheimer's control of his emotions and reactions. "I think he had no great reluctance about using people," says Manley. "But . . . it was an enjoyable experience because of the character of Robert to do it so adroitly. And I think that he . . . realized that the other person knew that this was going on . . . It was like a ballet . . . each one knowing the part and the role he's playing, and there wasn't any subterfuge in it."[38]

Priscilla Duffield, who welcomed office visitors and took notes on phone calls (unless the general said, "Get her off the line!"), sometimes heard the brutal note in Oppenheimer's voice but thinks it only bothered those with an exposed nerve. Leadership seemed to come naturally; sometimes he had to work at it when a particular program or a touchy personality was involved.[39]

Oppenheimer learned to finesse awkward situations such as the tendency of certain colleagues to converse publicly in German or Italian. When individual admonition was ignored, he addressed a collective reminder to seven distinguished physicists requesting that they and their families speak only English in public places. The restriction did not, of course, apply to their homes or wide open spaces, but use of a foreign language, if overheard by those not immediately connected with the project, aroused comment.[40]

Oppenheimer often dropped in unannounced at division and group meetings. He once joined a metallurgy session during an inconclusive argument over the type of refractory container to be used for melting plutonium. Although this was hardly familiar ground to a theoretical physicist, after Oppenheimer had listened for a time, he summed up the discussion so clearly that the right answer, though he did not provide it, was immediately apparent.[41]

Aspects of the phenomenon of leadership that correspondence does not reflect were summed up by Hans Bethe when he spoke at the memorial service for Oppenheimer in 1967. "Los Alamos might have succeeded without him, but certainly only with much greater strain, less enthusiasm, and less speed. As it was, it was an unforgettable experience for all the members of the laboratory. There were other wartime laboratories of high achievement . . . But I have never observed in any one of these other groups quite the spirit of belonging together, quite the urge to reminisce about the days of the laboratory, quite the feeling that this was really the great time of their lives."

"That this was true of Los Alamos was mainly due to Oppenheimer. He was a leader. It was clear to all of us, whenever he spoke, that he knew everything that was important to know about the technical problems of the laboratory, and he somehow had it well organized in his head. But he was not domineering, he never dictated what should be done. He brought out the best in all of us, like a good host with his guests. And because he clearly did his job very well, in a manner all could see, we all strove to do our job as best we could."

"One of the factors contributing to the success of the laboratory was its democratic organization. The governing board, where questions of general and technical laboratory policy were discussed, consisted of the division leaders (about eight of them). The coordinating council included all the group leaders, about 50 in number, and kept all of them informed on the most important technical progress and problems of the various groups in the laboratory. All scientists having a B.A. degree were admitted to the colloquium in which specialized talks about laboratory problems were given. Each of these three assemblies met once a week. In this manner everybody in the laboratory felt a part of the whole and felt that he should contribute to the success of the program. Very often a problem discussed in one of these meetings would intrigue a scientist in a completely different branch of the laboratory, and he would come up with an unexpected solution."

"This free interchange of ideas was entirely contrary to the organization of the Manhattan District as a whole . . . Oppenheimer had to fight hard for free discussion among all qualified members of the laboratory. But the free flow of information and discussion, together with Oppenheimer's personality, kept morale at its highest throughout the war."[42]

For those who never saw Oppenheimer at work inside the Tech Area fence, the mystique of his leadership included an element of his personal concern. He seemed to understand the uprooted feeling that afflicted newcomers, many of whom had left homes as pleasant as the Oppenheimers' own house in Berkeley. Dismayed by lack of privacy and recurrent milk, water, and power shortages, they were somewhat appeased by the knowledge that it was Oppenheimer who had included fireplaces and large closets in the original house plans. He no longer came to dinner bearing bouquets of flowers, the gesture for which he was famous among Berkeley hostesses, but he gave both employed and nonworking wives a sense that their presence and participation in the collective enterprise was important. He shared the anxiety over a rash of illnesses that afflicted the mesa as families from all over the country pooled regional germs and adjusted to local food and water and to the 7,300 foot altitude. When anxiety reached a peak in the autumn of 1943 with the death of a young chemist, wife of a group leader, from an unidentified form of paralysis, it was somewhat reassuring to know that Oppenheimer himself had been the first to visit the bereaved husband.

He also took a personal interest in happier events. An atmosphere not unlike that associated with shipboard romances resulted in several marriages after a few months' acquaintance, including that of Oppenheimer's secretary, Priscilla Greene, and Robert Duffield. "Robert worried a lot about marriages like ours," recalls Mrs. Duffield. When an abrupt summons to meet security officers in Cheyenne, Wyoming, prevented Oppenheimer from attending the Duffields' wedding, he asked Priscilla to drive him as far as Santa Fe so they might talk without interruption. She was touched by his fatherly advice, based as it was on less than three years' experience of marriage.[43]

OPPENHEIMER GRADUALLY ACQUIRED a competent administrative staff, but many questions needed his personal attention. One of these was salaries. At the beginning, established academic scientists received twelve-tenths of their university salary, usually based on ten months of teaching. Younger scientists were paid according to the OSRD scale, technicians at prevailing rates. Not every new recruit fitted these neat categories, and the personnel officer had to make exceptions[44] To make sure that his own case was not among them, Oppenheimer wrote to R. G. Sproul, president of the University of California.

[Los Alamos]
September 18, 1943

Dear President Sproul:

At the time when the special project in New Mexico was opened, my salary was set by the University, in consultation with representatives of the War Department, at $10,000 a year. I appreciated the action of the University in thus recognizing the very serious responsibilities which a director of such an undertaking would assume, and I think that you would agree that they are indeed considerable.

In peacetime I was, both at the University of California and at California Institute of Technology, a professor of physics and not a director of anything. Thus my present salary exceeds by a little over $200 a month that which I would get if we applied our usual formula to my peacetime salaries. I think that neither the University or I would want to regard work done for the Government of the United States in time of war as the occasion for any essential increase in income, and I am therefore suggesting that in the future my salary might be reduced in accordance with the procedure which we in general follow. In an enclosure I am giving the figures on the basis of which this should be determined.

I should like to take this opportunity to express to you on behalf of the workers on this project their appreciation for the support which the University has given it, under circumstances which have not always been easy and which have required so much both of judgment and of good will.

Very sincerely yours,

J. R. Oppenheimer

After consulting the university official in charge of the Los Alamos contract, Sproul replied that a salary reduction was up to the War Department, which had set the figure in the first place, though he and his colleague agreed that heavy responsibilities justified the higher figure. Groves acknowledged a copy of Oppenheimer's letter to Sproul with the comment: "I do wish to tell you how much I personally approve your attitude."[45]

IN THE AUTUMN of 1943 Oppenheimer and his staff were preparing for an event of international significance, the arrival of scientists associated with Britain's atomic weapons project known by the code name of Tube Alloys. In the period immediately following the discovery of fission, when nuclear research in the United States still lacked coherent direction, British physicists and their refugee colleagues were doing important theoretical and experimental work.

The outbreak of war and the mobilization of all Britain's resources for defense precluded development of a major atomic project, and in June 1942 Churchill and Roosevelt reached an informal agreement that the "research plant" for the atomic weapon should be located in the United States. There followed months of hard bargaining between Bush and Conant and their British counterparts over the degree of access that British scientists should have to research centers in the United States. Finally at Quebec in 1943 Churchill and Roosevelt decreed "full and effective collaboration" in bringing bomb development to a successful conclusion. A Combined Policy Committee was placed in charge, and James Chadwick was designated Head of the British Mission in Washington. Working with General Groves, Chadwick planned the transfer of many of Britain's highly qualified nuclear scientists to the parts of the Manhattan Project where they could be most useful. Those assigned to Los Alamos began arriving in December 1943. Eventually this group numbered nineteen, plus Chadwick and G. I. Taylor as consultants.[46]

Niels Bohr and his physicist son, Aage, were also nominally part of the British Mission by virtue of Bohr's appointment as consultant to Tube Alloys after he arrived in London in October 1943 following his escape from Nazi-occupied Denmark.

A brief note to Groves dealt with a minor aspect of the British delegation's arrival.

136 | TO LESLIE R. GROVES

[Los Alamos]
November 2, 1943

Dear General Groves:

After you gave me the list during your last visit of the men whom we may expect from the United Kingdom, it occurred to me that it might be wise before they arrive here to give them new names. This refers especially to Niels Bohr. I am thinking of the fact that mail will be addressed to them, that they may on occasion originate or receive long-distance calls, that they will be making some local purchases, and that for all these routine matters it would be preferable if such well known names were not put in circulation.

It has, in fact, troubled us some that we are forced to place calls for Dr. Conant, Fermi, Lawrence, etc. This does not happen very often, but in view of the fact that we try not to use these names over the telephone, the placing of the calls themselves seems to us rather unwise. I doubt whether at this late date it would be practicable to assign new names to those who have been associated with the project in the past. In the case of Bohr and Chadwick I think it would be advisable to do so before they get here.

Sincerely yours,

J. R. Oppenheimer

Fermi refused to take seriously his pseudonym of Henry Farmer, and the only aliases consistently used were Nicholas Baker for Bohr (or "Uncle Nick" to his former students) and James, or Jim Baker, for his son.

LOS ALAMOS, with its constant challenges to ingenuity and adaptability, proved to be a fine place to assess new talent, of which there was a good deal on hand. In May 1945 the average age of the scientific staff was 29.4 years; the age distribution curve peaked sharply at twenty-seven.[47] The newness of the field had attracted the young, and the policy of draft deferment for essential workers made them available when older men were already committed to other war research. Los Alamos also brought together people in fields that did not ordinarily overlap and was therefore a good recruiting ground for university departments and for the interdisciplinary research centers that proliferated after the war. The competition began early. Oppenheimer was still trying to lure people *to* Los Alamos when he tried to interest the chairman of the Berkeley physics department in a promising young theorist.

137 | TO RAYMOND T. BIRGE

[Los Alamos]
November 4, 1943

Dear Professor Birge:

In these war times it is not always easy to think constructively about the peace that is to follow, even in such relatively small things as the welfare of our department. I would like to make one suggestion to you which concerns that, and about which I have myself a very sure and strong conviction.

As you know, we have quite a number of physicists here, and I have run into a few who are young and whose qualities I had not known before. Of these there is one who is in every way so outstanding and so clearly recognized as such, that I think it appropriate to call his name to your attention, with the urgent request that you consider him for a position in the department at the earliest time that that is possible. You may remember the

268

name because he once applied for a fellowship in Berkeley: it is Richard Feynman. He is by all odds the most brilliant young physicist here, and everyone knows this. He is a man of thoroughly engaging character and personality, extremely clear, extremely normal in all respects, and an excellent teacher with a warm feeling for physics in all its aspects. He has the best possible relations both with the theoretical people of whom he is one, and with the experimental people with whom he works in very close harmony.

The reason for telling you about him now is that his excellence is so well known, both at Princeton where he worked before he came here, and to a not inconsiderable number of "big shots" on this project, that he has already been offered a position for the post war period, and will most certainly be offered others. I feel that he would be a great strength for our department, tending to tie together its teaching, its research and its experimental and theoretical aspects. I may give you two quotations from men with whom he has worked. Bethe has said that he would rather lose any two other men than Feynman from this present job, and Wigner said, "He is a second Dirac, only this time human."[a]

Of course, there are several people here whose recommendation you might want; in the first instance Professors Brode and McMillan.[b] I hope you will not mind my calling this matter to your attention, but I feel that if we can follow the suggestion I have made, all of us will be very happy and proud about it in the future. I cannot too strongly emphasize Feynman's remarkable personal qualities which have been generally recognized by officers, scientists and laity in this community.

With every good wish,

Robert Oppenheimer

a. Eugene Wigner was on the staff of the Met Lab from 1942 to 1945.
b. Robert Brode of the Berkeley physics department was a group leader at Los Alamos.

Birge replied that he could not make permanent appointments while so many tenured professors were still on leave. The department had a lot of lower division students, and he had hired people to teach them. However, he requested further information about Feynman.[48]

IN DECEMBER 1943 the Bohrs arrived for the first of their wartime visits to Los Alamos. The British regarded Bohr's attachment to their mission as helpful in implementing the Quebec agreement but were not sure that Groves would allow him full access to American laboratories unless he joined the Manhattan Project. Bohr himself wished to keep the British affiliation. Groves proved more tractable than expected, and Bohr was allowed to visit all parts of the project.[49] Nevertheless, Oppenheimer made sure that his contribution at Los Alamos was a matter of record.

138 | TO LESLIE R. GROVES

[Los Alamos]
January 17, 1944

Dear General Groves:

Dr. Baker [Niels Bohr] has left today and I think it appropriate to report to you briefly on his visit.

1. On the technical side Dr. Baker concerned himself primarily with the correlation and interpretation of the many new data on nuclear fission and related topics which have been obtained by this project. He left with us a brief report on the theoretical understanding of these data. It has been the point of view of this laboratory that in matters of such great importance, and where theories were involved which were new and unproven, all important quantities would have to be determined by experimental measurement, and I believe this policy was and is sound. Nevertheless, the advantage of some theoretical insight into the phenomena is very great indeed in that it enables us to evaluate experiments critically, to determine the relative priority of experiments, and in general to reduce the amount of futile discussion and waste motion. For all these reasons the work that Baker did for us should prove of very great value in the months to come. Baker concerned himself very little with the engineering problems of our program although he is of course aware of their importance and their difficulty.

2. By arrangement with Chadwick and me, Baker is to remain on the British payroll and all his expenses are to be paid by the British. A change in this arrangement will only be made if you or Dr. Chadwick see strong reasons to alter it.

3. I should like in a formal way to express my hope that Baker's collaboration with this project will continue, since it has been of great help to us and is likely to be so throughout the year.

4. By word and deed Dr. Baker has done everything he could to support this project and to indicate that he is sympathetic not only with its purposes and general method of procedure, but with the policies and achievements of the project's overall direction. I should like to make it quite clear that the effect of his presence on the morale of those with whom he came in contact was always positive and always helpful, and that I see every reason to anticipate that this will be true in the future.

Very sincerely yours,

J. R. Oppenheimer

What Oppenheimer did not mention to Groves were the hours spent discussing Bohr's conviction that the successful development of an atomic weapon would require a radical change in international relations and that Britain and the United States must make a generous offer to share its control if they hoped to avoid a disastrous arms race. Lecturing in 1963 on "Niels Bohr and his Times," Oppenheimer recalled: "He made the enterprise, which often looked so macabre, seem hopeful . . . [he spoke of] his own high hope that the outcome would be good, and that in this the role of objectivity, friendliness, cooperation, incarnate in science, would play a helpful part: all this was something we wished very much to believe."[50]

This first visit to Los Alamos lasted a few weeks; then Bohr and his son left for Washington and London. An April interview with Churchill was a painful failure. Bohr returned to the United States for a July talk with Roosevelt, which he mistakenly thought went much better, but when the two leaders met in September they not only dismissed Bohr's proposal to tell other Allied leaders about the bomb but directed that Bohr's movements be closely watched.[51]

Bohr's views deeply influenced Oppenheimer and a few others to whom he talked at Los Alamos. They became gospel to most Los Alamos scientists as soon as the successful test of July 16, 1945, relieved the pressure of work and freed them psychologically to ponder its meaning.

EARLY IN 1940 Rudolf Peierls and Otto R. Frisch, who was working with Peierls at Birmingham, had calculated the critical size of a uranium bomb and suggested ways of separating U^{235}. Peierls had a broad understanding of all aspects of Britain's Tube Alloys project. He had come to the United States in September 1943 to help decide how British scientists could best expedite bomb development and had stayed on as consultant to a research group at Columbia working on the gaseous diffusion process for separating U^{235}. Oppenheimer knew that Groves would respect the sound judgment of this brilliant, unassuming man.

139 | TO LESLIE R. GROVES

[Los Alamos]
February 14, 1944

Dear General Groves:

Dr. Peierls spent two and a half days at Site Y. Almost all of this time was taken up by conferences with members of the Theoretical Division and with the other members of the British mission.

1. One of the main purposes of Peierls' visit was to reach a decision on what parts of the work now being carried out in Britain should be contin-

ued. There was therefore a rather careful comparison of the methods and results of the British workers with ours, in so far as the British have been working on the same problems. No important discrepancies in results were revealed by this comparison. It was agreed that British analytical work on critical masses, multiplication rates and efficiencies could best be discontinued.

It was further agreed that their work on the optical analogy, although probably not of a character to justify its initiation at this time, might profitably be continued and should preferably be transferred to this laboratory. This would mean bringing Marshall, who has been in charge of the work in Britain, to this laboratory.[a] We should have him work under the general supervision of O. R. Frisch. Plans to effect this have been initiated.

It was further agreed that the detailed numerical calculations on the blast wave now in progress in Britain should be continued for some time. These are more laborious and less perspicuous than the methods used here, but should provide a reliable check.

2. The chief contribution made by Peierls to the work of this laboratory lay in the following. The methods used by the British for integrating the blast wave equations in all their complexity are applicable to the physically different but formally similar problem of the hydrodynamics of implosion. Since I am not satisfied with the adequacy of the methods now in use in this laboratory for studying this latter problem, we went into the technical aspects of the British methods in considerable detail with Peierls, and are planning to attack the implosion problem along these lines with the highest possible urgency.

Sincerely yours,

J. R. Oppenheimer

a. Frisch was already at Los Alamos. D. G. Marshall soon joined the British Mission there.

At Los Alamos the British scientists worked on many problems but principally on the implosion method of assembling the bomb. Implosion involved a sudden compression of a subspherical critical mass of fissionable material by detonating a surrounding high explosive layer. At the April 1943 conference, Seth H. Neddermeyer had offered a theoretical analysis which demonstrated the feasibility of the implosion technique. He had been encouraged by Oppenheimer to carry on experiments, although at the time the theoretical physicists and the explosives experts preferred to push work on the gun device. The "optical analogy" was that between the diffusion of neutrons and the behavior of light scattered from white particles dispersed in a transparent medium. Oppenheimer's concern about hydrodynamics was relieved by the arrival in May 1944 of British consultant G. I. Taylor, whose new theory of interface instability was useful in several areas.

Oppenheimer's comment on the laborious British method of calculating the blast wave reflected a general difference in approach. According to the historian of the British project, "The Americans had tended to obtain as many and as detailed results as possible with rather questionable methods while the British had erred in the opposite direction, obtaining too few results by fairly reliable methods."[52] In September 1943, when scientists were again allowed to compare progress, they found that the different approaches had, in fact, complemented each other.

A month after this report of Oppenheimer's, Peierls also moved to Los Alamos and soon became deputy head of the British group there, while Chadwick from Washington supervised all the British scientists working in the United States. Peierls noted with satisfaction that no distinction was made between members of the British and American teams and that the work was guided "by the necessity to get the best answer in the shortest possible time rather than by questions of formal organization and prestige."[53]

Peierls also enjoyed the resumption of personal contact with Oppenheimer which had begun as members of Pauli's group in Zurich in the spring of 1929. "Robert was one of those people," Peierls recalled recently, "who takes his job, but not himself, seriously." When the Oppenheimers gave a party for Lord Cherwell, Churchill's scientific adviser, Peierls unaccountably failed to receive an invitation. In Peierls' office next day, Oppenheimer apologized for this terrible mistake. "But," he added, "there is an element of relief in this situation: It might have happened with Edward Teller."[54]

UNDERSTANDABLY, Oppenheimer wrote few personal letters during the war. Los Alamos mail was censored, and residents were expected to correspond only with relatives and friends who would be alarmed by complete silence. Frank Oppenheimer, working at the Berkeley Radiation Laboratory and at Oak Ridge, knew what his brother was doing, and there was no one else who would expect regular letters. But in the spring of 1944 Oppenheimer acknowledged good news from members of a family—a mother and four daughters, not Oppenheimer relatives—whose migration from Germany he had assisted. A note written by one of the sisters in 1962 reminded him that "in 1940 you brought us all over and we could save our lives thanks to you."[55]

[Los Alamos]
April 5, 1944

Dear Anne and Hilde,

Thank you for your very good letters which I was extremely glad to have. The news of Anne's citizenship is indeed good, and I share your welcome for this and understand your pride.

It was very good of you to send back to me the money. I hope it has not meant a hardship for you and appreciate very much your wanting to do it. I hope that there will not be a time in the future when you will need it, but if that happens please let me know and I will try to make it available to you.

I have not written earlier because I have been away from Berkeley and probably shall be for the duration. I doubt whether I shall get to see you until the war is over, but I am looking forward to it then.

With all warm greetings and best wishes,

[Robert Oppenheimer]

MAJOR PEER DE SILVA, to whom Oppenheimer addressed the following stern note, was the intelligence officer assigned to assist him in enforcing security regulations applying to civilians under laboratory jurisdiction. In April 1944 Arthur L. Hughes was personnel director, though he would soon return to his post as chairman of the department of physics, Washington University, St. Louis. David Hawkins, a philosopher from the University of California, was responsible for liaison with the local representative of the Army, known as Post Administration. He gradually assumed broader responsibilities in the area of personnel and immediately after the war wrote the official history of Project Y.

141 | MEMORANDUM TO PEER DE SILVA

[Los Alamos]
April 21, 1944

It has come to my attention that you have on numerous occasions in the past offered your advice to Dr. Hughes on the form of his letters and on procedures adopted by him. I am informed by him and by Dr. Hawkins that the suggestions made by you have been incompatible with the effective functioning of his office. It would appear desirable to me that whenever in the future you wish to advise personnel of this laboratory on matters of security, you discuss the questions involved either with Dr. Hawkins or me. This, of course, does not apply to those many cases where individuals may wish to consult you, or to those specific problems which we have asked you to undertake.

J. R. Oppenheimer

IF OPPENHEIMER had any inclination to forget the quieter world of academic physics where he had felt so much at home, he would have been reminded by the active recruitment going on at Los Alamos. His strong recommendation of Richard Feynman for a postwar appointment at Berkeley was still being discussed six months later.

142 | TO RAYMOND T. BIRGE

[Los Alamos]
May 26, 1944

Dear Professor Birge:

Thank you for your long and explicit letter of May 11. I was very much interested in some of the more general remarks on the state of our department and the education of physicists generally. You must know that I feel a very deep concern at the almost total paralysis of academic scientific training. It will be many years before we shall have recovered from the ill effects of present policy and I can only wish you and the colleagues associated with you the very best of success in your efforts. It is true that as far as men of graduate standing are concerned, projects like the one with which I am connected and many others are providing a real training, but the highly organized and highly integrated character of the work of these projects will probably fail to give men that deep and independent curiosity and vision on which the best of research has in the past been based.

I must say that I am not nearly so much in sympathy with the attitude expressed toward Feynman. It is not an unusual thing for universities to make commitments to young men whom they wish to have after the war. I surely do not know of all the cases where such commitments have been made, even to members of this project, but there are three which come to mind: Christy has been offered an assistant professorship by Compton at the University of Chicago although he had no connection with the university before the war. Ramsey has been offered a position by Columbia University, to become effective after the termination of this project. Feynman,

275

as you know, has been offered an assistant professorship by Cornell.[a] In every case I believe that the university is willing to make a definite commitment and regards the acceptance of the scientist as a commitment. In every case I believe the scientist appreciates that the extension of an invitation to him is an act of generosity which in turn demands some loyalty on his part. The fact that this was not the case for Condon has been well known to me, but I have preferred to regard it as atypical.[b] It seems to me that commitments so made not only have precedent but have some sense since by them a relationship can be established between a man and an institution in which the elements of loyalty and confidence in the future play an appropriate part. It seems to me that this is one of the few ways in which institutions of learning which are devoted to the public good can distinguish themselves from more competitive and more predatory organizations. It also seems to me one of the ways in which a department can exercise an enlightened self-interest by offering a certain security to a man who has a great deal to offer it. If it is a policy of the University of California never to make such commitments, I believe that this policy is in error. It is true that the future of a state university is necessarily uncertain. It is true too that ours is a department which has justified a reputation as one of the great centers of physics in the country, and which has every reason to believe that its usefulness to society has been great enough to warrant continued support. It is also true that no additions have been made to the department during the war years. It would seem to me that under these circumstances too much of courage was not involved in making a commitment to a young scientist. It is thus with the greatest disappointment that I learn that our university and our department cannot follow this policy.

As for Feynman himself, I perhaps presumed too much on the excellence of his reputation among those to whom he is known. I know that Brode, McMillan, and Alvarez are all enthusiastic about him, and it is small wonder.[c] He is not only an extremely brilliant theorist, but a man of the greatest robustness, responsibility and warmth, a brilliant and a lucid teacher, and an untiring worker. He would come to the teaching of physics with both a rare talent and a rare enthusiasm. We have entrusted him here with the giving of a course for the staff of our laboratory. He is one of the most responsible men I have ever met. He does not regard himself as a privileged artist but as one of a group of hard working men for whom the development of physical science is an obligation, and the exposition both an obligation and a pleasure. He spends much of his time in the laboratories and is always closely associated with the experimental phases of the work. He was associated with Robert Wilson in the Princeton project and Wilson attributes a great part of the success of that project to his help. We regard him as invaluable here; he has been given a responsibility and his work carries a weight far beyond his years. In fact he is just such a man as we have long needed in

Berkeley to contribute to the unity of the department and to give it technical strength where it has been lacking in the past.

With every good wish,

J. R. Oppenheimer

a. Robert Christy received his Ph.D. from Berkeley in 1941, came to Los Alamos from the Met Lab, and went to Chicago after the war. Ramsey returned to Columbia, and Feynman went to Cornell.

b. Edward U. Condon received a Ph.D. from Berkeley in 1926, then spent a postgraduate year abroad. Condon joined the physics department at Princeton in 1928. He and Birge differed as to whether he had reneged on a firm commitment to Berkeley.

c. Brode, McMillan, and Alvarez, on leave from Birge's department, all held responsible posts in the Ordnance Division at Los Alamos.

EACH STEP ACCOMPLISHED brought new problems. Chemists and metallurgists had been working for six months in a specially constructed building with air-conditioning and meticulous dust control when Oppenheimer reassured Groves about the handling of highly toxic plutonium and its compounds.

143 | TO LESLIE R. GROVES

[Los Alamos]
June 27, 1944

Dear General Groves:

Thank you for your letter of June 19 in which you ask me to point out to the responsible workers in chemistry and metallurgy the necessity for the greatest care and scruple in handling the active materials we are now receiving. I have shown your letter to Dr. Kennedy and asked him again to bring this matter to the attention of his staff.

You will of course appreciate that we have taken the responsibility for this material, both because of its immense value and because of the great toxicity of some forms of it, with the greatest seriousness, and that all work in chemistry and metallurgy is being carried out in such a way as to minimize the danger of loss and contamination. We are trying to steer a course which insures the greatest safety compatible with technical progress and I hope that it will prove that our judgment in this has been sound.

Very sincerely yours,

J. R. Oppenheimer

One of the minor miracles of the Los Alamos venture was the mutual respect that developed between those two seemingly incompatible characters, Oppenheimer and Groves. Unlike some of his colleagues, Oppenheimer early learned not to quail during the general's periodic inspections. Groves' forthright defense of Oppenheimer in 1954 is well known, and in later years, he often used news items about Oppenheimer as an excuse to write a friendly note and remind him of their past association.

AN ALWAYS WELCOME VISITOR was James Conant who, as scientific adviser to the entire Manhattan Project, came to Los Alamos every three or four weeks during the final year of the war.

Charles A. Thomas, research director of the Monsanto Chemical Company, had coordinated research on the chemistry and purification of plutonium 239 at the Chicago Met Lab, Iowa State College at Ames, Berkeley, and Los Alamos. As the chemistry and metallurgy of plutonium became concentrated at Los Alamos, Thomas's role was less crucial.[56]

The focus of attention in mid-summer 1944 was on several ambitious experiments to study the implosion method of bomb assembly, but it is not obvious to which particular experiment this letter refers.

144 | TO JAMES B. CONANT

[Los Alamos]
August 3, 1944

Dear Dr. Conant:

We are looking forward to your visit on the seventeenth and will plan to meet you at the Chief at Lamy. I think it will be a good time for you to come and with luck we shall even have a rather important experiment going on in the days you are here. Your confidence in our future success is something that I would like to have checked against realities just as often as possible and I think that the next months will inevitably be a time when we shall value your advice and help to a very special degree.

I have the impression that we are not going to get very far with Charles Thomas, and that his own reluctance to become further involved in this project and the pressure put on him by his company will combine to keep him from very active participation in this work. I think that if anyone can change his mind on this it will be you.

We have had the first positive indications as far as our main program goes, and although the results have not been checked, they do lend some encouragement. By the time you are out we should know pretty well how sound they are.

Very sincerely yours,
Oppie

TOWARD THE END of the summer Oppenheimer had occasion to congratulate a second set of new citizens, this time in his Aunt Hedwig's family. He also had news of his own to report.

145 | TO HEDWIG STERN

[Los Alamos]
August 25, 1944

Dear Hedwig,

We were so happy to learn of the successful outcome on the citizenship. Kitty and I send you all our warmest congratulations. We know how much it means to you to have this settled after the long periods of uncertainty and trouble. I wish that we could be with you for a celebration but we will have to postpone that until our return to Berkeley.

Perhaps you know that we are expecting a child in November. Kitty has been very well and everything is good with us except that life is a little bit too busy for our taste.

My love to Alfred and to Lotte and my special love to you.

[Robert]

The Oppenheimers' daughter, Katherine, always called Toni, was born December 7, 1944, in the one-story frame hospital a quarter of a mile from her parents' home. Her birth certificate, like those of other Los Alamos war babies, listed the place of birth as Box 1663, Sandoval County Rural.

Within Los Alamos, the Oppenheimers lived much as did their neighbors, but with a difference: because they entertained many visitors, Kitty's name was high on the list at the maid service office which assigned the Indian and Spanish-American women who arrived each weekday morning by bus from the valley.

Even before a fence went up around their house, with a military patrol inconspicuously on duty, the Oppenheimers had more physical privacy than families in the four-unit apartments but even less time to enjoy it. Sel-

279

dom did they get to Perro Caliente, hidden tantalizingly behind the Sangre de Cristos, a thirty-mile crow's flight to the east. For Oppenheimer, even a short ride up into the Jemez with his wife on the horses they kept in the Ranch School stables was a luxury. Other couples exchanged dinners or went to so-called parties two or three evenings a week, but when Oppenheimer was not traveling or working late there was official entertaining, more pleasant but no less time consuming when the guests were old friends like Tolman, Lauritsen, Bohr, or Rabi.

Sometimes the Oppenheimers took their friends, or slipped away alone, down to the bridge at the Rio Grande for a dinner prepared by Edith Warner. Oppenheimer and Miss Warner, a quiet Pennsylvania Quaker and a dozen years his senior, had something in common. In 1922 both had come to New Mexico for their health, he to the Pecos, she to the Pajarito Plateau. Returning in 1928 determined to find a livelihood, Miss Warner became custodian of the Ranch School supplies deposited by the train that ran once or twice a day along the narrow gauge tracks on the west bank of the Rio Grande. Gradually she renovated the small adobe house that went with her job, filled it with Indian pots, Spanish rugs, and natural objects from nearby mesas; in it she opened a small store and tearoom. Sometimes friends or paying guests occupied a nearby house built for the purpose. Oppenheimer had stopped there on pack trips from Perro Caliente. In 1941 he took his wife to meet Miss Warner, and these brief encounters laid the basis for one of those special friendships for which he—and she—had such talent. They also met Tilano, a former governor of San Ildefonso Pueblo, two miles east across the river, who for some years had been Miss Warner's companion and helper with chores and garden.

The tracks of the "chili line" were removed in 1941. Gas rationing kept tourists away, and Miss Warner was wondering how she could manage financially when she learned that the Ranch School would close and that even the trickle of strangers still crossing the Rio Grande to her tearoom must stop. One evening Oppenheimer and General Groves dropped in. Discussing proposed eating facilities on the hill, Groves suggested that Miss Warner might run the dining room in the former School Lodge or the cafeteria for unmarried dormitory residents. In desperation she agreed to consider the proposal. Oppenheimer and Groves went away. In a few moments there was a knock on the door. Oppenheimer stood on the step, a tall figure in the winter moonlight. "Don't do it," he said, then turned and went back to the car.[57]

Shortly thereafter Oppenheimer made another proposal. By serving dinner to eight or ten people three evenings a week, Edith Warner could earn enough for her simple needs, but this was not what Oppenheimer stressed. Scientists and their wives would have few opportunities for evening diversion away from "The Hill"; she would be making a real contribution to the war effort. Miss Warner and General Groves agreed. The Oppenheimers had first choice of dates. By a thoroughly undemocratic and mysterious process, others were notified when their turn came to take guests there. All became in some measure her friends, and, as Oppenheimer had foreseen, returned to their thin-walled apartments refreshed in spirit by contact with Miss Warner, Tilano, and the peace of the little house by the river.

MOST MANHATTAN PROJECT scientists of draft age had been deferred through regular Selective Service procedures. After early 1944 the Los Alamos staff was augmented by members of the Army's Special Engineer Detachment (SED) composed of young men with technical training or experience who for a variety of reasons had not received draft deferment. This group, including college graduates and Ph.D.s, performed desperately needed services but presented laboratory personnel officers and the Post Command with new problems to adjudicate—housing for married SEDs, jobs for the wives, and conflicts between laboratory working hours and barrack duties. These disparities in privilege between civilian and military laboratory staff disturbed all concerned, including Oppenheimer.

146 | TO LESLIE R. GROVES

[Los Alamos]
August 30, 1944

Dear General Groves:

We have so often come to you with our troubles that I would like to tell you of one case in which they appear to be solved. The command of the SED, in the hands of Captain [T. O.] Palmer and under the general supervision of Major de Silva appears to have been in every way successful. I have had no complaints of the relations between the detachment and the laboratory and only words of appreciation ever since this arrangement has been in effect. My own opinion is that the tensions which had developed in the past are rapidly abating, with a corresponding gratifying improvement in the morale and effectiveness in the detachment and its work.

I should like you to know that all of us appreciate the actions which you took to bring this about.

Sincerely yours,

J R Oppenheimer

A day later Oppenheimer again wrote to Groves, this time about a significant technical accomplishment. The X-10 stocks referred to the plutonium from the small production unit at the Clinton Laboratories at Oak Ridge.

147 | TO LESLIE R. GROVES

[Los Alamos]
August 31, 1944

Dear General Groves:

I should like you to have a report on the status of our X-10 stocks. Our records show, according to Dr. Kennedy's recent study, that we have received a total of 51 grams of this material. The material has been used for approximately 2500 separate experiments. The overall loss per experiment has been about 1 per cent. The result is that we now have in stock or accounted for by loan to other laboratories, 36 of the original 51 grams.

I believe that on the whole the mastery of the techniques necessary for handling the product which we have obtained in the last months has justified the use to which the material has been put and the losses incurred therein. This is also the opinion of Dr. Kennedy. Some further loss is to be anticipated during the experimental phase of our studies of this material, and perhaps another 5 or 10 grams will disappear in this way, although I confidently hope that this is an overestimate. On the other hand, we are now in a position to carry through the operations necessary for final fabrication with a very high yield (99%) and to recover almost all that is not included in the yield. I therefore believe that the material which we have dissipated will be paid for many times over by the effectiveness with which we can deal with production lots when they become available.

Sincerely yours,

J R Oppenheimer

IN SEPTEMBER Oppenheimer received from Chairman Birge a long letter about staffing problems in the Berkeley physics department caused by uncertainty as to how long the Los Alamos contingent would be away. Substitutes on temporary appointments were getting restive. Oppenheimer's former student Joseph W. Weinberg had been approached about a tenured post elsewhere. He was doing an excellent job and could not be spared until Oppenheimer returned. Birge feared that the eventual termination of government projects would result in increased competition for peacetime jobs and that the untenured members of the department would leave before the tenured ones returned.[58]

148 | TO RAYMOND T. BIRGE

[Los Alamos]
September 27, 1944

Dear Professor Birge:

Thank you for your letter of September 23. I appreciate the gravity of the problem which you raise and wish that I might offer an easy solution. This, however, [is] not the case, and your most gloomy forebodings have a significant chance of being fulfilled.

First, as to the plans of the members of the department who are now here, —Alvarez, Brode, McMillan and Oppenheimer,—I cannot of course speak with certainty of what their future personal preferences and hopes may be. I believe that this project will continue with essentially undiminished priority for the duration, that is, for some months after hostilities cease. I know that during that time it will be hard for me to acquiesce in the release of anyone who is bearing a vital responsibility for the work, and that this is true of all the men in question. Miracles are of course possible, such as a decision by higher authority to discontinue the prosecution of this work, but I think that only a miracle could affect the status of the men with whom you are concerned. There is no point in my trying to estimate what the duration will be; you are in as good a position to do that as I. I may tell you that in my own planning I do not expect to be able to leave this work before the Spring of 1946, but this is merely based on what I read in the *Albuquerque Tribune* and the *Denver Post*.

As for the specific problem of Weinberg, it would be my feeling that we would either have to be prepared to continue his employment in the future at a salary not less than that which he is now receiving, and until such time as he accepted a new position, or we should have to allow him at the present time to accept any position which he regarded as satisfactory and likely to be permanent. I realize that this puts you in a very difficult position but I am sure that you will agree with me that it is the only honorable course. I do not wish to recommend that we make a commitment of the kind suggested above to Weinberg, but if in your opinion this is necessary for the welfare of the department, I shall understand and I shall make no objection.

I believe that your views about the OSRD will probably turn out to be justified. The point of view expressed by Dr. Bush is that after the defeat of Germany only such projects will be continued as are likely to contribute directly to the Japanese War. Knowing the natural conservatism of research organizations I believe that it will be sometime before there are marked cutbacks in the OSRD. When these do occur there may be something of an avalanche of scientists seeking re-employment.

It would seem to me that there is only one solution to the present difficulties which may reduce the temporary havoc in the department. If it can be anticipated that a somewhat larger department will be required in the postwar years, I should recommend very strongly adding members to the department at an early date. I am sure that at this time men who can now, or shortly, be released from their wartime duties will be glad to join us. In this way it may be possible to provide some continuity over the difficult months ahead.

This letter contains no information which bears on the program of the project here; nevertheless, since a false construction could be put on it I wish that you would regard it as classified and written to you for your guidance only.

Sincerely yours,

J. R. Oppenheimer

The impatience detectable in Oppenheimer's response can be attributed in part to Birge's earlier refusal to commit the department to so exceptional a candidate as Feynman. Oppenheimer was preoccupied with a recently completed reorganization of the Los Alamos Laboratory beside which the Berkeley problems seemed momentarily unimportant. The reply to Birge's next letter was less testy in tone.

149 | TO RAYMOND T. BIRGE

[Los Alamos]
October 5, 1944

Dear Professor Birge:

Thank you for your good letter of October 2. I am glad that you are going to take steps to increase the strength of the department, and feel confident that we will all appreciate the wisdom of this in days to come.

Several months ago Dr. Feynman accepted a permanent appointment with the Physics Department at Cornell University. I do not know details of salary and rank, but they are presumably satisfactory to him. I shall of course do my best to call to your attention any men who are available and whom we should want to recommend strongly for the department. I am afraid that at the present time this may involve some conflict since we are still eager to add to our personnel here and since in the nature of things I tend to go after the men in whom I have the greatest overall confidence. It is true that I do from time to time learn of cut-backs in OSRD projects and I am in a rather good position to find out about personnel. I shall do the very best I can.

With all good wishes,

J. R. Oppenheimer

BY EARLY SUMMER 1944 scientists developing the gun mechanism of bomb assembly were reasonably sure of success, but it was doubtful how soon there would be enough uranium for more than one bomb. Therefore, those who set laboratory priorities, that is, General Groves and the Military Policy Committee, decided that the implosion method employing plutonium, expected soon in sizeable quantities from the plant at Hanford, Washington, promised more bombs at an earlier date and should be pushed as an alternative. This decision prompted a major reorientation of the work of the laboratory which involved the rearrangement of divisions and the appointment of two associate directors, Captain William S. Parsons, USN, head of the Ordnance Division since May 1943, and Enrico Fermi, who lived at Los Alamos after September 1944.[59]

Some think Fermi arrived too late to have a marked effect on development of the bomb, although his broad understanding provided a valuable check on the work of others. Oppenheimer hoped that Fermi's commonsense and tempered judgment would mediate conflicting views that threatened occasionally to disrupt the generally harmonious atmosphere of the project. Two differences of opinion about priorities had left a residue of bitterness. One was Edward Teller's dissatisfaction with the small effort expended on developing a hydrogen weapon, "the Super." This was temporarily resolved by allowing Teller to pursue his own thoughts with support from anyone particularly eager to work on the problem. The other less publicized source of tension was between those taking a largely traditional ordnance approach to the problem of detonation and the theoretical and experimental physicists working on the novel implosion device. Oppenheimer's ability to understand divergent viewpoints and then reach his own conclusion was evident in the covering letter with which he forwarded to Groves an early autumn report from Captain Parsons.

[Los Alamos]
October 6, 1944

Dear General Groves:

I am glad to transmit the enclosed report of Captain Parsons, with the general intent and spirit of which I am in full sympathy. There are a few points on which my evaluation differs somewhat from that expressed in the report and it seems appropriate to mention them at this time.

1. I believe that Captain Parsons somewhat misjudges the temper of the responsible members of the laboratory. It is true that there are a few people here whose interests are exclusively "scientific" in the sense that they will abandon any problem that appears to be soluble. I believe that these men are now in appropriate positions in the organization. For the most part the men actually responsible for the prosecution of the work have proven records of carrying developments through the scientific and into the engineering stage. For the most part these men regard their work here not as a scientific adventure, but as a responsible mission which will have failed if it is let drop at the laboratory phase. I therefore do not expect to have to take heroic measures to insure something which I know to be the common desire of the overwhelming majority of our personnel.

2. I agree completely with all the comments of Captain Parsons' memorandum on the fallacy of regarding a controlled test as the culmination of the work of this laboratory. The laboratory is operating under a directive to produce weapons; this directive has been and will be rigorously adhered to. The only reason why we contemplate making a test, and why I have in the past advocated this, is because with the present time scales and the present radical assembly design this appears to be a necessary step in the production of a weapon. I do not wish to prejudge the issue: it is possible that information available to us within the next months may make such a test unnecessary. I believe, however, that the probability of this is extremely small.

3. The developmental program of the laboratory, whether or not it has been prosecuted with intelligence and responsibility, is still far behind the minimal requirements set by our directive. This fact, which rests on no perfectionist ideals for long-range development, means that there must inevitably be some duplication of effort and personnel if the various phases of our program,—scientific, engineering and military,—are to be carried out without too great mutual interference. It is for this reason that I should like to stress Captain Parsons' remark that a very great strengthening in engi-

neering is required. The organizational experience which the last year has given us is no substitute for competent engineers.

Sincerely yours,

J. R. Oppenheimer

One person who did not require explanations and understood Oppenheimer's need for moral support was James Conant. "Just a line to tell you once again how satisfactory I think everything is going at Y," he wrote on October 20, 1944. "In all seriousness, you are to be congratulated on the progress made and the organization as it now stands. I enjoyed my trip immensely, and I am particularly grateful to you and your wife for your hospitality."[60]

PRESIDENT ROOSEVELT died suddenly on April 12, 1945. Philip Morrison recently reconstructed the impact of the shattering event on the isolated, tightly-knit mesa community:
"By Thursday afternoon the news was everywhere. We had lost FDR. Now there was no one we knew up there at the top, where the view ought to be clearer. The war raged on in the Pacific, though it was smoldering to an end in Europe. The United Nations was assembling, evidently ignorant of fission weapons. Los Alamos could see ahead only a little way, out to the first test, for which we were urgently at work. The usual Sunday services at the movie theater would be heavily attended even by the unchurched scientists, for The Director would offer remarks in memorial for the man who had been our leader 'in an old and unperverted sense.'"
"Sunday morning found the mesa deep in snow. A night's fall had covered the rude textures of the town, silenced its business, and unified the view in a soft whiteness, over which the bright sun shone, casting deep blue shadows behind every wall. It was no costume for mourning, but it seemed recognition of something we needed, a gesture of consolation. Everybody came to the theater, where Opje spoke very quietly for two or three minutes out of his heart and ours."[61]

REMARKS AT MEMORIAL SERVICE FOR
PRESIDENT FRANKLIN D. ROOSEVELT

Los Alamos, April 15, 1945

When, three days ago, the world had word of the death of President Roosevelt, many wept who are unaccustomed to tears, many men and women, little enough accustomed to prayer, prayed to God. Many of us looked with deep trouble to the future; many of us felt less certain that our works would be to a good end; all of us were reminded of how precious a thing human greatness is.

We have been living through years of great evil, and of great terror. Roosevelt has been our President, our Commander-in-Chief and, in an old and unperverted sense, our leader. All over the world men have looked to him for guidance, and have seen symbolized in him their hope that the evils of this time would not be repeated; that the terrible sacrifices which have been made, and those that are still to be made, would lead to a world more fit for human habitation. It is in such times of evil that men recognize their helplessness and their profound dependence. One is reminded of medieval days, when the death of a good and wise and just king plunged his country into despair, and mourning.

In the Hindu scripture, in the Bhagavad-Gita, it says, "Man is a creature whose substance is faith. What his faith is, he is." The faith of Roosevelt is one that is shared by millions of men and women in every country of the world. For this reason it is possible to maintain the hope, for this reason it is right that we should dedicate ourselves to the hope, that his good works will not have ended with his death.

J. R. Oppenheimer

FROM LATE 1944 until the end of the war Oppenheimer was preoccupied with correlating the interlocking parts of the bomb project and with preparations for the July test of the implosion device. Technical memorandums of the period shed little new light on how he handled his job, and his correspondence file yields virtually no nontechnical letters. One exception is a reply to an apologetic letter from Wolfgang Pauli, whose secretary had mistakenly mailed an earlier request for a contribution to a proposed Bohr festschrift to Frank instead of to Robert.[62] As director of Project Y, Oppenheimer had acquired a vastly broadened knowledge of ballistics, metallurgy, procurement, and security, not to mention how to deal with people, but he was well aware how effectively the experience had removed him from the cutting edge of theoretical physics.

[Los Alamos]
April 16, 1945

Dear Pauli:

It was very good to have your letter and to know a little of what you are thinking and doing.

I have not been at all distressed about the Bohr-Festschrift and I am not completely sure that I should do anything about it. In the first place, I have never been in Copenhagen and therefore I am not probably one of those who should be writing, although like everyone else who has ever done any Physics, the debt to Bohr is beyond evaluation. In the second place, for the last four years I have had only classified thoughts and anything I could write would be somewhat antiquated and somewhat trivial, so that it is very far from clear to me that it could in any sense be regarded as an honor to Bohr to have it written. I don't know how other people are responding to this invitation, and if it is a matter of a token only, and you think it appropriate, I would be glad to do what I can. I could write a few pages, maybe less, on the analogy between the sensitization of photosynthesis on the one hand, and the internal conversion of gamma rays on the other, but it would not be very hot stuff. Would you let me have a word as to what you think I should do. My own thought is that it would be better for me not to contribute.

It was good to have your word of greeting for Kitty, and she sends both you and Franca her warmest greetings and her love. All of us are beginning to look forward to the time when we can get back to a little more normal way of living and to a little bit of Physics, which looks if anything more seductive for the fact that it has been cultivated so little in the last few years.

With all warm greetings,

Sincerely yours,

J. R. Oppenheimer

A note from Birge in May, congratulating Oppenheimer on election to the American Philosophical Society, was another reminder of a world not dedicated to lethal weaponry. Oppenheimer replied that he would soon be "sufficiently old and respectable properly to qualify for membership."[63]

OPPENHEIMER PLACED responsibility for the test of the implosion device, scheduled for mid-July, in the capable hands of the Harvard physicist Kenneth T. Bainbridge. Back in May 1944, he had accompanied Bainbridge and two Army officers on the first of several expeditions to select a test site. In two weapons carriers the group explored a remote area to the southwest of Los Alamos, getting caught in mountain snowdrifts and lost on the open desert. Oppenheimer enjoyed every moment of the rugged three-day trip, but he was too busy to go on any others.[64] Finally, a site was chosen in the desolate Jornado del Muerto near Alamogordo, New Mexico, some three hundred miles south of Los Alamos. Oppenheimer supplied the code name for the test: Trinity. In 1962, replying to General Groves' query about the origin of the name, Oppenheimer wrote: "I did suggest it . . . Why I chose the name is not clear, but I know what thoughts were in my mind. There is a poem of John Donne, written just before his death, which I know and love. From it a quotation:

> . . . As West and East
> In all flatt Maps—and I am one—are one,
> So death doth touch the Resurrection.

That still does not make Trinity; but in another, better known devotional poem Donne opens, 'Batter my heart, three person'd God.' Beyond this, I have no clues whatever."[65]

Bainbridge's aide was Frank Oppenheimer, transferred from Oak Ridge, he later explained, because there "I got to be a pretty good expediter."[66] The reunion brought satisfaction to Robert, but he was busy, and Frank was often away at Alamogordo.

The pressure and momentum of work, already great, intensified as preparations for the test moved forward. Los Alamos scientists now cite this as the principal reason why, after German defeat was imminent, they did not challenge the use of the bomb in Japan as did those at the Met Lab and, to a lesser extent, at Oak Ridge. There had been at least two abortive discussions. Robert Wilson remembers convening an "impact of the gadget" meeting, probably in the spring of 1944, but thereafter he yielded to Oppenheimer's plea that attention should not be distracted from completing the bomb. In March 1945, some forty-five people, among them former members of the American Association of Scientific Workers, discussed the postwar economic prospects for scientists and the social impact of atomic energy, but Oppenheimer conveyed his opinion that scientists restricted by security could not accomplish much, and the group disbanded after appointing a committee to revive the discussion as soon as secrecy was lifted.[67]

Oppenheimer cannot have relished this repressive role. He and Niels Bohr had discussed international ramifications by the hour, but he avoided specific planning for future applications of the sort embodied by scientists at Chicago and Oak Ridge in the "Prospectus on Nucleonics" of November 1944.[68] In September 1944, when Tolman, as chairman of the War Department's Committee on Postwar Recommendations, asked what Los Alamos people he should talk to, Oppenheimer gave him a dozen names but expressed doubt that any of them had very coherent thoughts about postwar work. "I can say this of certainty of myself," he added.[69]

But in the spring of 1945, as Groves' reports to the War Department became increasingly optimistic about the probability that two types of fission weapon would be ready for use against Japan in midsummer, Oppenheimer was drawn into decisions relating to their use and into the role of adviser on atomic policy. As a member of the Target Committee of civilian consultants, Air Corps officers, and Manhattan Project scientists, he was host to meetings at Los Alamos on May 10 and 11 at which the committee recommended that criteria for selection of targets should give priority to two considerations: maximum psychological effect to induce prompt Japanese surrender and proof of the devastating power of atomic weapons so that all nations would see the need for international cooperation.[70]

Oppenheimer also served on a scientific advisory panel to the War Department's Interim Committee, which was appointed in early May to plan postwar atomic policy. With the other panel members—A. H. Compton, Fermi, and Lawrence—Oppenheimer attended an Interim Committee meeting in Washington on May 31.[71] Correspondence does not document what Oppenheimer was thinking as he made the transition from technical administrator to consultant on national policy, but the minutes of this Interim Committee meeting partially fill the gap. In addition to providing technical data and estimates "Dr. Oppenheimer strongly urged that numbers of the present staff should be released to go back to their universities and research laboratories in order to explore the many ramifications of this field, to avoid the sterility of the present orientation to specific problems only, and to develop cheaper and simpler methods of production . . . Fundamental knowledge of this subject was so wide spread throughout the world that early steps should be taken to make our developments known to the world. He thought it might be wise for the United States to offer to the world free interchange of information with particular emphasis on the development of peace-time uses. The basic goal of all endeavors in the field should be the enlargement of human welfare. If we were to offer to exchange information before the bomb was actually used, our moral position would be greatly strengthened."[72]

Panel members were not present the next day when the Interim Committee authorized the use of the bomb on a combined military and civilian target in Japan, but before leaving Washington they drafted a memorandum on the organization of a domestic atomic energy agency and agreed to meet at Los Alamos on Saturday, June 16, to make recommendations for postwar research and development. As was to happen repeatedly in the next eight years, Oppenheimer's gift for succinct summary made him the obvious person to formulate the committee's conclusions. The panel's Los Alamos meeting produced three reports: one on long-range planning, another recommending that the Manhattan Engineer District continue operations pending establishment of a peacetime authority, and a third, drafted in response to a last-minute request from Interim Committee chairman George L. Harrison. On behalf of Secretary Stimson, Harrison asked the panel's opinion as to the technical feasibility of a proposal presented in a long memorandum dated June 11 which James Franck of the Met Lab had brought to Washington, urging that an atomic weapon be demonstrated to Japanese leaders in an uninhabited area prior to full military use. According to all accounts, this was the topic that chiefly occupied panel members during the weekend of June 16, with Lawrence being the last to abandon the search for an acceptable alternative to military use. Without waiting to complete the other reports, Oppenheimer informed Harrison that the panel was not persuaded that a demonstration would ensure a quick end to the Pacific war.[73]

The implosion bomb was tested at Alamogordo on July 16.[74] Teams of Los Alamos scientists took the components of the two bombs to the Pacific. The uranium bomb was dropped on Hiroshima on August 6, the plutonium implosion bomb on Nagasaki on August 9, and on August 15 hostilities ceased.[75]

Los Alamos tried to celebrate one of these events with a big party. Ambivalence accompanied success: not only was the party a dismal flop but people later disagreed about when it took place. Some said everyone was too exhausted after Alamogordo; others that no one celebrated Hiroshima. In after years, Oppenheimer recalled only that he had dropped by briefly, found a usually cool-headed young group leader vomiting in the bushes outside, and thought, "The reaction has begun."[76]

V | *"High promise . . . yet only a stone's throw from despair"*

LOS ALAMOS, AUGUST TO NOVEMBER 1945

WHILE WAITING FOR NEWS of Japan's capitulation after the bombing of Nagasaki, Oppenheimer worked on the final draft of the report on post-war planning which the Interim Committee's Scientific Panel was preparing for the secretary of war. Lawrence joined him at Los Alamos for the week-end to discuss the report. He found Oppenheimer weary, harrassed, and not optimistic.[1] Shortly thereafter Oppenheimer took the report to Washington and submitted it to Secretary Stimson with a covering letter.

152 | TO THE SECRETARY OF WAR

August 17, 1945

Dear Mr. Secretary:

The Interim Committee has asked us to report in some detail on the scope and program of future work in the field of atomic energy. One important phase of this work is the development of weapons; and since this is the problem which has dominated our war time activities, it is natural that in this field our ideas should be most definite and clear, and that we should be most confident of answering adequately the questions put to us by the committee. In examining these questions we have, however, come on certain quite general conclusions, whose implications for national policy would seem to be both more immediate and more profound than those of the detailed technical recommendations to be submitted. We, therefore, think it appropriate to present them to you at this time.

1. We are convinced that weapons quantitatively and qualitatively far more effective than now available will result from further work on these problems. This conviction is motivated not alone by analogy with past developments, but by specific projects to improve and multiply the existing weapons, and by the quite favorable technical prospects of the realization of the super bomb.

2. We have been unable to devise or propose effective military countermeasures for atomic weapons. Although we realize that future work may reveal possibilities at present obscure to us, it is our firm opinion that no military countermeasures will be found which will be adequately effective in preventing the delivery of atomic weapons.

The detailed technical report in preparation will document these conclusions, but hardly alter them.

3. We are not only unable to outline a program that would assure to this nation for the next decades hegemony in the field of atomic weapons; we are equally unable to insure that such hegemony, if achieved, could protect us from the most terrible destruction.

4. The development, in the years to come, of more effective atomic weapons, would appear to be a most natural element in any national policy of maintaining our military forces at great strength; nevertheless we have grave doubts that this further development can contribute essentially or permanently to the prevention of war. We believe that the safety of this nation —as opposed to its ability to inflict damage on an enemy power—cannot lie wholly or even primarily in its scientific or technical prowess. It can be based only on making future wars impossible. It is our unanimous and urgent recommendation to you that, despite the present incomplete exploitation of technical possibilities in this field, all steps be taken, all necessary international arrangements be made, to this one end.

5. We should be most happy to have you bring these views to the attention of other members of the Government, or of the American people, should you wish to do so.

Very sincerely,

J. R. Oppenheimer
For the Panel

When Oppenheimer returned to Los Alamos a week or so later, hall-ways, offices, and living rooms teemed with talk: war was now so terrible that effective steps to control it would have to be taken. He recognized the flowering of seeds that he and Niels Bohr had planted even though he had felt duty-bound to discourage organized discussion until the laboratory's mission was accomplished. Out of his hearing, much of the talk was pre-faced by, "Oppie says . . ."

Oppenheimer also found a pile of mail, including official congratula-tions and letters from old friends surprised to have found his name so prom-inently associated with the weapons that had ended the war. These also were laudatory, in keeping with the mood of a country suddenly at peace. A prompt reply went to the provost of the University of California.

153 | TO MONROE E. DEUTSCH

August 24, 1945

Dear Dr. Deutsch,

Thank you for your generous and thoughtful letter. You will well understand that for all of us this enterprise of the atomic bomb has been heavy with misgiving and concern, and that your words of encouragement were very specially welcome. We must share the hope that in the years to come men will be glad of this development, and find ways to adapt it to the great human problems of our time.

It will scarcely be news to you that the administration of the Los Alamos Project has been a constant and often fantastic misery to the University of California. Many circumstances of security, remoteness, and the inevitable mismatch of personalities, have contributed to this; and I know that I must often have seemed to be making a disproportionate contribution myself. You will understand that in this I was going no further than seemed to me essential for the prompt and effective fulfillment of our directives, and that I did not come lightly or irresponsibly to a position of feud with the officers of the University. Nevertheless I wish that you would express to them my profound regret that the project could not be operated in a spirit of greater mutual confidence and cordiality.

With every warm good wish,

[Robert Oppenheimer]

The differences between the university and the Los Alamos administration for which Oppenheimer apologized had revolved principally around personnel policies and procurement. Los Alamos staffing required many exceptions. If supplies and equipment did not arrive promptly, impatient scientists complained of inefficiency; university agents, coping with priorities and shortages, had found demands unreasonable. When recriminations became most bitter, Oppenheimer had intervened.[2]

WITHIN A FEW DAYS of his return from Washington, Oppenheimer and his wife drove to Santa Fe, then around the southern slopes of the Sangre de Cristos, and up the Pecos Valley to Perro Caliente for the nearest approximation to privacy and a holiday that they had enjoyed in three years. He took with him letters reestablishing links with the outside world and answered some of the more personal or pressing ones by hand or on the typewriter. One of the first replies was to his cousin, Lee Oppenheimer, son of his Uncle Emil.

154 | TO LEE OPPENHEIMER

Cowles [New Mexico]
August 25 [1945]

Dear Lee,

Thank you for your good letter, and its wise & generous words. Apart from the note of thankfulness, there are two things I'd want to say in answer: I'd no longer argue with you about the social sciences: I'd pray maybe, that you would have wisdom in this most difficult, most critical field of human thought. And as for what comes of these things we've been working on—hope, & if you have the opportunity, work—that they may come to a good end. Liberals or no, it is not in the bag.

It was sweet to hear from you; perhaps before long we'll see one another again. I hope so.

Robert

Another prompt reply—with fewer misspellings than in the Harvard days but typed in the same casual format—went to Herbert Smith, now headmaster of the Francis W. Parker School in Chicago. There had been enough contact since Oppenheimer's last surviving letter to Smith, from Cambridge, England, in 1926, to allow a first-name salutation.

Perro Caliente
August 26 [1945]

Dear Herbert,

It seemed appropriate, & very sweet, that your good note should reach me on the Pecos—we had come over for a few days after the surrender. Like so many of the beautiful things of which I learned first from you, the love of it grows with the years.

Your words were good to have. You will believe that this undertaking has not been without its misgivings; they are heavy on us today, when the future, which has so many elements of high promise, is yet only a stone's throw from despair. Thus the good which this work has perhaps contributed to make in the ending of the war looms very large to us, because it is there for sure.

There is some chance that after this we may be in the East—that would have the clear good that we might see one another more than over these last years. If I can at all, I shall come to visit you.

With all warm greetings to you & to May, and with my thanks for your wise kind letter.

Robert

Another old friend who preserved the note Oppenheimer wrote from Cowles was his Harvard classmate, Frederick Bernheim.

Cowles, N.M.
August 27 [1945]

Dear Fred,

It was good to have your note, singularly and pleasantly unaltered by the two decades. It was in Muenchen I saw you last, I think, one hell of a long time ago for Muenchen, even if not for you or me.

I'd like to come see you, & if I knew where to say, would most warmly return the invitation. Kitty—who is the vague marriage—read your note & said as how you must be a lovely fella.

We are at that ranch now, in an earnest but not too sanguine search for sanity. It ought to be, but it isn't, like the spring days when the paving would make a tentative show through the slush of Mt. Auburn St. There would seem to be some great headaches ahead.

Yours

Robert

IN THE ACADEMIC RECRUITING at Los Alamos, Oppenheimer himself was prime quarry. Through talks with Richard Tolman and Charles Lauritsen he knew they were eager that he should convert his prewar annual visits to Caltech into a full-time appointment. He was less sure about Caltech's official attitude or about its future direction with Robert Millikan preparing to retire after twenty-four years as president. Soon after Oppenheimer arrived at Perro Caliente, he communicated his reservations to his friend Lauritsen.

157 | TO CHARLES C. LAURITSEN

[Cowles, New Mexico
ca. August 27, 1945][3]

Dear Charlie,

In these days in the mountains we have had a chance to think a little of the personal things in the future. More and more we recognize how strong the personal arguments are for coming to Pasadena. But there are as you know many things which are vague in my mind about the Institute. Some of them no doubt must remain vague for a while, and some would be less vague if my past connections there had been less tenuous. Almost none of the questions I am writing are in themselves "conditions"; but I think it will be apparent that what we do will be affected by the answers collectively. The reason that I am looking this gift horse in the mouth is of course that the decisions now I am taking at least with the intention of permanence. For the Institute too that is necessary. I have talked a little with Willie [Fowler] and with Richard [Tolman] and am sending him a copy of this note. Millikan asked me to let him know before making up my mind. I am writing to you rather than to him, because we have been so close in all this, and you will understand what I have in mind. But please show him all or any parts of this letter, and enlist his aid if you want it in answering. Beyond this letter there will be nothing much I can say at this time.

1) What provisions will exist, what provisions do we hope may exist, for the support of graduate students? Since teaching such students is the only thing I can really "guarantee" of the future, this makes a lot of difference. In

the 30's the situation at the institute was not satisfactory I thought. How many graduate fellowships of one sort or another can there be in all physics? What sort of stipends will be available? What can we do to improve the situation if it needs improvement?

2) I proposed twice getting Rabi to the institute thinking it a good thing generally, and for us in particular a great source of strength. Has this fallen through? If so, is it lack of money, is it reluctance to add another jew to the faculty, is it a general feeling that he would not fit in? How would these things look a little later? Don't you yourself think it would be a good idea to bring a man, not ingrown in the institute, of such rare qualities as scientist and man?

3) Is it known or guessed who will be in charge of the institute, who will be chairman of the physics department, how institute policies may be made, whether and how I might be expected to participate?

4) How tight is the situation financially? Could we if we thought it wise go in for an electron acceleration program, or a boiler, or a big cyclotron? (I know we should not do everything, but these are just examples.)

5) What would the institute policy be in regard to salary? I want two things at this time: a salary that is good enough to stay put the rest of the days, without haggling, and one that expresses a certain enthusiasm about hiring me. I've had an offer from Columbia, seemingly very attractive in all its provisions about work. They would pay me 15000, and 2500 more for a research assistant of my choosing. I realize that the salary is quite out of line for the institute, but what would an in line salary be? The stipend for the assistantship I had in Berkeley before the war, and is one of the few definite things without which I would not take a job, even though in the first months I might not use it. What could be done about that? From Conant and Neumann I know that the Princeton Institute and Harvard are both working up to offering me jobs.[a] I have not encouraged them and think it most unlikely I'd go to those places. The Berkeley situation is peculiar as you know: my feeling is that it lies between the institute and Columbia.

6) Would the institute welcome and support, if in conscience we thought it right, my advisory participation in future atomic national policy? I am plenty worried about this, far more of course than about the personal things; and if there were a real chance of helping would want to feel that this was welcome. Of course there are many reasons why this might not be.

That is a long list of questions, some trivial and some as you can tell more profound: I don't expect complete or completely satisfactory answers to them all, but without a little help I certainly could not say yes: I would have a pleasant life, surely, but with such a high chance that it would turn useless before many years had passed. Do let me hear from you, either officially if that is possible, or in any other way, but before too long. If you could bring an answer to Los Alamos that would be good. I must leave there for the east toward the middle of the month, and by then ought in all probability to have things settled. Are you coming to Chicago for the panel meeting the 20th? I have many profound worries in that field, and would hope to have you there so very much.

Affectionately,

[Robert]

a. John von Neumann, noted mathematician and professor at the Institute for Advanced Study, was a Los Alamos consultant.

When Millikan wrote to Oppenheimer on August 31 about the keen "desire to have you an important part of the big job of the next three decades here" (which prompted an almost unprecedented salary offer), he addressed the questions about opportunities for individual work and collaboration that Oppenheimer had raised with Lauritsen. However, it was six weeks before Oppenheimer was ready to give Caltech a definite answer. Millikan had needed some persuading. A month earlier he had written Tolman questioning whether Caltech should offer Oppenheimer a job, on the grounds that he was not a good teacher, that his future contribution to theoretical physics was doubtful, that possibly Caltech had enough Jews on its faculty, and that two promising young men might be had for the same price.[4]

STILL AT PERRO CALIENTE, Oppenheimer replied to a letter from Lawrence about citations conferred by the city of Berkeley upon its two now world-famous citizens. After taking the Scientific Panel's report to Washington, he was far from optimistic. Reporting to Lawrence on what he had learned there, he also reflected upon the not entirely amicable exchange of views about his possible return to Berkeley that had occurred during Lawrence's last visit to Los Alamos.

158 | TO ERNEST O. LAWRENCE

Cowles [New Mexico]
August 30, [19]45

Dear Ernest,

Thank you for sending me your fine letter to the Mayor of Berkeley. I had earlier answered the note and resolution on behalf of the Berkeley people at Los Alamos, in the same vein of course as your answer, but not I think so good.

After our meetings I had a few days in Washington; it was a bad time, too early for clarity. I took our letter, after the revisions, to Bush and to Harrison—Conant, Stimson, [Karl] Compton were all away—and had an opportunity with them to explain in more detail than was appropriate in a letter what our common feelings were in this all important thing. I emphasized of course that all of us would earnestly do whatever was really in the national interest, no matter how desperate and disagreeable; but that we felt reluctant to promise that much real good could come of continuing the atomic bomb work just like poison gasses after the last war. To some extent the problems of the future are sharpened and made immediate by the situation at Y. All of us are willing to wait for a bit, and help with any plan that looks reasonable. But in the end this will have to be based on a national policy which is intelligible in its broad outlines to the men who are doing the work. I had the fairly clear impression from the talks that things had gone most badly at Potsdam, and that little or no progress had been made in interesting the Russians in collaboration or control. I don't know how seriously an effort was made: apparently neither Churchill nor Attlee nor Stalin was any help at all, but this is only my conjecture. While I was in Washington two things happened, both rather gloomy: the President issued an absolute Ukase, forbidding any disclosures on the atomic bomb—and the terms were broad—without his personal approval. The other was that Harrison took our letter to [James] Byrnes, who sent back word just as I was leaving that 'in the present critical international situation there was no alternative to pushing the MED [Manhattan Engineer District] program full steam ahead'. This may have been somewhat garbled in transmission, but I fear not. I shall try before our next meeting in Chicago to get the situation a little better in mind; perhaps you have already done that. But I do not come away from a profound grief, and a profound perplexity about the course we should be following.

We have been at the ranch some days now, and I'm beginning to recover a little of the sanity that had all but vanished by the weekend you visited Y. I have very mixed and sad feelings about our discussions on Berkeley. I meant them in a far more friendly, tentative and considerate spirit than they appeared to you; and was aware and tried to make you aware at the time that fatigue and confusion gave them a false emphasis and color. It may seem odd and wrong to you that the lack of sympathy between us at Y and the California administration over the operation of the project could make me consider not coming back: I think it would not have seemed so odd if you had lived through the history as we did, nor so hard to understand if you remembered how much more of an underdogger I have always been than you. That is a part of me that is unlikely to change, for I am not ashamed of it; it is responsible for such differences as we have had in the past, I think; I should have thought that after the long years it would not be new to you. In any case it seemed little more than honorable to tell you of the misgivings, however unfortunate the timing. My own thoughts and plans have not come clear, though they no doubt will. But it must be apparent that your own very strong, very negative reactions would, if confirmed, and quite apart from the views of others involved, tend to carry a considerable weight with me, since any fruitful future in Berkeley would have to depend, not on identity certainly, but on a certain mutual respect for non identical points of view.

Affectionately,

Robert

Oppenheimer the underdog had surfaced at least once at a prewar Berkeley physics department meeting. After a favorable vote on Lawrence's proposed expenditures for ever larger equipment, Oppenheimer remarked acidly, "Now I suppose I may order a gross of pencils." Lawrence's biographer, who tells this story, observes that something of the old camaraderie returned as the two men worked together in Washington on atomic energy legislation in the autumn of 1945, but their discussion at Los Alamos in the tense days following the Japanese bombings dramatized the deterioration of a once meaningful friendship.[5]

On his return to Berkeley following the conversation with Oppenheimer, Lawrence immediately reported its substance to Birge. Notes made by Birge at the time summarized Oppenheimer's reasons for not returning as follows: He had been foolish years ago and "got in bad" with Sproul and Deutsch; more recently there had been constant fighting with the university's representative over the running of Los Alamos; Birge had always been out of sympathy with him and with what he wanted to do and furthermore Birge should be replaced as chairman. Lawrence had angrily told Oppenheimer that he ought not to come back if he felt that way.[6]

Oppenheimer could afford to be cavalier, even a shade paranoid, about the return to Berkeley, for in addition to the pressure from Caltech, he had also been the object of a number of informal job feelers through which prestigious academic institutions avoid the stigma of outright rejection. In these weeks after Hiroshima, Oppenheimer was not the only Los Alamos scientist poised uneasily between the familiar and the unknown, nor was he the only one to conclude after a year or two that his first decision had been wrong. But his physical and spiritual exhaustion was deeper than most; on his shoulders rested more directly the burden of destruction in Japan, and his brief experience in Washington left him deeply worried about how his government would use its new power. Preoccupation with global problems contributed to the difficulty of deciding his personal future.

BEFORE RETURNING to Los Alamos Oppenheimer dashed off a hand-written note to an old friend, Marcelle Meyer Bier, a member of the family that had befriended his father as a teenage immigrant.

159 | TO MARCELLE BIER

Cowles, N.M.
August 31, 1945

Dear Marcy

Thank you for your sweet note—it was very good of you & good to have. Certainly it has been our hope, as it must now be for many others, that this work on the atomic bomb, coming after these terrible years of war, may serve as a real instrument in the establishment of peace. That is almost the only thing right now that seems to matter.

With every warm good wish

Robert Oppenheimer

IMMEDIATELY FOLLOWING HIROSHIMA and Nagasaki, scientists at all Manhattan Project sites began discussing the need to educate policy makers and the American public about the implications of atomic energy in order to prepare the way for establishment of a system of international control that would avoid an atomic arms race. With intersite communication still restricted, groups at the Met Lab, Clinton Labs at Oak Ridge, and Los Alamos produced almost identical statements of principles and purpose. Unexpectedly prompt publication on August 12 of Henry de Wolfe Smyth's report, *Atomic Energy for Military Purposes,* gave scientists reason to think that this campaign could begin at once, and when they learned of the presidential injunction against public discussion, which Oppenheimer had mentioned to Lawrence, they were puzzled and indignant. To members of the newly formed Association of Los Alamos Scientists (its acronym, ALAS, was stressed on the first syllable), Oppenheimer seemed the logical emissary to get their statement cleared for publication.[7]

[Los Alamos]
September 9, 1945

Dear Mr. Harrison:

During my recent absence from the laboratory a group of scientists prepared the enclosed statement, which they would like to have presented to the press. I have been informed that the views expressed in the statement are held very nearly unanimously; that of all the civilian scientists (something over three hundred) who could be reached, only three felt that they could not sign the statement.

Although I had no part in the organization of the group or the preparation of the statement, you will probably recognize that the views presented are in closest harmony with those I have discussed with the Interim Committee. It seemed to me desirable to give the Committee an opportunity to examine this statement, and at my suggestion it is being transmitted to you for that purpose. I should wish to subscribe to the opinion of the scientists here that freer and more enlightened public discussion of the problems raised by atomic power and atomic weapons would itself be in the public interest, and should therefore like to encourage the Committee to approve the publication of the enclosed statement. Nevertheless, I am aware that there may be circumstances unknown to me which could make a public discussion at this time a source of embarrassment to the Government, and that the Committee may feel that the publication of such a statement at this time would hamper rather than advance the efforts of the Government to secure an enduring peace.

With every good wish,

J. R. Oppenheimer

The letter to Harrison reflects none of the outrage over the President's ban on discussion of atomic energy publicly expressed in early September by some prominent Manhattan Project scientists, for example Harold Urey and Samuel Allison.[8] Oppenheimer was becoming what would, a few years hence, be called "an inside scientist." In the course of his work on the Interim Committee's Scientific Panel he had developed great confidence in the judgment of Secretary of War Stimson and his aide George Harrison and, despite his skepticism about Potsdam, he did not realize, with Stimson on the point of retirement, how rapidly their influence was being supplanted by that of advocates of a cold war posture. In any case, the ALAS statement was shown to the Cabinet, after which it became a state paper and could not be published.

ALAS members learned the fate of their carefully worded document only after Oppenheimer left on September 18 for a two-week stay in Washington. To angry letters and teletype messages from the ALAS chairman, he replied with assurances that ALAS views were fully shared by those in a position to influence policy. Meanwhile, ALAS members watched helplessly while the Clinton Labs group leaked its statement of purpose to the *New York Herald Tribune* for publication on September 26 and the Atomic Scientists of Chicago made a similar release immediately following the President's October 3 atomic energy message to Congress. When at last a revised ALAS statement did appear on October 14, it made the front page of the Sunday *New York Times* under the headline "400 Experts Decry Lone Atom Policy."

Oppenheimer joined ALAS as soon as he retired as director of the laboratory. Later he gave much tacit support to the national federation formed by the original site groups, but he continued to feel that he could work most effectively for international control of atomic energy as an adviser to the policy makers.[9]

IN WASHINGTON, when not answering aggrieved communications from his colleagues at Los Alamos, Oppenheimer was principally engaged in conveying the views of the Scientific Panel to members of the War Department staff who were drawing up legislation to establish a domestic atomic energy authority. His Los Alamos secretary, Anne Wilson (Priscilla Duffield's successor), went along to help him get out the panel's final report. "It was a very exhausting and exciting time," she later wrote Charles Lauritsen, "and I found myself at all times covered with admiration at what I thought to be the magnificent job he did there."[10]

Oppenheimer had already announced his intention to resign the directorship of Los Alamos as soon as a satisfactory successor could be found, but continued uncertainty about what he would do after that is reflected in letters written from Washington on September 29.

Washington, D.C.
September 29, 1945

Dear President Sproul:

It is not unnatural that in the last weeks several institutions should have approached me with invitations to join their faculties. These invitations have been in many ways attractive, in offering freedom and opportunity for effective work in my field of theoretical physics, research assistance, salaries ranging from two to three times my salary in the Physics Department in Berkeley, and the furtherance of associations grown cordial in common work on the atomic bomb projects.

It is not easy for me to know in what spirit to consider these invitations. Long years of collaboration and friendship in Berkeley have made ties of real strength. Yet I am aware of a certain lack of confidence on the part of the University for what it must inevitably have regarded as my indiscretions of the past. I am likewise aware of the conflicts which arose between me and officers of the University when I was in charge of the Los Alamos project. It would be wrong for me to return to Berkeley unless it seemed, to the administration of the University as well as to the Physics Department, that this was truly and unreservedly in their best interests, that I might play a useful part as scientist, teacher, and member of the academic community. It would seem wrong to me to return at a salary so out of proportion to those of the other institutions.

It is clearly in the interests of the University of California, as it is in those of all the others involved, that a decision be reached without delay, so that constructive plans may be made. I should therefore very much appreciate a frank expression of your views. I can well understand that these may be rather negative, and in that case should not want you to feel obligated to write an answer.

I am sending a copy of this note to Professor Birge, for his plans too are inevitably involved.

Very sincerely,

J. R. Oppenheimer

Washington, D.C.
September 29, 1945

Dear Professor Birge:

The enclosed somewhat melancholy letter will tell you as well as I can what the present state of my thoughts is about Berkeley, and my own future. I think you know how hard it would be for me not to return; I want you to have a word of assurance that if I do come back it will be with full confidence in you as Chairman of the Department and in the cordiality and effectiveness of our collaboration.

As you can see, I am worried about the wild oats of all kinds which I have sown in the past; nor am I quite willing in the future to be part of an institution which has any essential distrust or any essential lack of confidence in me. I think that only harm can come from ignoring this concern; and I hope that you will agree with me that in writing this letter to President Sproul I am laying a reasonable basis for all our futures, whatever they may be.

With warmest personal
greetings,

J. R. Oppenheimer

Enclosure

THOUGH STILL UNSURE about his welcome at Berkeley, Oppenheimer firmly closed the door, not for the first or last time, on an offer from his alma mater, a decision made difficult by his growing admiration and affection for its president, whom he addressed on less formal occasions as "Uncle Jim."

Washington, D.C.
September 29, 1945

Dear Dr. Conant:

Your good letter was here in Washington for me when I arrived, but I did not want to answer it precipitately. It was certainly as thoughtful, considerate, and understanding a letter as I have ever had; I no longer want to delay an answer in which I have an increasing sense of certainty.

Surely no situation could be more attractive than that which you outline at Harvard; but I know now, as I should have known earlier had not fatigue and confusion played too great a part, that I would like to go back to California for the rest of my days; that I have a sense of belonging there which I will probably not get over. I should have told you this a month ago, but I didn't know it then. I hope that the trouble to which this has put you will not have been entirely wasted, and that the delays will not have hurt the plans which Harvard is so wisely making for the future.

I should like to thank you for the extraordinarily friendly way in which you have come to this question, and assure you of my regret that I shall not have you as my boss in the times to come. That was one of the hardest things to say no to.

Very sincerely,

J. R. Oppenheimer

Though seemingly committed to California, Oppenheimer had yet to decide between institute and university. Birge's reply of October 6, singularly magnanimous in view of his correspondent's expressed desire to unchair him, tried to dispel any notion that Oppenheimer was not wanted in Berkeley. Segrè too seemed to feel unwanted, said Birge, adding, "I cannot understand how such misconceptions could have arisen. Is there something about the climate at Los Alamos that breeds them?" Oppenheimer seemed to do a lot of traveling; couldn't he come to Berkeley and discuss these matters?[11]

On October 16 Oppenheimer sent a nightletter to William Houston, chairman of physics at Caltech, which said in part: "Am formally and gratefully accepting professorship of physics at the Institute. Planning to arrive in Pasadena first week of November . . . Appreciated your fine letter."[12]

The tone of finality was deceptive. Still hopeful, Sproul and Birge extended Oppenheimer's leave of absence, and, indeed, by February 1946 he was negotiating his return to Berkeley. This took place the following August, with three days each month to be spent in Pasadena. Certainly Oppenheimer had spent too much time in Washington to give Pasadena a fair trial; perhaps the questions about Caltech raised earlier with Lauritsen had not been resolved. Possibly a phone call had something to do with it, in which Lawrence is quoted as saying, "Robert, when you get through wandering around, come on back home. Your old office is waiting, your old hat is on the rack, your desk hasn't been cleaned out."[13]

In April 1947 when Birge announced to his Berkeley colleagues that Oppenheimer had accepted the directorship of the Institute for Advanced Study in Princeton, he described this loss as "the greatest blow ever suffered by the department."[14]

In retrospect Oppenheimer viewed the move as inevitable: "I think that the charm went out of teaching after the great change of the war . . . For one thing I was always called away and distracted because I was thinking about other things, but actually I don't think I ever taught well after the war. I have a feeling that . . . my job . . . was to get a part of the next generation brought up and that job was done when I came [to Princeton]."[15]

EVEN AFTER the first flood of congratulations had subsided, Oppenheimer's correspondence reflected his new status as a statesman of science. On September 29 Albert Einstein wrote from Princeton recommending Emery Reves' *Anatomy of Peace,* which proposed a world federation with a strong military force as a means of preserving peace. To Einstein it was "unthinkable that we can achieve peace without a genuine supranational organization to govern international relations."[16]

164 | TO ALBERT EINSTEIN

October 10, 1945

Dear Dr. Einstein:

Thank you for your good letter of September 29th. I am in complete agreement with the views expressed by you, and in general agreement with those expressed in the accompanying letter of Mr. Reves'.

If I say "general agreement" I mean only this: the history of this nation up through the Civil War shows how difficult the establishment of a federal authority can be when there are profound differences in the structure and values of the societies it attempts to integrate. I therefore view the problem as more, rather than less, difficult than Mr. Reves suggests.

The statements attributed by you to me are not mine; nor, as a matter of fact, have I ever seen them. I have known, of course, of the existence of such views, and have attempted where possible to point out their inadequacies.

These views do not correspond to the advice which I, or my immediate colleagues, have given to the Government of the United States. We have been concerned rather with the problem of initiating those negotiations which might establish confidence and form the basis for a real unity. We have, I believe, from the first recognized the essentially political character of this problem, and regarded the development of the atomic bomb as of incidental, but perhaps decisive, importance in two respects:

1) Focusing more sharply the attention of the public on the dangers of international anarchy (and in particular on the dangers of competitive armament between two all-powerful nations).

2) Providing a new and specific point of discussion where agreement might be less difficult to achieve.

I should appreciate it very much if you could send us as many copies of Mr. Reves' book as you conveniently can. Very many of my associates at Los Alamos are profoundly concerned with these problems and would be grateful for help.

With every warm good wish,

J. R. Oppenheimer

The statement disclaimed by Oppenheimer was that of the Association of Oak Ridge Scientists, which called not for world government but for an international agency to control atomic energy. The Oak Ridge scientists claimed that their views were held by hundreds of scientists who had worked on the bomb, including Manhattan Project leaders; this led Einstein to assume that Oppenheimer was a signer. Within three months Oppenheimer became a principal contributor to the Acheson–Lilienthal Report on which the United States international control proposal was based.[17]

There is no large body of correspondence between Einstein and Oppenheimer, nor did they become intimate friends during the eight years they were colleagues in Princeton.

OCTOBER 16 was Oppenheimer's last day as director of the Los Alamos Laboratory. Under a brilliant New Mexico sky, virtually the entire population of the mesa assembled for an outdoor ceremony. On behalf of the laboratory, Oppenheimer accepted from General Groves the Secretary of War's Certificate of Appreciation and made a short speech: "It is our hope that in years to come we may look at this scroll, and all that it signifies, with pride."

"Today that pride must be tempered with a profound concern. If atomic bombs are to be added as new weapons to the arsenals of a warring world, or to the arsenals of nations preparing for war, then the time will come when mankind will curse the names of Los Alamos and of Hiroshima."

"The peoples of this world must unite, or they will perish. This war, that has ravaged so much of the earth, has written these words. The atomic bomb has spelled them out for all men to understand. Other men have spoken them, in other times, of other wars, of other weapons. They have not prevailed. There are some, misled by a false sense of human history, who hold that they will not prevail today. It is not for us to believe that. By our works we are committed, committed to a world united, before this common peril, in law, and in humanity."[18]

Each person on the payroll of Project Y received a dime-sized sterling silver pin stamped with a large "A" and a small "BOMB." President Sproul was there from Berkeley to accept his institution's by-no-means minor share of credit. Despite the university comptroller's signature on their paychecks, most of those present, unless they had struggled with personnel and procurement, had thought of themselves as working for their country—or for Oppenheimer. A perceptible titter swept the crowd when the Army chaplain concluded the final prayer with a booming, "Oh God, bless all schools and colleges, and especially the University of California."

Before Oppenheimer flew to Washington for a Senate committee hearing next morning, he dictated the nightletter accepting the professorship at the California Institute of Technology. On October 17 Norris E. Bradbury, Stanford University physicist, became director of the Los Alamos Laboratory. A commander in the Naval Reserve, Bradbury had been in charge of implosion research in the Explosives Division since September 1944.

Oppenheimer stayed in Washington for the remainder of the week, one of intense activity on the part of representatives of newly formed scientists' organizations who had gathered there to protest the military flavor of the War Department's May–Johnson bill establishing a domestic atomic energy commission which Oppenheimer and other panel members had endorsed. In addition to testifying at Senate and House committee hearings, Oppenheimer was occupied in trying to reconcile dissenting scientists to the bill. At the same time he was working with the War Department on amendments which would placate critics. In neither effort was he fully successful. However, along with Arthur Compton, who was equally concerned about this well-publicized revolt among their colleagues, Oppenheimer made sure that before the week was out the new secretary of war, Robert P. Patterson, publicly stated that with due regard to security, American scientists "should feel that it is proper for them as citizens to join actively in public consideration" of the political and social implications of atomic energy.[19]

Among remaining tasks awaiting Oppenheimer at Los Alamos was acknowledgment of the loyal and unstinting help he had received from key members of his staff. Into each letter went the note of personal solicitude that had marked the Oppenheimer style as leader. A particularly warm one went to David Dow, whose arrival in January 1944 had relieved the director of many nontechnical administrative burdens.

165 | TO DAVID DOW

October 29, 1945

Dear Dave:

Our association during the past two years has been so close, and my debt to you so varied and so great, that I think it right to send you a letter of appreciation.

Unlike most of the people at Los Alamos, you can have had little if any intellectual or technical satisfaction in your work. Helping to keep the place from running on the rocks, trying to find a common ground of understanding for all the many strong and disparate personalities, contributing your experience and your training as a lawyer, to a situation that came as near to defying legal control as any—all this has not been a bed of roses. You and I know that the loyalty and intelligence of all the people who made up the laboratory might well have been wasted, and the atomic bomb not been made, had we not worked together to provide an administration.

I know that in years to come you will think back at our miseries with contracts, with construction, with transportation, with personnel, and wonder how we could have lived through it. I know that for you, as for me, it was because of devotion to the purposes of the laboratory, to our country, and to those ideals of the scientists here, which made it possible to have the spirit of unity despite all personal difficulties and conflicts. I myself do not think that we would have survived at all without your help, and if it is any comfort to you to have those words written on paper you should have them.

I most earnestly hope that now that the emergency is over you will find it possible to return to the study of law and to have some of that academic tranquillity for which you yearn and for which the struggles of the last years, in my opinion, have made you rather rarely eligible.

With every warm good wish,

J. R. Oppenheimer

The letter to Charlotte Serber, wife of Oppenheimer's former student and colleague, herself a close friend in the Berkeley years, included some project history as well as recognition of an outstanding contribution.

166 | TO CHARLOTTE SERBER

November 2, 1945

Dear Charlotte:

It corresponds to my desires as a friend, and to my duties as the Director of the Los Alamos laboratory, to give you a word of appreciation for the work which you have done.

When we first discussed the formation of this laboratory we all knew that it would be peculiarly dependent on an adequate library, and on a library organized in the interests (the sometimes inconsiderate interests) of the scientists who would be the staff. We also knew of the problem—but I think we underestimated it—that would be presented by the necessity for maintaining a very complete file of classified documents, both those describing the work of the laboratory, and reports from elsewhere which might prove essential or helpful. Finally, we knew that the laboratory could not be run unless there was effective machinery for putting out the reports, the memoranda, and all of the other communications on which the understanding and the unity of the laboratory staff so largely depended. All of these have indeed presented real problems, not made easier by the absolute isolation which rendered us completely dependent on how the Library and Document Room were operated. They were not made easier by the frantic time schedules, which meant that it was never possible to wait for obtaining information, nor by the extraordinary technical variety and complexity of the matters in which we had an inevitable interest.

Perhaps the best way of saying how well you have discharged the responsibilities involved is this: I have never had a complaint of how the Library or Document Room were run, and in this large and often chaotic laboratory I have found that there was no reluctance on the part of the staff to enter such complaint at the slightest provocation. I think this is a tribute, not only to your administrative effectiveness, but to your good judgment, your foresight, and above all to your understanding of the problems with which we were faced and of the scientists who made up the laboratory. I think no single hour of delay has been attributed by any man in the laboratory to a malfunctioning, either in the Library or in the classified files. To this must be added the fact of the surprising success in controlling and accounting for the mass of classified information, where a single serious slip might not only have caused us the profoundest embarrassment but might have jeopardized the

313

successful completion of our job. I know that in carrying out these duties you have had the services of many able and loyal workers, but I also know that neither their ability nor their loyalty would have been effective without the guidance, support, and the good judgment which you gave them; and if they were loyal they had reason to be, because of your concern for them and for the work they were doing.

I do not know whether in any future time a job quite like this will exist anywhere in the world—it is a little hard to think that it will—but I know that the work that you have done will have seasoned you for many other perhaps easier undertakings, and increased your confidence in your own ability. Certainly it would be right that you take pride in a job well done— an integral part, and a most important one, in this strange, but rather heroic, undertaking.

Cordially,

Opje

ON THE EVENING of November second, Oppenheimer spoke to the members of the Association of Los Alamos Scientists. Some five hundred people packed the largest movie theater on "The Hill" to hear him. Years later, when former ALAS members were asked about postwar political activity, the answer invariably began (and sometimes ended) with "I remember Oppie's speech. . ."

SPEECH TO THE ASSOCIATION OF LOS ALAMOS SCIENTISTS
Los Alamos, November 2, 1945[20]

I am grateful to the Executive Committee for this chance to talk to you. I should like to talk tonight—if some of you have long memories perhaps you will regard it as justified—as a fellow scientist, and at least as a fellow worrier about the fix we are in. I do not have anything very radical to say, or anything that will strike most of you with a great flash of enlightenment. I don't have anything to say that will be of an immense encouragement. In some ways I would have liked to talk to you at an earlier date—but I couldn't talk to you as a Director. I could not talk, and will not tonight talk, too much about the practical political problems which are involved. There is one good reason for that—I don't know very much about practical politics. And there is another reason, which has to some extent restrained me in the past. As you know, some of us have been asked to be technical advisors to the Secretary of War, and through him to the President. In the course of this we have naturally discussed things that were on our minds and have been made, often very willingly, the recipient of confidences; it is not possible to speak in detail about what Mr. A thinks and Mr. B doesn't think, or what is going to happen next week, without violating these confidences. I don't think that's important. I think there are issues which are quite simple and quite deep, and which involve us as a group of scientists—involve us more, perhaps than any other group in the world. I think that it can only help to look a little at what our situation is—at what has happened to us—and that this must give us some honesty, some insight, which will be a source of strength in what may be the not-too-easy days ahead. I would like to take it as deep and serious as I know how, and then perhaps come to more immediate questions in the course of the discussion later. I want anyone who feels like it to ask me a question and if I can't answer it, as will often be the case, I will just have to say so.

What has happened to us—it is really rather major, it is so major that I think in some ways one returns to the greatest developments of the twentieth century, to the discovery of relativity, and to the whole development of atomic theory and its interpretation in terms of complementarity, for analogy. These things, as you know, forced us to re-consider the relations

315

between science and common sense. They forced on us the recognition that the fact that we were in the habit of talking a certain language and using certain concepts did not necessarily imply that there was anything in the real world to correspond to these. They forced us to be prepared for the inadequacy of the ways in which human beings attempted to deal with reality, for that reality. In some ways I think these virtues, which scientists quite reluctantly were forced to learn by the nature of the world they were studying, may be useful even today in preparing us for somewhat more radical views of what the issues are than would be natural or easy for people who had not been through this experience.

But the real impact of the creation of the atomic bomb and atomic weapons—to understand that one has to look further back, look, I think, to the times when physical science was growing in the days of the renaissance, and when the threat that science offered was felt so deeply throughout the Christian world. The analogy is, of course, not perfect. You may even wish to think of the days in the last century when the theories of evolution seemed a threat to the values by which men lived. The analogy is not perfect because there is nothing in atomic weapons—there is certainly nothing that we have done here or in the physics or chemistry that immediately preceded our work here—in which any revolutionary ideas were involved. I don't think that the conceptions of nuclear fission have strained any man's attempts to understand them, and I don't feel that any of us have really learned in a deep sense very much from following this up. It is in a quite different way. It is not an idea—it is a development and a reality—but it has in common with the early days of physical science the fact that the very existence of science is threatened, and its value is threatened. This is the point that I would like to speak a little about.

I think that it hardly needs to be said why the impact is so strong. There are three reasons: one is the extraordinary speed with which things which were right on the frontier of science were translated into terms where they affected many living people, and potentially all people. Another is the fact, quite accidental in many ways, and connected with the speed, that scientists themselves played such a large part, not merely in providing the foundation for atomic weapons, but in actually making them. In this we are certainly closer to it than any other group. The third is that the thing we made—partly because of the technical nature of the problem, partly because we worked hard, partly because we had good breaks—really arrived in the world with such a shattering reality and suddenness that there was no opportunity for the edges to be worn off.

In considering what the situation of science is, it may be helpful to think a little of what people said and felt of their motives in coming into this job. One always has to worry that what people say of their motives is not adequate. Many people said different things, and most of them, I think, had some validity. There was in the first place the great concern that our enemy might develop these weapons before we did, and the feeling—at least, in the early days, the very strong feeling—that without atomic weapons it might be very difficult, it might be an impossible, it might be an incredibly long thing to win the war. These things wore off a little as it became clear that the war would be won in any case. Some people, I think, were motivated by curiosity, and rightly so; and some by a sense of adventure, and rightly so. Others had more political arguments and said, "Well, we know that atomic weapons are in principle possible, and it is not right that the threat of their unrealized possibility should hang over the world. It is right that the world should know what can be done in their field and deal with it." And the people added to that that it was a time when all over the world men would be particularly ripe and open for dealing with this problem because of the immediacy of the evils of war, because of the universal cry from everyone that one could not go through this thing again, even a war without atomic bombs. And there was finally, and I think rightly, the feeling that there was probably no place in the world where the development of atomic weapons would have a better chance of leading to a reasonable solution, and a smaller chance of leading to disaster, than within the United States. I believe all these things that people said are true, and I think I said them all myself at one time or another.

But when you come right down to it the reason that we did this job is because it was an organic necessity. If you are a scientist you cannot stop such a thing. If you are a scientist you believe that it is good to find out how the world works; that it is good to find out what the realities are; that it is good to turn over to mankind at large the greatest possible power to control the world and to deal with it according to its lights and its values.

There has been a lot of talk about the evil of secrecy, of concealment, of control, of security. Some of that talk has been on a rather low plane, limited really to saying that it is difficult or inconvenient to work in a world where you are not free to do what you want. I think that the talk has been justified, and that the almost unanimous resistance of scientists to the imposition of control and secrecy is a justified position, but I think that the reason for it may lie a little deeper. I think that it comes from the fact that secrecy strikes at the very root of what science is, and what it is for. It is not possible to be a scientist unless you believe that it is good to learn. It is not good to be a scientist, and it is not possible, unless you think that it is of the highest value to share your knowledge, to share it with anyone who is interested. It is not possible to be a scientist unless you believe that the knowledge of the world, and the power which this gives, is a thing which is of intrinsic value to humanity, and that you are using it to help in the spread of knowledge, and are willing to take the consequences. And, therefore, I think that this resistance which we feel and see all around us to anything which is an attempt to treat science of the future as though it were rather a dangerous thing, a thing that must be watched and managed, is resisted not because of its inconvenience—I think we are in a position where we must be willing to take any inconvenience—but resisted because it is based on a philosophy incompatible with that by which we live, and have learned to live in the past.

There are many people who try to wiggle out of this. They say the real importance of atomic energy does not lie in the weapons that have been made; the real importance lies in all the great benefits which atomic energy, which the various radiations, will bring to mankind. There may be some truth in this. I am sure that there is truth in it, because there has never in the past been a new field opened up where the real fruits of it have not been invisible at the beginning. I have a very high confidence that the fruits—the so-called peacetime applications—of atomic energy will have in them all that we think, and more. There are others who try to escape the immediacy of this situation by saying that, after all, war has always been very terrible; after all, weapons have always gotten worse and worse; that this is just another weapon and it doesn't create a great change; that they are not so bad; bombings have been bad in this war and this is not a change in that—it just adds a little to the effectiveness of bombing; that some sort of protection will be found. I think that these efforts to diffuse and weaken the nature of the crisis make it only more dangerous. I think it is for us to accept it as a very grave crisis, to realize that these atomic weapons which we have started to make are very terrible, that they involve a change, that they are not just a slight modification: to accept this, and to accept with it the necessity for those transformations in the world which will make it possible to integrate these developments into human life.

As scientists I think we have perhaps a little greater ability to accept change, and accept radical change, because of our experiences in the pursuit of science. And that may help us—that, and the fact that we have lived with it—to be of some use in understanding these problems.

It is clear to me that wars have changed. It is clear to me that if these first bombs—the bomb that was dropped on Nagasaki—that if these can destroy ten square miles, then that is really quite something. It is clear to me that they are going to be very cheap if anyone wants to make them; it is clear to me that this is a situation where a quantitative change, and a change in which the advantage of aggression compared to defense—of attack compared to defense—is shifted, where this quantitative change has all the character of a change in quality, of a change in the nature of the world. I know that whereas wars have become intolerable, and the question would have been raised and would have been pursued after this war, more ardently than after the last, of whether there was not some method by which they could be averted. But I think the advent of the atomic bomb and the facts which will get around that they are not too hard to make—that they will be universal if people wish to make them universal, that they will not constitute a real drain on the economy of any strong nation, and that their power of destruction will grow and is already incomparably greater than that of any other weapon—I think these things create a new situation, so new that there is some danger, even some danger in believing, that what we have is a new argument for arrangements, for hopes, that existed before this development took place. By that I mean that much as I like to hear advocates of a world federation, or advocates of a United Nations organization, who have been talking of these things for years—much as I like to hear them say that here is a new argument, I think that they are in part missing the point, because the point is not that atomic weapons constitute a new argument. There have always been good arguments. The point is that atomic weapons constitute also a field, a new field, and a new opportunity for realizing preconditions. I think when people talk of the fact that this is not only a great peril, but a great hope, this is what they should mean. I do not think they should mean the unknown, though sure, value of industrial and scientific virtues of atomic energy, but rather the simple fact that in this field, because it is a threat, because it is a peril, and because it has certain special characteristics, to which I will return, there exists a possibility of realizing, of beginning to realize, those changes which are needed if there is to be any peace.

Those are very far-reaching changes. They are changes in the relations between nations, not only in spirit, not only in law, but also in conception and feeling. I don't know which of these is prior; they must all work together, and only the gradual interaction of one on the other can make a reality. I don't agree with those who say the first step is to have a structure of international law. I don't agree with those who say the only thing is to have friendly feelings. All of these things will be involved. I think it is true to say that atomic weapons are a peril which affect everyone in the world, and in that sense a completely common problem, as common a problem as it was for the Allies to defeat the Nazis. I think that in order to handle this common problem there must be a complete sense of community responsibility. I do not think that one may expect that people will contribute to the solution of the problem until they are aware of their ability to take part in the solution. I think that it is a field in which the implementation of such a common responsibility has certain decisive advantages. It is a new field, in which the position of vested interests in various parts of the world is very much less serious than in others. It is serious in this country, and that is one of our problems. It is a new field, in which the role of science has been so great that it is to my mind hardly thinkable that the international traditions of science, and the fraternity of scientists, should not play a constructive part. It is a new field, in which just the novelty and the special characteristics of the technical operations should enable one to establish a community of interest which might almost be regarded as a pilot plant for a new type of international collaboration. I speak of it as a pilot plant because it is quite clear that the control of atomic weapons cannot be in itself the unique end of such operation. The only unique end can be a world that is united, and a world in which war will not occur. But those things don't happen overnight, and in this field it would seem that one could get started, and get started without meeting those insuperable obstacles which history has so often placed in the way of any effort of cooperation. Now, this is not an easy thing, and the point I want to make, the one point I want to hammer home, is what an enormous change in spirit is involved. There are things which we hold very dear, and I think rightly hold very dear; I would say that the word democracy perhaps stood for some of them as well as any other word. There are many parts of the world in which there is no democracy. There are other things which we hold dear, and which we rightly should. And when I speak of a new spirit in international affairs I mean that even to these deepest of things which we cherish, and for which Americans have been willing to die—and certainly most of us would be willing to die—even in these deepest things, we realize that there is something more profound than that; namely, the common bond with other men everywhere. It is only if you do that that this makes sense; because if you approach the problem and say, "We know what is right and we would like to use the atomic bomb to persuade you to agree with us," then you are in a very weak position and you will not succeed, because under those conditions you will not succeed in delegating responsibility for the survival of men. It is a purely unilateral statement; you will find yourselves attempting by force of arms to prevent a disaster.

I want to express the utmost sympathy with the people who have to grapple with this problem and in the strongest terms to urge you not to underestimate its difficulty. I can think of an analogy, and I hope it is not a completely good analogy: in the days in the first half of the nineteenth century there were many people, mostly in the North, but some in the South, who thought that there was no evil on earth more degrading than human slavery, and nothing that they would more willingly devote their lives to than its eradication. Always when I was young I wondered why it was that when Lincoln was President he did not declare that the war against the South, when it broke out, was a war that slavery should be abolished, that this was the central point, the rallying point, of that war. Lincoln was severely criticized by many of the Abolitionists as you know, by many then called radicals, because he seemed to be waging a war which did not hit the thing that was most important. But Lincoln realized, and I have only in the last months come to appreciate the depth and wisdom of it, that beyond the issue of slavery was the issue of the community of the people of the country, and the issue of the Union. I hope that today this will not be an issue calling for war; but I wanted to remind you that in order to preserve the Union Lincoln had to subordinate the immediate problem of the eradication of slavery, and trust—and I think if he had had his way it would have gone so—to the conflict of these ideas in a united people to eradicate it.

These are somewhat general remarks and it may be appropriate to say one or two things that are a little more programmatic, that are not quite so hard to get one's hands on. That is, what sort of agreement between nations would be a reasonable start. I don't know the answer to this, and I am very sure that no a priori answer should be given, that it is something that is going to take constant working out. But I think it is a thing where it will not hurt to have some reasonably concrete proposal. And I would go a step further and say of even such questions as the great question of secrecy—which perplexes scientists and other people—that even this was not a suitable subject for unilateral action. If atomic energy is to be treated as an international problem, as I think it must be, if it is to be treated on the basis of an international responsibility and an international common concern, the problems of secrecy are also international problems. I don't mean by that that our present classifications and our present, in many cases inevitably ridiculous, procedures should be maintained. I mean that the fundamental problem of how to treat this peril ought not to be treated unilaterally by the United States, or by the United States in conjunction with Great Britain.

The first thing I would say about any proposals is that they ought to be regarded as interim proposals, and that whenever they are made it be understood and agreed that within a year or two years—whatever seems a reasonable time—they will be reconsidered and the problems which have arisen, and the new developments which have occurred, will cause a rewriting. I think the only point is that there should be a few things in these proposals which will work in the right direction, and that the things should be accepted without forcing all of the changes, which we know must ultimately occur, upon people who will not be ready for them. This is anyone's guess, but it would seem to me that if you took these four points, it might work: first, that we are dealing with an interim solution, so recognized. Second, that the nations participating in the arrangement would have a joint atomic energy commission, operating under the most broad directives from the different states, but with a power which only they had, and which was not subject to review by the heads of State, to go ahead with those constructive applications of atomic energy which we would all like to see developed—energy sources, and the innumerable research tools which are immediate possibilities. Third, that there would be not merely the possibility of exchange of scientists and students; that very, very concrete machinery more or less forcing such exchange should be established, so that we would be quite sure that the fraternity of scientists would be strengthened and that the bonds on which so much of the future depends would have some reinforcement and some scope. And fourth, I would say that no bombs be made. I don't know whether these proposals are good ones, and I think that anyone in this group would have his own proposals. But I mention them as very simple things, which I don't believe solve the problem, and which I want to make clear are not the ultimate or even a touch of the ultimate, but which I think ought to be started right away; which I believe—though I know very little of this—may very well be acceptable to any of the nations that wish to become partners with us in this great undertaking.

One of the questions which you will want to hear more about, and which I can only partly hope to succeed in answering, is to what extent such views— essentially the view that the life of science is threatened, the life of the world is threatened, and that only [by] a profound revision of what it is that constitutes a thing worth fighting for and a thing worth living for can this crisis be met—to what extent these views are held by other men. They are certainly not held universally by scientists; but I think they are in agreement with all of the expressed opinions of this group, and I know that many of my friends here see pretty much eye to eye. I would speak especially of Bohr, who was here so much during the difficult days, who had many discussions with us, and who helped us reach the conclusion that [it was] not only a desirable solution, but that it was the unique solution, that there were no other alternatives.

I would say that among scientists there are certain centrifugal tendencies which seem to me a little dangerous, but not very. One of them is the attempt to try, in this imperilled world, in which the very function of science is threatened, to make convenient arrangements for the continuance of science, and to pay very little attention to the preconditions which give sense to it. Another is the tendency to say we must have a free science and a strong science, because this will make us a strong nation and enable us to fight better wars. It seems to me that this is a profound mistake, and I don't like to hear it. The third is even odder, and it is to say, "Oh give the bombs to the United Nations for police purposes, and let us get back to physics and chemistry." I think none of these are really held very widely, but they show that there are people who are desperately trying to avoid what I think is the most difficult problem. One must expect these false solutions, and overeasy solutions, and these are three which pop up from time to time.

As far as I can tell in the world outside there are many people just as quick to see the gravity of the situation, and to understand it in terms not so different from those I have tried to outline. It is not only among scientists that there are wise people and foolish people. I have had occasion in the last few months to meet people who had to do with the Government—the legislative branches, the administrative branches, and even the judicial branches, and I have found many in whom an understanding of what this problem is, and of the general lines along which it can be solved, is very clear. I would especially mention the former Secretary of War, Mr. Stimson, who, perhaps as much as any man, seemed to appreciate how hopeless and how impractical it was to attack this problem on a superficial level, and whose devotion to the development of atomic weapons was in large measure governed by his understanding of the hope that lay in it that there would be a new world. I know this is a surprise, because most people think that the War Department has as its unique function the making of war. The Secretary of War has other functions.

I think this is another question of importance: that is, what views will be held on these matters in other countries. I think it is important to realize that even those who are well informed in this country have been slow to understand, slow to believe that the bombs would work, and then slow to understand that their working would present such profound problems. We have certain interests in playing up the bomb, not only we here locally, but all over the country, because we made them, and our pride is involved. I think that in other lands it may be even more difficult for an appreciation of the magnitude of the thing to take hold. For this reason, I'm not sure that the greatest opportunities for progress do not lie somewhat further in the future than I had for a long time thought.

There have been two or three official statements by the President which defined, as nearly as their in some measure inevitable contradictions made possible, the official policy of the Government. And I think that one must not be entirely discouraged by the fact that there are contradictions, because the contradictions show that the problem is being understood as a difficult one, is temporarily being regarded as an insoluble one. Certainly you will notice, especially in the message to Congress, many indications of a sympathy with, and an understanding of, the views which this group holds, and which I have discussed briefly tonight. I think all of us were encouraged at the phrase "too revolutionary to consider in the framework of old ideas." That's about what we all think. I think all of us were encouraged by the sense of urgency that was frequently and emphatically stressed. I think all of us must be encouraged by the recognition, the official recognition by the Government of the importance—of the overriding importance—of the free exchange of scientific ideas and scientific information between all countries of the world. It would certainly be ridiculous to regard this as a final end, but I think that it would also be a very dangerous thing not to realize that it is a precondition. I am myself somewhat discouraged by the limitation of the objective to the elimination of atomic weapons, and I have seen many articles—probably you have, too—in which this is interpreted as follows: "Let us get international agreement to outlaw atomic weapons and then let us go back to having a good, clean war." This is certainly not a very good way of looking at it. I think, to say it again, that if one solves the problems

323

presented by the atomic bomb, one will have made a pilot plant for solution of the problem of ending war.

But what is surely the thing which must have troubled you, and which troubled me, in the official statements was the insistent note of unilateral responsibility for the handling of atomic weapons. However good the motives of this country are—I am not going to argue with the President's description of what the motives and the aims are—we are 140 million people, and there are two billion people living on earth. We must understand that whatever our commitments to our own views and ideas, and however confident we are that in the course of time they will tend to prevail, our absolute—our completely absolute—commitment to them, in denial of the views and ideas of other people, cannot be the basis of any kind of agreement.

As I have said, I had for a long time the feeling of the most extreme urgency, and I think maybe there was something right about that. There was a period immediately after the first use of the bomb when it seemed most natural that a clear statement of policy, and the initial steps of implementing it, should have been made; and it would be wrong for me not to admit that something may have been lost, and that there may be tragedy in that loss. But I think the plain fact is that in the actual world, and with the actual people in it, it has taken time, and it may take longer, to understand what this is all about. And I am not sure, as I have said before, that in other lands it won't take longer than it does in this country. As it is now, our only course is to see what we can do to bring about an understanding on a level deep enough to make a solution practicable, and to do that without undue delay.

One may think that the views suggested in the President's Navy Day speech are not entirely encouraging, that many men who are more versed than we in the practical art of statesmanship have seen more hope in a radical view, which may at first sight seem visionary, than in an approach on a more conventional level.

I don't have very much more to say. There are a few things which scientists perhaps should remember, that I don't think I need to remind us of; but I will, anyway. One is that they are very often called upon to give technical information in one way or another, and I think one cannot be too careful to be honest. And it is very difficult, not because one tells lies, but because so often questions are put in a form which makes it very hard to give an answer which is not misleading. I think we will be in a very weak position unless we maintain at its highest the scrupulousness which is traditional for us in sticking to the truth, and in distinguishing between what we know to be true from what we hope may be true.

The second thing I think it right to speak of is this: it is everywhere felt that the fraternity between us and scientists in other countries may be one of the most helpful things for the future; yet it is apparent that even in this country not all of us who are scientists are in agreement. There is no harm in that; such disagreement is healthy. But we must not lose the sense of fraternity because of it; we must not lose our fundamental confidence in our fellow scientists.

I think that we have no hope at all if we yield in our belief in the value of science, in the good that it can be to the world to know about reality, about nature, to attain a gradually greater and greater control of nature, to learn, to teach, to understand. I think that if we lose our faith in this we stop being scientists, we sell out our heritage, we lose what we have most of value for this time of crisis.

But there is another thing: we are not only scientists; we are men, too. We cannot forget our dependence on our fellow men. I mean not only our material dependence, without which no science would be possible, and without which we could not work; I mean also our deep moral dependence, in that the value of science must lie in the world of men, that all our roots lie there. These are the strongest bonds in the world, stronger than those even that bind us to one another, these are the deepest bonds—that bind us to our fellow men.

A FEW DAYS after his farewell speech, Oppenheimer and his family left for Pasadena.

Down by the Rio Grande Edith Warner read Oppenheimer's talk. Until the war ended she and Tilano had asked no questions of their Los Alamos guests as they quietly served the simple dinners, but there had been intuitive understanding in that Quaker-Indian household that the activity on the Los Alamos mesa involved more than science and technology. The letter that followed Oppenheimer to Pasadena was at once a reminder of what he had accomplished and of the task that lay ahead.

167 | EDITH WARNER TO ROBERT OPPENHEIMER

November 25, 1945

Dear Mr. Opp,

Tilano's name for you is used with deep feeling. I have thought of you frequently and wished that your last visit had been less surrounded and interrupted by people. So it was especially satisfying to read your recent speech to the ALAS. I hope you do not mind my having it.

As I read, it seemed almost as though you were pacing my kitchen, talking half to yourself and half to me. And from it came the conviction of what

I've felt a number of times—you have, in lesser degree, that quality which radiates from Mr. Baker [Bohr]. It has seemed to me in these past few months that it is a power as little known as atomic energy, which has greatly increased man's need for it. It also seems that even recognition of it involves responsibility.

There are many things for which I would express my gratitude. Your trust in me not only solved an economic problem but greatly broadened my horizon. Your hours here mean much to me and I appreciate, perhaps more than most outsiders, what you have given of yourself in these Los Alamos years. Most of all I am grateful for your bringing Mr. Baker. I think of you both, hopefully, as the song of the river comes from the canyon and the need of the world reaches even this quiet spot.

May you have strength and courage and wisdom,

Edith Warner

Enclosed are a note for Kitty and a feather for Peter. Thank you.

Niels Bohr and Robert Oppenheimer in the 1950s. (Courtesy of Niels Bohr Institute, Copenhagen.)

Kitty and Robert Oppenheimer at the Rochester Conference on High Energy Physics, about 1951. (Courtesy of Oppenheimer Memorial Committee, Los Alamos, New Mexico.)

Robert Oppenheimer with his children, Toni and Peter, in Princeton, New Jersey, 1948. (Courtesy of Oppenheimer Memorial Committee, Los Alamos, New Mexico.)

Epilogue

Attachment to California had played a part in Oppenheimer's immediate postwar plans, but in October 1947 he assumed the prestigious post of director of the Institute for Advanced Study in Princeton, New Jersey. Apparently he had changed his mind since his 1935 visit to Princeton, when he wrote his brother, Frank, that the place was "a madhouse, its solipsistic luminaries shining in separate and helpless desolation." In Princeton he and Kitty, with their children, Peter and Toni, lived at Olden Manor, the director's residence on the edge of the Institute grounds. The spacious rooms of the large white frame house provided the right background for the Van Gogh that Robert had inherited; less imposing possessions, acquired over the years in California and New Mexico, gave an air of informal comfort. Robert had his library, Kitty a greenhouse, Peter, in due course, a photographic studio, and Toni a stall for her pony, to whom a visitor once found her feeding hot cocoa from a delicate French porcelain cup. Francis Fergusson, seeing his old friend for the first time as head of a family, watched in amazement as Robert, surrounded by adults conversing brilliantly, shifted his attention the moment Peter or Toni entered the room. Not every father could do that, thought Fergusson.[1]

During part of two summers after moving to Princeton, Oppenheimer lectured in Berkeley, and for a few years he made regular visits to the Pecos Valley in New Mexico. The Christmas holidays of 1951 were spent in the Virgin Islands, where Oppenheimer shared with Kitty and the children his youthful enthusiasm for sailing. The New Mexico ranch was not sold, but the Caribbean, and eventually a house of their own on the island of St. John, became the Oppenheimers' winter and summer holiday retreat.

In many respects Oppenheimer's postwar career followed a pattern common among successful scientists of his generation. He became an administrator and a consultant on national policy. He received appropriate honors and awards. He traveled in the United States and abroad, usually to attend meetings and give lectures. He enjoyed the contacts and the amenities of life in an academic community. Decreased scientific output could be explained by the time-consuming nature of administration and committee work and rationalized by the then widely accepted myth that a scientist's productive life ends at thirty.

In Oppenheimer's case, this typical pattern was affected throughout, and at certain points radically, by his personal history and by his special relationship to the atomic bomb. After the war many scientists who had been employed in war research and development engaged in vigorous campaigns to educate American voters: they stressed the need for international control of atomic energy and rallied public support for the legislation that established a domestic atomic energy commission controlled by civilians. Oppenheimer was often consulted by the younger men who organized these efforts, but, avoiding open advocacy, he preferred to take advantage of his direct access to decision makers. In the belief that nuclear weapons would henceforth dominate international relations and that a rational nuclear policy could be developed only on the basis of technical information, he continued to serve as a confidential adviser to those who made policy, as he had done in the final months of the war. He was not alone among prominent scientists in adopting this role, so gratifying to self-esteem, but for a time he was the most visible and probably the most influential of the insiders.

When Oppenheimer gave the informal talk to the Association of Los Alamos Scientists in November 1945, his advice was already being sought by State Department officials who were negotiating with Great Britain and the Soviet Union on exchange of atomic information and the establishment of a United Nations Atomic Energy Commission (UNAEC). In early 1946 he served on the Board of Consultants to the secretary of state's Committee on Atomic Energy, where his ideas—and, through him, those of Niels Bohr—strongly influenced the so-called Acheson-Lilienthal report, on which was based the international control plan presented by the United States to the UNAEC in June 1946. He was a member of a UNAEC subcommittee of scientists which reported unanimously in September 1946 that effective international control was technically feasible, but this was the only significant agreement in the long, politically dominated control negotiations. By the end of 1947, when Oppenheimer resigned as science adviser to the United States representative to the UNAEC, he was admitting privately that international control was a hopeless cause. He continued to support the principle and in 1952-53 he chaired a State Department panel on disarmament.

At the same time, Oppenheimer served on committees and panels dealing with domestic policy in which atomic energy was a factor. By far the most important of these appointments was his six-year term on the General Advisory Committee (GAC) to the United States Atomic Energy Commission (AEC), which succeeded the Manhattan Engineer District on January 1, 1947. He was elected chairman at the GAC's first meeting on January 3 and held this post until his term expired in July 1952. He was concurrently a member of the atomic energy committee of the Research and Development Board of the Department of Defense and chaired panels on long-range objectives and on military objectives in the field of atomic energy. He served on advisory and review panels for the Air Force and on the Science Advisory Committee of the Office of Defense Mobilization.[2] In fact, Oppenheimer became a kind of Pooh-Bah of atomic energy: because he summarized discussions so succinctly and was often staying in Washington for another meeting next day, fellow panel members gladly delegated report writing to him; sometimes this meant that Oppenheimer was reporting to Oppenheimer. After his term on the GAC ended in 1952, he became an AEC consultant without specific assignment.

By 1954 Oppenheimer was a highly respected figure, admired for his unique wartime contribution and for unstinting service to his country in time of peace. As director of the Institute for Advanced Study, he was regarded as the archetypical intellectual, identified with the pursuit of knowledge. His talks and articles on atomic energy and the place of science in the realm of ideas had reached a large audience. So firmly established was his position as a symbol of leadership and service that news of the suspension of his security clearance by the United States Atomic Energy Commission, first published in the *New York Times* on April 12, 1954, was greeted with shocked disbelief within the scientific community and by the general public. The *Times* article also stated that a hearing was beginning that day before a special three-member AEC personnel security board to determine the validity of charges that Oppenheimer's leftwing activities and associations in the late 1930s made it unwise to trust him with classified information.

For years Oppenheimer had been aware of this Damoclean sword; it fell on December 21, 1953, four and a half months before the *Times* announcement, when he was summoned to Washington and told of the AEC's plans. A letter of December 23 from AEC General Manager Kenneth D. Nichols informed him that his clearance, which was due to expire or be renewed the following July, would be withdrawn in thirty days unless he requested a hearing. The letter set forth the charges in detail, adding to the points about undesirable prewar associations the charge that after 1949, when the AEC rejected the General Advisory Committee's unanimous recommendation against a crash program to develop the hydrogen bomb, his lack of enthusiasm for the project had deterred some scientists from working on it.

During the holidays Oppenheimer and his wife consulted at length with lawyers and friends, and he decided to ask for a hearing. On March 4, 1954, he submitted a formal reply to Nichols' letter. The Personnel Security Board, chaired by Gordon Gray, began to survey the record on April 5 and, with Oppenheimer as the first witness, commenced closed sessions on April 12. The hearing ended on May 6. On May 27 the board conveyed to the AEC its two-to-one recommendation that Oppenheimer's clearance should not be reinstated. On June 28 the commission, by a vote of four to one, confirmed this conclusion, making clear that although they regarded Oppenheimer as a security risk, his loyalty was not in doubt. His clearance was revoked three days before it was due to expire.

Meanwhile, on June 15 the Government Printing Office released copies of the transcript of the hearing and related documents—over one thousand pages of small print.[3] Of the scientists called to testify, a few had expressed doubts about Oppenheimer's judgment and discretion and agreed that he had not encouraged work on the H-bomb. The majority of witnesses, including distinguished past and present colleagues in science and government, had testified unequivocally to his loyalty and to his positive role as an adviser.

The transcript also revealed the lengthy questioning to which Oppenheimer himself had been subjected. The antagonism infused into the proceedings by AEC counsel had been so obvious that Oppenheimer's usual command of language and of the *mot juste* had deserted him at critical junctures. He was especially disconcerted by questions relating to the contents of surreptitiously recorded conversations between him and security investigators during the war and to his testimony before the House Un-American Activities Committee in 1949. During these inquiries about the loyalty of other scientists, he had acknowledged that several of his family members, prewar intimates, associates, and acquaintances had been leftwingers or communists in the 1930s. In response to probing into his earlier statements, Oppenheimer sometimes gave awkward and ambiguous replies.

Defense witnesses had not heard Oppenheimer's testimony, but they began to talk privately about the inquisitorial atmosphere of the proceedings. Subsequent disclosures would document the more concrete forms of inequity that converted an informal hearing into a trial without due process: information available to government lawyers had been withheld from defense counsel, there had been delays in providing Oppenheimer's lawyers with transcripts of testimony, and offices in which he sought legal advice had been bugged.[4]

Even before the full story was known, the attempt to discredit Oppenheimer was vigorously denounced, not only by his admirers, but by people who had never really liked him. He was seen by some observers as a martyr to McCarthyism, by others as partner to a kind of Faustian bargain. His predicament suggested that scientists, or indeed intellectuals in any field, did not belong in government. However, scientists did not disappear from Washington. Rather, new administrators, whose values and priorities differed from those of the officials who had so consistently enlisted Oppenheimer's advice, gradually assumed control of atomic policy and sought out scientists with views more congenial to their own. This phenomenon had already been apparent in the tapering off of Oppenheimer's committee appointments before his clearance was suspended. Under earlier AEC management, "the Oppenheimer case" might never have come up.

To friends who saw him during and after this ordeal, Oppenheimer made no secret of the anguish it caused him and his family, though he never discussed this publicly. The standardized acknowledgment with which he replied to scores of letters expressing sympathy and outrage was brief and noncommital. Perspective, if not solace, came with time. His reaction to Heinar Kipphardt's play based on the transcript of the hearing was that the author tried to convert a farce into a tragedy.[5]

Two Princeton friends, one of whom saw Oppenheimer almost daily for years, agree that he rode the crisis surprisingly well and that if it changed him the change was for the better. He did not become a model of humility, but he was less often arrogant and showed more understanding of other people. Physically, he changed less than photographs sometimes suggest. One day he looked haggard and drawn; the next he appeared robust and attractive, the way he had as a young man.[6]

Some commentators have portrayed Oppenheimer as defeated or disgraced, but the dignity with which he conducted himself after the AEC verdict and the absence of bitterness from any public statement refutes either judgment. In November 1963, just before John F. Kennedy was killed, Oppenheimer learned that he would receive the AEC's Enrico Fermi Award for outstanding contributions to atomic energy. On December 2, when the award was presented by President Johnson, his words of thanks had been carefully phrased. "I think it is just possible, Mr. President, that it has taken some charity and some courage for you to make this award today. That would seem to be a good augury for all our futures. These words I wrote down almost a fortnight ago. In a somber time, I gratefully and gladly speak them to you."[7]

Oppenheimer's productivity in theoretical physics diminished sharply in the postwar years. He published few papers after 1942, and in the absence of this rudimentary indicator, the significance of his postwar contribution is not easily established. Encouragement and criticism had been hallmarks of his teaching. Although he taught no courses after 1947, he continued to encourage, criticize, and help others to recognize solutions. To the Institute for Advanced Study he brought successive groups of brilliant young people who met in his office to discuss problems in theoretical physics as profound and intractable as those he had tackled with his students in the 1930s. Some of these recruits received permanent institute appointments.

In 1947 Oppenheimer helped initiate a series of small annual conferences on fundamental problems in physics which expanded by demand into the successful Rochester conferences on high-energy physics. A significant segment of Oppenheimer's postwar papers in the Library of Congress consists of correspondence with younger physicists who sent him for comment the drafts of articles on topics he had opened up years earlier. Many of his contemporaries continued to defer to his judgment and to value his analytic skills. Hans Bethe recalled that "Oppenheimer was always there [at the institute] to stimulate, to discuss, to listen to ideas. Even when he was busiest with public affairs, he knew what was most important in physics. It was forever astonishing how quickly he could absorb new ideas and single out the most important point."[8] Some members of the new generation, however, found his influence on physics less constructive. Encouragement and criticism were both infused with a personal style that tended to promote his own viewpoint, which sometimes seemed intolerant of others' and too "philosophical" or even "irrelevant" to the young theorists grappling with current problems in a rapidly changing field. This modus operandi evoked varied responses which are still being sorted out by the participants.

During the first two decades of what Oppenheimer and many others termed "the atomic age," he emerged as an eloquent interpreter of the implications of atomic energy and of the cultural value of science. In at least 120 public lectures, commencement addresses, radio and television talks and interviews, and magazine articles, Oppenheimer expanded on the theme of his farewell talk at Los Alamos, that atomic energy constituted both a peril and a hope. He also explained, philosophically and poetically, the principles of the physics of fundamental matter he had helped to formulate in the 1920s and 1930s, and he explored the relation of these ideas to knowledge derived from the arts and the humanities. His ideas reached wide audiences through publication of his 1953 Reith Lectures for the British Broadcasting Company as a book, *Science and the Common Understanding,* and a collection of eight lectures delivered between 1946 and 1954, *The Open Mind.*[9] Oppenheimer combined this public role of interpreter of science with his less visible role as critic and nurturer of scientists, and prior to 1954, as government adviser.

Friendship continued to play an important part in Robert Oppenheimer's life. In addition to the large parties that his position at the institute entailed, there was much informal entertaining at Olden Manor. His letters contained cordial invitations for lunch, dinner, or the weekend. Among the school and college friends who came from time to time were Jane Didisheim Kayser, William Boyd, and John Edsall. Francis Fergusson, living on the outskirts of Princeton, again became an intimate friend. The classicist Harold Cherniss was a permanent institute member; the link with him went back to 1929, that with his wife, Ruth, to childhood. Robert Serber and I. I. Rabi were nearby at Columbia University. Oppenheimer kept in touch also with California friends, especially the Lauritsens and Tolmans. Richard Tolman died in 1948, but Ruth remained a cherished confidante. After her death in 1957 the Pasadena house, which held so many happy memories for Oppenheimer, belonged to Robert and Jean Bacher, who offered him the same warm welcome he had always found there. The home of Dorothy McKibbin in Santa Fe was another haven of warmth and renewal.

Niels Bohr, H. A. Kramers, Wolfgang Pauli, and Hans Bethe were but a few of the longtime associates in physics who enjoyed Oppenheimer's hospitality, officially at the institute, as friends at Olden Manor. His already wide acquaintance was greatly enlarged by contacts in Washington, at the United Nations, and the institute. Among the valued new friends were Justice Felix Frankfurter and the poet Archibald MacLeish.

Not all of his former associates felt as comfortable with Oppenheimer the man of affairs as they had with the charming companion in Berkeley or the unpredictable host at Perro Caliente. Those who had been with him at Los Alamos adapted most easily to the transformation.

By mid 1965 Oppenheimer began to think about retiring as director of the Institute for Advanced Study. He submitted his resignation early in 1966 when a malignant throat tumor required surgery and radiation therapy. Letters he wrote in the ensuing months show a realistic appraisal of the progress of his illness, the guarded optimism with which he welcomed a brief remission in the summer, and throughout a determination to maintain as long as possible his connection with physics at the institute, his commitments to other organizations, and communication with his friends. Robert Oppenheimer died at his home in Princeton on February 18, 1967.

Notes

Introduction

1. New York City records contain a birth certificate for "Julius R. Oppenhiemer [sic]," born April 22, 1904; Philip M. Stern with Harold P. Green, *The Oppenheimer Case: Security on Trial* (New York: Harper & Row, 1969), p. 7n. The heading on Oppenheimer's Harvard College transcript reads: "J (initial only) Robert Oppenheimer"; Office of the Registrar of Harvard College, Cambridge, Mass. Interview with Frank Oppenheimer by Alice Kimball Smith, April 14, 1976.

2. Interview with Paul Horgan by Alice Kimball Smith, March 3, 1976, pp. 16, 17. Communication from Frank Oppenheimer, June 1979. Interview with Francis Fergusson by Alice Kimball Smith, April 21, 1976.

3. Interview with Frank Oppenheimer, April 14, 1976.

4. Ibid.

5. Interview with J. Robert Oppenheimer by Thomas S. Kuhn, November 18, 1963. All quotations from Oppenheimer in this chapter are taken from this interview, pp. 1–4. Excerpts from the Oppenheimer interview in this volume have been verified with the original tape and may differ slightly from the transcript. In some instances sentence order has been rearranged to relate to points mentioned in the letters and commentary. See Sources and Style at the back of this volume.

6. "Remembering J. Robert Oppenheimer," editorial in *The Reporter* [Ethical Culture School publication], 15, no. 4 (April 1967).

7. Interview with Herbert W. Smith by Charles Weiner, August 1, 1974. Interview with Jane Didisheim Kayser by Charles Weiner, June 4, 1975. Interview with Fergusson, April 21, 1976. Herbert W. Smith remained on the staff of the Ethical Culture School as teacher and high school principal until 1938.

8. Interview with Horgan, March 3, 1976, pp. 16, 17.

9. Interview with Herbert W. Smith by Alice Kimball Smith, July 9, 1975.

10. Denise Royal, *The Story of J Robert Oppenheimer* (New York: St. Martin's Press, 1969), pp. 22–23. Interviews with Smith, August 1, 1974, July 9, 1975.

11. Interview with Kayser, June 4, 1975.

12. R[obert] O[ppenheimer] '21, "The Bazaar," *Inklings,* February 1921, p. 28. Interview with Fergusson, April 21, 1976.

13. Interview with Kayser, June 4, 1975.

14. Interview with Horgan, March 3, 1976, pp. 1, 4, 5, 28, 37.

15. Ibid., p. 17.

16. Interviews with Smith, August 1, 1974, July 9, 1975. Interview with Kayser, June 4, 1975. Interview with Fergusson, April 21, 1976.

17. Interview with Smith, August 1, 1974.

18. Oppenheimer to Mrs. Fermor S. [Peggy Pond] Church, November 21, 1958, Warner File, Box 76, J. Robert Oppenheimer Papers, Manuscript Division, Library of Congress, Washington, D.C.

I. "Work . . . frantic, bad and graded A"

1. Interview with J. Robert Oppenheimer by Thomas S. Kuhn (hereafter cited as interview with JRO), November 18, 1963, pp. 3–6.

2. Interview with Francis Fergusson by Alice Kimball Smith, April 21, 1976.

3. Fergusson to Smith, Thursday, *ca.* November 1921, made available to the editors through the courtesy of Herbert W. Smith.

4. Interview with William C. Boyd by Alice Kimball Smith, December 21, 1975, p. 20. J. Robert Oppenheimer, Harvard College transcript, Office of the Registrar of Harvard College, Cambridge, Mass. "Harvard University Descriptive Catalogue," *Harvard College Catalogue, 1922–23,* Harvard University Archives, Pusey Library, Cambridge, Mass.

5. Interview with JRO, November 18, 1963, pp. 5, 7, 8.

6. Interview with John T. Edsall by Charles Weiner, July 16, 1975, pp. 1–2, 4–6. Interview with JRO, November 18, 1963, p. 9. Harvard Student Liberal Club File, Harvard University Archives.

7. Interview with JRO, November 18, 1963, p. 7.

8. Fergusson to Smith, fall 1922, made available to the editors through the courtesy of Herbert W. Smith.

9. Interview with Herbert W. Smith by Alice Kimball Smith, July 9, 1975.

10. Interview with Herbert W. Smith by Charles Weiner, August 1, 1974. Interview with Smith, July 9, 1975.

11. Kayser to Smith, June 13, 1974, made available to the editors through the courtesy of Herbert W. Smith.

12. Inez Pollak to Smith, January 14, 1923. Kitty and Inez Pollak to Smith, January 28, 1923. Made available to the editors through the courtesy of Herbert W. Smith.

13. Interview with Frank Oppenheimer by Alice Kimball Smith, April 14, 1976.

14. Frederick Bernheim to Alice Kimball Smith, August 3, 1976. Interview with Bernheim by Charles Weiner, October 27, 1975, pp. 8, 27.

15. Interview with Bernheim, October 27, 1975, pp. 7–8.

16. Interview with George Stevens by Alice Kimball Smith, April 21, 1976.

17. Interview with JRO, November 18, 1963, pp. 6, 7.

18. "Minutes of Physics Department meeting, June 6, 1923," Division of Physics Record, and Lyman to Oppenheimer, June 8, 1923, Correspondence of the Director of the Physics Laboratory, Harvard University Archives. The editors are grateful to Katherine R. Sopka for drawing attention to this quotation in her thesis, "Quantum Physics in America, 1920–1935" (Ph.D. diss., Harvard University, 1976), n. 3.118.

19. Interview with JRO, November 18, 1963, p. 8. Pierce was professor of physics at Harvard.

20. Ibid., p. 10.

21. J. Robert Oppenheimer, Harvard transcript.

22. Interview with Fergusson, April 21, 1976. Interview with Smith, August 1, 1974. Interview with Paul Horgan by Alice Kimball Smith, March 3, 1976, p. 18.

23. Interview with Boyd, December 21, 1975, pp. 1–2.

24. Denise Royal, *The Story of J Robert Oppenheimer* (New York: St. Martin's Press, 1969), pp. 15, 19. Communication from Frank Oppenheimer, June 1979.

25. Interview with Smith, August 1, 1974.

26. Interview with Bernheim, October 27, 1975, p. 12. Interview with Boyd, December 21, 1975, p. 10. Interview with Horgan, March 3, 1976, p. 18.

27. Interview with Frank Oppenheimer, April 14, 1976.

28. Interview with Horgan, March 3, 1976, pp. 13–15. Frank Oppenheimer was also on this memorable voyage.

29. Interview with Boyd, December 21, 1975, p. 10. Interview with Bernheim, October 27, 1975, p. 10.

30. Interview with Horgan, March 3, 1976, pp. 19, 21.

31. Interview with Jeffries Wyman by Charles Weiner, May 28, 1975, pp. 10, 2–4.

32. Ibid., pp. 2–3, 14.

33. Interview with Frank Oppenheimer, April 14, 1976. Interview with Horgan, March 3, 1976, p. 3. Interview with Fergusson, April 21, 1976.

34. Interview with Horgan, March 3, 1976, pp. 24, 34–35.

35. Interview with Bernheim, October 27, 1975, pp. 7, 14–15.

36. Ibid., pp. 34–35.

37. Ibid., pp. 14, 15–16.

38. Interview with Boyd, December 21, 1975, pp. 3–4, 9.

39. Interview with JRO, November 18, 1963, pp. 8, 9.

40. Ibid., pp. 7, 9, 10.

41. Interview with Babette Oppenheimer Langsdorf by Alice Kimball Smith, December 1, 1976.

42. Interview with Wyman, May 28, 1975, pp. 7, 16. Interview with Bernheim, October 27, 1975, p. 30. Interview with Boyd, December 21, 1975, p. 15.

43. Interview with Boyd, December 21, 1975, p. 9. Interview with Bernheim, October 27, 1975, p. 8. Bernheim to Alice Kimball Smith, August 3, 1976.

44. Interview with Wyman, May 28, 1975, pp. 10–11.

45. For reference to President Lowell's recommendation and for a discussion of the position of Jews in American physics at this time, see Daniel J. Kevles, *The Physicists* (New York: Alfred A. Knopf, 1978), pp. 210–213; see also Samuel Eliot Morison, *Three Centuries of Harvard, 1636–1936* (Cambridge: Harvard University Press, 1936), pp. 417, 421–422.

46. Interview with Boyd, December 21, 1975, p. 10.

47. Bernheim to Alice Kimball Smith, August 3, 1976. Interview with Boyd, December 21, 1975, pp. 9–10.

48. J. Robert Oppenheimer, Harvard transcript.

49. Interview with Bernheim, October 21, 1975, pp. 28–29.

50. Interview with Horgan, March 3, 1976, pp. 23–24, 33. Interview with Francis Fergusson by Alice Kimball Smith, April 23, 1975.

51. Communication from Frank Oppenheimer, June 1979.

52. Interview with JRO, November 18, 1963, pp. 6, 7.

53. Ibid., p. 5.

54. Ibid., p. 9.
55. Ibid., p. 15.
56. Oppenheimer to Lord Russell, April 18, 1962, Bertrand Russell File, Box 62, Oppenheimer Papers.
57. Interview with JRO, November 18, 1963, p. 5.
58. In medieval times the term *tripos* referred to the three-legged stool on which the examiner sat; later it applied to the candidate, and finally to the examination; *Encyclopedia Britannica,* 11th ed., s.v. "Cambridge, [England]" and "Examinations."
59. J. Robert Oppenheimer, Harvard transcript.
60. Ibid.
61. Interview with Bernheim, October 27, 1975, p. 14.

II. "Making myself for a career"

1. Interview with J. Robert Oppenheimer by Thomas S. Kuhn (hereafter cited as interview with JRO), November 18, 1963, pp. 13, 14. J. J. Thomson was professor of experimental physics and until 1919 had been director of the Cavendish Laboratory, where he continued to do research. He had been master of Trinity College since 1918.
2. Bridgman to Rutherford, June 24, 1925, Percy W. Bridgman Papers, Harvard University Archives, Pusey Library, Cambridge, Mass. The Bridgman–Oppenheimer correspondence included or cited in this volume was located by Katherine R. Sopka and made available to the editors through the courtesy of Gerald Holton.
3. Bridgman to Oppenheimer, June 24, 1925, Bridgman Papers.
4. Consuelo Chaves Summers to Alice Kimball Smith, October 29, 1976.
5. Interview with Paul Horgan by Alice Kimball Smith, March 3, 1976, pp. 6–8.
6. Interviews with Francis Fergusson by Alice Kimball Smith, April 23, 1975, and April 21, 1976.
7. Smith to Fergusson, *ca.* early fall 1925, made available to the editors through the courtesy of Francis Fergusson.
8. Interview with JRO, November 18, 1963, pp. 14–16. Ebenezer Everett was Thomson's mechanic and laboratory assistant. James Chadwick was then assistant director of radioactive research at the Cavendish. Erwin Schrödinger, who at that time was professor of physics at the University of Zurich, was the inventor of wave mechanics.
9. Interview with Frederick Bernheim by Charles Weiner, October 27, 1975, pp. 19–21.
10. Interview with John T. Edsall by Charles Weiner, July 16, 1975, pp. 13–14, 17.
11. Interviews with Fergusson, April 23, 1975, and April 21, 1976.
12. Interview with Edsall, July 16, 1975, p. 18.
13. Ibid., pp. 26, 29, 30–31.
14. Ibid., pp. 20, 26–27, 30, 31. Interview with Jeffries Wyman by Charles Weiner, May 28, 1975, pp. 21–22.
15. Interview with Edsall, July 16, 1975, pp. 24, 27. Denise Royal relates the

poisoned apple story to a Christmas holiday trip to Corsica with Wyman and to Robert's refusal to return to England by way of Rome: "A twinkle shown [sic] in Robert's eyes. 'I left a poison apple on Blackett's table. I have to get back before he does,' was Robert's whimsical way of saying he had some work to do for Blackett"; Denise Royal, *The Story of J Robert Oppenheimer* (New York: St. Martin's Press, 1969), pp. 35–36.

16. Interview with Fergusson, April 21, 1976.

17. Interview with Edsall, July 16, 1975, p. 19. Interview with Fergusson, April 21, 1976.

18. Interview with JRO, November 18, 1963, p. 16. Ralph Howard Fowler, a mathematical physicist, was a lecturer at Cambridge. He was Rutherford's son-in-law.

19. Ibid., pp. 17, 21. Niels Bohr, a central figure in world physics and a major contributor to quantum theory, was director of the Institute for Theoretical Physics at the University of Copenhagen.

20. Ibid., p. 18.

21. Interview with George Uhlenbeck by Charles Weiner, January 8, 1977. Interview with JRO, November 18, 1963, p. 18.

22. Ibid., pp. 18, 21.

23. Interview with JRO, November 20, 1963, p. 4. Richard Courant was director of the mathematics institute at the University of Göttingen. In 1926–27 Werner Heisenberg was a lecturer at the University of Copenhagen, working with Niels Bohr. He had previously been Born's assistant at Göttingen. When Robert met him Heisenberg was only twenty-five, yet he had already made fundamental contributions to the development of quantum mechanics. Gregor Wentzel was professor of physics at the University of Leipzig. Wolfgang Pauli, another major figure in the development of quantum mechanics, was a *privat dozent* at the University of Hamburg.

24. J. Robert Oppenheimer, *Science and the Common Understanding* (New York: Simon and Schuster, 1953), p. 35.

25. Interview with Robert Serber by Charles Weiner, May 25, 1978.

26. Oppenheimer, *Science and the Common Understanding*, p. 64.

27. Born to Stratton, February 13, 1927, Office of the President File, Institute Archives and Special Collections, Massachusetts Institute of Technology Libraries, Cambridge, Mass. The editors are grateful to Katherine Sopka for drawing attention to this quotation in her thesis, "Quantum Physics in America, 1920–1935" (Ph.D. diss., Harvard University, 1976), p. 3.46. Referring to Oppenheimer, Dirac, and Pascual Jordan, the physicist Earle H. Kennard wrote a Cornell colleague that "there are three young geniuses in theory here, each less intelligible to me than the others"; Kennard to R. C. Gibbs, March 3, 1927, quoted in Daniel J. Kevles, *The Physicists* (New York: Alfred A. Knopf, 1978), p. 217.

28. Interview with JRO, November 20, 1963, p. 5.

29. Ibid., p. 4.

30. P. A. M. Dirac, "Recollections of an Exciting Era," in *History of Twentieth Century Physics*, ed. Charles Weiner, Proceedings of the International School of Physics "Enrico Fermi," Course 57 (New York: Academic Press, 1977), pp. 139–140.

31. Interview with Margaret Compton by Alice Kimball Smith, April 3, 1976.

32. Interview with JRO, November 20, 1963, p. 5.

33. Bridgman to Oppenheimer, April 3, 1927, Bridgman Papers. John Slater was an assistant professor of physics at Harvard.

34. Interview with JRO, November 20, 1963, p. 18.

35. Kemble to Lyman, June 9, 1927, Folder K 1927, Box 8, Correspondence of the Director of the Physics Laboratory, Harvard University Archives. Quoted in Sopka, "Quantum Physics," p. 3.47 and n. 3.124.

36. Dirac, "Recollections," p. 140. Oppenheimer to George Uhlenbeck, June 18, 1927, made available to the editors through the courtesy of George Uhlenbeck. Oppenheimer to Samuel Goudsmit, July 16, 1927, Microfilm 61, Section 5, Archive for History of Quantum Physics, American Philosophical Society, Philadelphia, Pa., and other repositories cited in Sources and Style, at the back of this volume.

37. Interview with Else Uhlenbeck by Alice Kimball Smith, April 20, 1976.

38. Communication from Frank Oppenheimer, June 1979.

39. Philip M. Morse, *In at the Beginnings: A Physicist's Life* (Cambridge, Mass.: MIT Press, 1977), p. 87.

40. Interview with Edsall, July 16, 1975, p. 34. Interview with William C. Boyd by Alice Kimball Smith, December 21, 1975, pp. 7, 19.

41. *Hound and Horn: A Harvard Miscellany*, 1, no. 4 (June 1928): 335.

42. Interview with Helen C. Allison by Alice Kimball Smith, December 7, 1976.

43. Oppenheimer to Maj. Gen. Kenneth D. Nichols, March 4, 1954, in U.S. Atomic Energy Commission, *In the Matter of J. Robert Oppenheimer: Transcript of Hearing before Personnel Security Board, Washington, D.C., April 12, 1954, through May 6, 1954* (Washington, D.C.: Government Printing Office, 1954), p. 7. Lyman to Oppenheimer, April 10, 1928, Corr., Dir. of Physics Lab., HUA.

44. Interview with JRO, November 20, 1963, pp. 18, 19.

45. Neva E. Reynolds to Oppenheimer, August 16, 1928. Reynolds to Wallace Lund, August 29, 1928. Copies in International Education Board Papers, Rockefeller Archive Center, Pocantico Hills, N.Y.

46. Neva E. Reynolds to W. W. Brierley, October 15, 1928, International Education Board Papers.

47. Interview with Frank Oppenheimer by Alice Kimball Smith, April 14, 1976.

48. Interview with Herbert W. Smith by Charles Weiner, August 1, 1974.

49. Interview with JRO, November 20, 1963, pp. 19–21.

50. Ehrenfest to W. E. Tisdale, January 12, 1929, International Education Board Papers. Tisdale was secretary of the International Education Board.

51. Interview with JRO, November 20, 1963, p. 22. In 1927 Heisenberg had become professor of theoretical physics at the University of Leipzig; Felix Bloch and Rudolf Peierls both studied with him. In Zurich Peierls and Oppenheimer became friends: they sailed together on the lake and discussed many matters other than physics. Interview with Rudolf Peierls by Alice Kimball Smith, March 4, 1975.

52. Interview with JRO, November 20, 1963, p. 22.

53. W. J. Robbins to Oppenheimer, April 30, 1929, International Education Board Papers.

54. Log of W. E. Tisdale, September 4, 1929, International Education Board Papers.

55. Robbins to Oppenheimer, April 30, 1929, International Education Board Papers.

III. "Physics and the excellences of the life it brings"

1. Interview with J. Robert Oppenheimer by Thomas S. Kuhn (hereafter cited as interview with JRO), November 20, 1963, p. 18.

2. Ibid., pp. 30–31.

3. Interview with Frank Oppenheimer by Alice Kimball Smith, April 14, 1976. Denise Royal, *The Story of J Robert Oppenheimer* (New York: St. Martin's Press, 1969), p. 44.

4. Interview with Else Uhlenbeck by Alice Kimball Smith, April 20, 1976.

5. Interview with JRO, November 20, 1963, p. 19. Interview with Frank Oppenheimer, April 14, 1976.

6. *The Fieldglass* [Fieldston School yearbook], 1930, p. 50.

7. Interview with Helen C. Allison by Alice Kimball Smith, December 7, 1976.

8. Interview with Else Uhlenbeck, April 20, 1976.

9. Interview with Wendell H. Furry by Charles Weiner, August 9, 1971.

10. Jean Bacher to Alice Kimball Smith, December 1, 1976.

11. Bureau of Vital Records, City of New York, to Charles Weiner, January 13, 1978. Interview with Herbert W. Smith by Charles Weiner, August 1, 1974. Interview with Frank Oppenheimer, April 14, 1976.

12. Interview with Else Uhlenbeck, April 20, 1976.

13. Interview with Leo Nedelsky by Alice Kimball Smith, December 7, 1976.

14. Ibid.

15. Interview with Furry, August 9, 1971.

16. Interview with Edwin and Ruth Uehling by Charles Weiner and Alice Kimball Smith, October 10, 1975.

17. Robert Serber, "The Early Years," in I. I. Rabi et al., *Oppenheimer* (New York: Charles Scribner's Sons, 1969), pp. 17–20.

18. Interview with JRO, November 20, 1963, p. 31.

19. Interview with Frank Oppenheimer, April 14, 1976.

20. Communication from Frank Oppenheimer, June 1979.

21. Postcard made available to the editors through the courtesy of Frank Oppenheimer.

22. Charles Weiner, "1932—Moving into the New Physics," *Physics Today*, 25 (May 1972): 40–49. Daniel J. Kevles, *The Physicists*, pp. 222–235.

23. Interview with Edwin and Ruth Uehling, October 10, 1975.

24. Serber, "The Early Years," p. 14.

25. Interview with Else Uhlenbeck, April 20, 1976.

26. Oppenheimer to Uhlenbeck, January 1934, Archive for History of Quantum Physics, American Philosophical Society, Philadelphia, Pa., and other repositories cited in Sources and Style at the back of this volume.

27. Frank Oppenheimer to Alice Kimball Smith, November 29, 1976.

28. See Charles Weiner, "A New Site for the Seminar: The Refugees and American Physics in the Thirties," in *The Intellectual Migration: Europe and America,*

1930–1960, ed. Donald Harnish Fleming and Bernard Bailyn (Cambridge: Harvard University Press, 1969), pp. 190–234.

29. Interview with Furry, August 9, 1971.

30. Interview with JRO, November 20, 1963, p. 31.

31. Interview with Furry, August 9, 1971. Interview with Robert Serber by Charles Weiner and Gloria Lubkin, February 10, 1967, pp. 6–7. Interview with Edwin and Ruth Uehling, October 10, 1975.

32. Interview with Edwin and Ruth Uehling, October 10, 1975. Serber, "The Early Years," p. 19. Interview with Felix Bloch by Charles Weiner, August 15, 1968, pp. 17–20.

33. Interview with Else Uhlenbeck, April 20, 1976.

34. Ibid.

35. Serber, "The Early Years," p. 19.

36. Interview with Edwin and Ruth Uehling, October 10, 1975.

37. Interview with Frank Oppenheimer, April 14, 1976.

38. "Celebration of the Sixtieth Birthday of Albert Einstein," *Science,* 89 (April 14, 1939): 335.

39. Oppenheimer to Cassidy, January 15, 1951, Cassidy File, Box 26, J. Robert Oppenheimer Papers, Manuscript Division, Library of Congress, Washington, D.C.

40. Interview with Edwin and Ruth Uehling, October 10, 1975. Interview with Philip Morrison by Charles Weiner, February 7, 1967, pp. 13–14. Interview with Furry, August 9, 1971.

41. Serber, "The Early Years," pp. 19–20.

42. Interview with Edwin and Ruth Uehling, October 10, 1975.

43. Interview with Frank Oppenheimer, April 14, 1976.

44. Oppenheimer to Maj. Gen. Kenneth D. Nichols, March 4, 1954, in U.S. Atomic Energy Commission, *In the Matter of J. Robert Oppenheimer: Transcript of Hearing before Personnel Security Board, Washington, D.C., April 12, 1954, through May 6, 1954* (Washington, D.C.: Government Printing Office, 1954), p. 8 (hereafter cited as AEC, *Hearing*).

45. Interview with Nedelsky, December 7, 1976.

46. Communication from Frank Oppenheimer, June 1979.

47. Oppenheimer to Nichols, March 4, 1954, in AEC, *Hearing,* pp. 8, 9.

48. *Science–Supplement,* 84 (November 20, 1936): 9; [Carl Anderson], "Concerning Mesotrons," memorandum [to Millikan?], December 29, 1943, and R. A. Millikan to A. Westgren, January 6, 1944, Nobel Prize Folders, Box 12, Millikan Papers, California Institute of Technology Archives; interview with Carl D. Anderson by Charles Weiner, June 30, 1966, pp. 19–29. Experiments by J. C. Street and E. C. Stevenson at Harvard also provided evidence for the existence of the meson.

49. J. R. Oppenheimer and J. F. Carlson, "On multiplicative showers," *Physical Review,* 51 (February 15, 1937): 220 (received December 8, 1936).

50. Robert Oppenheimer, "Thirty Years of Mesons," *Physics Today,* 11 (November 1966): 52.

51. Bureau of Vital Records, City of New York, to Charles Weiner, January 13, 1978.

52. Stern to Oppenheimer, October 14, 1966, H. Stern File, Box 69, Oppenheimer Papers.

53. Bohr to Oppenheimer, January 7, 1938, Bohr Scientific Correspondence, Niels Bohr Institute, Copenhagen, and Reel 24, BSC, Archive for History of Quantum Physics.

54. Oppenheimer to Nichols, March 4, 1954, in AEC, *Hearing,* p. 9. Oppenheimer to Robert Brady, June 10, 1938, and June 23, 1938, Center for the Study of the Consumer Movement, Consumers Union, Mount Vernon, New York.

55. Oppenheimer, "Mesons," p. 55. Interview with Robert Serber by Charles Weiner, May 25, 1978. Note handwritten by Millikan on Oppenheimer to Millikan, January 1, 1939 (letter 104).

56. Six of these notes located by the editors are not included in this volume. They are in the possession of William A. Fowler and will be deposited in the California Institute of Technology Archives.

57. Glenn T. Seaborg, "Public Service and Human Contributions," in Rabi et al., *Oppenheimer,* pp. 48–49.

58. "Minutes of the Seattle, Washington, Meeting, June 18–21, 1940," *Physical Review,* 58 (July 15, 1940): 187.

59. Oppenheimer to Nichols, March 4, 1954, and testimony by Katherine Oppenheimer, AEC, *Hearing,* pp. 10, 571–574. Communication from Robert Serber, August 1979.

60. Myer Solis-Cohen, "The American Descendants of Samuel Binswanger" (n.p., 1957), p. 9, Coa-Com File, Box 24, Oppenheimer Papers. Harvard College, Class of 1926, *Twenty-fifth Anniversary Report* (Cambridge: Harvard University Printing Office, 1951). Telegram from Molly and Ernest Lawrence to Oppenheimer, November 1, 1940, Folder 9, Carton 14, Ernest O. Lawrence Papers, Bancroft Library, University of California, Berkeley, Cal.

61. Oppenheimer to Nichols, March 4, 1954, and testimony by Katherine Oppenheimer, AEC, *Hearing,* pp. 11, 921.

62. Interview with John T. Edsall by Charles Weiner, July 16, 1975, p. 40.

63. *New York Times,* September 25, 1941, p. 27; September 26, 1941, p. 25; September 28, 1941, p. 8; October 2, 1941, p. 27.

64. Testimony by J. Robert Oppenheimer, AEC, *Hearing,* p. 131.

IV. "These terrible years of war"

1. Interview with Paul Horgan by Alice Kimball Smith, March 3, 1976, p. 33.

2. This history is covered in the early chapters of Richard G. Hewlett and Oscar E. Anderson, Jr., *A History of the United States Atomic Energy Commission,* vol. 1: *The New World, 1939–1946* (University Park, Pa.: Pennsylvania State University Press, 1962).

3. Lawrence to Compton, October 14, 1941, and October 17, 1941, Folder 19, Carton 27, Ernest O. Lawrence Papers, Bancroft Library, University of California, Berkeley, Cal. Oppenheimer to Compton, December 8, 1941, Folder 19, Carton 27, Lawrence Papers.

4. Millikan to Oppenheimer, March 25, 1942, Box 25.1, Robert A. Millikan Papers, California Institute of Technology Archives, Millikan Library, Pasadena, Cal.

5. Interview with John H. Manley by Alice Kimball Smith, December 30, 1975, pp. 1–3.

6. Interview with Robert F. Bacher by Alice Kimball Smith, March 16, 1978.

7. Conversation with John H. Van Vleck, May 30, 1978.

8. Oppenheimer to Manley, July 1, 1942, Manley Correspondence from Oppenheimer File, Box 50, J. Robert Oppenheimer Papers, Manuscript Division, Library of Congress, Washington, D.C.

9. *Manhattan District History: Project Y, the Los Alamos Project,* vol. 1: David Hawkins, *Inception until August 1945* (Los Alamos: Los Alamos Scientific Laboratory, Report LAMS-2532, vol. 1, December 1, 1961), 1.3 (hereafter cited as *Los Alamos Project,* vol. 1).

10. Hewlett and Anderson, *New World,* p. 104. Arthur H. Compton, *Atomic Quest* (New York: Oxford University Press, 1956), pp. 127–128.

11. Interview with Manley, December 30, 1975, p. 3.

12. For a detailed discussion of the planning and operation of the Los Alamos Laboratory, see Hewlett and Anderson, *New World,* chap. 7; *Los Alamos Project,* vol. 1, chap. 1.

13. Edwin M. McMillan and Elsie B. McMillan, "Early Days at Los Alamos" (unpublished manuscript of talks given at the University of California at Santa Barbara, February 20, 1975), pp. 2–3.

14. Hewlett and Anderson, *New World,* pp. 34, 41–42.

15. Leslie R. Groves, *Now It Can Be Told: The Story of the Manhattan Project* (New York: Harper & Row, 1962), pp. 61–63.

16. Oppenheimer to Hans A. Bethe, October 19, 1942, Bethe File, Box 20, Oppenheimer Papers.

17. For the background of the Seaborg–Oppenheimer exchange see Hewlett and Anderson, *New World,* pp. 109–110.

18. According to McMillan, when Groves and Dudley were in Berkeley on November 1 and again on November 4, the Los Alamos site had not been selected; McMillan and McMillan, "Early Days," p. 4.

19. Groves' account places the trip in October; *Now It Can Be Told,* pp. 63–67. The November 16 date was established by McMillan on the basis of Dudley's travel records; McMillan and McMillan, "Early Days," p. 5. The Atomic Energy Commission's historians also place it in mid-November (Hewlett and Anderson, *New World,* p. 229), which fits Oppenheimer's statement to Manley that he and McMillan were going "next week."

20. McMillan and McMillan, "Early Days," pp. 6–9. Groves later wrote McMillan that he had never heard of the Los Alamos site until Oppenheimer suggested it on November 16; ibid., p. 7. Hewlett and Anderson state that Los Alamos was already on Dudley's list; *New World,* p. 229.

21. Peggy Pond Church, *The House at Otowi Bridge: The Story of Edith Warner and Los Alamos* (Albuquerque, N.M.: University of New Mexico Press, 1959), chaps. 1, 12. Roland A Pettitt, *Los Alamos—Before the Dawn* (Los Alamos, N.M.: Pajarito Publications, 1972), pp. 47–58.

22. Bethe to Oppenheimer, December 22, 1942, Bethe File, Box 20, Oppenheimer Papers.

23. Bernice Brode, "Tales of Los Alamos," *Los Alamos Scientific Laboratory Community News,* June 2, 1960, through September 22, 1960. Laura Fermi, *Atoms in*

the Family: My Life with Enrico Fermi (Chicago: University of Chicago Press, 1954), chaps. 20–23. Eleanor Jette, *Inside Box 1663* (Los Alamos, N.M.: Los Alamos Historical Society, 1977) McMillan and McMillan, "Early Days." Unless otherwise indicated, comments on community life at Los Alamos are based on the recollections of one of the editors, Alice Smith, who lived there from July 1943 to January 1946.

24. This letter is printed in full in *Los Alamos Project,* vol. 1, app. 1, pp. 313–315.

25. Interview with Bacher, March 16, 1978. Hewlett and Anderson, *New World,* pp. 230–232.

26. *Los Alamos Project,* vol. 1, 1.10.

27. McMillan and McMillan, "Early Days," p. 3.

28. Interview with Priscilla Duffield by Alice Kimball Smith, January 2, 1976.

29. Interview with Dorothy McKibbin by Alice Kimball Smith, January 1, 1976.

30. *Los Alamos Project,* vol. 1, 1.26–1.51.

31. Ibid., 1.52–1.93.

32. Communication from John H. Manley, June 11, 1979.

33. Roosevelt to Oppenheimer, June 29, 1943, F.D. Roosevelt File, Box 62, Oppenheimer Papers.

34. *Los Alamos Project,* vol. 1, 1.26, 3.16, 7.21.

35. Interview with Bacher, March 16, 1978.

36. *Los Alamos Project,* vol. 1, 3.20.

37. See especially memorandum from Lt. Col. Boris T. Pash to Lt. Col. John Lansdale, Jr., June 29, 1943, in U.S. Atomic Energy Commission, *In the Matter of J. Robert Oppenheimer: Transcript of Hearing before Personnel Security Board, Washington, D.C., April 12, 1954, through May 6, 1954* (Washington, D.C.: Government Printing Office, 1954), pp. 821–822 (hereafter cited as AEC, *Hearing*). For Oppenheimer's 1954 testimony and records of the 1943 interrogations, see ibid., pp. 143–149, 845–886; and Haakon Chevalier, *Oppenheimer: The Story of a Friendship* (New York: George Braziller, 1965), pp. 44–47. For a discussion of the security angle of the June 1943 trip to Berkeley, see Philip M. Stern with Harold P. Green, *The Oppenheimer Case: Security on Trial* (New York: Harper & Row, 1969), pp. 47–48.

38. Interview with Manley, December 30, 1975, p. 8.

39. Interview with Duffield, January 2, 1976.

40. Memorandum from Oppenheimer to Bethe, Bloch, Rossi, Segrè, Staub, Teller, Weisskopf, August 9, 1943, Folder 380.01, Military Records, MED, National Archives, Washington, D.C.

41. Conversation with Cyril S. Smith.

42. Hans A. Bethe, "Oppenheimer: 'Where He Was There Was Always Life and Excitement,'" *Science,* 155 (March 3, 1967): 1082.

43. Interview with Duffield, January 2, 1976.

44. On salaries at Los Alamos see *Los Alamos Project,* vol. 1, 3.37–3.41, 3.56–3.58.

45. Sproul to Oppenheimer, October 4, 1943, President's Files, University Archives, Bancroft Library, University of California, Berkeley, Cal. Groves to Oppenheimer, September 24, 1943, Groves File, Box 36, Oppenheimer Papers. A memo

from Oppenheimer to Groves, October 13, 1943, suggests that the salary remained unchanged; R. G. Sproul File, Box 69, Oppenheimer Papers.

46. Vannevar Bush, *Pieces of the Action* (New York: William Morrow & Co., 1970), p. 282. Hewlett and Anderson, *New World,* chap. 8. Margaret Gowing, *Britain and Atomic Energy, 1939–1945* (New York: St. Martin's Press, 1964), chaps. 4, 5, 9, and app. 4, "Articles of Agreement Governing Collaboration between the Authorities of the U.S.A. and the U.K. in the matter of Tube Alloys."

47. *Los Alamos Project,* vol. 1, graph 1, p. 297.

48. Birge to Oppenheimer, November 26, 1943, Birge File, Box 20, Oppenheimer Papers.

49. Gowing, *Britain and Atomic Energy,* pp. 248–250.

50. Quoted in Alice Kimball Smith, *A Peril and a Hope: The Scientists' Movement in America, 1945–1947* (Chicago: University of Chicago Press, 1965), p. 6.

51. Ibid., pp. 6–13. Gowing, *Britain and Atomic Energy,* pp. 347–366. Martin J. Sherwin, *A World Destroyed: The Atomic Bomb and the Grand Alliance* (New York: Alfred A. Knopf, 1975), pp. 105–110.

52. Gowing, *Britain and Atomic Energy,* p. 261.

53. Quoted in ibid., p. 262.

54. Interview with Rudolf Peierls by Alice Kimball Smith, March 4, 1975.

55. Ilse Meyers to Oppenheimer, May 20, 1962, Me file, Box 48, Oppenheimer Papers.

56. *Los Alamos Project,* vol. 1, 8.4–8.14

57. Sometime before her death in 1951 Miss Warner told this story to Dorothy McKibbin; interview with McKibbin, January 1, 1976. See also Church, *House at Otowi Bridge,* pp. 29–31.

58. Birge to Oppenheimer, September 23, 1944, Raymond T. Birge Folder, General File, Lawrence Papers.

59. *Los Alamos Project,* vol. 1, 9.1–9.17. Hewlett and Anderson, *New World,* pp. 246–254.

60. Conant to Oppenheimer, October 20, 1944, Record Group 227, OSRD, S-1 Committee, Bush–Conant File, Box 3033, National Archives, Washington, D.C.

61. Communication from Philip Morrison, August 1979. Remarks at Memorial Service for President Franklin D. Roosevelt, Los Alamos, April 15, 1945, Folder 9, Carton 14, Lawrence Papers.

62. Pauli to Oppenheimer, April 16, 1945, W. Pauli File, Box 56, Oppenheimer Papers.

63. Birge to Oppenheimer, May 9, 1945, and Oppenheimer to Birge, May 14, 1945, University of California: 1943–47 File, Box 230, Oppenheimer Papers.

64. Kenneth T. Bainbridge, "Orchestrating the Test," in *All in Our Time: The Reminiscences of Twelve Nuclear Pioneers,* ed. Jane Wilson (Chicago: Bulletin of the Atomic Scientists, 1975), pp. 209–211.

65. Oppenheimer to Groves, October 20, 1962, Groves File, Box 36, Oppenheimer Papers. Lansing Lamont states that one evening when Bainbridge phoned Oppenheimer that the Alamogordo site had been chosen and a code name was needed, Oppenheimer happened to be reading a John Donne sonnet which begins: "Batter my heart, three person'd God: for you / As yet but knock, breathe, shine, and

seek to mend." Lamont does not give his source; *Day of Trinity* (New York: Atheneum, 1965), p. 70. As of January 9, 1979, Bainbridge in a conversation with Alice Kimball Smith was unable to confirm the story of the phone call.

66. Interview with Frank Oppenheimer by Charles Weiner, February 9, 1973, p. 87.

67. Smith, *A Peril,* pp. 60–62.

68. For portions of this, known as the Jeffries Report, see ibid., app. A.

69. Oppenheimer to Tolman, September 20, 1944, OSRD Committee on Post War Policy, Box 186, Oppenheimer Papers.

70. Sherwin, *A World Destroyed,* pp. 229–230.

71. Ibid., pp. 202–209. Hewlett and Anderson, *New World,* pp. 356–359.

72. Sherwin, *World Destroyed,* app. L, "Notes of the Interim Committee Meeting, May 31, 1945," p. 299.

73. Ibid., pp. 202–216 and app. L. Hewlett and Anderson, *New World,* pp. 356–360, 365–369. Smith, *A Peril,* pp. 41–50.

74. Principal sources for descriptions of the test are the eyewitness accounts of well-briefed *New York Times* reporter William L. Laurence and Brig. Gen. Thomas F. Farrell of Groves' staff; *New York Times,* September 26, 1945, pp. 1, 16; Groves, *Now It Can Be Told,* app. 8, "Memorandum for the Secretary of War, July 18, 1945," pp. 435–438.

75. For a well-documented account of decisions and diplomacy relating to these events, see Sherwin, *A World Destroyed,* passim.

76. On the reaction at Los Alamos, see Smith, *A Peril,* pp. 76–77.

V. "High promise . . . yet only a stone's throw from despair"

1. Herbert Childs, *An American Genius: The Life of Ernest Orlando Lawrence* (New York: E. P. Dutton & Co., 1968), p. 366.

2. *Manhattan District History: Project Y: the Los Alamos Project,* vol. 1: David Hawkins, *Inception until August 1945* (Los Alamos Scientific Laboratory Report, LAMS-2532, vol. 1, December 1, 1961), 3.59–3.81 passim.

3. The approximate date assigned to this letter is based on the internal evidence that it was written during the Perro Caliente vacation and in time for Millikan to respond to its contents in a letter of August 31.

4. Millikan to Oppenheimer, August 31, 1945 (p. 1 dated 1941, p. 2 correctly dated 1945), California Institute of Technology: 1941–47 File, Box 230, Oppenheimer Papers. Millikan to Tolman, July 31, 1945, Box 28.8, Millikan Papers.

5. Childs, *American Genius,* pp. 371–373, 376.

6. Raymond T. Birge, "History of the Physics Department," mimeographed (Berkeley, Cal.: University of California, n.d.), vol. 5: "The Period 1942–1950," chap. 17, p. 6.

7. For an extended account, see Alice Kimball Smith, *A Peril and a Hope: The Scientists' Movement in America, 1945–1947* (Chicago: University of Chicago Press, 1965), chap. 2.

8. Ibid., pp. 88–90.

9. Ibid., pp. 116–120, 144.

10. Wilson to Lauritsen, October 24, 1945, carbon copy in Box 1.9, Charles C.

Lauritsen Papers, California Institute of Technology Archives, Millikan Library, Pasadena, Cal.

11. Quoted in Birge, "Physics Department," vol. 5, chap. 17, p. 9.

12. Telegram from Oppenheimer to Houston, October 16, 1945, California Institute of Technology: 1941–47 File, Box 230, Oppenheimer Papers.

13. Millikan to Oppenheimer, February 20, 1946, California Institute of Technology: 1941–47 File, Box 230, Oppenheimer Papers. Childs, *American Genius,* pp. 375–376.

14. Birge, "Physics Department," vol. 5, chap. 17, p. 11.

15. Interview with J. Robert Oppenheimer by Thomas S. Kuhn, November 20, 1963, p. 32.

16. Einstein to Oppenheimer, September 29, 1945, as quoted in *Einstein on Peace,* ed. Otto Nathan and Heinz Norden (London: Methuen & Co., 1963), pp. 338–339.

17. Ibid., p. 338. *New York Herald Tribune,* September 26, 1945, pp. 1, 12. Smith, *A Peril,* pp. 451–460.

18. *Los Alamos Project,* vol. 1, 20.7.

19. For a fuller discussion of Oppenheimer's involvement with the May–Johnson bill and the initial stages of the postwar scientists' movement, see Smith, *A Peril,* chap. 3 passim.

20. An eight-page, undated, printed copy is entitled, "A Speech Given by J. R. Oppenheimer at a Meeting of the Association of Los Alamos Scientists, Los Alamos, New Mexico, November 2, 1945." Los Alamos Scientists, Association of, November 2, 1945 File, Box 262, Oppenheimer Papers. Below the title was printed the following: "This material is not for public release. A revised version will probably appear soon in one of the scientific journals." The editors have found no evidence of such publication.

Epilogue

1. Interview with Francis Fergusson by Alice Kimball Smith, April 23, 1975.

2. A list of government committees and panels on which Oppenheimer served was prepared for the Atomic Energy Commission's Personnel Security Board in 1954; see Security Case File, 1953–1967, Boxes 198 and 199, J. Robert Oppenheimer Papers, Manuscript Division, Library of Congress, Washington, D.C.

3. U.S. Atomic Energy Commission, *In the Matter of J. Robert Oppenheimer: Transcript of Hearing before Personnel Security Board, Washington, D.C. April 12, 1954, through May 6, 1954* (Washington, D.C.: Government Printing Office, 1954).

4. Philip M. Stern, with the collaboration of Harold P. Green, *The Oppenheimer Case: Security on Trial* (New York.: Harper and Row, 1969).

5. Ibid, p. 457. Kipphardt's play, written in German, was first performed in Germany in 1964. An English translation, *In the Matter of J. Robert Oppenheimer,* was published in New York in 1968 by Hill and Wang.

6. Interview with Fergusson by Alice Kimball Smith, April 21, 1976. Interview with Harold Cherniss by Alice Kimball Smith, April 21, 1976, pp. 23–24.

7. Oppenheimer's original words, jotted down when he thought the award

would come from President Kennedy, read "some charity, some courage, and some humor." He showed this draft to Alice Kimball Smith the evening after Kennedy was shot.

8. Hans A. Bethe, "Oppenheimer: 'Where He Was There Was Always Life and Excitement,'" *Science,* 155 (3 March 1967): 1081. Freeman Dyson provides illuminating perspectives on Oppenheimer's style and role at the institute in his autobiography, *Disturbing the Universe* (New York: Harper and Row, 1979), pp. 69–83.

9. *Science and the Common Understanding* (New York: Simon and Schuster, 1954). *The Open Mind* (New York: Simon and Schuster, 1955).

Sources and Style

Letters

Letters appearing in this volume are listed below by number, recipient, date, and source. Unless otherwise indicated, all letters were written by Robert Oppenheimer. If no source is given, letters were obtained from the recipient; copies of most of them have been deposited as a supplement to the Oppenheimer collection in the Library of Congress.

1. Herbert W. Smith, October 2, 1922
2. Herbert W. Smith, November 14, 1922
3. Herbert W. Smith, January 6, 1923
4. Herbert W. Smith, January 12, 1923
5. Herbert W. Smith, January 21, 1923
6. Herbert W. Smith, January 28, 1923
7. Herbert W. Smith, February 11, 1923
8. Herbert W. Smith, February 18, 1923
9. Herbert W. Smith, March 31, 1923
10. Herbert W. Smith, May 2, 1923
11. Herbert W. Smith, May 15, 1923
12. Edwin C. Kemble, May 24, 1923, Physics Laboratory Papers, Harvard University Archives
13. Herbert W. Smith, May 30, 1923
14. Francis Fergusson, June 14, 1923
15. Francis Fergusson, July 17, 1923
16. Francis Fergusson, August 16, 1923
17. Francis Fergusson, September 16, 1923
18. Francis Fergusson, September 28, 1923
19. Paul Horgan, September 28, 1923
20. Paul Horgan, October 6, 1923
21. Herbert W. Smith, October 6, 1923
22. Paul Horgan, [October 1923]
23. Herbert W. Smith, November 2, 1923
24. Herbert W. Smith, [ca. November 1923]
25. Herbert W. Smith, December 1, 1923
26. Herbert W. Smith, [winter 1923-24]
27. Francis Fergusson, Christmas, 1923
28. Herbert W. Smith, [ca. January 22, 1924]
29. Herbert W. Smith, [late winter 1924]
30. Herbert W. Smith, [ca. March 1924?]
31. Herbert W. Smith, [ca. April 10, 1924]
32. Herbert W. Smith, [ca. October 1924]
33. Herbert W. Smith, [ca. January 1925]

34. Herbert W. Smith, February 25, [1925]
35. Francis Fergusson, April 25, [1925]
36. Percy W. Bridgman, June 13, 1925, Bridgman Papers, Harvard Archives
37. R. E. Priestley, [*ca.* June 1925], Board of Graduate Studies, University of Cambridge
38. Percy W. Bridgman, June 29, 1925, Bridgman Papers, Harvard Archives
39. Francis Fergusson, July 20, [1925]
40. Herbert W. Smith, [*ca.* August 8, 1925]
41. Percy W. Bridgman, August 29, 1925, Bridgman Papers, Harvard Archives
42. R. E. Priestley, August 30, 1925, Board of Graduate Studies, Cambridge
43. Percy W. Bridgman, September 5, 1925, Bridgman Papers, Harvard Archives
44. R. E. Priestley, September 16, 1925, Board of Graduate Studies, Cambridge
45. Francis Fergusson, November 1, [1925]
46. Francis Fergusson, November 15, [1925]
47. Herbert W. Smith, December 11, [1925]
48. Francis Fergusson, January 23, [1926]
49. Francis Fergusson, March 7,[1926]
50. Frank Oppenheimer, [*ca.* late spring 1926]
51. R. E. Priestley, August 18, 1926, Board of Graduate Studies, Cambridge
52. Francis Fergusson, November 14, [1926]
53. Edwin C. Kemble, November 27, [1926], Archive for History of Quantum Physics (AHQP)
54. Percy W. Bridgman, February 12, [1927], Bridgman Papers, Harvard Archives
55. George Uhlenbeck, March 12, [1927], AHQP
56. Paul Dirac, November 28, [1927], Dirac Papers, Churchill College Library, University of Cambridge
57. Edwin C. Kemble, February 16, [1928], AHQP
58. Frank Oppenheimer, [March 1928]
59. Theodore Lyman, April 21, 1928, Physics Papers, Harvard Archives
60. Theodore Lyman, May 7, 1928, Physics Papers, Harvard Archives
61. Percy W. Bridgman, May 16, 1928, Bridgman Papers, Harvard Archives
62. International Education Board, August 2, [1928], International Education Board Papers (IEB), Rockefeller Archive Center
63. Research Fellowship Board in Physics, August 25, 1928, IEB Papers
64. Frank Oppenheimer, December 30, [1928]
65. International Education Board, January 3, 1929, IEB Papers
66. W. J. Robbins, January 23, 1929, IEB Papers
67. W. J. Robbins, February 4, 1929, IEB Papers
68. Robert A. Millikan, February 12, 1929, Millikan Papers, California Institute of Technology Archives
69. Frank Oppenheimer, May 6, [1929]
70. W. J. Robbins, May 14, [1929], IEB Papers
71. Frank Oppenheimer, September 7, [1929]
72. Frank Oppenheimer, October 14, [1929]
73. Frank Oppenheimer (from Julius Oppenheimer), March 11, 1930

74. Frank Oppenheimer, March 12, [1930]
75. Frank Oppenheimer, August 10, [1931]
76. Ernest O. Lawrence, October 12, [1931], Lawrence Papers, Bancroft Library, University of California, Berkeley
77. Ernest O. Lawrence, October 16, [1931], Lawrence Papers
78. George Uhlenbeck, November 29, 1931
79. Ernest O. Lawrence, January 3, 1932, Lawrence Papers
80. Frank Oppenheimer, [*ca.* January 1932]
81. Frank Oppenheimer (from Julius Oppenheimer), January 18, 1932
82. Frank Oppenheimer, March 12, [1932]
83. Frank Oppenheimer, [*ca.* fall 1932]
84. Robert A. Millikan, March 5, 1933, Millikan Papers
85. Niels Bohr, June 14, 1933, Niels Bohr Scientific Correspondence, Niels Bohr Institute, University of Copenhagen
86. Frank Oppenheimer, October 7, [1933]
87. George Uhlenbeck, [fall 1933], AHQP
88. Frank Oppenheimer, January 7, [1934]
89. Theodore von Karman, [*ca.* March 1934], von Karman Papers, California Institute of Technology Archives
90. George Uhlenbeck, [*ca.* March 1934], AHQP
91. Ernest O. Lawrence, [April 30?, 1934], Lawrence Papers
92. Edwin A. Uehling, May 12, [1934]
93. Frank Oppenheimer, June 4, [1934]
94. Frank Oppenheimer, July 31, [1934]
95. George Uhlenbeck, [*ca.* fall 1934], AHQP
96. Frank Oppenheimer, January 11, [1935]
97. Ernest O. Lawrence, [*ca.* early spring 1935], Lawrence Papers
98. Robert A. Millikan, April 19, 1937, Millikan Papers
99. Ernest O. Lawrence, [April 1937], Lawrence Papers
100. George Uhlenbeck, June 29, [1937]
101. Louise Oppenheimer Singer, October 21, [1937]
102. Robert Oppenheimer (from Niels Bohr), December 20, 1937, Niels Bohr Scientific Correspondence
103. Mildred Edie, May 29, [1938], Center for the Study of the Consumer Movement, Consumers Union, Mount Vernon, N.Y.
104. Robert A. Millikan, January 1, [1939], Millikan Papers
105. William A. Fowler, [January 28?, 1939]
106. George Uhlenbeck, February 5, [1939]
107. Louise Oppenheimer Singer, April 26, [1939]
108. William A. Fowler, [September 9, 1939]
109. F. Wheeler Loomis, May 13, 1940, Physics Department Records, Archives, University of Illinois, Urbana
110. Ruth and Edwin Uehling, July 4, [1940]
111. William A. Fowler, [spring 1941]
112. Edwin and Ruth Uehling, May 17, [1941]
113. F. R. Coudert, Jr., October 13, 1941, Franz Boas Papers, American Philosophical Society Library

114. Ernest O. Lawrence, November 12, 1941, Lawrence Papers
115. Robert A. Millikan, March 20, [1942], Millikan Papers
116. Robert F. Bacher, June 10, 1942, J. Robert Oppenheimer Papers, Manuscript Division, Library of Congress
117. John H. Van Vleck, June 10, 1942, Oppenheimer Papers
118. Edward Teller, September 11, 1942, Oppenheimer Papers
119. John H. Manley, October 12, 1942, Oppenheimer Papers
120. Robert Oppenheimer (from Glenn T. Seaborg), November 3, 1942, Oppenheimer Papers
121. Glenn T. Seaborg, November 6, 1942, Oppenheimer Papers
122. John H. Manley, November 6, 1942, Oppenheimer Papers
123. James B. Conant, November 30, 1942, Records of the Office of Scientific Research and Development (OSRD), Record Group 227, National Archives
124. Hans and Rose Bethe, December 28, 1942, Oppenheimer Papers
125. James B. Conant, February 1, 1943, Oppenheimer Papers
126. I. I. Rabi, February 26, 1943, OSRD Records
127. Enrico Fermi, March 11, 1943, Oppenheimer Papers
128. Robert Bacher, memorandum, April 28, 1943, Oppenheimer Papers
129. Leslie R. Groves, memorandum, April 30, 1943, Oppenheimer Papers
130. Wolfgang Pauli, May 20, 1943, Oppenheimer Papers
131. Robert Oppenheimer (from Wolfgang Pauli), June 19, 1943, Oppenheimer Papers
132. Franklin D. Roosevelt, July 9, 1943, Oppenheimer Papers
133. Richard C. Tolman, July 23, 1943, Oppenheimer Papers
134. Robert Oppenheimer (from Leslie R. Groves), July 29, 1943, Oppenheimer Papers
135. Robert G. Sproul, September 18, 1943, Oppenheimer Papers
136. Leslie R. Groves, November 2, 1943, Oppenheimer Papers
137. Raymond T. Birge, November 4, 1943, Lawrence Papers
138. Leslie R. Groves, January 17, 1944, Oppenheimer Papers
139. Leslie R. Groves, February 14, 1944, Oppenheimer Papers
140. Anne and Hilde Meyers, April 5, 1944, Oppenheimer Papers
141. Peer de Silva, April 21, 1944, Oppenheimer Papers
142. Raymond T. Birge, May 26, 1944, Oppenheimer Papers
143. Leslie R. Groves, June 27, 1944, Oppenheimer Papers
144. James B. Conant, August 3, 1944, OSRD Records
145. Hedwig Stern, August 25, 1944, Oppenheimer Papers
146. Leslie R. Groves, August 30,1944, Manhattan Engineer District, Military Records, National Archives
147. Leslie R. Groves, August 31, 1944, Oppenheimer Papers
148. Raymond T. Birge, September 27, 1944, Oppenheimer Papers
149. Raymond T. Birge, October 5, 1944, Oppenheimer Papers
150. Leslie R. Groves, October 6, 1944, Oppenheimer Papers
151. Wolfgang Pauli, April 16, 1945, Oppenheimer Papers
152. Secretary of War, August 17, 1945, Oppenheimer Papers
153. Monroe E. Deutsch, August 24, 1945, Oppenheimer Papers

Speech by Robert Oppenheimer to Association of Los Alamos Scientists, November 2, 1945, Oppenheimer Papers

Some of Robert Oppenheimer's pre-1942 letters were handwritten; others he typed himself. Almost all of the letters after 1942 were typed by a secretary; most of those from the Library of Congress collection are carbon copies. Misspellings and typographical errors have been silently corrected, and punctuation has been changed in some instances. Oppenheimer's British usage, Germanic word order, and French, Spanish, and German words have been retained. Deletions of portions of letters are indicated by ellipses; brackets have been used around dates, surnames, signatures, and other information supplied by the editors. Oppenheimer's scientific writings are identified in the letters and commentary by year and order of publication, for example: [1927e]. Full citations are given in the list of Scientific Papers.

Interviews

Some of the interviews conducted for this edition were intended as a permanent oral history archive which will be useful to scholars working on related topics. These interviews were tape recorded, transcribed, sent to the interviewee for review and correction, and returned with permission to deposit the final typed copy in the oral history collection of the Massachusetts Institute of Technology Libraries. In addition, use has been made of oral history interviews conducted in the early 1960s for the Archive for History of Quantum Physics and in the period 1964–1974 for the Center for History of Physics of the American Institute of Physics.

Interviews deposited in archives and used in preparing the commentaries in this volume are: *

Carl D. Anderson by Charles Weiner (CW), June 30, 1966, AIP
Frederick Bernheim by CW, October 27, 1975, MIT
William C. Boyd by Alice Kimball Smith (AKS), December 21, 1975, MIT
Harold Cherniss by AKS, April 21, 1976, MIT
John T. Edsall by CW, July 16, 1975, MIT
Paul Horgan by AKS, March 3, 1976, MIT
John H. Manley by AKS, December 30, 1975, MIT

Philip Morrison by CW, February 7, 1967, AIP
Frank Oppenheimer by CW, February 9, 1973, AIP
J. Robert Oppenheimer by Thomas S. Kuhn, November 18, 1963, and No-
vember 20, 1963, AHQP
Robert Serber by CW and Gloria Lubkin, February 10, 1967, AIP
Jeffries Wyman by CW, May 28, 1975, MIT

*AHQP: Archive for History of Quantum Physics, available at the following repositories:
American Institute of Physics, New York; American Philosophical Society Library, Philadelphia; Bancroft Library, University of California, Berkeley; Tate Laboratory of Physics, University of Minnesota, Minneapolis; Niels Bohr Institute, University of Copenhagen.

AIP: Center for History of Physics, American Institute of Physics, New York.

MIT: Institute Archives and Special Collections, Massachusetts Institute of Technology
Libraries, Cambridge.

In addition, interviews were conducted by the editors during the period
1975–1978 with the following persons (transcripts or notes are retained by the
editors):

Helen C. Allison
Robert F. Bacher
Ruth Meyer Cherniss
Margaret H. Compton
Priscilla Duffield
Francis Fergusson
Jane Didisheim Kayser
Babette Oppenheimer Langsdorf
Dorothy McKibbin
Jeannette Mirsky
Philip Morrison
Leo Nedelsky
Frank Oppenheimer
Peter Oppenheimer
Yvonne Blumenthal Pappenheim
Rudolf Peierls
Melba Phillips
Inez Pollak
Robert Serber
Herbert W. Smith
George Stevens
Edwin A. Uehling
Ruth Uehling
Else Uhlenbeck
George Uhlenbeck

Ellipses in quotations from interviews indicate omissions in the interviewee's
statements; brackets indicate substitutions or additions to clarify meaning or to provide continuity. Page numbers are cited when a typed transcript of the interview has
been deposited.

Scientific Papers by Robert Oppenheimer

1926a   On the quantum theory of vibration-rotation bands. *Proceedings of the Cambridge Philosophical Society,* 23 (1925-1927): 327–335 (received May 24, 1926).

1926b   On the quantum theory of the problem of the two bodies. *Proc. Camb. Phil. Soc.,* 23 (1925-1927): 422–431 (read July 26, 1926).

1926c   Quantum theory and intensity distribution in continuous spectra. *Nature,* 118 (November 27, 1926): 771 (dated October 30, 1926).

1926d   Quantentheorie des kontinuierlichen Absorptionsspecktrums. *Naturwissenschaften,* 14 (December 24, 1926): 1282 (dated November 1, 1926).

1927a   Zur Quantentheorie kontinuierlicher Spektren. *Zeitschrift für Physik,* 41 (1927): 268–293 (received December 24, 1926).

1927b   Zur Quantenmechanik der Richtungsentartung. *Zeit. f. Phys.,* 43 (1927): 27–46 (received March 8, 1927).

1927c   Bemerkung zur Zerstreuung der α-Teilchen. *Zeit. f. Phys.,* 43 (1927): 413–415 (received April 30, 1927).

1927d   Zur Quantentheorie der Molekeln (with M. Born). *Annalen der Physik,* 4th ser., 84 (1927): 457–484 (received August 25, 1927).

1927e   On the quantum theory of the polarization of impact radiation. *Proceedings of the National Academy of Sciences,* 13 (December 15, 1927): 800–805 (communicated October 26, 1927).

1928a   Three notes on the quantum theory of aperiodic effects. *Physical Review,* 31 (January 1928): 66–81 (dated August 1927).

1928b   On the quantum theory of the capture of electrons. *Phys. Rev.,* 31 (March 1928): 349–356 (dated December 1927).

1928c   On the quantum theory of the Ramsauer effect. *Proc. N. A. S.,* 14 (March 15, 1928): 261–262 (communicated February 21, 1928).

*1928d   On the quantum theory of field currents. *Phys. Rev.,* 31 (May 1928): 914.

1928e   On the quantum theory of the autoelectric field currents. *Proc. N. A. S.,* 14 (May 15, 1928): 363–365 (communicated March 28, 1928).

1928f   On the quantum theory of electronic impacts. *Phys. Rev.,* 32 (September 1928): 361–376 (dated May 1928).

1929   Über die Strahlung der freien Elektronen im Coulombfeld. *Zeit. f. Phys.,* 55 (1929): 725–737 (received May 6, 1929).

*1930a   Why does molecular hydrogen reach equilibrium so slowly? (with H. Hall). *Phys. Rev.,* 35 (January 1, 1930): 132–133.

1930b   Note on the theory of the interaction of field and matter. *Phys. Rev.,* 35 (March 1, 1930): 461–477 (received November 12, 1929).

1930c   On the theory of electrons and protons. *Phys. Rev.,* 35 (March 1, 1930): 562–563 (dated February 14, 1930).

* Abstract of paper presented at meeting of the American Physical Society.

1930d   Two notes on the probability of radiative transitions. *Phys. Rev.*, 35 (April 15, 1930): 939–947 (received March 4, 1930).

*1931a   Selection rules and the angular momentum of light quanta. *Phys. Rev.*, 37 (January 15, 1931): 231.

*1931b   Note on the statistics of nuclei. *Phys. Rev.*, 37 (January 15, 1931): 232–233.

1931c   Note on the statistics of nuclei (with P. Ehrenfest). *Phys. Rev.*, 37 (February 15, 1931): 333–338 (received December 23, 1930).

1931d   Relativistic theory of the photoelectric effect, part II: Photoelectric absorption of ultragamma radiation (with H. Hall). *Phys. Rev.*, 38 (July 1, 1931): 57–59, 71–79 (received May 7, 1931).

*1931e   Photoelectric absorption of ultra-gamma radiation (with H. Hall). *Phys. Rev.*, 38 (August 1, 1931): 589.

1931f   Note on light quanta and the electromagnetic field. *Phys. Rev.*, 38 (August 15, 1931): 725–746 (received June 26, 1931).

1931g   On the range of fast electrons and neutrons (with J. F. Carlson). *Phys. Rev.*, 38 (November 1, 1931): 1787–1788 (dated October 9, 1931).

*1932a   On the range of fast electrons and neutrons (with J. F. Carlson). *Phys. Rev.*, 39 (March 1, 1932): 864–865.

1932b   The impacts of fast electrons and magnetic neutrons (with J. F. Carlson). Phys. Rev., 41 (September 15, 1932): 763–792 (received July 18, 1932).

*1933a   The disintegration of lithium by protons of high energy. *Phys. Rev.*, 43 (March 1, 1933): 380.

1933b   On the production of the positive electron (with M. S. Plesset). *Phys. Rev.*, 44 (July 1, 1933): 53–55 (dated June 9, 1933).

1933c   The production of positives by nuclear gamma-rays (with L. Nedelsky). *Phys. Rev.*, 44 (December 1, 1933): 948–949 (dated November 18, 1933).

*1934a   On the production of positives by nuclear gamma-rays (with L. Nedelsky). *Phys. Rev.*, 45 (January 15, 1934): 136.

1934b   On the theory of the electron and positive (with W. H. Furry). *Phys. Rev.*, 45 (February 15, 1934): 245–262 (received December 1, 1933).

1934c   The production of positives by nuclear gamma-rays—errata (with L. Nedelsky). *Phys. Rev.*, 45 (February 15, 1934): 283.

*1934d   The theory of the electron and positive. *Phys. Rev.*, 45 (February 15, 1934): 290.

1934e   On the theory of the electron and positive (with W. H. Furry). *Phys. Rev.*, 45 (March 1, 1934): 343–344 (dated February 12, 1934).

1934f   On the limitations of the theory of the positron (with W. H. Furry). *Phys. Rev.*, 45 (June 15, 1934): 903–904 (dated June 2, 1934).

1934g   On the scattering of the Th C″ γ-rays (with C. C. Lauritsen). *Phys. Rev.*, 46 (July 1, 1934): 80–81 (dated June 12, 1934).

1935a   Are the formulae for the absorption of high energy radiations valid? *Phys. Rev.*, 47 (January 1, 1935): 44–52 (received November 12, 1934).

1935b   Note on charge and field fluctuations. *Phys. Rev.*, 47 (January 15, 1935): 144–145 (received December 3, 1934).

* Abstract of paper presented at meeting of the American Physical Society.

1935c Note on the production of pairs by charged particles. *Phys. Rev.*, 47 (January 15, 1935): 146–147 (received December 3, 1934).

1935d The disintegration of the deuteron by impact. *Phys. Rev.*, 47 (June 1, 1935): 845–846 (received March 29, 1935).

1935e Note on the transmutation function for deuterons (with M. Phillips). *Phys. Rev.*, 48 (September 15, 1935): 500–502 (received July 1, 1935).

*1936a On the elementary interpretation of showers and bursts. *Phys. Rev.*, 50 (August 15, 1936): 389.

*1936b The density of nuclear levels (with R. Serber). *Phys. Rev.*, 50 (August 15, 1936): 391.

1937a On multiplicative showers (with J. F. Carlson). *Phys. Rev.*, 51 (February 15, 1937): 220–231 (received December 8, 1936).

1937b The disintegration of high energy protons (with G. Nordheim, L. W. Nordheim, and R. Serber). *Phys. Rev.*, 51 (June 15, 1937): 1037–1045 (received March 22, 1937).

1937c Note on the nature of cosmic-ray particles (with R. Serber). *Phys. Rev.*, 51 (June 15, 1937): 1113 (dated June 1, 1937).

1937d Note on nuclear photoeffect at high energies (with F. Kalckar and R. Serber). *Phys. Rev.*, 52 (August 15, 1937): 273–278 (received May 19, 1937).

1937e Note on resonances in transmutations of light nuclei (with F. Kalckar and R. Serber). *Phys. Rev.*, 52 (August 15, 1937): 279–282 (received May 19, 1937).

1938a Note on boron plus proton reactions (with R. Serber). *Phys. Rev.*, 53 (April 15, 1938): 636–638 (received February 1, 1938).

1938b On the stability of stellar neutron cores (with R. Serber). *Phys. Rev.*, 54 (October 1, 1938): 540 (dated September 1, 1938).

1939a On massive neutron cores (with G. M. Volkoff). *Phys. Rev.*, 55 (February 15, 1939): 374–381 (received January 3, 1939).

1939b Discussion—Behavior of high energy electrons in cosmic radiation by C. G. Montgomery and D. D. Montgomery. *Reviews of Modern Physics*, 11 (July–October 1939): 264–266.

1939c On continued gravitational contraction (with H. Snyder). *Phys. Rev.*, 56 (September 1, 1939): 455–459 (received July 10, 1939).

1939d On pair emission in the proton bombardment of flourine (with J. S. Schwinger). *Phys. Rev.*, 56 (November 15, 1939): 1066–1067 (dated October 29, 1939).

1940a The production of soft secondaries by mesotrons (with R. Serber). *Phys. Rev.*, 57 (January 15, 1940): 75–81 (received November 3, 1939).

*1940b On the applicability of quantum theory to mesotron collisions. *Phys. Rev.*, 57 (February 15, 1940): 353.

1941a On the spin of the mesotron. *Phys. Rev.*, 59 (March 1, 1941): 462 (dated February 14, 1941).

* Abstract of paper presented at meeting of the American Physical Society.

1941b   On the selection rules in beta-decay. *Phys. Rev.*, 59 (June 1, 1941): 908 (dated April 25, 1941).

1941c   On the interaction of mesotrons and nuclei (with J. Schwinger). *Phys. Rev.*, 60 (July 15, 1941): 150–152 (received June 19, 1941).

*1941d Internal conversion in photosynthesis. *Phys. Rev.*, 60 (July 15, 1941): 158.

*1941e The high energy soft component of cosmic rays (with R. F. Christy). *Phys. Rev.*, 60 (July 15, 1941): 159.

*1941f Multiple production of mesotrons by protons (with E. C. Nelson). *Phys. Rev.*, 60 (July 15, 1941): 159–160.

*1941g On the internal pairs from oxygen. *Phys. Rev.*, 60 (July 15, 1941): 164.

1941h   The mesotron and the quantum theory of fields. In Enrico Fermi et al., *Nuclear Physics*. Philadelphia: University of Pennsylvania Press. Pp. 39–50.

*1942   Pair theories of meson scattering (with E. C. Nelson). *Phys. Rev.*, 61 (February 1 and 15, 1942): 202.

1946   Reaction of radiation on electron scattering and Heitler's theory of radiation damping (with H. A. Bethe). *Phys. Rev.*, 70 (October 1 and 15, 1946): 451–458.

1948a   The multiple production of mesons (with H. W. Lewis and S. A. Wouthuysen). *Phys. Rev.*, 73 (January 15, 1948): 127–140 (received October 2, 1947).

1948b   Note on stimulated decay of negative mesons (with S. T. Epstein, R. J. Finkelstein). *Phys. Rev.*, 73 (May 15, 1948): 1140–1141 (received February 5, 1948).

1949   Discussion on the disintegration and nuclear absorption of mesons: remarks on μ-decay. *Rev. Mod. Phys.*, 21 (1949): 34–35.

1950   Internal conversion in the photosynthetic mechanism of blue green algae (with W. Arnold). *Journal of General Physiology*, 33 (1950): 423–435.

* Abstract of paper presented at meeting of the American Physical Society.

Bibliography

BETHE, HANS A. Oppenheimer: where he was there was always life and excitement. *Science,* 155 (March 3, 1967): 1080–1084.

———. J. Robert Oppenheimer 1904–1967. *Biographical Memoirs of Fellows of The Royal Society,* 14 (1968): 391–416.

BIRGE, RAYMOND T. History of the Physics Department. Vols. 3–5 (1928–1950). Berkeley: University of California, n.d. (mimeographed).

CHILDS, HERBERT. *An American Genius: The Life of Ernest Orlando Lawrence.* New York: E. P. Dutton, 1968.

CHURCH, PEGGY POND. *The House at Otowi Bridge: The Story of Edith Warner and Los Alamos.* Albuquerque: University of New Mexico Press, 1959.

COMPTON, ARTHUR H. *Atomic Quest.* New York: Oxford University Press, 1956.

GOWING, MARGARET. *Britain and Atomic Energy: 1939-1945.* New York: St. Martin's Press, 1964.

GROVES, LESLIE R. *Now It Can Be Told: The Story of the Manhattan Project.* New York: Harper & Row, 1962.

HEILBRON, JOHN L. Quantum historiography and the Archive for History of Quantum Physics. In *History of Science: An Annual Review of Literature, Research and Teaching,* vol. 7. Cambridge: W. Heffer & Sons, 1968. Pp. 90–111.

HEWLETT, RICHARD G., AND OSCAR E. ANDERSON, JR. *The New World, 1939-1946.* Vol. 1 of *A History of the United States Atomic Energy Commission.* University Park: Pennsylvania State University Press, 1962.

KEVLES, DANIEL J. *The Physicists.* New York: Alfred A. Knopf, 1978.

KUHN, THOMAS S., JOHN L. HEILBRON, PAUL FORMAN, AND LINI ALLEN, EDS. *Sources for History of Quantum Physics: An Inventory and Report.* Philadelphia: The American Philosophical Society, 1967.

LAMONT, LANSING. *Day of Trinity.* New York: Atheneum, 1965.

Manhattan District History: Project Y: The Los Alamos Project. Vol. 1, David Hawkins, *Inception until August 1945.* Los Alamos: Los Alamos Scientific Laboratory Report LAMS-2532, December 1, 1961.

MICHELMORE, PETER. *The Swift Years: The Robert Oppenheimer Story.* New York: Dodd, Mead, 1969.

OPPENHEIMER, J. ROBERT. *Science and the Common Understanding.* New York: Simon and Schuster, 1954.

———. *The Open Mind.* New York: Simon and Schuster, 1955.

PEIERLS, RUDOLF. J. Robert Oppenheimer. In *Dictionary of Scientific Biography,* vol. 10. New York: Charles Scribner's Sons, 1974. Pp. 213–218.

RABI, I.I., ROBERT SERBER, VICTOR F. WEISSKOPF, ABRAHAM PAIS, AND GLENN T. SEABORG. *Oppenheimer.* New York: Charles Scribner's Sons, 1969.

ROSSI, BRUNO. *Cosmic Rays.* New York: McGraw Hill, 1964.

ROYAL, DENISE. *The Story of J Robert Oppenheimer.* New York: St. Martin's Press, 1969.

Bibliography

SEIDEL, ROBERT W. Physics research in California: the rise of a leading sector in American physics. Ph.D. diss., University of California, Berkeley, 1978.

SHERWIN, MARTIN J. *A World Destroyed: The Atomic Bomb and the Grand Alliance.* New York: Alfred A. Knopf, 1975.

SMITH, ALICE KIMBALL. Los Alamos: focus of an age. *Bulletin of the Atomic Scientists,* June 1970, pp. 15–20.

———. *A Peril and a Hope: The Scientists' Movement in America, 1945-1947.* Chicago: University of Chicago Press, 1965.

SOPKA, KATHERINE R. Quantum physics in America, 1920–35. Ph.D. diss., Harvard University, 1976.

STERN, PHILIP M., WITH HAROLD P. GREEN. *The Oppenheimer Case: Security on Trial.* New York: Harper & Row, 1969.

UNITED STATES ATOMIC ENERGY COMMISSION. *In the Matter of J. Robert Oppenheimer: Transcript of Hearing before Personnel Security Board, Washington, D.C., April 12, 1954, through May 6, 1954.* Washington, D.C.: Government Printing Office, 1954. Paperback edition, Cambridge: MIT Press, 1971.

WEINER, CHARLES, ED. *History of Twentieth Century Physics.* Proceedings of the International School of Physics "Enrico Fermi," course 57. New York: Academic Press, 1977.

———. A new site for the seminar: the refugees and American physics in the 1930s. In Donald Harnish Fleming and Bernard Bailyn, eds., *The Intellectual Migration: Europe and America, 1930-1960.* Cambridge: Harvard University Press, 1969.

WILSON, JANE, ED. *All in Our Time: The Reminiscences of Twelve Nuclear Pioneers.* Chicago: Bulletin of the Atomic Scientists, 1975.

Index

Abelson, Philip H., 208-209, 209n, 230
Acheson-Lilienthal Report, 310, 328
Ackley, John Kenneth, 218, 219
Adler, Felix, 2-3, 8, 137
Agassiz Museum, Harvard, 17
Alamogordo, N. M., *see* Trinity test
Albuquerque, N.M., 8
Allard, Louis, 54, 55n
Allen, Alexander, 248, 249n
Allison, Samuel K., 148, 243, 246n, 304
Alvarez, Luis W., 217 and n, 247, 276, 277n, 283
American Association for the Advancement of Science, 148n
American Association of Scientific Workers, 219, 220, 290
American Committee for Democracy and Intellectual Freedom (ACDIF), 218
American Philosophical Society, 289
American Physical Society, 146, 154, 169, 213
Analysis of Mind (Russell), 24
Anatomy of Peace (Reves), 309
Anderson, Carl D., 160, 193, 197, 199
Anderson, Herbert L., 236, 238n
Ann Arbor, *see* University of Michigan at Ann Arbor
Anna Karenina (Tolstoy), 70

Army, U.S.: and contracts for Los Alamos, 243, 248; living facilities provided by, 244-245; on commissions for senior scientists, 247, 249, 256; role of defined, 247-249; Special Engineer Detachment, 281. *See also* Groves, Gen. Leslie R.; Military Policy Committee
Artzibasheff, Boris, 42, 43n, 46
Association of Los Alamos Scientists (ALAS), 303; statement by, 304-305; JRO's farewell speech to, 315-325, 328
Association of Oak Ridge Scientists, 305, 310
Atomic bomb: preliminary work on, 222; and OSRD, 222-223; fast neutron research, 223-228; centralized laboratory for research on, 229, 231; predetonation and problem of impurities, 234-235, 239-241; gun device, 260, 272, 285; implosion, 272-273, 278, 285; test of implosion device, 286, 288, 289-290, 292; views on use of, 290-291; choice of targets, 291; proposal to demonstrate only, 292; bombing of Hiroshima and Nagasaki, 292; question of postwar work on, 301; JRO's ALAS talk on impact of, 315-325. *See also* Fission; Los Alamos Laboratory; Trinity test
Atomic energy, postwar policy on, 293-294; JRO's trips to Washington on, 300-301;

Index